DEEP
TEXT

Praise for *Deep Text*

"Remarkably useful—a must-read for anyone trying to understand text analytics and how to apply it in the real world."
—Jeff Fried, CTO, BA Insight

"A much-needed publication around the largely misunderstood field of text analytics ... I highly recommend *Deep Text* as required reading for those whose work involves any form of unstructured content."
—Jim Wessely, President, Advanced Document Sciences

"Sheds light on all facets of text analytics. Comprehensive, entertaining, and enlightening. Reamy brings together the philosophy, value, and virtue of harnessing text data, making this volume a welcome addition to any professional's library."
—Fiona R. McNeill, Global Product Marketing Manager, Cloud & Platform Technology, SAS

"One of the most thorough walkthroughs of text analytics ever provided."
—Jeff Catlin, CEO Lexalytics

"Reamy takes the text analytics bull by the horns and gives it the time and exposure it deserves. A detailed explanation of the complex challenges, the various industry approaches, and the variety of options available to move forward."
—Bryan Bell, Executive VP, Market Development, Expert System

"Written in a breezy style, *Deep Text* is filled with advice on the role of text analytics within the enterprise, from information architecture to interface. Practitioners differ on questions of learning systems vs. rule-based systems, types of categorizers, or the need for relationship extraction, but the precepts in Tom Reamy's book are worth exploring regardless of your philosophical bent."
—Sue Feldman, CEO, Synthexis

"A must read for anybody in the text analytics business. A lifetime's worth of knowledge and experience bottled up for us to drink at our own pace. Enjoy!"
—Jeremy Bentley, CEO, Smartlogic

DEEP TEXT

USING TEXT ANALYTICS
to Conquer Information Overload,
Get Real Value From Social Media,
and Add Big(ger) Text to Big Data

TOM REAMY

Medford, New Jersey

First Printing

Deep Text: Using Text Analytics to Conquer Information Overload, Get Real Value From Social Media, and Add Big(ger) Text to Big Data

Library of Congress Cataloging-in-Publication Data

Names: Reamy, Tom.
Title: Deep text : using text analytics to conquer information overload, get real value from social media, and add big(ger) text to big data / by Tom Reamy.
Description: Medford, New Jersey : Information Today, Inc., 2016.
Identifiers: LCCN 2016010975 | ISBN 9781573875295
Subjects: LCSH: Data mining. | Text processing (Computer science) | Text files—Analysis. | Big data. | Social media. | Electronic data processing.
Classification: LCC QA76.9.D343 R422 2016 | DDC 006.3/12—dc23
LC record available at https://lccn.loc.gov/2016010975

Printed and bound in the United States of America

President and CEO: Thomas H. Hogan, Sr.
Editor-in-Chief and Publisher: John B. Bryans
Project Editor: Alison Lorraine
Production Manager: Tiffany Chamenko
Production Coordinator: Johanna Hiegl
Marketing Coordinator: Rob Colding
Indexer: Nan Badgett

Interior Design by Amnet Systems
Cover Design by Denise Erickson

infotoday.com

Contents

PART 3   TEXT ANALYTICS DEVELOPMENT

PART 4   TEXT ANALYTICS APPLICATIONS

PART 5   ENTERPRISE TEXT ANALYTICS AS A PLATFORM

TABLES AND FIGURES

Tables

Figures

Foreword

"Text analytics" is commonly used to refer to a clutch of quite diverse computer-aided techniques for extracting insight out of large volumes of unstructured text. The techniques, and their practitioners, come from diverse disciplines—information science and information retrieval, data science, statistics, knowledge organization, taxonomy and indexing, and more. The applications are equally diverse, from large scale machine-assisted categorization of knowledge bases, to business intelligence insights from market data, to patent mining for R&D analysts, to sentiment analysis for marketeers, to e-Discovery techniques for litigators.

It is a vibrant, complex, and highly technical field, often appearing mysterious to nonpractitioners. And where there is mystery, there is room for magical thinking, sleight of hand, and unrealistic expectations about what the technology can do, accompanied by an underappreciation of the human analyst's role in guiding the algorithms toward robust and valid insights.

While there are several books available on automated text mining and text analytics techniques and applications, this is the first from a text analytics expert with deep experience in knowledge management and knowledge organization. Here's why this is important. The various machine techniques for analyzing the contents of text in unstructured documents understand parts of speech and semantic rules, and can be told about document structure within any given genre. They can compare documents for similarity and difference, and, using statistical techniques, they can identify keyword strings that may be used to characterize documents or clusters of documents. But there are two very important things they don't know how to do, namely, tracking problems of polysemy (the same terms being used to mean different things) and synonymy (different terms being used to mean the same thing).

Polysemy and synonymy usage occur in the habits and patterns of the subcultures of document writers and consumers, represented by their localized working languages. In genomics, for example, specialists commonly reuse common-language names for gene sequences without any centralized nomenclature control; in consequence, the same name can refer to entirely different gene sequences across different species. Another example might be the document author who habitually uses local short forms that she knows her audience will understand, but that a more distant reader may not.

Machine techniques on their own can be excellent at picking up meanings from within well defined corpora, but once you are trying to understand concepts across very diverse corpora, the machines need to be sensitized by their human handlers to the contextual cues that create significant differences in language and meaning. The varieties of expression need to be mapped to each other using content models, taxonomy structures, or other forms of vocabulary control. These structures are what overcome the problems of polysemy and synonymy, and they allow the analyst to navigate the landscape in a purposeful and flexible way.

This is the realm of the taxonomist and the knowledge organization professional, whose expertise is in understanding and framing differences in context, and in creating language models to enable insights to be extracted in robust and transparent ways across large and diverse sets of unstructured data, and diverse communities of content producers. This is what moves the machine from being a producer of descriptive strings that hold unpredictable value for the analyst to a producer of reliable meaning and insight. And this is what is needed for text analytics to be scalable, reliable, and effective in its support of business goals.

I am very excited that Tom Reamy has at last brought order and clarity to this field using the tools and insights of knowledge organization. This book is written with the practitioner in mind and is full of practical examples and wisdom born of deep experience. In the process, Reamy takes the field of text analytics from a fragmentary clutch of diverse techniques, with very little methodological consistency, toward what he calls a "deep-text" approach—a framework that integrates well-established knowledge organization methodologies with a portfolio or toolkit approach to the use of methods and techniques, and that is focused on getting repeatable value from a text analytics infrastructure, as distinct from the ad hoc project-driven approaches that are so typical today.

Patrick Lambe
April 2016

Patrick Lambe is the author of *Organising Knowledge: Taxonomies, Knowledge and Organisational Effectiveness* (Chandos 2007) and co-author of *The Knowledge Manager's Handbook* (Kogan Page 2016). He is a founder of the Innovations in Knowledge Organisation conference (www.ikoconferen.org) and he consults, researches, and teaches in the field of knowledge organization and knowledge management. Patrick is based in Singapore.

Acknowledgments

After publishing a number of articles over the years, I thought it would not be too difficult to make the step up to writing a book. Boy, was I wrong! It turned out to be more difficult than I imagined, and it would not have been possible at all without the help of a great many people. This help came in many guises and consisted of both large and small contributions. I want to deeply thank all of the people who have helped write this book, one way or another, and if I don't mention you by name, forgive me, but I can only plead the usual rushing to meet a deadline.

First, I want to thank all of the following people for agreeing to be interviewed, and for providing extremely valuable insights into their companies, the overall market for text analytics, and ideas about its future direction:

Trevor Carlow, SAP
Margie Hlava, Access Innovations
Richard Mallah, Cambridge Semantics
Fiona McNeill, SAS
Sartendu Sethi, SAS
Fiona Mitchell, SAS
Meta Brown, Consultant
Jeff Caitlin, Lexalytics
Jeremy Bentley, Smartlogic
Catherine Havasi, Luminoso
Mary McKenna, Textwise
Jim Wessely, Consultant
Tom Anderson, OdinText
Daniel Mayer, Temis
Bryan Bell, Expert System
David Schubmehl, IDC
Boris Evelson, Forrester
Seth Grimes, Market Analyst—Text Analytics
Sue Feldman, Synthexis

I learned a great deal from all of you, especially those of you who disagreed with me. In addition to the interviews, I've had many discussions with a number of you at various conferences, including my own, Text Analytics World—and mostly over a glass or two of fine wine. Thank you.

In addition, I want to thank the consultants who have participated in one or more projects for my company, the KAPS Group. Thanks for making us successful and for putting up with my management style. I especially want to thank Marcia Morante and Jim Wessely, who have been with me on a number of projects. I also want to thank Evelyn Kent, Heather Hedden, Barbara Deutsch, Wendi Pohs, and Michael Kilgore for their help during the company's critical phases. Thanks as well to Laurie Wessely, Diana Bradley, Marlene Rockmore, Deborah Hunt, Heather Dubnik, Barbara Brooker, Donna Cohen, Kyle Nicholls, Deborah Plumley, Cheryl Armstrong, and Melanie Reamy.

And, of course, thanks to all the clients who hired us and allowed us to develop our skills, along with new ideas and solutions. I also want to express my gratitude for all the conferences, especially Information Today and Text Analytics World. Thank you for inviting me to speak and allowing me to try out lots of ideas, including developing a three-hour workshop on text analytics that was the initial basis for this book (with a lot more additions than I thought).

In addition, I would like to thank those people without whom the book would never have any readers—the ITI staff: John B. Bryans, Tiffany Chamenko, Beverly Michaels, Alison Lorraine, Johanna Hiegl, Rob Colding, and Denise Erickson.

I also want to thank the following for their direct contributions in reviewing a number of chapters in the book. These reviews covered everything from grammar and syntax (not my strong suit), and more importantly, the flow of the presentation. They provided a number of ideas for content, as well. These reviewers include Jim Wessely, Evelyn Kent, and Melanie Reamy. And a special thanks to Stefanie Mittelstadt, who did a wonderful job reviewing multiple chapters and providing invaluable suggestions for both flow and content.

Finally, I have to thank my wife, Melanie Reamy, without whose help and support this book would not have been written. She not only contributed in multiple ways but also provided the material and emotional support that I needed. And she put up with too many obsessive-compulsive and just plain cranky days. Thank you.

Introduction

It has become a common assertion that 80% of valuable business information can be found in unstructured text. Exactly how this was determined is a little unclear, but it's huge and very obviously growing with the explosion of social media. Considering the dramatic increase in the amount of unstructured text we are witnessing, I would not be surprised to learn the figure is actually closer to 90%.

We can get a good idea of the value that organizations place on their ability to handle the 10%–20% of information in structured data by the amount of research and activity in the area of data and databases. According to the Bureau of Statistics, there were 118,700 database administrators in the United States in 2012.[1] According to the same source, employment of database administrators is projected to grow 15% by 2022.

In addition, a Google search of database management degree programs turned up 114 different programs—and that doesn't include the vastly more numerous certification and training programs for database administrators and/or programmers.

So if organizations are spending that amount of money and devoting that many resources to handle their structured data—which only contains 10%–20% of valuable business information—imagine how much they're spending on getting the maximum value out of all that unstructured text. It must be a gigantic number, right?

Not exactly. The truth is we have absolutely no precise idea how much money and resources are being devoted to dealing with unstructured text. Nobody has considered that it is significant enough to track—*yet*.

But I do remember a statistic saying that companies devoted 0.5 people (on average) to support their efforts for search, which is one of the primary unstructured text applications.

Text analytics, in its broadest sense, is *the* major tool for dealing with unstructured text other than the human brain—and there are only a handful of degree programs that cover unstructured text in any depth and they focus mainly on text mining as part of a computer science degree. Instead of large database associations with thousands of members, we have a few small groups,

1

such as Text Analytics Summit and Text Analytics World, with their relatively tiny conferences (as compared to the attendance for database conferences).

Baffling, Isn't It?

So, what could explain this baffling lack of attention and effort to get value from all that unstructured text? There are a few possible factors.

First, most of the people that I talk to don't know what text analytics is, and those who actually do recognize the term think that it's basically tracking nice and negative things that people say on Twitter about their company or their products.

Another factor is that for data there are established and common artificial languages, like SQL, that create a platform for both learning and developing applications, and thus developers can build on the work of hundreds of others. Yes, there are variations, but compared to the vendor-specific chaos within text analytics, these are minor.

But the real answers lie with the complexity of text—unstructured text is orders of magnitude more complex than simple data. In addition, text analytics (the primary tool for dealing with unstructured text) has yet to develop a systematic, explicit set of techniques that enable organizations to extract the value and meaning out of their unstructured text. Right now, text analytics is more of an art than a science. It requires programming ... and poetry. It requires the ability to write in an artificial language—like SQL or R—and at the same time understand the nuances of meaning in natural languages that range from relatively formal business-speak to the vitriolic rantings found in much of social media. It also requires the ability to apply all of that within useful business contexts for the purpose of creating applications that actually produce value.

Because of the complexity of text, text analytics will probably never be as easy to learn as database design and programming. But we can build a better foundation for text analytics to improve not only how we train people in text analytics, but how we understand the business value of text analytics as a whole.

I hope that one step in the right direction is the writing of this book.

Text Analytics and Text Mining

I suppose at this point I ought to offer at least a preliminary definition of what text analytics really is. There is only one problem: *There's no real consensus about what text analytics really is.*

First of all, there's a lot of confusion over the terms *text mining* and *text analytics*. That modern arbiter of usage, Wikipedia, considers text analytics as a synonym for text mining (I disagree). In fact, the Wikipedia entry is entirely dominated by a mathematical, text mining approach:

> Text mining, also referred to as *text data mining*, roughly equivalent to text analytics, refers to the process of deriving high-quality information from text ... The overarching goal is, essentially, to turn text into data for analysis, via application of natural language processing (NLP) and analytical methods.[2]

Text analytics doesn't even merit its own entry! Instead, it is currently under text mining's subheader, *text mining and text analytics*:

> The term is roughly synonymous with text mining ... The latter term is now used more frequently in business settings while "text mining" is used in some of the earliest application areas, dating to the 1980s, notably life-sciences research and government intelligence.
>
> The term text analytics also describes that application of text analytics to respond to business problems ... It is a truism that 80% of business-relevant information originates in unstructured form, primarily text. These techniques and processes discover and present knowledge—facts, business rules, and relationships—that is otherwise locked in textual form, impenetrable to automated processing.[3]

I find it interesting that, even as they tout the similarity of text mining and text analytics, the two entries for "text mining" and "text mining and text analytics" are significantly different. "Text mining" is fundamentally "about extracting data from unstructured text" while "text mining and text analytics" is about how to "discover and present knowledge" locked within text.

You don't have to be a doctrinaire knowledge management (KM) devotee of the data-information-knowledge-wisdom hierarchy to see that there is a big difference between "extracting data" and "discovering knowledge." So, even the entries that claim that they are "roughly synonymous" point to clear differences. I guess it revolves around just how rough the "roughly synonymous" really is—because it looks positively mountainous to me!

When you dive into the specifics of these definitions, the first thing to note is how data-oriented the first one is. For example, the phrase "text data mining"—it's almost as if they can't bring themselves to only talk about text, something I've seen all too often.

Text data mining *is* a good description of one particular technique—extracting entities from unstructured text, then applying data processing methods for a variety of purposes. However, even in a strict text mining approach, counting and discovering patterns in text is often more important than extracting data from the text.

And when you look at the broader concept of text analytics, extracting data *is* an important part of text analytics—but it's only one part. What's missing is the concept of *meaning*—and two of the other biggest application areas within text analytics: search and sentiment. Or, I should say that it *does* include them, but only the simplest approaches to them, ignoring the whole richness (and messiness) of language. The dangers of this approach can be seen in early sentiment analysis applications, which just took dictionaries of positive and negative words and counted them up.

The results? Barely above chance.

As it turns out, to do a good job of extracting data from text, you have to take into account the linguistic and cognitive elements of text. In other words, you have to capture the context around those entities to use them in more intelligent and sophisticated ways. These contexts can be anything, from simple negation, "I didn't love the product," to more complex conditionals, such as "I would have loved this product if it had not been for the keyboard."

The early applications just saw "love" and "product" near each other—and so rated them as positive.

In addition to the differences in approach to the nuances of language, text mining and text analytics have a couple of other major differences. The first is that the applications built with the two techniques tend to be very different. Text mining applications really are much more data oriented, while text analytics powers applications, like search and e-Discovery, which deal with language and meaning far more than data.

The second difference is in terms of the skills and backgrounds of the practitioners. Text mining has more to do with math and statistics, while text analytics builds on language and taxonomies. You find very different people with different skills and experiences in the two fields.

What Is Text Analytics?

I don't want to get bogged down in terminology wars regarding what text analytics actually is, but I think it is important to emphasize the need for two terms that, while they can often be used together to build better applications, refer to very different techniques and different applications. However, the two fields do share a number of common elements, which complicates things. Perhaps what we need is a new term that encompasses both? If you have any candidates, please send them to me and maybe we'll have a contest.

In the meantime, it seems to me that *text analytics* is the broader term, so I will use it to refer to the entire field, except where noted. I will discuss text mining as a part of text analytics, but it is not something that we will devote much time to (see Chapter 1 for more on this).

So here goes: Briefly and generally, text analytics is the use of software and content models (taxonomies and ontologies) to analyze text and the applications that are built using this analysis.

To add more detail to the definition, let's take a look at some of the basic within text analytics. One basic is to simply count the words of various types and discover patterns within the text (text mining). These counts and patterns can be used to gain a variety of insights into the documents as well as the people writing the documents. These counts and patterns can be used to characterize such things as the educational or expertise level of the writer, or even whether the writer is telling the truth—people who are lying tend to use the word "I" less often than people telling the truth.

In addition, text analytics can be used to extract data of all kinds, such as people, companies, products, events, etc., from unstructured text. That data can then be incorporated into all the structured data techniques and applications we've developed. In other words, Big Text can make Big Data even bigger! Extraction can be used as part of text mining patterns, but can also be used directly in applications such as search, where extraction is used to capture *multiple metadata values*—and which in turn support one of the successful approaches to search, *faceted navigation*.

Another set of techniques can be used to generate summaries of large sets of documents to provide a much more manageable and useful approach than having to read through them all. These summaries can range from simple general characterizations (often used in search applications) to complex one- to five-page characterizations of all the key information contained in each 200-page document.

Finally, text analytics can be used to characterize the content of unstructured text by subject matter (major and minor topics) and by positive and negative sentiment. This is often the most difficult thing to do but also the most valuable if done correctly. Frequently referred to as "auto-categorization," it can be used to do far more than categorize a document.

This functionality is really the heart and brain of text analytics. It is the technique that adds depth and intelligence to our analysis of text by capturing and utilizing the context around individual words for better text mining, extraction, sentiment characterization, and all the other potential uses of text analytics. Understanding context is at the heart of the human understanding of meaning, and without it, text analytics is severely restricted in scope and value.

Is Deep Learning the Answer?

Deep learning is the current hot topic in artificial intelligence and is associated with successes like IBM's Watson. It is an approach that is also being applied to the analysis of unstructured text of all kinds.

However, the technique is actually based on neural networks, which is something that we explored starting in the '80s. The difference now is primarily scale—the huge jumps in processing speed and storage enable us to build much more complex neural networks. This scale is what has led to some major successes in AI and text analysis, but it also has some major limitations. It is very good for discovering patterns, both perceptual and linguistic, but it has not been as successful with conceptual problems.

With all the hype about deep learning, I used to think that I was one of the very few that had doubts about how far you could go with this approach. However, I just came across a very good article in the *MIT Technology Review* titled "Can This Man Make AI More Human?"[4]

The article discusses Gary Marcus, who is taking a different approach to AI by trying to apply how children learn. Children don't learn by being exposed to millions of examples and discovering the common patterns within those millions. They basically learn by developing a rule and generalizing it—and then learning how to apply it better by learning the exceptions to the rule. And the key to those exceptions is that it is not a *what* in the form of simply a list of exceptions, but a *why*, as in why the exception needs to be recognized. The article asks the question, "But is deep learning based on a model of the brain that is too simple?" And the answer is *yes*. The article goes on to state:

These systems need to be fed many thousands of examples in order to learn something ...

In contrast, a two-year-old's ability to learn by extrapolating and generalizing—albeit imperfectly—is far more sophisticated ... Clearly the brain is capable of more than just recognizing patterns in large amounts of data: It has a way to acquire deeper abstractions from relatively little data.

The article goes on to describe a situation that is very similar to what I found in text analytics, which is that deep-learning methods are extremely powerful (and better than human) in identifying things, like faces and even the spoken words in audio recordings, but they are not even close to human capabilities when dealing with the meaning of those words. As the article puts it:

A deep-learning system could be trained to recognize particular species of birds in images or video clips, and to tell the difference between ones that can fly and ones that can't. But it would need to see millions of sample images in order to do this, and it wouldn't know anything about why a bird isn't able to fly.

And in this case, what is true for AI is also true for text analytics: *Deep learning is not enough by itself.* On the other hand, it is definitely a powerful technique that can be combined with other techniques, such as those found within text analytics. To continue to use the brain example, "In other words, the brain uses something like a deep-learning system for certain tasks, but it also stores and manipulates rules about how the world works so that it can draw useful conclusions from just a few experiences."

Text Analytics, Deep Text, and Context

For text analytics, a better approach is what I call *deep text* (yes, I'm somewhat stealing the term, but it's a good one). Like Marcus' approach to AI, deep text is an approach that focuses on developing rules and applying those rules to unstructured text. Of course, the rules that we develop in a deep-text approach are nowhere near as sophisticated as our two-year-old human—at least not yet, but it is a much more powerful approach than some text analytics vendors take with their overuse of example documents and statistics.

A text analytics rule might be something like this: "If you see any of the sets of words that represent a particular concept within the same paragraph or section and you don't see any of another set of words that would change the meaning, then this indicates this concept is present and is an important one for this document."

This approach focuses on rules (and the exceptions to rules) to characterize the meaning in text, as well as doing a more sophisticated job of extracting key entities and concepts. For example, if a human brain is reading a paper on pharmaceutical companies and sees the word "pipeline," it automatically (or unconsciously) knows that it means a product pipeline, not an oil and gas pipeline. Since we still don't know how to construct a human mind except the old fashioned way, we have to tell our AI and text analytics applications how to look at the context around a word and use that context to determine the meaning of that word for this instance. This context (and the rules that characterize it) needs to look at multiple contextual dimensions or layers, from the words immediately before and after "pipeline," to words in the same sentence or paragraph—and within an overall document context as well.

Context and rules are the key concepts in a deep-text approach to text analytics. In succeeding chapters, we'll dive more deeply into what this approach means and how to do text analytics in a way that goes beyond simple text mining. However, since there is really not a good overall book on text analytics, our focus will be on thoroughly understanding all the different approaches. Hopefully by the end of the book, you will have a good general knowledge of what text analytics is all about and also be able to see how a deep-text approach to text analytics is key to its success.

We will also cover everything, from how to get started in text analytics and how to develop text analytics, to the kinds of applications you can build with text analytics, wrapping it all up with the best way to approach incorporating text analytics within an enterprise.

Who Am I?

Text analytics is still a young and developing field and it is not clear what the best background to have really is (though most of the consultants I hire have library science backgrounds). The reality is people in text analytics can come from a variety of backgrounds and experiences. My particular path is one that I would not necessarily recommend to anyone else, but it worked out well for me.

My academic experience was long and varied as I was one of those professional students who really didn't want to graduate because they were having too much fun learning. When I did finally get an undergraduate degree, I had the requirements and credits for three degrees—English, philosophy, and the history of ideas. My official degree was in the field of history of ideas, in which I earned a master's and ABD ("all but dissertation").

I was hard at work writing my dissertation on a somewhat obscure German philosopher/thinker named Ernst Cassirer when I was seduced by the work that was going on in the Stanford AI program—and by their promise that they were only a couple of years away from modeling common-sense knowledge. I sold my car and a few other possessions, moved out of too-expensive Palo Alto, and bought my first computer and began to explore AI and programming.

It didn't take too long to realize that they were not two years away—or even two decades as it turned out. But it was too late, and I embarked on a career of consulting, mostly in educational software, though my first two "products" were two science-fiction computer games that I designed and programmed (they didn't sell all that well, but they did win a couple of awards). This period ended with one of the few full time jobs I've ever had programming educational software.

This was followed by working with two colleagues to start an educational training software company. Unfortunately, we launched our first product just as California was going into a major recession. End of that story.

So it was back to consulting, with more of a focus on helping companies design their approach to information, rather than programming. There was also another short full-time job with Charles Schwab organizing their intranet and developing a corporate taxonomy. This, too, fell victim to a recession.

That was followed by creating my second company (and the one that I still am working for), KAPS Group. The group was me and a number of other consultants that I met over the years. The initial focus was developing taxonomies and consulting on their use in search and other applications. While my company still does taxonomy consulting, the focus has shifted to text analytics, with an early project working with software from Inxight.

Since then, I've worked on a large number of projects for clients in business and government, during which I and my consultants have learned how to do text analytics of all kinds. I've also been speaking about text analytics at a variety of conferences, including Taxonomy Boot Camp, Enterprise Search Summit, KMWorld, Semantic Technology, and others.

In addition to talks on specific aspects of text analytics, I've also been offering a three-hour workshop on what text analytics is and what you can do with it. Since 2013, I've served as program chair for a conference devoted to text analytics, Text Analytics World.

My company now partners with many leading text analytics vendors. Having a wide range of different vendor technologies as well as working on projects from news aggregation to analyzing social media for sentiment about different phones and plans was exciting, and it also led me to realize that the field of text analytics needed something.

I decided that what the field needed was a firmer foundation, both theoretical and practical, and so I decided to write this book. There were other reasons as well, chiefly that most people I meet (outside of conferences) don't know what it is and don't have any idea of what you can do with it.

In addition, I've seen too many people that have been charged with doing text analytics—often with no training or background—do it pretty badly. And then they blame the software, or they come to the conclusion that text analytics is not worth doing, and so they drop the whole thing.

I'm distrustful of claims that some new technology will "revolutionize everything," but I do think that text analytics done well (deep text) has the potential to take the chaos and messiness of unstructured text and turn it into an incredibly valuable asset for business, government, academic research, and, who knows, perhaps even art.

Plan of the Book

The book is divided up into five parts with three chapters each.

Part 1: Text Analytics Basics

The first part, Text Analytics Basics, lays the foundation for the rest of the book. In Chapter 1 (What is Text Analytics?), I present a broad definition of text analytics that includes text mining, auto-categorization, and sentiment analysis among other features and capabilities. In this chapter, I also discuss the importance of content models (taxonomies and ontologies, etc.) and metadata as a basic component of adding structure to unstructured text. I also briefly discuss the technology behind text analytics (which we will go into more detail in Chapter 2). The chapter closes with a quick look at broad text analytics application areas, including enterprise search, social media (including voice of the customer), and a variety of applications that can be built with text analytics.

In Chapter 2, we take a much deeper look at the actual functionality on which text analytics rests. This includes text mining, but we don't go into as much depth on this functionality, both because it is significantly different from all the others and it has been well covered in other books. Text mining is more mathematical than linguistic.

Entity extraction is one of the basic functionality areas of text analytics in which software is used to basically extract data from all that unstructured text. The software is set up to extract noun phrases of various kinds, such as people, organizations or companies, and a whole range of other types of entities. In addition to simple entities, the software can also be used to extract facts which consists of sets of entities and relationships between them. For example, you might extract a person's name and then also their address and phone number. More advanced facts might include the relationships between two companies, for example, they are competitors and/or merger candidates.

Another basic functionality that we cover in this chapter is summarization in which software can be set up to summarize large documents into more manageable and general form. Currently this is an underutilized functionality, but that could very well change in the near future. A summary could be a simple two- or three-sentence, high-level summary that might be used in a search results list to take the place of the snippet (the first 100 or 200 words of the document). On the other hand, a summary could be a five- to 10-page document that captures all the essential information in large documents, enabling editors or analysts to quickly scan large collections in relatively short periods of time.

Sentiment analysis uses text analytics software to determine or capture the positive or negative sentiment being expressed in social media, such as Twitter or blogs. This has been one of the hottest areas in text analytics for the last few years, and the field has matured lately with more advanced rule-based analysis that replaced simple positive and negative vocabulary dictionaries. These early efforts were barely above chance, but it led to an explosion of companies that offered an easy development path. However, as we shall see, easy text analytics is basically a contradiction in terms—if you want meaningful results.

The last, and in many ways the most important and complex, functionality is normally called "auto-categorization." This name came from the early focus on search applications in which the software characterized the primary topics—or the *aboutness*—of documents in a search results list. However, this functionality is really at the heart of advanced text analytics, and thus can be used to make all the other pieces smarter. This functionality can be based on everything, from categorization by comparing targets with sample documents, to building sophisticated rules using each vendor's proprietary language.

In Chapter 3, we switch gears to talk about the business value of text analytics, which is often analyzed in terms of the return on investment, or ROI of text analytics. Text analytics is really a foundation technology that supports a variety of ways to get value from that most underutilized resource, unstructured text. This makes doing ROI calculations a bit complex, but still doable. In fact, when you do ROI calculations, the only real problem is the numbers are so high that it is sometimes hard to believe for many people—believe it!

We look at the basic benefits of text analytics in three main areas: enterprise search, social media applications, and a range of text analytics–based applications. We then explore the question, "If text analytics is so powerful and produces so much value, why isn't everybody doing it?" As you might expect, the answers are many and varied. We end this chapter with the discussion of how best to sell the benefits of text analytics by, in some cases, going beyond the numbers in order to make the case at the C-level. Success stories are still a great way to convince people at all levels.

Part 2: Getting Started in Text Analytics

In this part we cover how to get started in text analytics with research into both the current text analytics software market and research into your organization's information environment and needs.

Chapter 4, Current State of Text Analytics Software, covers the early history and current state of the text analytics market. This market is characterized by a number of themes, including that the market is a very fragmented one with no dominant leader. Another theme looks at the factors contributing to the growth of the market as well as the variety of applications and offerings by various vendors. We look at current trends in the market, and we also look at what the obstacles are that are holding back an even more dramatic growth in the market.

Chapter 5, Text Analytics Smart Start, discusses the issues that organizations should pay attention to when getting started in text analytics. We then discuss the methodology that my company has developed to help people do both the necessary research and an initial evaluation of which software will work best in their organization. This methodology can be applied to both enterprise text analytics and social media applications.

Finally in this chapter, we discuss the design of the text analytics team that will do the initial selection and form the basis for future development.

Chapter 6, Text Analytics Software Evaluation, discusses the unique requirements for text analytics software, which is unlike most traditional software in that it deals with that messy language stuff. The unique nature of text analytics software calls for a two-part process, which consists of a fairly traditional market evaluation, but culminates in a proof of concept (POC). The POC is the essential part of the methodology, both for making the best purchasing decision and for creating the foundation for future development. We end the chapter by looking at two example evaluation projects.

Part 3: Text Analytics Development

In Part 3, we consider how to build on the aforementioned foundation; in other words, we ask "What is the actual development process that goes into text analytics applications?"

Chapter 7, Enterprise Development, focuses on developing categorization capabilities, as that is what poses the most complex development challenges. This development starts with analyzing enterprise content and any existing content structure or taxonomies that exist within the enterprise. This preliminary phase also includes developing a powerful understanding of users and what their information needs and behaviors are. We then cover the actual development process, which typically involves a number of cycles of develop-test-refine until you are ready for prime time. The chapter also covers a major topic—maintenance and governance—which too often is treated almost as an afterthought. The chapter ends by looking at the development process for entity and/or fact extraction, which, while much simpler than categorization, has a number of specific issues and techniques.

Chapter 8, Social Media Development, analyzes what is required to do advanced sentiment analysis and other social media development processes. In this chapter we use a number of example projects, including a project that looked at the extremely varied and creative ways of expressing positive and negative sentiments in a number of social media sites dedicated to expressing our love-hate for our phones. We also cover the basic development process, which is very similar to the process for categorization, but with a number of specific differences. We end this chapter with discussing what the current major issues are in social media development.

Chapter 9, Development: Best Practices and Case Studies, adds a level of concreteness to the discussion by looking at a number of specific projects that my company has worked on and tries to capture the best practices lessons that came out of those projects. The very first project we did, a news aggregation application, was both a successful project and an incredible learning experience as we developed a number of best practices and learned which ones to discard. We then look at two enterprise projects that were very similar—while one a major success, the other a major failure. No one likes to talk about failures, but you can learn a great deal about what does *not* work in text analytics by studying them.

Part 4: Text Analytics Applications

In this part, we cover the full range of text analytics applications, or as many as we can since the number and variety of applications continues to dramatically grow. We'll cover three main areas of applications: enterprise search, which will focus on faceted navigation, a broad range of text analytics applications, or *InfoApps* as they're also referred to, and lastly, social media applications.

Chapter 10, Text Analytics Applications—Search, starts with a description of the futility of trying to make search work—*without* dealing with the whole dimension of meaning. Without text analytics, search engines are stuck with dealing with words as essentially "stupid chicken scratches."

There have been two major advances in search—aside from technical advances, which do little to improve the quality of search—Google and faceted navigation. Unfortunately, within the enterprise, Google's PageRank algorithm doesn't work—and that leaves us with faceted navigation. Faceted navigation has the potential to dramatically improve search, but it has one major flaw—it requires an enormous amount of metadata. What this means is that most successful implementations have been on commercial websites, where they could use their product catalogs to supply all the necessary metadata. There is, however, a solution for search within the enterprise, which is using text analytics to generate all the necessary metadata to make faceted navigation really function.

Enterprise taxonomies are another approach that had a great deal of potential but ran into a major problem—the gap between the taxonomy and the content. In other words, having a well-designed taxonomy is only half the solution—someone has to apply the taxonomy to documents and there the success story is much more problematic. One approach is to combine text analytics with content management to develop a hybrid of automatic and human tagging.

We conclude the chapter by looking at how text analytics can enable us to look beyond individual documents and incorporate the characteristics of an overall corpus of documents, as well as dividing up documents into smaller and more meaningful sections.

Chapter 11, Text Analytics Applications—InfoApps, discusses some of the most interesting and most valuable applications that can be built with text analytics. These applications include things like business intelligence, e-Discovery, and fraud detection, all of which incorporate text analytics to some degree. Often with these applications, the text analytics components are largely hidden, as vendors offer the application and do the text analytics development themselves.

In addition to these hidden text analytics applications, there are a number of other applications in which the text analytics components are more explicit. One area that has seen a lot of success is the analysis of documents for characterizing expertise levels to build applications that can range from knowledge management expertise location applications to enhancing HR's evaluation of potential employees.

A less dramatic, but economically powerful application is using text analytics to uncover all the duplicates and near-duplicate documents that are typically found within enterprises today. Finally, we talk about different kinds of automatic and semiautomatic summarization that can be done with text analytics. These summaries can be used to enhance the use of unstructured documents in the enterprise, both by reducing the reading burden of wading through multiple large documents (most of which have little importance), and by creating richly-structured summarizations of documents that can support new applications.

Chapter 12, Text Analytics Applications—Social Media, discusses the huge and growing number of applications that are being built to discover sentiment and other insights into customers and competitors. We start out by exploring the unique characteristics of the social media world of extremely wild, and at times incoherent text found in Twitter and other social media posts. Getting beyond the poor quality of text is one of the major challenges in this area. As with most text analytics application areas, the other main challenge is to develop more in-depth models to support more sophisticated understanding of what this text means. For example, even categorizing something as short as a tweet as either positive or negative oversimplifies the ideas and sentiment in those tweets, almost to the point of uselessness.

If done well, however, social media provides a rich environment for applications, such as customer relationship management (CRM), and in particular voice of the customer (VOC) applications. As a second-generation set of applications are being developed, they are moving beyond simple positive and negative to much deeper psychological characterizations. In addition, another area of huge value is behavior prediction in which, for example, it is possible to distinguish customers who are likely to cancel from those simply trying to get something from you.

Part 5: Enterprise Text Analytics as a Platform

In the final part, Enterprise Text Analytics as a Platform, we discuss the best overall approach to text analytics. The question is whether to approach text analytics as a series of independent applications, or to develop an enterprise text analytics platform that can support all those applications.

Chapter 13, Text Analytics as a Platform, starts with a discussion of different approaches to text analytics and comes to the conclusion that—while the application-infrastructure dichotomy is really more of the spectrum—for most organizations, looking at text analytics as a semantic infrastructure is really the best approach. We present the arguments in favor of a strategic versus a tactical approach, and/or a platform or a project approach. The key argument is that even if you tend to favor tactical and project approaches, you still need to develop an overall strategic vision of what text analytics can do for your organization in order to come up with the best decisions.

We then present a number of arguments in favor of an infrastructure platform approach. One key factor is that unstructured text is growing in size and complexity, and it is found throughout the organization, not in any one department, but everywhere. The other key argument is that we have tried the tactical/project approach for years, and it made little headway in gaining real value out of all the unstructured text within and outside the enterprise.

Chapter 14, Enterprise Text Analytics—Elements, describes what an infrastructure platform approach to text analytics would look like in most organizations. We describe what the main features of enterprise text analytics (ETA) are and introduce the concept of a semantic infrastructure. Virtually all modern organizations have developed a technical infrastructure for dealing with information, which is a necessary component, but without a semantic infrastructure, the ability to deal with information will be extremely limited. Briefly, a semantic infrastructure consists of all the elements that deal with and support the use of language or semantics for the organization. This can include taxonomies and ontologies as well as other communication models.

We then present a kind of thought experiment that describes what an enterprise text analytics department might look like and where that ETA department might be located within the organization. This chapter also describes what the basic skill requirements are for doing text analytics and the best way to obtain these skills. We also discuss who the best candidates are for text analytics training.

The chapter then expands that discussion to include who are the best and natural partners and contributors to text analytics in other parts of the organization. This chapter describes some of the backgrounds of these partners and contributors. These key backgrounds can include cognitive science as well as various language studies. In addition, training departments often can play a key role, both in developing text analytics and integrating it within the organization. Finally, we look at the contributions of IT and the data—or structured information— groups.

This chapter continues with a quick look at the technology of an ETA group. This technology model includes not only the text analytics software itself but also enterprise search, enterprise content management, and of course, SharePoint. The chapter concludes with a look at what the range of services are that this ETA group could offer to the organization, and how you might create an ETA department or group.

Chapter 15, Developing ETA—Semantic Infrastructure, dives more deeply into what a semantic infrastructure is and how it can deliver value to the organization. We start with how important an understanding of the content within the organization is, how to create a content map of what you have, and why and how it is used. We also discuss how to develop content models, including taxonomies that can power text analytics. We also discuss what the implications of text analytics are for those content models and taxonomies, specifically that neither simple, one-dimensional taxonomies nor five-level taxonomies with thousands of nodes are very useful.

Mapping the content in the organization is one key step, but the second key component is to map all the various communities, both formal and informal, within the organization. It is important to understand the information needs and behaviors of all these communities in order to develop an ETA solution. We use the metaphor of the neocortical community model in which most communication takes place within small communities, but there is also a need for some intercommunity communication (communities can be anything from a group within a department to an informal special-interest group).

The chapter concludes by looking at how to add depth and intelligence to our understanding of these communities with a cognitive deep research effort. The final point is that when dealing with something like semantics and information, it is extremely practical to pay attention to this cognitive theoretical depth.

Conclusion

In the conclusion, we review and discuss a number of the major themes of the book, including the relationship of text mining and text analytics, the importance of integration for doing text analytics—in choosing your methodology as well as the kinds of content—and some of the important themes for development and application of text analytics. We end with a look at the future of text analytics in general, and specifically how text analytics and cognitive computing can mutually enrich each other.

We also explore the idea of *deep text* as the key to doing advanced text analytics. There are three essential characteristics of deep text:

- Linguistic and cognitive depth
- Integration of multiple techniques, methods, and resources
- Platform/infrastructure

These three characteristics are essential for doing text analytics in a way that goes beyond simple word counting. They are the keys to adequately modeling the rich complexity of natural language. They are also the key to the future of text analytics, whether it will continue to be a mildly interesting set of techniques, or whether it will fulfill its potential to dramatically improve our ability to integrate unstructured text into an ever-growing range of applications.

Endnotes

1. Bureau of Labor Statistics, U.S. Department of Labor, *Occupational Outlook Handbook, 2014-15 Edition*, Database Administrators.

2. "Text mining." Wikipedia. https://en.wikipedia.org/wiki/Text_mining.

3. "Text mining and text analytics." Wikipedia. https://en.wikipedia.org/wiki/Text _mining#Text_mining_and_text_analytics.

4. Knight, Will. "Can This Man Make AI More Human?" *MIT Technology Review*, January/February, 2016. www.technologyreview.com/featuredstory/544606/can-this-man-make-ai-more-human/.

PART 1

Text Analytics Basics

CHAPTER 1

What Is Text Analytics?

And Why Should You Care?

So, what is text analytics? And why should you care? Well, the why part is pretty easy. Text analytics can save you tens of millions of dollars, open up whole new dimensions of customer intelligence and communication, and actually enable you to make use of a giant pile of what is currently considered mostly useless stuff: *unstructured text*.

The "what is" question is a little more complicated, but stick with me and I'll try to give you a good answer in 25 pages or less.

What Is Text Analytics?

About 90% of the time when I tell people what I do—*text analytics*—there is an awkward silence, followed by a kind of blank look. Then, depending on the personality of the person, there is often an "oh, what is that?" Or, there is a sort of muttered, "oh." And then, they start looking for the nearest exit. In other words, it's not a very good icebreaker or conversation starter.

Now, I'm not overly fond of precise definitions of an entire complex field of study, especially one as new and still morphing as text analytics. But I would like to be able to tell people what it is I do, and so I guess I'd better take a stab at defining it.

Actually it's not just the layperson on the street who could use a new definition of text analytics, but there seems to be a great deal of disagreement among those professionals who claim to do text analytics as to what exactly it is. Text analytics encompasses a great variety of methods, technologies, and applications, so it shouldn't be too much of a surprise that we haven't quite nailed it down yet.

To make matters worse, there are all sorts of claimants for the title of "what I do is the REAL text analytics." For one, "text mining" often claims to deal with all things text. Then, the so-called "automatic categorization" companies will tell you that they do all you need to do with text. And finally, the "semantic technology" or the "semantic web" people not only claim the word semantic as their own but also that what they do is *the* essential way of utilizing unstructured text.

I'm also a firm believer in Wittgenstein's notion of family resemblances, that is, for any complex field, there is no one or two essential characteristics, but rather a family of overlapping characteristics that define what it is—yet another reason why I'm suspicious of attempts to define something as complex as text analytics in a one-sentence definition.

But, we still have to try.

Text Analytics Is ...

In my view, the term *text analytics* should be defined in the broadest possible way. Almost anything that someone has described as text analytics belongs within the definition.

In essence, what we're trying to do is *add structure to unstructured/semistructured text*—which includes everything from turning text into data, to diving down into the heart of meaning and cognition, through to making that text more understandable and usable.

My "big tent" definition of text analytics includes, for example:

- Text mining
- The latest mathematical, vector space, or neural network model
- The grunt work of putting together vocabularies and taxonomies
- The development of categorization rules, the application of those rules, advanced automated processing techniques— everything from your company's official anti-discrimination policy to the chaos of Twitter feeds
- The development and use of sophisticated analytical and visual front ends to support analysts trying to make sense of the trends in 20 million email threads, or the political and social rantings of millions of passionate posters, both evil and heroic (depending on your point of view)

So, with all those caveats (or quibbles) in mind, the essential components of "big tent" text analytics are:

- Techniques – linguistic (both computational and natural language), categorization, statistical, and machine learning
- Semantic structure resources – dictionaries, taxonomies, thesauri, ontologies

- Software – development environment, analytical programs, visualizations
- Applications – business intelligence, search, social media ... and a whole lot more

We will go into each of these components in more detail, but one thing they all have in common: They are all used to process unstructured or semi-structured text. And so, the fifth essential component of text analytics is:

- Content – unstructured or semi-structured text, including voice speech-to-text

The output of all this text processing varies considerably. A short list includes:

- Counting and clustering words in sets of documents as a way of characterizing those sets
- Analyzing trends in word usage in sets of documents as part of broader analyses of political, social and economic trends
- Developing advanced statistical patterns of words and clustering of frequently co-occurring words, which can be used in advanced analytical applications—and as a way to explore document or results sets
- Extracting entities (people, organizations, etc.), events, activities, etc., to make them available for use as data or metadata, specifically:
  - Metadata to improve search results
  - Turning text into data, such that all our advanced data analytical techniques can be applied
- Identifying and collecting user and customer sentiment, opinions, and technical complaints to feed programs that support everything customer—customer relations, early identification of product issues, brand management ... and even technical support
- Analyzing the deeper meaning and context around words to more deeply understand what the word, phrase, sentence, paragraph, section, document, and/or corpus is about—this is perhaps the most fundamental and the most advanced technique that is used for everything from search ("aboutness") to adding intelligence or context to every other component and application of text analytics

Content and Content Models

With a name like text analytics, it should come as no surprise that the primary content of text analytics is … *text!* But having said that, we haven't said much, so let's look a little more deeply. The stuff that text analytics operates on is all kinds of text from simple notepad text to Word documents and websites, blogger forum posts, Twitter posts, and so on. In other words, anything that can be expressed in words (and can be input into a computer one way or another) is fair game for text analytics.

What we don't deal with are things like video, although there are a number of applications that incorporate video into a text analytics application, either by generating a transcript of all the spoken words in a video and/or operating on any text metadata descriptions of the video.

Text analytics also does not deal directly with data, although again, there is an enormous amount of data incorporated into text analytics applications at a variety of levels.

This type of text is often referred to as *unstructured text*, but that is not really accurate. If it were really unstructured text, we wouldn't be able to make any sense out of it. A slightly more accurate description would be *semi-structured text*, which is what a lot of people call it.

However, this does not really capture the essence of the kinds of text that text analytics is applied to. Only someone raised in a world in which databases rule would come up with the term *semi-structured*. More accurate terms would be *multi-structured*, or even *advanced-structured* (OK, that's probably a bit much).

The reality is, this type of text is structured in a wide variety of ways, some fairly primitive and simple, and still others exemplifying the height of human intelligence.

Let's start with the primitive and simple structure of the text itself. In most languages, ranging from English to Russian to Icelandic, the first level of structure consists of *letters*, *spaces* and *punctuation marks*. We won't be dealing much at the level of letters, although in English and other similar languages, spaces are how we define the second level of structure—*words*. Also, punctuation marks are important—particularly for the third level of structure, namely *phrases*, *clauses*, *sentences* and *paragraphs*—and this is where the concept of *meaning structures* comes into play.

For obvious reasons, words—the second level of meaning structure—are the basic unit that we deal with in text analytics, normally in conjunction with the third-level meaning structure of phrases, clauses, sentences, and paragraphs. We don't want to get too bogged down in linguistic theory, but we do use words, phrases, clauses, sentences, and paragraphs in text analytics rules.

For example, a standard rule would be to look for two words within the same sentence, and count them differently than finding those two words separated by an indeterminate amount of text. In other words, it is usually more important to find two words in the same sentence than two words in different sentences that happen to be within five words of each other.

The next level of meaning structure is that of *sections* within documents, which can be defined in a wide variety of ways and sizes, but this is where it gets really interesting in terms of text analytics rules. Structuring a document in terms of sections typically improves readability, but it can also lead to very powerful text analytics rules.

For example, in one application we developed rules that dynamically defined a number of sections, which included things like abstracts, summaries, conclusions, and others. The words that define these sections were varied and so had to be captured in a rule, but then that gave us the ability to count the words, phrases and sentences that appeared in those sections as more important than those in the simple body of the document.

Metadata—Capturing and Adding Structure

The last type of structure is *metadata*—data or structure that is added to the document, either by authors, librarians, or software. This includes things such as title, author, date, all the rest of the Dublin Core,[1] and more. Currently, the most popular and successful approach to metadata is done with what are called *facets*—or faceted metadata.

Metadata may not have the exalted meaning of metaphysics and the like, but nevertheless, it is a fundamental and powerful tool for a whole variety of applications dealing with the semantic structure of so-called unstructured text.

What text analytics does in the area of metadata is twofold. First, it incorporates whatever existing metadata there is for a document into its own rules. For example, if there is an existing title for a document, then a text analytics rule can count the words that appear in the title as particularly significant for determining what the document is all about.

The second role for text analytics is to overcome the primary obstacle to the effective use of metadata—actually tagging documents with

The Meaning of "Meta"

Whenever I write about metadata, I'm always struck by the variety of meanings that the word "meta" has accumulated over the centuries. These meanings range from the mundane—metadata is data about data—to the sublime of metaphysics and all the associated uses based on the fundamental meaning of something higher than normal reality.

On a more personal note, it always reminds me of weird little facts that we pick up. As an undergraduate student, I decided that rather than take the standard French or Spanish as my foreign language, I would study ancient Greek. I'm still not sure why I did, but my guess is it had something to do with the fact that I was also reading James Joyce's *Ulysses* at the time. Whatever the reason, I took two-and-a-half years of it!

And that is where I came across this weird little fact about the word "meta:" In Greek, "meta" has a few basic meanings, but these meanings really took off after a librarian in Alexandria attempted to categorize all of Aristotle's works. He had just finished the volume/scroll on physics, and the next work he picked up was this strange work on the nature of reality. And so the story goes: He didn't know what to call it, so he called it *metaphysics*, which in Greek simply meant "the volume that came after the volume on physics." A humble beginning for a word that has come to mean so much.

good metadata values. In particular, this is an issue for faceted metadata applications, which require massive amounts of metadata to be added to documents.

We will explore this topic in more detail in Chapter 10, Text Analytics Applications, but the basic process that has had the most success is to *combine human tagging with automatic text analytics-driven tagging.* This hybrid approach combines the intelligence of the human mind with the consistency of automatic tagging—the best of both worlds.

Text analytics is also ideally suited to pulling out values for facets, such as "people" and "organizations," that enable users to filter search results more effectively (see Chapter 10 for more on facets and text analytics). Text analytics can also pull out more esoteric facets, such as for one project where we developed rules to pull out all the mentions of "methods"—everything from analytical chemical methods to statistical survey methods.

However, the most difficult (but also the most useful) metadata are *keywords* and/or *subject*—in other words, what the document's key concepts are and what the document is about. This is where text analytics adds the most value.

Subject and keywords metadata are typically generated by the text analytics capability of auto-categorization, which we will more fully discuss later in the chapter.

Text analytics uses a variety of meaning-based resources to implement auto-tagging and other metadata assignments. The basic resource is some type of controlled vocabulary, which can be anything, from a simple list of allowed values (names of states or countries) to fully-developed taxonomies.

There is a rich literature on taxonomies (see the bibliography), but the basic idea is that a *taxonomy is a hierarchical structure of concepts* (or events, actions or emotions) used to add a dimension of meaning to the analysis of text documents. Taxonomies are typically used in text analytics to provide a structure for sets of rules that can be applied to the text documents, where each node in the taxonomy will contain rules that categorize the documents as belonging to that node or not.

We will deal with how text analytics utilizes and creates content structure in Chapter 7, Text Analytics Development, and Part 5—Enterprise Text Analytics as a Platform.

Technology / Text Analytics Development Software

Theoretically, text analytics could be done by hand with teams of librarians or indexers, but the reality is it's only possible to do with some fairly sophisticated technology in the form of software. This software operates on a number of levels. The initial stage is simply structuring all the text into words, words into sentences, and finally into paragraphs. In most languages, including English, this is very simple: Words are defined by spaces, sentences by end-of-sentence code (period), and paragraphs by end of paragraph codes (hard return, followed by new indented text).

All text analytics software is able to perform these basic processes. In addition, the other basic process that virtually all text analytics software includes is part of speech characterization—characterizing words as articles, prepositions, nouns, verbs, and so on.

There are many books on the underlying technology used to accomplish these analytical tasks, so we won't be covering that level in this book.

One of the amazing things about the field of text analytics is that you can actually build a great many extremely valuable applications just on this very, very simple set of capabilities. Some applications, for example, build characterizations of document types based on simple word counts of various parts of speech. In fact, one of the most advanced applications I've seen uses the patterns and frequencies of articles and prepositions (so-called "function words") to build very sophisticated models that can do things, like determine the gender of the writer, and establish the power relationship of the writer to the addressee.[2]

However, in addition to these basic text processing capabilities, the field of text analytics has recently added a range of capabilities, including noun phrase extraction, auto-categorization, analyzing the sentiment of documents, and more.

We will cover those capabilities in finer detail in the next chapter, but will first take a look at the software development environment that is used to build on these basic text processing capabilities. The basic development processes are mostly the same for both text mining and text analytics at the initial stages. The differences show up at the end/analytical stage. The overall process is shown in the following list:

Basic Development Processes for Both Text Mining and
Text Analytics:

1. Variety of text sources – web, email, document repositories, etc.

2. Document fetching/crawling processes

3. Preprocessing – categorization, feature/term extraction, sentiment, etc.

4. Processed document collection – machine processing

Text Mining:

5. Apply various algorithms, refine – pattern discovery, trend analysis

6. Basic user functionality – filters, query, visualization tools, GUI, graphing, etc.

Text Analytics:

   7. Application – search, sentiment analysis, variety of application front ends

While text mining (TM) and text analytics (TA) share a lot of the initial processing stages and functions, different applications normally call for different approaches to those processing steps. For example, while both TM and TA employ categorization rules, they are typically different types of rules. TM categorization rules are almost always statistical, machine-based rules while TA rules often add explicit, human-created rules. As the title of the book implies, we will be focusing on TA in this book.

The following screenshot (Figure 1.1) shows one development environment for text analytics software. Most text analytics development environments share the majority of functions but, of course, being separate and competing companies, they all do it slightly differently. This makes life interesting for those of us who work with and partner with multiple text analytics companies.

Figure 1.1 shows the vocabulary and taxonomy (or ontology) management functions that most text analytics development environments utilize. There is a taxonomy on the left, and associated with each node are broader, narrower and related terms. In this example, the phrase "adult

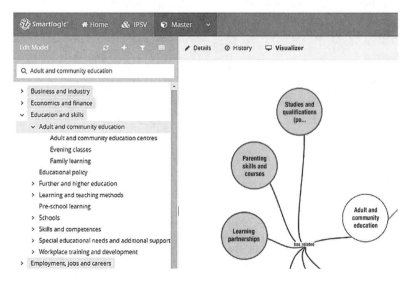

Figure 1.1   Development Environment 1

and community education" is a narrower term of "education and skills," and the phrases, "adult and community education centres" and "evening classes" are its narrower terms. Of course, each software vendor uses different terminology to refer to the various parts—and typically have slightly different components—but all have the same basic features.

In addition, there are various standard features for basic project development, such as project functions and rudimentary editing functions.

Typically, there is also a variety of features for loading test text files and/ or source text files. These text file collections can be used for developing initial categorization rules as well as for testing and refining those rules. This is usually done by running various tests that apply categorization or extraction rules to sets of text files and presenting the results in a variety of screens, showing pass/fail, scores, and other analytical results that also tend to vary by vendor.

The following screen from a different vendor (Figure 1.2) shows a development environment having rules associated with the taxonomy nodes. These rules can be simple lists of terms that you would expect to show up in documents about that topic, but not in other related topics. Or, they may include various advanced rules.

In many ways, these rules are essentially saved searches that can be applied to sets of documents that in turn can be used in a search application to help find specific documents. But they can also be used for a variety of other applications, where the goal is not to find a specific document, but to categorize sets of documents which can then be fed into applications,

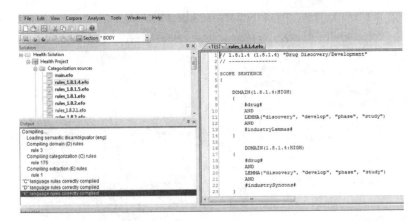

Figure 1.2   Development Environment 2

which might, for example, analyze the overall sentiment expressed in that document set.

Also, these categorization rules are typically orders of magnitude more complex and sophisticated than those of almost all searchers, with the possible exception of professional librarian searchers.

The following screen (Figure 1.3) shows one of those advanced rules as well as other common features in text analytics development environments.

On the left side of the screen is an area labeled "categorizer," which is used to manage a taxonomy that will provide the structure of the set of rules to be applied to documents. Below "categorizer" is an area labeled "concepts," where rules for extracting specific text or types of texts are developed and managed. The area to the right contains the actual rules that are used to categorize and/or extract from the target documents.

In addition to these basic development features, text analytics software typically includes functions to generate rules from a set of training documents. These rules can be statistical and/or sets of terms. In addition, some software has functions that attempt to automatically generate subcategories of the particular taxonomy.

Another basic set of functions enables developers to run and manage the testing environment, where rules are tested against a variety of documents and the results can then be analyzed. These tests then become the means to refine the rules.

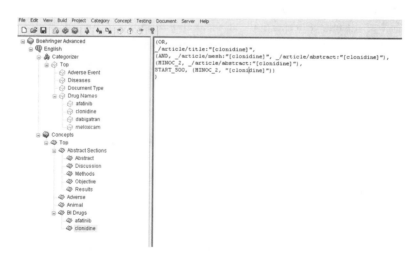

Figure 1.3 Categorization Rules

Text Analytics Applications

Text analytics by itself provides no real value—it is only the range of applications that can be built with text analytics that can help companies deal with the ever-growing mess of unstructured content. In fact, a couple of representatives I interviewed for this book took exception to my characterization of them as a text analytics vendor. One expressed that text analytics is not really a field, but only a component found within various applications. Another representative explained that their company sold applications and services—*not* text analytics—even though those applications and services depended entirely on their text analytics capabilities.

While I agree that text analytics does not provide direct value (except for those of us who find it fun and occasionally profitable), I disagree with the notion that text analytics is not a field (more on that in the Conclusion). In fact, it seems to me that one factor slowing the development of text analytics is an underappreciation of the uniqueness of the skills and capabilities that go into successful text analytics.

A good way to look at text analytics is that text analytics is a platform for building applications, and one thing is certainly true—text analytics applications continue to grow in both number and in the value that organizations are realizing from those applications. At this stage, the only limits seem to be the creativity of application designers and the still unconquered difficulty of intelligently processing all that messy unstructured text—the linguistic messiness problem.

We will take a deeper look at these applications and the role of text analytics in their development in Part 3, but generally, text analytics-based applications fall into four major areas:

1. Search, particularly enterprise search
2. Voice of the customer and other types of social media analysis
3. Search-based applications
4. Embedded applications

Enterprise Search

In the area of enterprise search, text analytics improves search by improving the quality of metadata, improving the efficiency of metadata generation, and lowering the cost of generating all that metadata. One thing has become very clear in the last 10-plus years since just after the turn of the century—enterprise search will never get better without more metadata and better metadata—and this is what text analytics brings to the table.

The three elements of text analytics that are used to improve search are *summarization*, *extraction*, and *auto-categorization*.

Summarization can enhance search results displays by providing a better characterization of the document in the results list than simple snippets. Snippets, the first 50 or so words of a document, can sometimes provide a reasonable clue as to the content of the document, but just as often will be almost meaningless gibberish. There are other more complex kinds of summarization that can be anything from an automatically-generated table of contents to descriptions of all the important concepts and entities in the document.

Extraction can be used to generate large amounts of metadata for each document, and this metadata can be used to develop the one approach to enterprise search that has shown promise—*faceted search*, or faceted navigation. Faceted search works very well, particularly compared with traditional enterprise search with its rather woeful relevance ranking, but one limit is simply the effort to generate all the metadata needed for the various facets. Text analytics changes that by lowering the cost to automate or semiautomate the process while also improving the quality and consistency of the metadata.

Extraction can feed traditional facets like "people" and "organization," where the software extracts all the names of people and organizations, enabling users to filter search results based on those facets. The text analytics-generated metadata can also be combined with other types of metadata that could normally be generated in a content management system, such as "author," "date," and other system metadata.

Auto-categorization can be used to populate the most difficult (and in many ways the most important) facet, which is "topic" or "subject." "Subject" can be used for both what the document is about and/or the major ideas within that document. This is where auto-categorization is primarily used and it can generate this metadata much more cheaply (and consistently) than hiring a team of out-of-work librarians or part-time taggers.

In addition, auto-categorization can also be used to improve the quality of the metadata generated by extraction through disambiguation rules and the ability to utilize context in much more sophisticated ways than simple catalog-based extraction.

Companies and organizations have spent millions of dollars buying one new search engine after another—and the results continue to disappoint. It is text analytics that has the promise of actually making enterprise search work.

Social Media—Voice of the Customer

Early social media applications consisted primarily of counting up positive and negative words in social posts of all kinds. These words were simply read out of dictionaries of positive ("good," "great," etc.) and negative terms ("terrible," and the ever popular "sucks"), which made the applications very easy to develop.

Unfortunately, it also made these applications rather stupid—and, if not useless, certainly much less valuable than the early bandwagon enthusiasts claimed. On the other hand, it was the beginning of what would become a major new avenue for enterprises to monitor and capture customer (and potential customer) feedback, along with their mindset to better meet their needs.

Thus it is text analytics in the broadest sense that makes this entire field possible—imagine trying to hire enough people to go through hundreds of thousands to millions of Twitter and/or blog posts per day!

While it was possible to get some value from the early simplistic approaches, the field only began to deliver real value when more sophisticated text analytics capabilities were applied. As was true of extraction, social media analysis needed the added intelligence of the full suite of text analytics capabilities to disambiguate, as well as to otherwise take into account the rich context, within which sentiment—or the voice of the customer—was being expressed. For example, with early approaches, the phrase, "I would have really loved this new laptop if it wasn't for the battery," would very likely have been classified as a positive sentiment—"love" and "new laptop" are within a few words of each other—and there are no sentiment words next to "battery."

Fortunately, we are currently in a more mature stage of social media applications, and while they are more difficult to develop, they deliver much more value. The applications include *voice of the customer*—monitoring social posts for positive and negative customer reactions to basic product features, the features of new product releases, new marketing campaigns, and much more.

Search-Based Applications

Search-based applications is a term that basically refers to using search as a platform for building a whole variety of different applications. These applications include things like e-Discovery, business intelligence, and developing rich dashboards for everything from marketing to scientific research. The idea is to build on search engines' capability of dealing with unstructured text to enrich applications that previously could only utilize structured data.

It is very interesting that in the early discussions of search-based applications, the need for text analytics was included as one component. Unfortunately, as search engine companies jumped on the idea as a natural way to extend their value, they tended to downplay the need for text analytics as something that emphasized the need for an element besides the search engine itself. Software companies seemed loathe to admit that something apart from their product was needed to really make search work. This is perhaps one reason why the idea of search-based applications has not made as much progress as it could have.

Incorporating unstructured text into this class of applications requires that we move beyond simple search results lists, which, as a number of people have discovered, is something that you need text analytics for. Even if you incorporate the results of a search engine's output into other applications, those results are still based on very simplistic relevance ranking calculations. Just as text analytics is needed to make enterprise search work, it is also needed to make search-based applications work. In fact, a better term might be "text analytics–based applications."

Embedded Applications / InfoApps

In addition to using text analytics (with or without a search engine) as a platform for applications, one new trend is to embed text analytics directly into them. These applications, which are somewhat of a second generation of applications built on top of search-based applications, have been termed *InfoApps* by Sue Feldman, who has a wonderful way with nomenclature.

Since the output of text analytics is normally simple XML, it is relatively easy to integrate these capabilities into other applications. The first example of that integration was with enterprise search itself. The second early integration was with content management software to help generate metadata.

The new generation of InfoApps takes the output from text analytics and embeds them directly into applications that are similar to the search-based applications, but doesn't require an actual search engine platform. Some examples of this type of application:

- Use text analytics for processing a few hundred thousand proposals to pull out all the important facts, like names of the bidder (architects, subcontractors), key dates, project costs, addresses and phone numbers, etc., and make that data available for a wide range of applications.

- Use text analytics to analyze tens of millions of emails between vendors and suppliers to uncover key information, which can be used for anything from buttressing a legal claim to discovering unclaimed discounts owed by the supplier.
- Use business intelligence and customer intelligence for combining data and text processing in order to gain a more complete picture of what is going on in a particular market and/or what specific competitors are doing. This is often paired with sentiment to look into how customers are reacting to new products or marketing campaigns.
- Use your imagination! If you have a lot of unstructured text (and who doesn't?), there will likely be a way for text analytics to do anything from improving your current processes to creating whole new application areas.

We will be taking a deeper look at these kinds of applications in Part 4, but the basic situation is that unstructured text continues to constitute 80%–90% of valuable business information—and the only real way to get good value out of all that text is with text analytics. Text analytics is basically a foundation or platform capability that can be integrated with a whole variety of other application areas and other fields (like semantic technology or Big Data).

As we shall see in later chapters, text analytics can, or should be, a rare combination of approaches and skills—one that incorporates standard IT programming skills with deep academic linguistic skills and a deep appreciation for the complexity of language and actual day-to-day communication.

With that in mind, let's start to take a deeper look at all the elements of this rich and dynamic new field in the next chapter.

Endnotes

1. "DCMI Home: Dublin Core® Metadata Initiative (DCMI)." Dublincore.org, 2015.
2. Pennebaker, James W. *The Secret Life of Pronouns: What Our Words Say about Us.* New York: Bloomsbury Press, 2011.

CHAPTER 2

Text Analytics Functionality

There are a number of core high-level capabilities that in recent years have come to be an essential part of text analytics. Currently, there are five major core capability areas within text analytics:

1. Text mining (including clustering)
2. Extraction
3. Summarization
4. Sentiment analysis
5. Categorization (or auto-categorization)

There are also a number of lower-level capabilities that can be used to support these five. One core functionality is the basic level technique of *clustering*—or finding clusters of co-occurring words within documents and sets of documents. This is basic in the sense that it underlies a number of techniques, from text mining to the so-called auto-taxonomy generation feature that a lot of text analytics vendors offer.

At a high level, the core capabilities can be distinguished by the text units that they operate on, the complexity of the operation, and the types of analysis performed.

Text mining primarily operates on very low level textual units— words, and occasionally sentences and paragraphs. The words are categorized into simple semantic categories, such as parts of speech (nouns, verbs, etc.).

Extraction of various kinds mostly operates at a higher level, with units such as noun phrases—as well as even more advanced linguistic constructions to extract things like events and facts.

Summarization is also a higher-level capability that operates on more of a semantic level. However, in terms of its practical uses, this functionality is more of a support feature—and one that many vendors are dropping from their software.

Sentiment analysis also operates primarily with phrases—and the phrases tend to be significantly more complex than those in simple extraction. This kind of capability is a combination of higher-level extraction and some of the simpler high-level language constructs that are found in auto-categorization.

Finally, *auto-categorization* operates on the highest level of semantic abstraction, as it tries to understand or characterize the meaning of text.

Let's take a deeper look at each of these five.

Text Mining

While text mining is a major capability for text analytics—indeed, for many it is pretty much all of text analytics with everything else playing a supporting role—we will not be covering it with quite the same depth as the other four. The two major reasons for this are: 1) text mining is the outlier with its emphasis on math over language (among other differences), and 2) unlike the rest of text analytics, the field of text mining has been well covered in multiple books, including a very good one titled *The Text Mining Handbook* by Ronen Feldman and James Sanger.[1]

What text mining does is analyze documents and sets of documents by counting up all the words, then mapping the frequency of those words—this is really the heart of text mining. It sounds simple, but there is a lot of preprocessing that can categorize those words (into sets of concepts) and limit the analysis of those words to only the significant ones.

In the world of text mining, the other four basic capabilities of text analytics listed above are normally considered preprocessing. In the words of Feldman and Sanger:

> Although text mining preprocessing operations play the critical role of transforming unstructured content of a raw document collection into a more tractable concept-level data representation, the core functionality of the text mining system resides in the analysis of *concept co-occurrence* patterns across documents in a collection.[2]

Once you have a map of all the words in a document and/or an entire corpus, there is a variety of highly-sophisticated analytical techniques that can be applied to this word count map, and this enables a broad range of applications to be built. It is in these analytical techniques that the real difference between text mining and text analytics lies.

These applications might include tasks like tracking the changes in a document collection or comparing the differences between two documents to determine the level of similarity. These differences might be used to answer questions, such as:

- What is the general trend of news topics between two periods?
- Are the topics the same or widely different between the two periods?
- Can emerging and disappearing topics be identified?

One of my new favorite studies is a research project that counted pronoun frequency in a broad range of text over the last century, which revealed that there has been a steady increase in the use of the word "I" in U.S. society. Depending on your political leanings, that might explain a lot. On the other hand, another study indicated that people who are lying are less likely to use the word "I." Does that mean we are becoming more truthful *and* more egotistical as a society? We'll just have to do some more studies!

In addition to counting words (refer to Figure 2.1), the other major capability of text mining is in generating clusters of co-occurring terms. A great deal of advanced mathematical analysis goes into generating these

	D1			f_x Descriptive Terms
	A	B	C	D
1	#	Percentag	Freq	Descriptive Terms
2	1	34%	766	optimization
3	2	13%	298	+ driver, + device, + mechanism, + layout, + mobile device, + drive force, + lithography, + drive development, hard-drive, + multiprocessor, + fabrication, + parallel, performance analysis, + mobile phone, + hardware platform
4	3	7%	152	+ router, + technology, + memory, + mechanism, + component, hardware, + optimization
5	4	1%	15	dram, + memory, + hardware implementation, + router, hardware, + technology, + component
6	5	15%	344	+ mechanism, + memory, + hardware description language, + hardware optimization, + hardware parameter show, + component, + hardware component, hardware overhead, + keyboard, + hardware system, + drive, + parallel, hardware complexity, performance analysis
7	6	7%	156	+ microprocessor, + pipeline, + firmware, + hardware modification, + hardware trap, hardware-software, device reliability, hardware support, hardware, + hardware implementation, vlsi, + hardware platform, + drive, + drive architecture, + keyboard
8	7	11%	245	hardware, + hardware unit, + drive resource management issue, hardware availability, hardware development, + hardware precision, + hardware basic, hardware design, + hardware resource, hardware acceleration, + hardware configuration
9	8	10%	217	+ component, + technology, + mechanism, + parallel, + optimization
10	9	4%	87	+ equipment, hardware cache due, + router, hardware, + memory, + device, + component, + technology, + mechanism, + optimization
11				

Figure 2.1   Text Mining Clustering

clusters. The cluster then becomes a second order of structure, which can subsequently be fed into the advanced analysis that is the real heart of text mining.

In other areas of text analytics, a taxonomy is normally used to provide an initial structure. Clusters and taxonomies each have their own advantages and disadvantages. The biggest advantage of clusters of co-occurring terms is that the process of generating them is relatively automatic—relatively, in that there is always some human preprocessing or contribution.

Clusters of co-occurring terms also have the advantage because they are based on actual text, rather than on artificial constructs applied to text. This allows clusters to be more dynamic, changing as the text changes. In addition, clusters are a more flexible structure than a rigid hierarchical taxonomy, which can be an advantage in certain types of applications and in specific kinds of text.

On the other hand, many of these advantages can also be disadvantages, depending on the application. The main drawback to clusters is lack of precision and the difficulty of human understanding regarding the basis of the cluster. For example, in Figure 2.1, it is hard to see what "performance analysis," "mobile phone," and "hardware platform" have in common, other than the fact that they appear close to each other in a sufficient number of documents. On the other hand, a taxonomy node can be given an explicit definition that is understandable and more precisely defines the essential characteristics of membership for that node.

In addition, the fact that clusters are based on specific text also limits the types of applications that can be built using clusters rather than taxonomies. For example, taxonomies can be used in search applications across a wide range of text content since they are based on a higher level of abstraction, while clusters are more tightly tied to specific sets of content. Also, taxonomies can normally be developed to more granular levels than clusters.

For now, the main point is that text mining is somewhat of an outlier in the overall field of text analytics. Text mining tends to be more mathematical than linguistic, and it shares more in common with data analysis than text analysis. As well, text mining tends to utilize a lower level of semantic analysis of the text even in its use of preprocessing. At best, text mining deals with the meaning of individual words—and sometimes phrases—but not sentences or paragraphs.

However, as we shall see later, combining text mining with other text analytics capabilities enables applications to take advantage of the strengths of each and overcome their limitations.

Entity (etc.) Extraction

Extraction of various elements—or *entities*—from text is similar to text mining in a number of ways, particularly in terms of the basic units on which it operates, in other words, relatively simple words and phrases.

Extraction tends not to use the context around those words, although as we shall see later on, there is some use of context to do things like disambiguation.

Extraction is essentially a way to pull data out of unstructured text and make it available for all the advanced data analysis techniques that have been developed over the years. However, this text-extracted data can also be used in a wide range of other applications.

In terms of techniques, there are three basic types of extraction that are commonly found in text analytics software: 1) noun phrase or entity extraction (which can include concepts, events, etc.), 2) regular expression extraction, and 3) fact extraction. We'll take a look at the basic features of each.

Noun Phrase / Entity Extraction

Basically, *noun phrase* or *entity extraction* is the capability of identifying and extracting particular types of entities such as people or organizations. There are two basic methods of entity extraction that differ dramatically in how they are implemented.

The first type is extraction of known entities, which are typically based on catalogs or lists of entities, along with their spelling variations. They are relatively simple, but can be tedious and resource-intensive to implement.

The following display (Figure 2.2) shows a list of country names—i.e., known entities—along with the variations of those names. This type of extraction might be part of an application that is looking for any mention of particular countries, which can then feed a variety of different applications—everything from news alerts about those countries, to various analytical applications looking to do a trend analysis of mentions of groups of countries mapped, to anything from an economic event, to [fill in your favorite].

The second type of entity extraction is the extraction of unknown entities. In place of lists or catalogs of terms, this type of extraction is usually based on rules. An example of an entity extraction rule is seen in the following screenshot (Figure 2.3). What the rule states is, "if you see a word that begins with a capital letter, and it is followed by the word 'said,' then that capitalized word is very likely to be a person." The logic of the rule

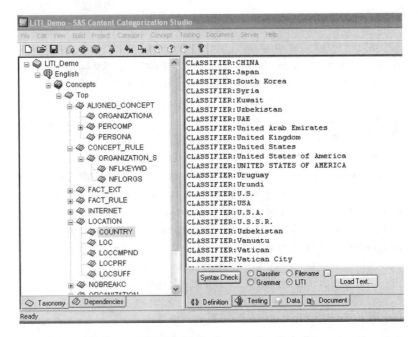

Figure 2.2   Entity Extraction List

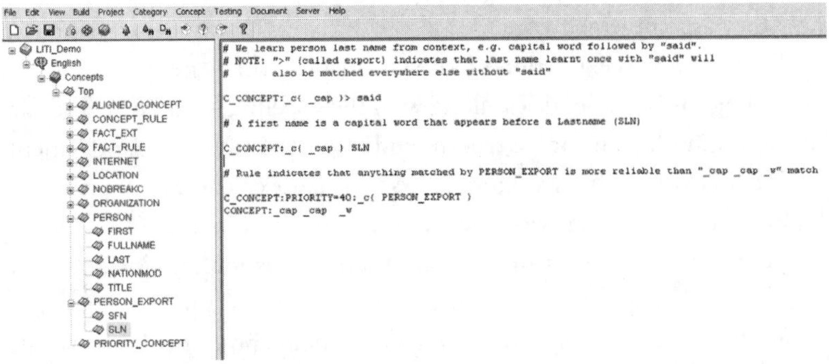

Figure 2.3   Entity Extraction Rules

is that more often than not, if "whatever" is saying something, then "whatever" is referring to a person.

Of course, this will also bring in some false hits. Think of the case where someone describes a company (instead of a person) that is saying something. This illustrates how important it is to remember that text analytics rules are *rarely* developed to work by themselves or in isolation.

So in this case, the rule could be refined with a simple Boolean NOT rule that would exclude all known organization names and reduce the number of false hits.

In the case of unknown entities, the trade-off is between the power of being able to find entities (even when you don't have a list of them all) and the lower accuracy of rules-based entity extraction. For example, trying to generate a database or catalog that covers all names of all people is a daunting task. The type of rule described above could save people from a lot of development costs.

In fact, trying to develop a database of all possible human names is both extraordinarily difficult and highly questionable as an undertaking. A colleague did try to develop a database of all first names, enjoying the luxury that comes from being a university professor with a lot of free labor (otherwise known as "students"). The database was something on the order of 30,000 names, and she thought that they actually had well over 90% of all possible first names covered. Of course, with the recent trend towards ever more creative first names, that number is probably going down.

And that does not count last names (apparently a whole lot more possibilities), and then, of course, there's the dauntingly high number of possible combinations. So we will likely continue to need these kinds of rules, but at the same time we have to realize that most real-world situations will be a combination of different rules and different types of rules.

Which type of rule to use will depend very much on the type of application and the type of content being analyzed. For example, if the application was only interested in finding names of people within their own organization—and that list of names already existed in an HR database—then it would be a simple matter to import it into an application. Very often, the two types of extraction can be combined, where you may develop a catalog of names of people, or organizations (or whatever), and then supplement that by a rule such as the one described above.

Regular Expression Extraction

There is another type of extraction that is often used in text analytics, namely for various *regular expressions*. In the following example (Figure 2.4), a regular expression operator, REGEX, is being used to extract any URLs found in the target text. This type of extraction is actually a combination of lists and rules, which combines the power of both, but with the restriction that it only works for certain well-formed entities.

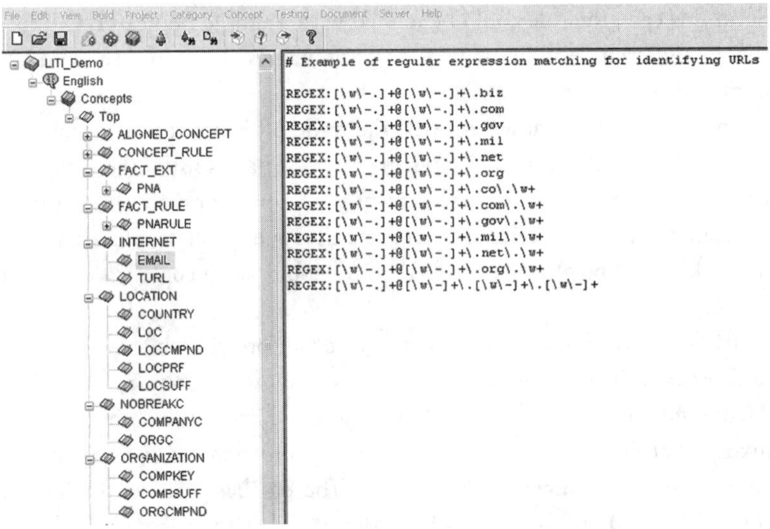

Figure 2.4   Entity Extraction—REGEX

In this example, there are a small, limited number of types of URLs designated by specific text, such as ".biz" or ".mil." The other parts of the rule basically state that if you find any series of words followed by the specific designations, then count it as a URL and extract it.

Regular expression extraction can be combined with other entity extraction capabilities and/or used for the same kinds of applications. It has the ability to find known entities without developing a full list and the ability to find unknown entities with a much greater accuracy than the rules-based entity extraction described above. The best of all possible worlds—but only for entities for which you can find expressions with a predictable pattern.

Fact Extraction

Fact extraction is a functionality that builds on entity extraction. In the following example (Figures 2.5 and 2.6), there are three components. In the first and third parts, the software looks for names of companies or other organizations. This can be a combination of a database of company names or a rules-based extraction. The middle part of the rule is the most complex, and what it is looking for is a variety of text phrases that indicate that the relationship between the two organizations or companies is one of a merger or an acquisition.

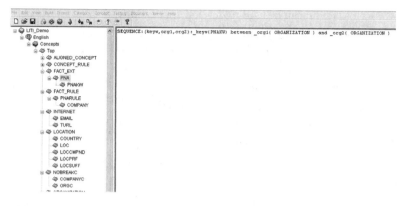

Figure 2.5   Fact Extraction—Basic

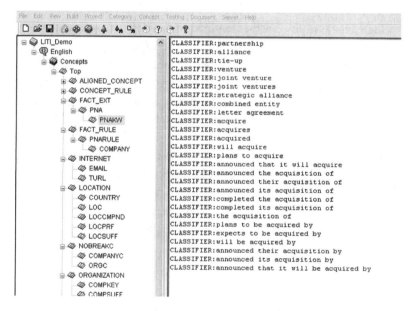

Figure 2.6   Fact Extraction—Verbs

There are quite likely tens of thousands of ways for a single sentence to express this sort of relationship, but by abstracting out from the non-essential parts of the sentence, the rule can develop a manageable set of key terms. So, rather than look at individual sentences, the rule looks at a manageable number of ways of expressing a merger and/or acquisition relationship between two organizations.

Fact extraction can be used to develop applications, such as a news alert looking for any kind of announcement about mergers and acquisitions, but it can also be used to feed into semantic technology and ontology-based applications. This is the sort of application that was developed for the BBC Olympics coverage, which still stands as one of the most cited and successful actual ontology-based applications.

One of the most powerful and interesting uses of fact extraction is in developing the ability to reason about relationships based on an ontology model that captures a variety of essential relationships. In the example above, a "company" ontology could model a wide range of attributes, such as companies that have employees who get paid by the company, companies that make profits or losses, companies that have presidents and CEOs (who themselves have a whole variety of characteristics—names, salaries, etc.), and much more.

These relationships can then be used in a variety of applications that "connect the dots," such as a simple look-up of an employee's personal information—even if that information is in a separate document or database. Or, it might be possible to derive various implications from the relationships, such as if a person is fired from a company, they no longer receive a salary. The possible relationships are limitless—the trick to date has been to decide which ones are important in which context.

In my experience, using fact extraction to feed semantic web applications is a technique with huge potential that is still often largely under-utilized. I believe that semantic web applications will continue to have unrealized potential until there is a stronger, deeper integration of text analytics, ontology development, and semantic technology.

Summarization

Summarization is one of the lesser known and cited capabilities of text analytics. One of the early uses for summarization was to create a replacement for snippets in search results lists. Search results typically list the titles of the documents, dates and snippets, which are often the first 50–100 words of the document. Snippets are rarely useful, particularly since the beginnings of documents are very often some structural element. Some search engines will take 50–100 words around the first instance of the search query, which is better, but often not very useful.

Summarization is one of those capabilities that is largely hidden from control by the user, and is based on a set of rules of varying sophistication.

There has been a great deal of research into processes and algorithms to improve automatic summaries, but most still require a human post-processing stage.

There are two basic types of summarization: *dynamic* and *static*. Dynamic summarization works in conjunction with the search query, the software looking at the words around the occurrence of the search term as it locates the most important sentences to use in the summarization. Other typical rules involve taking the first sentence of the paragraph, which contains one or more instances of the search query term, then combining it with other sentences or sentence fragments that contain the search query term.

This sort of summarization clearly works best with well-written documents, such as formal documents and/or news stories with well-written first paragraph sentences. It is perhaps because of this limitation that many text analytics companies no longer offer summarization as part of their platforms.

Static summarization doesn't start with a search query but rather tries to create a general summary of a document. This approach attempts to discover the key ideas of the document and organize the summary around them. As text analytics platform companies drop support for dynamic summarization, the trend is shifting towards companies developing more fully automated static summarization capabilities. This shift is accompanied by an application focus that is moving from search to other types of applications.

One common application is in document review, in which the software creates summaries that enable human reviewers to determine whether it is worth their valuable time to look into that specific document. Text analytics can be used in most of those cases to filter the number of documents requiring human review to more manageable numbers, or in other applications, the summary can function as a substitute for the full document.

For example, in one application, we used text analytics to pull out 30 or 40 key pieces of information in a set of documents, and presented that to a client in the midst of an important decision on whether to bid on a project or not.

This is one of the many application areas of text analytics that doesn't sound very exciting, though it can actually save millions of dollars in employee hours, and at the same time, produce better results.

Sentiment Analysis // Social Media Analysis

Sentiment analysis has been a major focus for text analytics for the last few years as companies have begun to monitor various social media streams, particularly those dealing with a company's products. Social media streams such as Twitter, forums, blogs and other social media provide a wealth of data not otherwise available. In fact, sentiment analysis has already been through one hype-bust cycle as it was going to "revolutionize everything"—but then it crashed to earth as so many high-tech "revolutions" have done in the last 20 or 30 years. We're now entering the familiar phase of building more realistic—and ultimately more valuable—applications.

In its simplest form, sentiment analysis is the use of software to characterize and/or extract various kinds of positive and negative sentiments from text. Sentiment analysis started with very simple rules which tried to score the positive and negative polarity expressed in text. The early applications simply used generic dictionaries of positive and negative terms. This was easy to do, but had very limited application. One fascinating example of what you can do with this simple approach is in the New York Times article of October 28, 2015.[3] They ranked the words of our current political candidates as positive or negative as well as on a complexity scale.

These dictionaries of positive and negative words were of limited value, and so have been supplemented with more context-dependent expressions. Positive expressions can be everything from a simple "that camera is very good" to "the quality of the image in this camera is somewhat superior to other models" and even more complex expressions. And, of course, negative expressions can be everything from "this camera sucks" to highly original and scathing insults, questioning everything from the parentage of the people who made the camera to their right to qualify as fully human.

In addition to simple positive and negative sentiments, other more advanced approaches include trying to characterize and capture more complex emotional states using techniques such as appraisal theory (see Chapter 8 for more details). These more complex emotions include things like sad, angry, disappointed, and even so depressed they should be watched carefully.

Another advance over simple positive and negative sentiment judgments has been the development of more sophisticated scoring systems instead of binary judgments. A lot of the early work in this area was done with restaurant and movie reviews that had overall scores along with text. You might see anything from four stars to nine out of 10 for positive reviews, or four piles of excrement (or insert your favorite insulting image), or simply only two out of 10 for negative reviews.

Sentiment Methods

There are a variety of methods used to characterize sentiment in text, and they range on a familiar scale from fully automatic to human/automatic hybrids. Most organizations have moved beyond simple positive and negative keywords.

More advanced approaches include a number of sophisticated statistical approaches in which every word is given a vector value in order to come up with a composite score of positive or negative sentiment for the entire document. These approaches begin with selections by humans of good example sets of documents exemplifying positive or negative judgments. While these approaches tended to be more accurate than simple positive and negative keywords, they also suffered from a number of limitations, particularly for advanced sentiments.

As has often been the case in text analytics, the best answer is usually a combination of approaches, marrying deeper semantics and better models along with rules-based approaches. In the following diagram (Figure 2.7), you can see a number of the elements of this approach.

What you have on the left is a hierarchy of products and features of products. These features typically correspond to either the most popular features of the product or the features that the company is primarily interested in. In the example above, we have camera features, such as quality, usability, image, price, and so forth. Under each feature, there are positive, negative, and neutral terms or phrases.

Associated with each sentiment area on the right, there are a number of phrases and terms extracted from documents (training sets) to capture the typical positive or negative comments.

The typical development cycle for these sorts of applications is for humans—specifically subject matter experts—to select those training sets that are great examples of positive, negative and neutral statements about the particular products and product features. The software typically begins with a simple dictionary, or a more complex semantic network of positive and negative terms, and applies that to the text.

In addition to the positive and negative phrases that the software extracts from sample documents, it is also possible to build categorization-like

	Type	Rule Body
File Edit View Build Help		

Training Corpora
Statistical Model
Polarity Keywords
Product

		Type	Rule Body
⊟ Product	1	CLASSIFIER ∨	really is an improvement
⊟ iPhone	2	CLASSIFIER ∨	iPhone is great
⊟ Feature	3	CLASSIFIER ∨	worked great
⊟ value	4	CLASSIFIER ∨	I love the features
Positive	5	CLASSIFIER ∨	very happy
Negative	6	CLASSIFIER ∨	Great phone
Neutral	7	CLASSIFIER ∨	The iPhone 4 is remarkable
⊟ features	8	CLASSIFIER ∨	I love the features
Positive	9	CLASSIFIER ∨	screen is the best
Negative	10	CONCEPT_R! ∨	(DIST_5, "screen", "_c{best}")
Neutral	11	CLASSIFIER ∨	Great phone, it's easy to use
⊟ ease	12	CLASSIFIER ∨	
Positive	13	CLASSIFIER ∨	
Negative	14	CLASSIFIER ∨	
Neutral	15	CLASSIFIER ∨	
⊟ battery	16	CLASSIFIER ∨	
Positive	17	CLASSIFIER ∨	
Negative	18	CLASSIFIER ∨	
Neutral	19	CLASSIFIER ∨	
⊟ Feature Polarity	20	CLASSIFIER ∨	
	21	CLASSIFIER ∨	
	22	CLASSIFIER ∨	
	23	CLASSIFIER ∨	
	24	CLASSIFIER ∨	

Figure 2.7   Sentiment Analysis Basic

rules that capture more general kinds of comments. For example, a rule might look for any word that means "terrible" within the same sentence as any word that means "support." These kinds of rules enable the software to take into account context, and can be more complex, such as "if you see any of these various sets of words in the same sentence with any words that describe a feature, then count it as positive, unless you also see any qualifying or negating phrases."

Auto-Categorization / Auto-Classification

Without the ability to categorize, we could not function at all, either in the physical world or in our social and intellectual lives. An understanding of how we categorize is central to any understanding of how we think and how we function, and therefore central to understanding what makes us human.[4]

—George Lakoff, *Women, Fire, and Dangerous Things: What Categories Reveal about the Mind*

The last text analytics capability we will discuss is usually called *auto-categorization*, and in many ways, it is the most fundamental and the most advanced of all the text analytics capabilities. It is also one that is rather unfortunately named in that auto-categorization is only one of the uses for the underlying capability. For now, we will continue to use the term auto-categorization until a better term is developed. Hopefully, that new term will come soon (perhaps I'll start that contest I mentioned in the Introduction) since that major arbiter of terminology, Wikipedia, has inactivated the term.[5]

In an earlier discussion, I came up with "contextual analysis," which has been adopted by one vendor, but that is more about the software and what it does than the act of categorizing a document. Until then, I'll stick with auto-categorization. But stay tuned.

Whatever we call it, auto-categorization is a capability that is fundamental to text analytics, both because it can be used to create the most valuable applications, and because it is a feature that adds intelligence and depth to all the other text analytics capabilities. In other words, auto-categorization is really the brains of the outfit.

The key idea is encapsulated in the title, "*Thinking Fast and Slow,*"[6] where author Daniel Kahneman describes two systems of the brain. One (System 1) excels in fast pattern matching, and the other (System 2) excels in slower, more analytical tasks, such checking the validity of a logical argument. In the world of text analytics, auto-categorization is System 2.

One of the fundamental uses for auto-categorization is to characterize the "aboutness," or subject, of a document and/or capture the key ideas of the document. It can also be applied to sections of the document, paragraphs, sentences, or even phrases. In many ways, this is the most advanced kind of judgment about text. It is certainly the closest to human-type judgment among all text analytics capabilities. Not surprisingly, it is also the most difficult to do well.

In some ways, it is similar to artificial intelligence (AI) in trying to reproduce results that are similar to advanced human judgments. Of course, back in the 1980s, artificial intelligence was "only a couple years away from being able to model human intelligence." Some of us are still waiting, but luckily text analytics auto-categorization does not need a complete model of human intelligence, and we can forge ahead and make progress now.

In fact, one much simpler way to think about auto-categorization, particularly those approaches based on categorization rules, is that they are essentially saved search queries that can be applied to new text. For example, you might have a very simple rule that says: IF you find the phrase "service plan" OR "customer support plan" AND (the name of one of your plans), THEN the document is about one of your company service plans.

Categorization Methods

Auto-categorization typically starts with some type of taxonomic structure. It can be as simple as a list of 20 or 30 topic areas, or it can be as complex as a six- or seven-level taxonomy with thousands of nodes. The basic approach is to develop a categorization capability for each topic area or taxonomy node. For example, in the following display (Figure 2.8), there is a simple one-level taxonomy of specific diseases. Associated with each disease is a rule that can be used to determine which specific documents are about that disease.

There are a number of approaches to doing auto-categorization, some of which are more advanced than others. As with sentiment analysis, the first step is usually selecting example documents called "training sets" that are good examples for specific categories. In the example above, subject matter experts would pick anywhere from 10, 50, or perhaps 100 documents that are good examples of documents dealing with each particular disease.

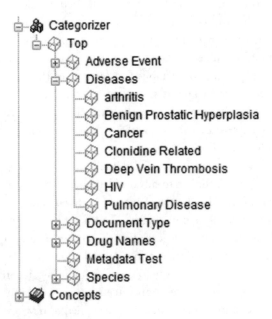

Figure 2.8   Basic Categorization

The software then analyzes those documents and creates a statistical signature of the training set documents, which can then be compared to new documents to determine if they belong to the same category.

This is often touted as the easiest way to do categorization. However, very often the results are not particularly good. In cases where there are a few very distinct categories, categorization by training sets can be adequate, but with more categories—and particularly when the categories are not sufficiently distinct and/or are more granular, this method usually fails to provide sufficient accuracy.

The next simplest approach to auto-categorization is to take those initial training documents and pull out specific terms—either unique terms or terms that can distinguish one category from another—and present them to a human editor, who can then refine the list of terms.

In the following list, the rule is simply a list of terms and phrases that the software (or a human editor) found in the initial training sets—ideally terms that show up in the target documents but not in the general collection of documents.

```
tyrosine kinase inhibitor,

epidermal growth factor receptor,

EGFR,

non-small cell lung cancer,

breast cancer,

glioblastoma,

head cancer,

neck cancer,

colorectal cancer,
```

This list of terms and phrases can then be applied to new documents, and if the new documents contain enough of those terms, then the new document is considered as belonging to that category. Of course, there is a lot more to deciding whether specific documents belong to a category or not, including use of various search-type functionality such as relevance ranking.

Categorization using unique terms and phrases can also be supplemented in most software by developing rules in addition to the terms. The simplest forms use the basic Boolean operators AND, OR, NOT to build auto-categorization rules. However, by combining all three operators, some fairly complex rules can be built, such as IF ("cancer" OR "glioblastoma")

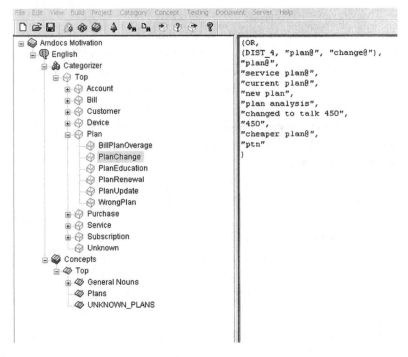

Figure 2.9   Simple Categorization Rule

AND ("neck" OR "head" OR "breast") AND NOT ("research" OR "fundraising") THEN count it as a hit.

However, most text analytics software adds more advanced operators to build even more complex rules. One of the more common operators is some variant of the DIST operator in Figure 2.9, which looks at the distance between two words or phrases. Of course, each vendor has their own proprietary syntax (DIST_5, NEAR_5, or <1:5>). Perhaps we need to develop a common standard terminology, like SQL?

Regardless of what it is called, this operator can be used to increase the power of the rule dramatically. In the following example (Figure 2.9), one part of the rule says to only count a hit if the word "plan" appears within four words of the word "change." This kind of rule can be used to eliminate a large number of false positives.

And, of course, combining Boolean operators with these more advanced operators can be used to develop even more complex rules as seen in the next example (Figure 2.10). These more complex rules are typically much more accurate than simple lists of keywords or sample documents.

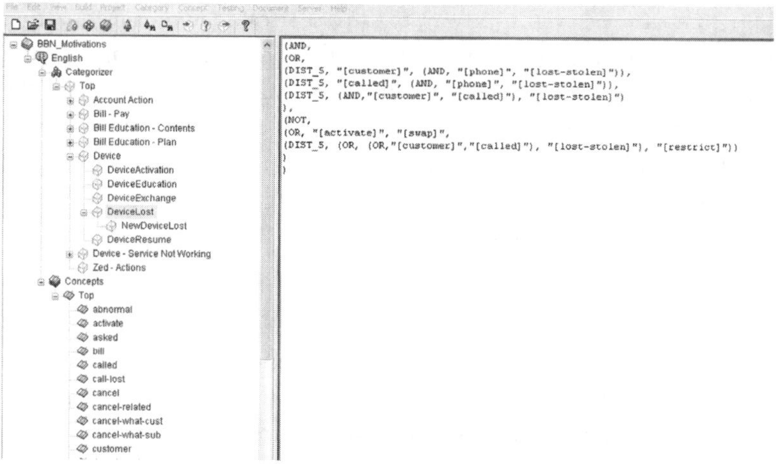

Figure 2.10   Advanced Categorization Rule

Another type of rule uses one of the other powerful capabilities of auto-categorization, which is to add structure to unstructured content by building rules to identify sections of the document. In one project I worked on, we analyzed the document set and came up with a limited number of words that, when used by themselves, indicated that the text following was an abstract or similarly important section.

Abstract,	Summary,
ABSTRACT,	Background:,
Introduction,	Aim,
Background,	SUMMARY,

Once you add this sort of structure to unstructured text, there are a number of ways to use the structure to enhance auto-categorization as well as other applications. For instance, you may want to give the keywords that appear in the abstract much more weight than words found within the body of the text. We will go more deeply into these kinds of advanced rules in Chapter 7.

In addition to categorizing documents against a taxonomy, another primary use of categorization rules is to disambiguate some of the other capabilities of text analytics software. For example, in entity extraction, one of the common problems is distinguishing between different meanings of the same word. For example, the word "Ford" might refer to a car, to a person, to a company, or even to a way to cross a stream. Auto-categorization rules can be used to distinguish which of those meanings is being used in a particular document or sentence by examining the context around the occurrence of that term. So, if the sentence or paragraph contains other words that refer to parts of cars, or to company activities, or to the person holding a particular position, then those words can be used to disambiguate between the meanings of the word "Ford."

Supplemental Auto-Functions

In addition to the five text analytics capabilities discussed above, a number of text analytics software development platforms offer supplemental functions that can be used to "automatically" create a starting taxonomy and/or suggest new taxonomy nodes to be added to a current taxonomy. These automatic taxonomies are really multiple clusters of clusters of co-occurring terms with some rules used to create relatively *orthogonal*—or *exclusive*—sets.

This type of functionality can be very useful for exploring new documents and exposing some interesting connections between new terms and old. Very useful—but if anyone tells you that the automatic taxonomy is a "real" taxonomy and can replace (not supplement) human-developed taxonomies, don't believe them.

Endnotes

1. Feldman, Ronen, and James Sanger. *The Text Mining Handbook: Advanced Approaches in Analyzing Unstructured Data.* Cambridge: Cambridge University Press, 2007.

2. Ibid, page 8.

3. "Ted Cruz as Beowulf: Matching Candidates with the Books They Sound Like." *The New York Times,* October 28, 2015.

4. Lakoff, George. *Women, Fire, and Dangerous Things: What Categories Reveal about the Mind.* Chicago: University of Chicago Press, 1987.

5. Wikipedia: Auto-categorization. (Note: *This page is currently inactive and is retained for historical reference.* Either the page is no longer relevant or consensus on its purpose has become unclear. To revive discussion, seek broader input via a forum, such as the village pump, https://en.wikipedia.org/wiki/Wikipedia:Village_pump. August, 2015.)

6. Kahneman, Daniel. *Thinking, Fast and Slow.* New York: Farrar, Straus and Giroux, 2011.

The Business Value of Text Analytics

As we saw in the last chapter, text analytics involves difficult and often expensive software. It requires significant resources and more importantly, resources that very often companies don't have prior to undertaking a text analytics project. All of this raises some critical questions: Why do text analytics—and what are the possible benefits? In other words, what is the return on investment, or ROI, of text analytics?

The answer is not a simple one, in part because there are a broad range of different types of applications that text analytics can support—from fixing search to understanding your customers and what they are talking about, to how they feel about your products or your campaigns or your company, to understanding your competitors and what they are working on, to what people are saying about them, their products, and more. And that's just the regular applications—there are new ones being developed every day with one of the hot areas being combining unstructured text with structured data—especially Big Data applications.

The problem of measuring ROI is slightly different in each of these different cases and, in addition, there are well-known difficulties within each area. On the one hand, many analysts are arguing that measuring ROI of, for example, social media campaigns, is the wrong measure. On the other hand, the early enthusiasm for sentiment analysis seemed to stumble when people began asking what the real business value was.

To understand the business value of text analytics, we need to focus our questions more precisely. We need to look at the situation in each of the different application areas of text analytics. We will do this in the rest of the chapter, but it can be helpful to also take a look at the basic business logic of text analytics.

The Basic Business Logic of Text Analytics

The basic business logic is simply:

1. Companies are overwhelmed by enormous and growing amounts of unstructured text.

2. Most of this unstructured text is not being utilized or at least not fully utilized.

3. Text analytics is (among other things) a way of adding structure to all that unstructured text.

4. Adding structure to unstructured text turns it from a problem (information overload) into a (whole set of) solutions.

OK, that is easy—end of chapter.

Well, maybe it's not quite *that* simple.

The amount of unstructured text is growing daily. The standard that 80% of all important business information is in unstructured text—Word documents, notes of various kinds, and so on—is in need of an update. With the rise of more social media text and data, this figure is more like 90%.

It would seem fairly obvious that if you have an enormous amount of unstructured text—and the best way to get value from all that text is to add structure—and the best way to add structure is text analytics—then the benefits of text analytics are clear. Of course, it is never that simple, and we need to always make the case for the value of text analytics.

Is Asking About ROI the Wrong Question?

In a lot of ways, asking about the ROI of text analytics is really asking the wrong question. It's kind of like asking, what is the ROI for having a human resources department? Or more fundamentally, what is the ROI for organizing your company?

Imagine if companies simply went out and hired thousands of people, at the start of each day putting them all in a single, giant room. Then, as each new task came up, managers would go hunting through this mass of people to try to find the right person for that particular job. After the right people had been chosen, they would try to figure out which ones were best suited for managing the project and which ones were best for actually implementing the project. In other words, what if you had to figure out what the employee hierarchy was every single day?

In essence, this is what people are doing now with unstructured content. The only way to get real value out of unstructured content is to add structure. And the best, most economical way to add structure to unstructured content is through text analytics, or more often, hybrid solutions that combine text analytics with human effort.

Benefits in Three Major Areas

There are three major areas in which text analytics can provide significant benefits to an organization: enterprise search, social media, and multiple text analytics–powered applications, some of which used to be called search-based applications.

Even though it seems obvious that unstructured text is a woefully underutilized resource and that adding structure is the best way to get value from that resource, we still need to be careful and creative about how we justify text analytics, particularly because the reality is that text analytics has an enormous potential for transforming the way organizations work, not only for developing whole new ranges of applications, but for incorporating the social dimension of customers in new and exciting ways.

In addition, these benefits fall into two broad categories:

- Cost savings and/or productivity enhancements
- Applications that generate new revenues and/or create new opportunities

Each organization will have a different balance and a different set of benefits, and so it is important to take a deep look at how text analytics will work within your organization.

Also, since text analytics is a platform for multiple applications, it makes sense that the benefits case needs to be made for each area of application that can be built on it. If you just look at one application, the cost/benefits calculation might not look too good. Although it is amazing how often even one application can justify the cost of an entire text analytics platform. And when you start adding them all together, the case becomes overwhelmingly good.

Justifying each application that text analytics can drive is beyond the scope of this book and is a never-ending task, but the arguments for large classes of applications have been pretty well-developed.

Case One: Enterprise Search

One of the most fundamental (and largest) areas of applications for text analytics is in enterprise search, which constitutes between 30%–50% of text analytics applications, depending on which pundit or researcher you talk to. So let's take a closer look at the benefits that text analytics can bring to enterprise search.

First of all, enterprise search is also largely an infrastructure application that, when done correctly, involves a search engine, content management, taxonomies and other forms of metadata. And the reality is that today, enterprise search has failed to live up to its potential as multiple surveys have demonstrated.[1] What we typically see in company after company is growing dissatisfaction with enterprise search, until finally the company decides it's time to try a new search engine. Then they go out, do a stand-ard search engine initiative, and end up buying a new search engine. This increases "satisfaction in search" for anywhere from a few months to a year or two, or until the dissatisfaction begins to grow and grow, in part as the amount of content grows and grows. Text analytics has the potential to end this search engine dance by enabling new ways to add meaning to search and getting organizations past that familiar refrain, "enterprise search *sucks!*"

In addition, another information technology that often works with enterprise search is enterprise *content management* (CM), which also has the potential to greatly improve search. Unfortunately, content manage-ment has also largely failed to live up to its potential. While content man-agement has done quite a good job of storing documents, its track record in enabling the location of those documents has been pretty dismal. Con-tent management should be the place where we add the metadata that is required to enable us to find those documents, but the reality is that most metadata projects—particularly asking authors to add keywords to documents as they publish them into the content management system, or CMS—have been failures.

Adding metadata is not a task that most authors want or are very good at. They may be subject matter experts, but selecting good keywords to enable nonexperts to find those documents is not a skill that very many people have. In addition, they usually balk at the extra work of categoriz-ing their documents, and have been very creative in finding ways to get around the onerous task. The result is more often than not, very terrible and/or missing metadata.

Adding text analytics to content management is one of the most effec-tive ways to use content management to improve search, as we shall see in Chapter 10. The basic answer is that text analytics can automatically or semiautomatically add metadata to content—and it can add lots of

metadata that support the most important new approach to search—
faceted search.

The other component that was supposed to improve search is adding
taxonomies to the mix. I have to admit that I used to believe that this was
the best answer, and spent a few years developing taxonomies for organizations, which, while they helped somewhat, were rarely worth the effort and
time. The basic problem was not with the taxonomy, but with trying to
apply the taxonomy to documents, in other words, manual tagging with
all its well-known problems.

We'll focus more on the specific issues with search, content management,
and taxonomies in Chapter 10, but the basic answer is that text analytics
can be the foundation that finally drives success in enterprise search, content management, the use of taxonomies, and generating good metadata.

The basic model is that text analytics incorporates taxonomies, and can
be used to develop ways to apply the taxonomy—automatically or semiautomatically—inside a content management workflow and/or within a
search engine. It can also be used to extract large varieties of metadata to
feed a faceted search.

Using these approaches, it is possible to greatly enhance the accuracy
and usefulness of enterprise search. Finally!

OK, So We Fix Search—So What?

At this point a good skeptic might ask: OK, so we fix search—but what
does that actually mean in real business value? Well, we have had an answer
for a number of years in a couple of studies done by International Data
Corporation (IDC).[2] IDC looked at three main areas in which bad search
was costing organizations:

- The amount of time people spend searching (and thus not
  working, but getting paid)
- The re-creation of documents in cases where employees could
  not find the document they needed
- And finally, the cost of bad business decisions and/or poor
  quality work as a result of not getting the right information

What they found when they looked at the amount of time employees spent searching was that about 50% of the time spent on searching
was the result of a bad search engine. In other words, a reasonable search
engine should, on average, be able to find documents in half the time typically spent by modern organizations. Based on their assumptions about

the average salary and the amount of time the typical employees spend searching, this costs the average organization $2,500 per person per year.

They also estimated that the need to re-create documents which could not be found was costing organizations an average of $5,000 a year per person. And this only looked at the time it took to re-create the document, but often another cost that could be even higher is the proliferation of duplicate (and even worse, near-duplicate) documents. These duplicates not only pollute search results lists, but can lead to even worse problems when people use the wrong version of the document. This can lead to anything from a legal liability to what IDC calls a "bad quality decision," which can have enormous consequences.

Now we come to the third IDC category of cost: the results of bad quality decisions at work. This is an area that is much harder to quantify, but they came up with some conservative estimates of about $15,000 a year per person that bad search was costing organizations. Of course, it could also be much more.

There is a famous story of a pharmaceutical company that spent hundreds of millions of dollars because of a bad search.[3] We don't know just how apocryphal the story is, and losing that much money because of a bad search is beyond the experience of most of us, but still, bad business decisions because of bad search can be amazingly expensive.

When you add up just the three primary areas (and there are more), it comes out to about $22,500 a year per employee. In other words, bad search is making more than the minimum wage and you have one of these minimum-plus wage earners for every employee in your organization. That's a lot of waste! It's time to fire them!

If text analytics could improve the results of search by only 30%, that is a savings of $6.75 million a year per every 1,000 employees. This is, of course, a pretty generic estimate; exactly how much improvement text analytics can achieve will vary considerably based on type of content, type of searches, the amount of effort put into the text analytics solution, and so on. However, in projects that I have seen, the improvements have been closer to 50%—equating to $11 million dollars a year per every 1,000 employees.

The cost of text analytics software can vary dramatically, but an average is in the low six figures, or around $100,000 plus development costs (that could double or triple that for a new search application). The return on investment is still in the neighborhood of $6.5 million a year per 1,000 employees! That's a pretty good ROI.

Getting Your Money's Worth

In addition to the productivity and related savings of adding text analytics to enterprise search and enterprise content management, there is the argument that organizations have spent enormous amounts of money on enterprise search and enterprise content management—but they are not getting anywhere near full value from those investments. By adding a relatively small additional cost, text analytics enables organizations to finally get the full value from those earlier investments.

Text analytics can also put an end to that all-too-frequent search engine dance of buying-trying-crying-buying. So, one of the benefits of spending $100,000 on text analytics is to save organizations from spending $500,000 to $1 million every few years on a search engine that doesn't work, or a content management system that users find ways to circumvent in that all-important element of adding metadata. For smaller organizations, the proportions will likely be the same, just divide by X—say $50,000 for text analytics—and $125,000 to $200,000 in savings. Smaller organizations probably don't need any of the above, but you might grow, so stay tuned.

Case Two: Social Media Applications

Aside from search, social media analysis is the other big set of applications in text analytics. This has been one of the hottest areas in the field over the last few years. Many more companies have jumped on the social media bandwagon and are doing sentiment analysis in order to understand what people are saying about their company and their products. It also led to the second major burst of new text analytics companies coming into existence, based on simple sentiment analysis along with some more or less advanced data analytics.

So it might seem that this area doesn't need any significant justification, but the reality is it's already gone through one hype-and-bust cycle as companies jumped on the bandwagon before discovering that it was actually hard to achieve real business value from simple sentiment analysis that monitors Twitter feeds and blogs.

Now, however, the business value is being realized as people develop more sophisticated methods of sentiment analysis and ways to analyze social media for valuable information beyond the simple "do people like or dislike a feature of my product?" This new generation of social media text analytics applications has found its path into the organization in a variety of ways.

In the early days of sentiment analysis (2004–2008), sentiment added a much-needed dimension to early marketing attempts to track the number of mentions or site visits that the company or its products got. As the article titled "Sentiment Analysis: Measuring Social Media and Content Marketing ROI" informs us, it quickly became apparent that mentions were not a very good measure:

> For example, when Progressive was involved in a social media nightmare last year, its online mentions may have skyrocketed, but the sentiment behind them was predominately negative. If the company were simply measuring mentions and website visits, it would have a very incomplete picture of its brand presence.[4]

In the past, mentions and web traffic reports were supplemented by very basic positive-negative sentiment characterization, which, while an improvement, were still too simplistic. All they did was count the number of positive and negative words in documents or posts. This is a lot like past search engines counting the number of times a search term appeared in a document and then presenting that as a measure of relevancy. Pretty dumb.

These early sentiment applications had very low accuracy because they failed to take into account the complexity of sentences. For example, the sentence, "I would have loved [product name], except it has a short-lived battery," might be characterized as positive because it has "loved" and the product name in the same document and in close proximity. On top of that, "short-lived" might not even show up in their generic dictionary of negative terms, since it is very context-specific.

The obvious next step was to develop more advanced rules that could look at the context around those positive and negative terms—but the reality is that sentiment accuracy is still fairly low (though always improving). This has led to a shift away from sentiment expressions as a standalone measure in favor of the use of multiple other indicators, such as number of fans, number of retweets, and even web traffic—if it is only part of the measurement.

While there has been progress in enhancing sentiment and other social media with text analytics, the reality is that it is very difficult to actually measure ROI from social media. For example, the following marketing study asked 500 executives of leading companies what they measured to track the impact of social media. The overwhelming majority of companies track a variety of indirect indicators, such as the number of fans or lead generation, but only 7% tried to measure direct sales. The basic problem is that is it very hard to measure direct sales figures, and so most companies don't even try.

The survey responses of what they tracked were:

26% fans, followers, and supporters

25% web traffic

16% lead generation

10% reduced cost of customer support

7% value of sales generated through social media programs[5]

This difficulty in measuring direct ROI doesn't seem to have slowed the rush to get on the social media bandwagon—and with good reason.

It is not surprising that marketing, sales and other departments continue to invest in social media monitoring programs. After all, social media offers direct access to that most precious of commodities—customers, both real and potential.

As the previously-cited "Sentiment Analysis" article put it:

Social media supports existing business goals & objectives.

Every customer touch point can be enhanced by social media

Public relations/corporate communications/crisis management

Marketing (including email marketing, newsletters, etc.)

Customer service

Human resources

Lead generation/sales

Event planning/management

Market research

Mobile apps[6]

What Are the Benefits of Social Media Analysis?

As for the benefits of *social media analysis*, the first thing to understand is what social media can actually do for your business. Many companies have realized that social media does *not* generally function as an engine for direct sales—and so they are moving away from strict return on investment (ROI) metrics. From 2012 to 2014, the proportion of marketers using a revenue-per-customer metric on social media fell, from 17% to just 9%.

This doesn't mean that metrics cannot and should not be used, or that ROI can't be measured for certain aspects of social media marketing, but it does mean that you have to take a holistic view when trying to gauge ROI through social media analysis.

The first major benefit that text analytics brings to social media is an enhanced ability to do sentiment analysis. Text analytics adds depth and intelligence to sentiment analysis, helping it move beyond the early simplistic sentiment characterization. For more on how this is done, see Chapter 8, and for more on social media applications, see Chapter 12.

Social media measurements can be added to traditional measures, such as site visits, open rates, conversions, and more. What social media analysis—like other text analytics–based applications—adds to these traditional measures is a deeper look at the context around those simple numbers. Traditional measures mostly deal in correlations, while social media analysis can often add a deeper understanding of why customers feel the way they do—and provide greater insight into their current and predicted behavior.

In addition, text analytics can be applied to social media for a large and growing number of applications that have little to do with sales and marketing. Companies can monitor online conversations in Twitter, blogs, and product forums for a variety of insights, including not just negative feedback, but ideas for new products or features and services. To understand what people really want requires applications to go beyond just sentiment analysis.

Monitoring social media more broadly can also provide insights, like early warning of issues with a particular product or feature and allow the company not only to respond to criticism, but get an early start on improving their product before the negativity gets too widespread and set in the public's mind.

The range of possible applications and benefits includes:

- A strong social presence can help build brand awareness.
- Companies can engage directly with customers, helping build brand loyalty.
- They can monitor the online conversation about their products and services, garner feedback, and respond to criticism.
- It can boost search engine optimization (SEO) and traffic to your main corporate website.
- Using social media effectively can also be an essential part of the localization process, if you are reaching out to foreign markets.

In an article from Text Analytics Summit, they listed the following areas where text analytics adds value:

- Attrition rate management and reduction
- Customer satisfaction
- Customer management effectiveness
- Enhancing predictive modeling and other data processes
- Maintaining or increasing long-term revenues
- Managing brand perception
- Marketing campaign evaluation
- Product design insights[7]

Social Media Examiner's 2013 Social Media Marketing Industry Report[8] found that 89% of marketers surveyed said that their social media efforts had generated more exposure for their businesses. The second major benefit was an increase in traffic, reported by 75% of respondents. 69% used social media to gain marketplace intelligence, and 65% used it to increase the loyalty of fans and customers.

Clearly, the business value of social media and our ability to measure it continues to grow dramatically.

Text Analytics–Based Application Benefits

Text analytics–based applications, including what have been called search-based applications, InfoApps, and embedded applications, have many benefits—including one big advantage when trying to justify the investment—*they can actually produce income!* Not just productivity gains, or being able to listen to your customers, but real income.

Not all text analytics–based applications produce direct income, but rather than try to make an abstract case for cost savings for the whole class of applications, it is probably a better idea to just share some stories of real-world applications that can give you an idea of the range and variety of ways that text analytics can produce incredible benefits. This is particularly true because companies rarely make a big effort to actually calculate the ROI of these applications—usually the savings are extremely clear.

So, Let's Just Share Some Stories

During my career in text analytics, I've come across many stories, several of which I share with you here.

Email Audit Application: A company created a service business where they analyzed millions of emails for their clients, looking for indications that the client was owed money by one or more of its vendors. All they had to do was look through 20 million emails for various indicators that one of those emails contained evidence that their client was owed money. They initially used a fairly standard search engine but decided to convert to a text analytics solution.

The benefits from adding text analytics included increased speed and accuracy of the audit process and improved efficiency of each auditor. Auditors were then able to process more emails and have a higher quality work with fewer false hits. This led to a win-win-win scenario of reduction in manual labor costs, more bonuses for individual auditors, and higher profits for the company.

Processing Construction Proposals: A construction firm was receiving up to 700,000 construction proposals a year in lengths of up to 1,000 pages each. They processed these proposals by hand into a standard format, developed rich summaries for them, and made them available to their customers. They pulled information such as the architect's name and address, bid date, and specific information about any special circumstances regarding the project.

Text analytics increased the speed of their processing while reducing the amount of human errors. They were also able to minimize their labor costs and increase their profits.

Predicting Customer Behavior: In this application, text analytics was used to analyze hundreds of thousands of customer support notes and predict which customers were likely to cancel their accounts based on conversation dynamics with customer support reps. For this application, rules were developed that distinguished between customers likely to cancel and those merely threatening to cancel in order to get something. This was done by looking for bargaining words—"I'll cancel *unless…*" and "stop doing this *or…*" in the same sentence or phrase as the word "cancel" itself.

As with a lot of applications, text analytics was combined with other indicators such as number of phones, frequency of previous behaviors, etc., but it was the text analytics piece that added the intelligence.

Fraud Detection: In this case, courtesy of SAS, a company in Belgium using a variety of different detection techniques reduced fraud by 98%, leading to a savings of €1 billion per year. This was another high-volume case where tax auditors had to analyze hundreds of millions of transactions a year. Impossible without text analytics!

Improving Customer Support: A Hong Kong call center was able to monitor 2.6 million calls and 98,000 emails to uncover hidden relationships among complaints, spot trends before they became a major problem, and generally produce good intelligence about their customer complaints.

The analysis of all this unstructured text went from weeks—and in some cases even months—to a matter of minutes. This not only saved them enormous amount of time and enabled them to reduce costs, but because of the sheer speed, they were also able to write additional analyses and get better information, which in turn enabled them to make better decisions and develop smarter strategies.

While these very high-volume applications lead to very high ROI, it's also possible to get great results using much smaller amounts of content.

Creating a Newsletter(s): One of the earliest applications was to use text analytics to scan news feeds (could be anything from 900 to a few thousand words), then analyze them to either automatically or semiautomatically create newsletters for various customers. This might involve 6,000–10,000 articles a day—more than what human editors can typically do. Subscriptions to the newsletter could then be sold—a business model currently being followed by quite a few companies, from Dow Jones to new startups.

This type of application can also be done within the enterprise, which, while not generating direct income, can enrich employees in a variety of ways—from keeping up with important company news to keeping up with the latest external news in targeted areas.

Duplicate Documents: Another common application is to use text analytics to scan content repositories of hundreds of thousands to millions of documents, then tag those documents that are duplicates (or worse, near-duplicates). This might not sound like a major advance, but as we discussed, part of the poor performance of enterprise search can be traced to these duplicates. Estimates for the value of this type of application can run into the millions for large organizations.

Finding the Right Expert: Another common application is in the area of knowledge management, which has struggled with issues of maintaining expertise profiles for one of their standard applications—expertise location. Applying text analytics, to both documents that employees write and any internal social media groups where they post, enables these expertise profiles to be created automatically. This produces better profiles with less effort.

Several of these applications were ones that my company worked on, with several others provided by various text analytics vendors and partners.

These are just a few of the growing number of applications that companies are using text analytics to create.

It is becoming more and more clear that text analytics is capable of having a huge impact on organizations today—and that this impact is growing dramatically. It is also clear that text analytics is essential for developing these kinds of applications—and that the full range of applications is something that we are still barely beginning to understand.

All that raises a critical question: *If the benefits of text analytics are so obvious, then why isn't text analytics as widespread as database software?* In other words, why isn't everyone doing it?

Why Isn't Everyone Doing It?

As with any complex field, the reasons as to why everyone isn't doing text analytics are many and varied. Let's look at a few.

What Is It?

Many people still don't know what text analytics is. There are a surprising number of companies that simply are not aware of text analytics. In other cases, they have only heard about one particular application of text analytics: typically sentiment analysis or social media analysis. Those who have heard about text analytics often lack the depth of knowledge necessary to understand how it can help them. (And that is just one of my reasons for writing this book.)

You Actually Are, You Just Don't Know It

You actually are doing text analytics! You just don't know it yet—or you're calling it something else.

I am always amazed at how often I go into an organization, invited by one department or another, to explore using text analytics for some new initiative, and in my usual preliminary process of researching their current information environment, I discover that they already have two or three text analytics projects going on simultaneously—*without being aware of it.*

This is particularly true if each project started with a tightly designed initial focus, such as a social media customer listening project done by the marketing department (for a better approach, see Chapter 13: Text Analytics as a Platform). They may have chosen a particular text analytics vendor who is well known in the social media area, while the legal department has selected a different vendor noted for their work in the legal arena. In that case, you have IT supporting both products—without realizing that one product could do both.

Another common situation is where text analytics is embedded in a search engine, usually in a very limited and/or primitive way, and the focus is on the application. So, if the organization is asked if they have text analytics, the answer is *no*—even though there is an e-Discovery application that uses this primitive text analytics built right into the search engine.

We Don't Do That Here

One reason companies maintain an attitude of "we don't do that here" and don't undertake projects using text analytics is that they don't value the kinds of things you can do with it. In some cases, they've never jumped on the social media bandwagon. In other cases, there is a legitimate argument that they don't really need the kind of applications that text analytics can support. Perhaps they are a small company and they don't really need a new search engine, or they don't have any sophisticated compliance or legal needs, or they don't do any business intelligence or customer intelligence. However, the number of companies that fall into this category is definitely getting smaller and smaller.

If IT Doesn't Know What It Is, It Doesn't Exist

Since text analytics involves software, the IT department is very often the starting point for many organizations. This brings up another difficulty in making the case for text analytics, which is that text analytics software is different from the majority of software that IT departments are used to dealing with. The difference is this software is designed to deal with language, meaning, and cognition in ways that tend to go beyond traditional IT expertise. So, selling the importance of text analytics software to IT department very often fails due to this unfamiliarity.

This is in contrast to typical data and database projects, which are easier to understand. Language is much more complex than data, and text analytics projects tend to be more complex than standard data projects.

I Don't Believe It

One reason that companies don't undertake text analytics projects is that they simply don't believe the kinds of ROI numbers that come out of various studies. This is related to not really knowing much about text analytics, being skeptical, and seeing it as just another fad solution that will either disappear or not lead to the kind of profound benefits that advocates are claiming.

For example, some of us remember when corporate intranets were going to completely revolutionize the way organizations did business. The current reality is that most corporate intranets don't provide much more business value than an easy way to publish what today's lunch menu is—not exactly revolutionary! (OK ... maybe that's a bit overstated—intranets *are* an important communications platform, but *revolutionary?*)

Of course, a related effect is that some companies don't see text analytics as revolutionary, so it can't be very important. You will notice that as amazing and powerful and (insert your favorite adjective) that text analytics is, I have not claimed that text analytics is the next revolution. I don't know about you, but I'm a bit tired of "revolutions." Doesn't anyone believe in evolution anymore?

Productivity Improvements Get No Respect

Another factor that makes it difficult to justify the expense and complexity of text analytics is that for one large class of applications, the value of text analytics is primarily in the area of productivity gains (which sounds pretty mundane—but is that why it gets no respect?). Helping employees work smarter and faster, while a common value in organizations, is harder to justify than an application that shows up immediately on the bottom line or in financial statements. Especially when that bottom line increase means a promotion for those involved. If a CEO sees a personal plus, the project is easy to justify.

It's Too Complex

Complexity is probably the only semilegitimate argument, unlike the ones above. Not having a simple argument for the benefits of text analytics is among the reasons why text analytics has been slow to be adopted by organizations, according to a number of people I interviewed for this book.

One of the basic reasons is that text analytics is primarily a platform or infrastructure for a wide variety of applications. While this makes text analytics all the more valuable, in a world that's oriented around specific projects, it makes making the case for text analytics even more difficult.

In addition, text analytics is essentially an interdisciplinary activity. It calls for contributions from a variety of players:

- IT to make the software work
- Information professionals like librarians or taxonomists to develop structures for text analytics applications

- In more advanced applications, linguists to understand the subtleties of language
- Business groups, ranging from sales to technical support to HR and others, to provide input into the design and focus of text analytics projects
- Data analysts to help make sense of it all
- Often other groups as well

In addition to the individual contributions of each of these groups, text analytics calls for a deeper interdisciplinary communication between the groups. Since most organizations don't have a "semantic infrastructure department," per se, text analytics projects call for a level of interdisciplinary cooperation that goes beyond what typically exists in them.

However, the real danger in this case is not that text analytics is too complex and costs too much (the actual payoff is way greater than the cost), but rather that companies will implement their text analytics project in the wrong way. And the wrong way is *not* planning for complexity—which is about the only way to do text analytics and not see an enormous payoff.

It's Too Expensive

The catch here, of course, is what does the "too" in "too expensive" really mean? There is no doubt that the software is still pretty expensive (with full implementations running into six figures for the software alone), and then there's the cost of implementing. On the other hand, when you look at the kind of cost savings, new applications, and all the other benefits of text analytics that we've covered so far, it could be legitimately be said that, for most companies, it's way too expensive not to buy and implement text analytics.

Selling the Benefits of Text Analytics
Going Beyond the Numbers

The advantages of text analytics are becoming more and more obvious, and studies like the IDC report provide good hard figures for the benefits of text analytics and can be used to sell them within the organization. However, if it were that simple, text analytics would be everywhere. But numbers don't tell the whole story—and numbers can lie.

In selling the benefits of text analytics—and in addition to these kinds of numerical studies—one good way to capture the impact, particularly of bad decisions and bad quality work, is to add or generate stories that reflect the negative results of this bad quality work. There are many stories about the cost of bad quality information. Good stories have a way of not only capturing the monetary cost but also capturing the imagination of the people who are making the decisions about software purchases for their organization.

It is always a good idea to look for stories within your own organization in order to justify the cost of text analytics applications or initiatives. Real-life stories with people who are known and/or situations that are known to the decision-makers can carry an enormous amount of power.

In a recent workshop on text analytics, when I told the famous pharmaceutical story, the 12 or so people around the room nodded and seemed to get the idea. Then, one of the participants told a similar story that had much less financial impact but was taken from their organization with software and systems that they all knew and had used. The effect was electric—not polite nods of agreement but loud exclamations and an immediate chatter of questions and comments.

The famous story that I tell, however, is a good place to start the process of generating those internal stories. This story, about the cost of bad search, has to do with a pharmaceutical company that was investigating whether or not to initiate the development of a new drug. They conducted multiple searches of existing literature to see if anyone else had worked with this drug and what the possible side effects and efficacy might be. Of course, what they were mainly interested in seeing was if anybody else had already started work on this drug.

As the story goes, nothing particular was found as a result of their searches, and so the company embarked on a five-year development campaign to develop this new drug. Near the end of that five-year period, someone conducted a follow-up search and—either because of the better search engine or more public documents—found that in fact, another company had already tried to develop that drug and found that it didn't work.

Now, most bad searches don't add up to the tens or hundreds of millions of dollars involved in a five-year drug development effort, but there are many stories of lesser, though still enormous impacts of the cost of bad search.

In addition to developing stories of the results of bad search, bad customer experiences, or failed applications, another good tactic for understanding the value of text analytics and selling value to upper management is to convert the money into other measures. For example how many additional full-time employees could a company hire with an extra $6.5 million a year? Another measure might be how much savings could be passed on to customers by lowering costs and driving up sales as your company underbids its rivals, paying greater dividends to your stockholders, or giving your employees bonuses or raises.

Making the Case at the C-level

Even though the arguments for text analytics are pretty compelling, the majority of companies have not yet instituted a text analytics initiative. One reason for this, as mentioned earlier, is that it can be very difficult to make the case for text analytics, particularly for the company's C-level executives, which can include but are not limited to the CEO, CFO, and CTO.

There are a number of issues in trying to sell the benefits of text analytics to C-level executives. The first is this is not an area they typically understand very well. The language of text analytics is very often completely foreign to someone who is primarily concerned with the management and direction of the strategy of the company. Even CTOs, while they might understand the actual software used in text analytics, rarely understand the linguistic or cognitive issues involved.

C-level executives also tend to view text analytics as not business-critical, as a lot of it does not *seem* to directly contribute to the bottom line—at least not at first glance. This is changing with the focus on social media for marketing, but not for the kind of platform that is usually the best way to approach text analytics. They also tend to think of the semantics involved in text analytics as simply extra work without much benefit.

In addition, the kind of productivity gains that are often cited for text analytics are either simply not believed or the belief is that if employees just worked better or harder, they could easily overcome this without a major change in the way they do business.

Another issue is that even though text analytics can be used to create assets for the company, these assets (taxonomies, metadata, and the capability to categorize and add metadata to documents) are not well-recognized. They are also not tangible benefits and don't show up in typical accounting bottom lines. This is probably something that should change as we live in a so-called information age, but that will probably have to wait and is really a separate issue.

Another issue is that very often CTOs tend to think that since they can install and manipulate the software, they can do all the other tasks as well—even without any experience in things like categorization, linguistics, and cognitive science. So to make the case to C-level executives, we not only need the kinds of numbers and stories that can be used to justify text analytics as mentioned earlier, but we also need to educate them about the nature of semantics and language and cognitive science that form the heart of text analytics.

We also need to let them know that doing semantics is, in fact, difficult as well as highly valuable. Without this education, executives can not only underestimate (and therefore not assign sufficient resources), but they also tend toward the mistaken perception that "anybody can do it" and assign the wrong resources, such as only using IT people who know code very well but don't know language or categorization.

Dangerous Issues in Selling the Benefits of Text Analytics

We don't want to step into the danger zone and oversell the idea that text analytics will automatically solve everything (something I have been accused of) and that everyone will immediately see great benefits if they would only undertake text analytics initiatives. There are a number of dangers, for example, by doing text analytics in ways in which companies don't realize the benefits.

The first of these is approaching text analytics as just a standard software project. As we'll discuss in Part 5—*text analytics is really infrastructure*—and is best approached in that way. It may be that you can start with small, easy-to-do projects in order to build support, but if you only do that, you won't see the real benefits of text analytics.

As well, approaching each project as simply an independent project will very likely mean you will not be able to build on prior projects, and you will end up duplicating efforts and costs. I am always amazed by how little communication there is between groups within the same company, which makes it very easy to have three different projects buying their own software and having to learn everything from scratch.

Yet another danger is not assigning enough resources to develop an initial text analytics initiative and even more importantly, the resources to continue to refine and maintain text analytics applications.

Danger also exists in using the wrong resources. Text analytics tends to need a range of skills and experiences including IT, library and linguistic skills, taxonomy skills, and subject matter expertise. One common mistake that organizations make is thinking that all they need is IT and subject matter expertise. But as I've said numerous times, subject matter expertise is very different from the skill of being able to categorize that subject matter expertise as well as develop the taxonomic structures and good metadata that text analytics needs.

It is also a danger to start with the wrong elements, particularly in the area of taxonomies. A lot of organizations start with a bad taxonomy and assume that it will be easy to fix as they go along. The bad taxonomy, for example, might be one that is way too big and complex, which makes it difficult and expensive to apply. Or it may be that the taxonomy is really just a simple list of significant concepts and doesn't add any structure to help organize their content.

Categorization particularly works best with taxonomies with very orthogonal categories. If your taxonomy has multiple overlapping categories all mixed together, it becomes very difficult to create good categorization rules as there's too much overlap—and people can't tell the difference, much less a poor semiartificial intelligence mind.

In the area of social media, the dangers of overselling very basic and primitive implementations became quickly obvious and led to the first disillusionment with text analytics. The good news is that this was followed by social media analysis applications which were much more sophisticated with things like appraisal taxonomies rather than simple positive and negative dictionaries and particularly in combining social media analysis with other data-driven analysis.

This approach—and others like it—enabled sentiment analysis to achieve a level of accuracy that could make it deliver real business value by accurately monitoring customer sentiment about products, features of products, and even new ad campaigns.

Summary

To sum up, the benefits of text analytics are compelling but complex. As such, it requires some careful thought, not only to make the case(s) but to make it in a way that resonates with all the audiences in your organization, from the CEO and CTO to those who will be implementing all those amazing applications to all the myriad end users.

Different arguments need to be developed for different use cases, not only because they produce different kinds of benefits and have different costs to develop but also because different parts of your organization tend to respond to different kinds of arguments. Not only that, but these parts also speak different languages (marketing, HR, etc.) and they see the world through different lenses.

For example, marketing departments will understand the benefits of social media analysis and applications but might not see much benefit in a better enterprise search. IT might see the value of text analytics–fueled search but may dismiss many advantages of some of the applications built with that search, like duplicate documents or expertise location. A knowledge management (KM) or library group loves the idea of expertise location, especially if it could model tacit knowledge, but dismisses sentiment analysis as too fuzzy.

On the other hand, the best way to approach text analytics is to build a text analytics platform that can support the full range of applications and presumably appeal to all. While this will return the most value and the best ROI, this approach is also (sometimes) the most difficult to make the case for—at least until there is that text analytics department in every organization.

Until then, the best thing you can do is to take an all-of-the-above approach to building the case for text analytics. In other words, it finds your documents, finds new customers, sells your products, builds new products, and washes your dishes while taking out the dog. Well, most of that is true.

And remember, money talks, but stories talk even better.

Endnotes

1. "Findwise Enterprise Search and Findability Survey 2014." Findwise.com. 2014. www.findwise.com/findwise-enterprise-search-and-findability-survey-2014 -findability-day-2014.

2. "2013 Social Media Marketing Industry Report: How Marketers Are Using Social Media to Grow Their Businesses." *Social Media Examiner*, 2013.

3. A good summary of search studies, including the IDC study, can be found on the Search Technologies website: www.searchtechnologies.com/enterprise-search -surveys.

4. Cretella, Emily. "Sentiment Analysis: Measuring Social Media and Content Marketing ROI." Thepitagroup.com. March 14, 2013. blog.thepitagroup.com/2013 /sentiment-analysis-measuring-social-media-and-content-marketing-roi/.

5. Center for Marketing Research, University of Massachusetts.

6. Cretella, Emily. "Sentiment Analysis: Measuring Social Media and Content Marketing ROI." Thepitagroup.com. March 14, 2013. blog.thepitagroup.com/2013 /sentiment-analysis-measuring-social-media-and-content-marketing-roi/.

7. Pitts, Mark, Farouk Ferchichi, Matthew P.T. Ruttley, and Ramkumar Ravichandran. "Executive Lessons on Modern Text Analytics." Presentation, 13th Annual

Text Analytics Summit West 2014, San Francisco, November 4, 2014. (Note: The whitepaper from Text Analytics Summit was prepared by: Geoff Whiting, Principal, GWhiting.com, and Alesia Siuchykava, Project Director, Data Driven Business, and can be accessed via www.analyticsearches.com/site/files /776/66977/259607/711763/Business_Case_for_Text_Analytics_8.2014.pdf.)

8. "2013 Social Media Marketing Industry Report: How Marketers Are Using Social Media to Grow Their Businesses." *Social Media Examiner*, 2013.

PART 2

Getting Started in Text Analytics

CHAPTER 4

Current State of Text Analytics Software

This book is based mostly on my experience and that of my company, the KAPS Group. This experience includes doing text analytics development projects for a broad variety of clients both large and small. We did strategy consulting on how to best approach text analytics solutions development—all the way from enterprise search to knowledge management applications—and we successfully forged partnerships with a large number of text analytics software vendors, providing professional services to help clients implement our partner's software.

Although the KAPS group has conducted research for a number of clients trying to select the best text analytics software, I do not consider myself a market analyst. So to deepen that research for this chapter, I conducted a number of interviews with representatives of text analytics software companies as well as other consultants and market analysts for IDC and Forrester.

That said, keep in mind that, unless otherwise noted, the opinions expressed in this chapter and the rest of the book are mine. And, yes, I have lots of them.

A Short (Personal) History of Text Analytics

I would like to jump-start the discussion of the current state of text analytics by taking a quick look at its recent history—and part of my reasons for doing so are personal. My academic background centers around a field called "history of ideas," and so I always like to start with the historical foundation of an idea. In addition, there is that well-known quote that is almost always misquoted as "Those who do not study history are condemned to repeat it."[1]

This is neither the time nor place for a full history of the development of text analytics—though it would be interesting to uncover why the field is called "text analytics."[2] That said, what follows is my personal experience and understanding—others may or may not agree.

What's in a Name?

According to an article on the Decision Analyst website, text analytics as a field started in World War II, but was originally called *content analysis*.[3] However, the article also talks about text mining and text analytics as equivalent—another indication that we need a new name for the field?

Out of Insight (Inxight) Comes a New World

The birth of commercial text analytics can be traced—as so much else in the information arena—to Xerox PARC (otherwise known as Palo Alto Research Center). The first really successful commercial company (in my experience) in text analytics was called Inxight, and in what now has become a tradition, many people from Inxight came from Xerox PARC. There were other companies, of course, but this was one of the leaders—particularly in terms of developing a full text analytics development platform.

Text analytics, like so much in the world of computer science and information, started out not in the garage, but in the academic world. There was a great deal of research going on in various universities surrounding text analytics, with a primary focus centering on NLP—or *natural language processing*—approaches. NLP looks at language primarily from a mathematical and/or statistical perspective.

What Inxight did was to move text analytics from this very academic-and-NLP approach to a platform based on auto-categorization, entity extraction, and the realm of search and metadata. The company did a whole lot of things very, very well in terms of developing a really great product based on advanced text analytics techniques. They seemed to be quite successful, and although one decision was perhaps not good for Inxight, it turned out to be very good for the field as it established a major part of it: They took one of their signature applications for entity extraction, called ThingFinder, and licensed it to a whole range of individuals and entities. Many of those companies took ThingFinder, put some front ends on it, and became competitors.

What followed was an explosion of companies, all based primarily on entity extraction. Many were successful for a while, but the field became extremely chaotic and saw many companies come and go.

Case in point: In 2008, my company did a software evaluation project for a client in which we looked at all the current text analytics companies to select the best one for them. We took a broad look at the overall market and then an even more careful look at about 20 companies. Three years later, we did a similar evaluation project for a new client and when we looked at the list of companies used for the 2008 project, almost half had gone out of business.

Of those, the lucky or good ones were bought and integrated into new companies, or in some cases, incorporated into other products. Inxight itself was bought (twice!)—first by Business Objects to fuel their business intelligence offerings, which was in turn purchased by SAP. Inxight mostly disappeared for a while, but in the last few years, SAP has come to the very good conclusion that the original Inxight text analytics platform was a really good product in its own right.

Early Applications

During the early 2000s, the two most common applications were news aggregation and enterprise search. One of my company's early projects was for a company scraping news stories from about 5,000 websites, then aggregating them into a variety of newsletters for different associations. Working with their editors, we developed a number of taxonomies for each association area, such as education, consumer packaged goods, and others. We then developed auto-categorization rules for each node in the taxonomy. These rules were then applied to the incoming stories, and the resulting categorized news stories were sent to editors.

In this particular case, the value of the categorization was immediately obvious—the amount of time it took the editors to create a newsletter went from four hours to 20 minutes.

For the other early application—enterprise search—the payoff was not as obvious. "The problem with search" was certainly severe enough—companies struggled when trying to find information within growing repositories of unstructured content. And as we see, this dynamic of extreme need, but not particularly successful applications, is something that continues to this day. The application of text analytics to enterprise search has certainly helped, but lack of support due to the difficulty of making the ROI case was and continues to be a difficult sell.

Over the following few years, enterprise search, news applications, and a number of other search-based applications within the enterprise drove a slow but steady growth of text analytics applications. Early on, there was an additional track—a variety of applications using primarily text mining techniques, combined with data analytics in the area of customer intelligence.

Getting Sentimental

The next really big movement in the text analytics field was driven by *sentiment analysis*. In fact, sentiment analysis was the first hot topic having to do with text analytics—which led to the development of a number of new companies taking very basic text analytics platforms and using them to analyze sentiment in social media.

This early approach to sentiment analysis was simply to create dictionaries of positive and negative words, then count the number of each found in forum posts and other social media. This was enough to generate a great deal of excitement as companies began to track all those nasty and occasionally good things people were saying about a company, its products, or whatever else was being tracked. As long as they didn't require too much accuracy, everyone seemed to be happy, at least for a while.

Still, the excitement lasted long enough to create the first major hype cycle for text analytics, but as people began to realize the limitations of this approach—as well as the difficulty of actually tying these positive and negative sentiments to real business value—the inevitable slide into the trough of disillusionment began.

Since then, sentiment analysis has been slowly developing as a field in three ways. The first was to add more and more intelligence into the analysis, instead of just counting up positive and negative words. People had begun realizing that sophisticated sentiment analysis required a deeper understanding of the context around these words.

The second development was to move beyond simple sentiment and identify more sophisticated emotions like disappointment. This was helped by the development of more sophisticated emotion taxonomies, and while this deeper analysis continues to struggle with such advanced expressions like counterfactuals and satire, its level of sophistication has improved dramatically.

The third development was to take basic sentiment analysis techniques and apply them to understanding actual behavior, including such fundamentals as why people bought particular products or what really infuriated people about their expensive (and now malfunctioning) products.

The shift from enterprise text analytics to sentiment analysis and other social media applications was driven by a number of factors, including that social media applications were easier to do. There was also an obvious payoff—getting direct insight into customers and/or early warnings of potential technical or psychological problems with products.

Enterprise text analytics, on the other hand, was largely being presented as a productivity gain by helping people find needed information and/or reducing the amount of time that they wasted looking through giant repositories of unstructured content. Even though, as mentioned in Chapter 3, IDC and others did some wonderful analysis showing how much money this was costing companies, selling this benefit to CEOs and CIOs turned out to be a difficult sell.

Current State of Text Analytics

That's probably enough history, so let's take a look at the current state of text analytics. We'll start with an overview of the overall market for text analytics, the current companies offering text analytics, and the variety of different applications for text analytics. We will survey a number of surveys on text analytics market, including overall satisfaction ratings. And finally, we'll look at future trends in text analytics and obstacles that the field currently faces.

Overall Text Analytics Market

We will be using a number of surveys on text analytics by Seth Grimes and a Hurwitz report on the current text analytics market, a survey I did at the Text Analytics World conference, as well as the interviews discussed at the beginning of the chapter.

I have to admit that a book is probably not the best place for the latest market analysis (by the time his book is published a lot of any specific analysis will likely be out of date), so what I'm going to do here is look at a number of broad themes and trends within the overall text analytics market.

Theme Number One: A Fragmented Market

The first thing to note is that the text analytics market is an extremely fragmented market. There are no dominant companies either in terms of sales or techniques, though with the development of the Watson platform, IBM has moved to the top of companies offering advanced text analytics techniques.

Text analytics firms range from a whole host of small startup companies, to a number of established and well-funded mid-tier companies, and finally, to large, well-established companies like IBM and SAS.

In addition, the primary focus of these companies varies significantly. In his latest survey, Seth Grimes decided to lump all the various companies together, which makes sense when looking at the overall market. But when analyzing the market for clients, I normally break down the market into seven major categories (although there is a lot of overlap and companies are constantly morphing):

- Taxonomy vendors offering some text analytics capabilities
- Text mining
- Extraction and analytics vendors
- Sentiment and social media vendors
- Full-platform vendors
- Open source
- Embedded text analytics software

Next, we'll take a quick look at each of the seven categories.

Taxonomy Management Software

Before there was text analytics there was taxonomy and taxonomy management software. There is a close relationship between taxonomy and text analytics, where a number of companies started offering taxonomy management software and afterward added a basic text analytics functionality. The latest example is a very successful taxonomy management company, Pool Party, which currently offers a full suite of text analytics capabilities.

Another trend is that a number of taxonomy management software companies were bought and incorporated into text analytics offerings. The last major purchase was Smartlogic, which acquired taxonomy management firm Schema Logic.

These days, this category seems to be largely going away, both in actuality and from reports prepared for text analytics clients. In part, this is due to most text analytics platform vendors having at least a fairly well-developed taxonomy management capability built into their software. If you don't go with the full platform vendor, or if you have a very large taxonomy, you may want to look into adding this capability.

Text Mining Software

Companies predominantly or exclusively offering text mining software comprise one of the largest categories in the market. It is also the earliest developed approach, and therefore in many ways, is the most mature.

However, it is also somewhat of an outlier, as text mining succeeds largely by ignoring all the complexities of language and instead treats documents as bags of words to which very advanced statistical techniques are applied. In essence, *text mining treats text as data.*

The amazing thing is how much valuable analysis can be done with this approach—and how many incredibly valuable insights can be created with it.

On the other hand, as the most mature part of the market, there is not really a lot to distinguish between different companies based solely on their text mining capabilities. Differences between companies tend to revolve around the range of analytical techniques available, usability, the strength and stability of the company, and, of course, price.

Extraction and Analytics Vendors

Extraction is similar to text mining in that the basic approach is to avoid as much of the linguistic complexity as possible, instead using entity or noun phrase extraction to pull data out of unstructured text. As mentioned previously, many companies started by using Inxight's ThingFinder and then developed various analytical front ends.

The viability of extraction-only companies is highly questionable, considering the number of them that went out of business. Today, most vendors don't advertise themselves as primarily extraction, but sell their products, services and analytical tools—you must look behind the scenes to realize that their only text capabilities are entity or noun phrase extraction. In addition, the need for disambiguation is what pushes these companies to add more complete text analytics capabilities.

Sentiment and Social Media Vendors

Sentiment and social media companies constitute the largest component in the overall text analytics market. In an interview, an analyst for Forrester reported they are tracking over 100 companies in this space, which they see as not only indicative of the level of interest but also of the immaturity of the market. There is also a great deal of difference in their ability to utilize more advanced techniques than simple positive and negative word counting.

The market for sentiment/social media companies is extremely volatile, so proceed with caution when selecting a vendor that will support the development of more advanced techniques (and try to assess whether or not that vendor will be around in two years).

A major decision for enterprises looking to add sentiment and social media analysis is whether to buy a dedicated package from one of these vendors or the usually more expensive full platform from text analytics companies.

Full-Platform Vendors

Full-platform vendors typically offer all of the above—text mining, entity extraction, social media analysis—and in addition, they offer the poorly named auto-categorization capability (with which you can do a whole lot more besides simply automatically categorizing documents).

In the interest of disclosure, this is the area that I know best, and I have done most of my work with these vendors. Perhaps this is why I feel these companies offer the best approach to doing text analytics applications, but it also seems that the market is beginning to agree with me—more and more companies are adding the full range of functionality even if they only started with entity extraction or sentiment analysis.

Within this category of companies, there are roughly three different scales—very large enterprise text/analytical software, midrange enterprise text/analytical software, and a few small startup type organizations—many of which will likely be bought in the next year or two if their technology is good enough.

Open-Source Software

In addition to commercial vendors, open-source software provides another approach for developing your own text analytics capabilities. There are a couple of different sources, but there don't seem to be many differences between them.

Obviously, open source will only appeal to companies with the technical expertise to develop their own capabilities. More often than not in my experience, open source is used to develop a particular product rather than for broad internal use.

In his 2014 report, Seth Grimes sees open source as a major avenue in the text analytics space. My experience has been that open source is a great way to get started in text analytics—if you have the right internal resources and culture. I've also seen that many companies start out looking at open source, and after some initial development, they run up against major roadblocks and either abandon text analytics or turn to one of the commercial vendors.

Stay tuned …

Embedded Text Analytics Software

Another category of companies offers specific products, such as business intelligence and customer intelligence platforms, within which text analytics capabilities are embedded. I include them in this analysis, in part because enterprises that are exploring buying BI or CI software should or can consider either developing their own with text analytics software, or at least look at the issue of integrating BI or CI with other text analytics-based products.

The pluses and minuses for buying stand-alone applications versus full-platform are pretty well known, although the final decision will rest on many factors internal to each company.

More on the Text Analytics Market

There is a great deal more that can be said about all the various aspects of the text analytics market space, but there are two reasons for not going into more detail right now. The first is that by the time this book is published, the market will have changed. The second is that I would be happy to help you dive more deeply into the market in order to decide your best approach to text analytics—all you have to do is hire my company, and I will be glad to help out ;-)

Theme Number Two: Market Continues to Grow

The overall market for text analytics continues to grow at a very healthy pace—about 25%–40% growth according to industry watcher Seth Grimes.[2] This opinion is shared by the Hurwitz Victory Index Report, which also analyzes various factors behind the growth.[4]

Growth Factors

The Hurwitz report lists four major factors driving the growth in text analytics, the first being a growing and better understanding of the value of the technology. I would add that it is not just the technology that people are understanding better but the overall process and the incredible variety of applications that can be built with it. If this is true, it is particularly good news as it has the potential to overcome one of the main obstacles to wider adoption of text analytics—the lack of a strategic vision.

The second factor is the maturing of the technology. Again, I would say it's not just the technology that's maturing but the process of developing and applying text analytics as a whole. My own experience has been that this maturing process is very uneven—there have been major advances in text mining, but in other areas it has been spotty. As well, it seems to me that the technology supporting new applications is definitely maturing, while the development environment lags somewhat behind.

The third factor they cite is the rise of social media, which clearly has been a major driver in the growth of text analytics. Social media has seen advances in basic text analytics techniques as well as new analytical and mathematical techniques.

The fourth factor they mention is increasing computing power, enabling the analysis of ever larger data sets within reasonable and/or economic timeframes. It has also supported new types of applications, particularly advances in integrating unstructured text and structured data.

While I generally agree that these factors are helping fuel the continued growth of text analytics, I'm also struck by the technology focus of these factors. What this tells me: While there have been significant technology advances, the underlying difficulty of dealing with messy and complex language has not seen a whole lot of advances.

Seth Grimes' 2014 report also cites increases in computing power and data availability as major growth factors. He also mentions increasing automation, which will allow greater integration in such areas as online commerce, customer support, health service delivery, and other applications.

In addition to these two factors, Seth also cites open-source text analytics and the API economy as factors that lower entry barriers and provide additional flexibility. As noted, my own experience has been that while open source and the API economy do lower the barriers to getting started in text analytics, more often than not companies that take this path run into roadblocks when they try to go from pilot projects to full-scale project or product development.

Market Drivers

In addition to technology drivers, Seth Grimes cites a number of market drivers. The first market driver is customer interactions—in other words, more and more companies are adding text analytics to customer service and customer experience applications.

His second market driver regards channel solutions—this is when companies not only utilize standard surveys but add a full range of options such as social media, news, chat, and voice. This enables companies to collect data across the full set of customer touch points.

The third market driver is new consumer and market insights in which companies are using text analytics to enrich new or next-generation market research.

A fourth market driver is that early adopters of text analytics, healthcare, medicine, and biotechnology are continuing to push ahead with the development of new kinds of applications and sophisticated new approaches.

The fifth and last market driver is the whole arena of search and search-based applications in which traditional search-based approaches are being expanded to provide a platform for a huge range of applications.

Theme Number Three: Variety of Applications

Nothing shows the overall health and vibrancy of the text analytics market and the multiple benefits that the text analytics can deliver than a look at the incredible variety of applications that companies around the world are developing.

I've included here the results of a report and two surveys in which respondents were asked to list any applications that they were planning or had developed.

The first survey is from the Seth Grimes 2014 Text Analytics Report, for which the following question was asked: What are your primary applications where text comes into play?

Voice of the customer/customer experience – 39%

Research (not listed) – 38%

Brand/product/reputation management – 38%

Competitive intelligence – 33%

Search, information access, or question answering – 29%

Customer/CRM – 27%

Content management or publishing – 25%

Online commerce including shopping, price, etc. – 16%

Life sciences or clinical medicine – 15%

e-Discovery – 14%

Insurance, risk management, or fraud – 13%

Other – 11%

Insurance, risk management, or fraud – 13%

Product/service design, quality assurance, etc. – 10%

Financial services/capital markets – 9%

Intellectual property/patent analysis – 8%

Law enforcement – 6%

Military/national security/intelligence – 5%

I have to admit that I don't quite believe the 5% figure for military/national security/intelligence. After all, what self-respecting spy agency would publicly admit to using these tools?

It reminds me of the early days of text analytics when text analytics vendors would proudly announce that InQTel (the buying/research entity that supported various intelligence agencies), had bought their product. And, of course, they were being truthful up to a point, but the reality is that InQTel had also bought the text analytics software from every single one of their competitors. Not a particularly ringing endorsement.

I'm not surprised by the fact that social media and customer experience were number one in his survey—this is an area that Seth is heavily involved in, and so there was likely some bias in the sample.

Of course, the same is true for the survey that I did in 2013, which was a small survey of attendees and potential attendees of a text analytics conference I've been chairing since 2013, Text Analytics World. While things are changing fast in the field, it is still probably generally indicative of the general market. Here are some of the results regarding important areas:

Predictive analytics and text mining – 90%

Search and search-based apps – 86%

Business intelligence – 84%

Voice of the customer – 82%

Social media – 75%

Decision support, knowledge management – 81%

Big Data – 70%

Finance – 61%

Call center, tech support – 63%

Risk, compliance, governance – 61%

Security, fraud detection – 54%

Of course, this is not a scientific survey and, in this case, the sample is quite biased as it was sent to people who had mostly signed up, not for TAW but for PAW, or Predictive Analytics World. This probably explains the number one category, predictive analytics and text mining and perhaps as well the high rankings for business intelligence and Big Data.

However, even from this small sample, the one thing that stands out is that there is no one application that is dominant. This is true both for my survey and for Seth Grimes' survey. Rather, there is a broad variety of applications fulfilling all sorts of business needs. What this suggests is that text analytics is really a platform for applications, which means that it should be approached as an infrastructure, not a simple application. (We'll look at this in more detail in Part 5: Enterprise Text Analytics as a Platform.)

The second conclusion is that while the specific order might vary in both of these surveys and others that I've seen, the most common applications include a number of areas, such as social media, customer intelligence and voice of the customer, enterprise search and search based applications, and a few others depending on how they are described.

A good summary of the common leading applications and the incredible variety of text analytics applications is found in the Hurwitz Victory report. They list the highlights of some of the popular uses for text analytics:

- Marketing – VOC, social media analysis, churn analysis, market research, survey analysis
- Business – competitive intelligence, document categorization, HR (voice of employee), records retention, risk analysis, website faceted navigation
- Industry-specific – fraud detection, e-Discovery, warranty analysis, medical research

In addition to the variety of applications, there is also a huge range of sources that are being used in the various text analytics applications. So, for example, in the Seth Grimes 2014 text analytics reports, the following sources are listed by the respondents in response to the question: What textual information are you analyzing or do you plan to analyze?

Blogs (long form and micro) – 61%

News articles – 42%

Comments on blogs and articles – 37%

Customer/market surveys – 38%

Online forums – 36%

Facebook postings – 32%

Online reviews – 31%

Scientific or technical literature – 31%

Email and correspondence – 26%

Contact center notes or transcripts – 22%

Chat – 20%

Employee surveys – 20%

Website feedback – 16%

While the predominance of social media content (rather than enterprise content) is probably slightly skewed, it is nevertheless likely to be an accurate reflection of the overall content that enterprises are exploring.

Growth of the Text Analytics Market

The field of text analytics as a whole is doing quite well, and it continues to grow, continues to solve a variety of business problems, and enables the creation of a huge range of applications. However, not all is rosy in the field of text analytics.

First of all, while text analytics continues to grow, the rate of growth has somewhat slowed. In addition, at the text analytics conferences, Text Analytics Summit and Text Analytics World, attendance was down in 2014.

There is also evidence in the Seth Grimes 2014 report in the section on user satisfaction: the ratings were generally pretty good, with some specific exceptions, but again the overall ratings were down. One thing I found very interesting is that the overall experience and satisfaction rating is higher than it was for any of the individual components. Table 4.1 shows the Grimes report survey topics and results.

Table 4.1   Text Analytics Survey from Seth Grimes 2014

Text Analytics Areas	Satisfied or Completely Satisfied	Disappointed or Very Disappointed
Overall satisfaction	74%	4% (0% Very)
Ability to solve business problems	65%	10%
Technology performance	58%	16%
Professional services and support	54%	15%
Accuracy of results	54%	25%
Technology ease-of-use	50%	29%

I'm not sure how you get overall satisfaction at 74%, while the highest subcategory is at 65%. Was it the wording of the questions or some weird psychology? We will have to wait for the next survey.

Clearly the bottom three are areas that continue to limit the growth of text analytics. While ease-of-use got the lowest scores, it seems to me that the accuracy of results is even more of an issue. Some of the comments included things like:

- We are very dissatisfied with the products on the market, and so, are stuck with our current solution.

- Powerful tool, but the poor user interface makes me less confident about championing results.

- I have been doing text analytics since 1984, and I have yet to find an environment that meets my requirements for knowledge extraction.

Obstacles for the Field of Text Analytics

Even though text analytics continues to grow and has huge potential, still there are significant obstacles that are slowing down the growth of the field. So let's take a look at some of them.

Lack of Clarity and Strategic Vision

At Text Analytics World 2013, one of my survey questions was "What factors do you see as holding back adoption of text analytics?" The number one answer: "Lack of clarity about text analytics and its business value" (47% response rate), and when that is coupled with "Lack of senior management buy-in" (8.5%), this was by far the most common answer.

It's hard to sell to companies when they don't have a clear idea of what text analytics is and what it can do, how to do it, and the business value of doing it (though hopefully this book will put an end to all that!). But aside from the difficulty of making sales of products and/or services in text analytics, another problem is that this lack of clarity and strategic vision can lead companies into having unrealistic expectations about what text analytics can do and the effort it takes to do it—including having the right resources available.

The best way I've found to overcome this obstacle is described in the next chapter as a Smart Start that begins with an articulated strategic vision of text analytics within their organization based on research into their content, their users, and their applications. This is then coupled with a pilot that gives them an immediate practical win.

Text Analytics Is Strategic—the United States Prefers Projects

One issue I've seen in my practice is that the best approach to text analytics is to view it as a strategic platform or infrastructure for a variety of applications (see Part 5 for more on this idea).

The difficulty is that most enterprises in the U.S. tend to think more at the project level, so rather than build a text analytics platform that supports the entire range of potential applications, enterprises buy and implement a business intelligence application, a customer support application, a voice of the customer application, and so on. This raises the cost of doing text analytics and also tends to reduce the quality within each application area. Interestingly enough, according to a number of vendors I interviewed, the situation is significantly different in Europe where the infrastructure argument seems to find more resonance.

Text Analytics Is Infrastructure—It Requires Interdisciplinary Collaboration

A related issue is that an infrastructure approach to text analytics requires a high level of interdisciplinary collaboration between different groups within the enterprise. This includes IT, business groups, marketing—and something that is often missing in U.S. enterprises: a library.

I would and have argued that this kind of interdisciplinary collaboration is, in general, a good thing and something that more companies should do more of. In particular, text analytics is something that, when done correctly, can help establish a pattern and a culture of interdisciplinary collaboration that can bring great value to pretty much any kind of enterprise.

However, this brings up another major point with text analytics, which is that there are a lot of ways to do it wrong—working with wrong expectations, the wrong overall approach, inadequate resources, the wrong resources—the list goes on.

Some good news on the interdisciplinary collaboration front is that Stanford is now offering a combination English-Computer Science degree, which is definitely a step in the right direction. I'd like to see library science added into that, but one step at a time.

Text Analytics Is Context Dependent—It Requires Customization

One of the major problems with text analytics is that, despite what many vendors will tell you, there are really no out-of-the-box solutions that are worth much of anything. There is no automatic taxonomy generation, no automatic theme detection, and there is no automatic sentiment analysis. Yes, many or most vendors have all of these features in their software—and every one of them requires significant customization in order to get results that are much beyond random chance.

As noted above, text analytics is heavily context dependent—and that includes the content, the organization of the content (taxonomies/ontologies), and the questions that the various enterprises want to answer. In addition, the organization has its own private language with specialized vocabularies and, of course, all those shorthand acronyms that are meaningless outside the context of that particular organization.

I recall one vendor touting their software to a client of mine. They were quite proud of the fact that their software could accurately categorize the content that we were looking at with no customization whatsoever. The automatic categorization suggested that the documents were about telecommunications. And to give them their due, the documents were about telecommunications—because this was a telecommunication company and virtually all their documents were "about" telecommunications. In other words, the categorization added no value whatsoever, and getting to a level of granularity below "this is a telecommunications document" would require significant customization.

Usability of the Software

Another obstacle to the wider adoption of text analytics software that is cited in a variety of surveys as well as in my interviews is *usability*. As a partner to many of the leading text analytics vendors, I've had to learn to use a lot of different text analytics software with dramatically different front ends and approaches. Among the leading vendors, there tends to be a rough equivalence in terms of basic functionality, but each one does it differently.

So, sorry partners, but I can attest personally that, yes, usability leaves a lot to be desired. And while some packages are easier to use than others, they could all benefit from some significant usability makeovers.

Here I'll say that I don't think the fault lies so much in software developers as it does with the single biggest obstacle for text analytics: It deals with language in all its messy glory.

Biggest Obstacle—Complexity of Language

The single most important obstacle (and the factor that underlies many of the other obstacles) is the complexity of language in and of itself.

The human brain, growing up in rich social context, is a powerful language learning tool—and yet it takes the brain years of often awkward practice to become adept at language use. The situation for computer-based learning is, despite the speed of machine learning and processing, much more difficult. As well, computers have not had tens of thousands of years of evolving language capabilities, so it is not surprising that machine learning approaches continue to struggle to build applications with a deep and real-world understanding of language—in fact, they have a long history of failed attempts to automate language understanding. The hubris of early AI has been well documented, with people like John McCarthy predicting in 1962 that in 10 years, AI would replace him as a university professor and researcher. Not quite!

And for language handling, the claims were equally overly optimistic to say the least. For example, it was assumed that it would be very easy to develop automated translation programs, but it was quickly discovered that language was a little more complicated. My favorite story about automated translation is the translation of proverbs from Russian to English and back. The program would take the statements, translate from English to Russian, and then translate back. The results were a lot of fun: "The spirit is willing, but the flesh is weak" came back as "The vodka is OK, but the meat is spoiled." Literally correct, but hardly true to the original meaning.

There have been a number of advances in trying to model language as companies tried to overcome this rich complexity, but machine-based approaches are still largely stuck with treating documents as "bags of words." They are good at finding statistical patterns of individual words and simple combination of words, but don't even try to deal with anything deeper than a simple dictionary lookup of the meaning of the word.

One of the key concepts that's missing from this "bag of words" approach is the incredibly rich variety of contexts within documents—contexts that determine which of many meanings are correct or even more basically, how combinations of words work together to create a rich sentence or paragraph-based meaning.

For more on this, there is a good article by Walid Saba, "Text Analytics and Semantic Technology—Myth versus Reality," in which he looked at some of the hype and abuse that has marred the field of text analytics since its beginning. One point he makes (and that I completely agree with) is that there's something seriously wrong with the name "semantic technology" in that there is very little, if any, semantics in semantic technology.

In a section of the article titled "Natural Language Processing is Not for Hackers," he discusses some of the difficulties in AI for text analytics dealing with the complexity of language:

> No one as of yet has developed software that can understand ordinary spoken language, and, notwithstanding the fancy looking voice-enabled mobile apps, any talk of question/ answering software, or software systems that can understand the *sentiment* people express in free-form text, is just that: talk![5]

We pretty much know how to overcome this particular obstacle, but as usual the devil is in the details. We know we need to add more intelligence with multiple modules that combine memory with new input. And we know we have to develop newer and better ways for the system to learn so we don't have to solve the impossible task of mapping out every possible combination of words. And we're making progress with all of these tasks, but we still have a long way to go to figure out the best ways to add intelligence and learning to our artificial minds as regards the complexity and nuances found in language.

We will be discussing the details of a lot of these approaches throughout the rest of the book, including which ones seem to work best and where we need significant new breakthroughs, but there's just one thing to remember: If someone comes to you and tells you that their software automatically, out of the box, does everything you need for text analytics, run screaming from the room.

Current Trends in Text Analytics

Both the surveys that we've been looking at and my interviews include sections on current trends. Of course, the danger, as noted, is that by the time this book is published, current trends will be recent history, and the new current trends might be a deepening of the trend, a repudiation of the trend, or just simply different trends altogether.

In the two surveys, the primary focus is the future of the text analytics market, though they do discuss some current trends in the area of capabilities. One of the interesting things that I found regarding the current trends sections of both surveys is that virtually none of the trends they see as coming in the near future do much to alleviate the primary obstacles holding back the field that we discussed in the previous section.

Market Trends
Social Media Analytics

Both the Grimes and the Hurwitz surveys see social media as a major driver in the text analytics market. The Hurwitz survey cites that they found over 100 companies devoted exclusively to social media analysis—too many for them to analyze in their report.

As quite a few sources have noted, social media has already gone through one hype cycle but it does seem to be gearing up for another significant growth period. Hopefully, this one will have more substance than the first. And according to Hurwitz, they see this happening with, for example, new techniques being developed to move beyond simple positive and negative sentiment and creating things like an eleven-point scale of sentiment. Another similar approach is the development of appraisal taxonomies.

Search and Content Management

Another trend that both surveys (and my experience) see is the continued use of text analytics to enhance search and content management. This has always been one of the major areas of text analytics and should see continuing growth in the coming years.

This trend is not as new and exciting as what's going on in social media, nor will it see as rapid growth, but it should continue to grow at a significant pace.

There is no single new technology or technique that will dramatically change the use of text analytics in these areas, but rather there is an ongoing maturing and deepening of approaches and techniques—particularly in the area of a deeper understanding of language.

Cloud-Based Products and Services

Both surveys also see cloud-based products and services as a significant trend in the near future as more and more companies are offering these services as part of their repertoire. In addition to existing products and services, some companies like Clarabridge have become almost exclusively cloud based.

In addition to offering products and services through the cloud, another trend is the use of cloud-based servers as tools for development. As I write this, we are engaged in doing a pilot for a client in which our development environment sits on one of our vendor partner's cloud-based server. This particularly helps when we have a team spread across the country—or around the globe.

Embedded Text Analytics

Another trend that Seth Grimes identifies as a major driver is the growth of embedded text analytics. These are applications in which the text analytics is "behind the scenes," providing functionality for applications, like business intelligence or customer intelligence.

There seems to be a growth area, both in terms of the number of applications and also the variety of new applications that are incorporating or embedding text analytics as a major part of their functionality. In this case, if there are unstructured text sources that are significant, then text analytics should be a big part of those applications.

As one can imagine, it is difficult to track the number of these applications since companies don't always identify their applications as text analytics empowered—and the people using these applications don't think of themselves as using text analytics, either. Nevertheless, these applications will likely continue to be a major part of the text analytics market.

Capabilities Trends

In addition to market trends, there are also major trends in text analytics capabilities and techniques.

Integration of Text and Data

There are a lot of drivers behind the move to do more integration of text and data, and one big one is all the hype (and substance) around Big Data. Everyone wants to be seen as doing Big Data, but of course, Big Text is even bigger then Big Data. The drawback is that it is a lot harder to build Big Text applications. Big Data is not just about the size but is based on new techniques like Hadoop to handle all that data. Unfortunately, there is no comparable new technique for Big Text.

This integration is happening in a variety of ways. At the application level it's possible to simply combine insights from both the analysis of data and the analysis of text. For example, one common use is to use Big Data to gain more insights into what a certain population is doing, then combining that with insights from Big Text as to why people are behaving that way.

At the actual analytical level, one trend is that is it possible to extract more and more data from text and then apply all the powerful new techniques that have been developed for Big Data applications.

In addition to providing more data by extracting it from text, it's also possible now to do more advanced kinds of extraction like fact extraction, in which the relationship between two data elements is extracted as well as the data. In addition, it is possible to do even more advanced kinds of extraction in which, for example, you might find the name of the person on page one, their salary on page three, and their address in the appendix. The trick in these advanced cases is resolving the coreference problem, and is, knowing that the salary on page three refers back to the person on page one.

Cognitive Computing—Deep Learning

Another major trend built on advanced capabilities is *cognitive computing*. This is a concept and approach that's gaining more and more press—and they have their own conference as well. Cognitive computing takes advantage of the power of Big Data, which, when coupled with what is called *deep learning*, has the potential for producing extremely smart applications.

Skeptics point out that so-called deep learning is really just neural networks, an AI technique in existence since the '80s. One of the big differences is simply the amount of data that can now be processed and incorporated into these neural networks, making them a much more powerful tool.

No discussion of trends would be complete without mentioning Watson, the new Jeopardy champion. It was an amazing feat and Watson will have a major impact on the future of text analytics. One aspect of Watson that I find most significant is the use of dozens or hundreds of specialized modules, each of which offers a potential answer to each question. The trick is then to develop methods of evaluating all of those answers.

One issue that will likely determine the scope of Watson's impact is developing ways to speed up and reduce the cost of adapting Watson to new subject areas. It has taken years and a huge effort to develop Watson for healthcare, but if the cost and time come down, this could change everything.

Rise of Open-Source Text Analytics

The rise of open-source text analytics is a trend that both surveys see as significant. One point is, as companies incorporate open-source text analytics into their organizations, that it provides a platform for innovation and experimentation with new approaches to text analytics and with new approaches for incorporating text analytics into new kinds of applications.

As noted, my experience leads me to agree that this is a great argument for using open source, but where I have doubts is in the use of open-source text analytics to actually produce mature applications. Talking to clients, I found that almost all organizations that start exploring open source eventually abandon the platform for one of the more commercial offerings.

It will be interesting to see if open source can become a platform for fully-developed applications. As I see it, the real obstacle to developing mature applications is not mastering the technology, but once again the need to master the complexity of language.

All the Little Trends

In addition to these major trends, the surveys and interviews mentioned a lot of smaller, more specific trends—some of which might turn out to be bigger than the big trends. So here, in no particular order, is a quick list of other trends:

Rise of graph databases – This has been predicted for a number of years, so perhaps it's time for it to come true.

Enterprise listening – The application of social media, voice of the customer, and approaches to employees.

Siri-style question-answering – This will likely be applied in more and more contexts.

Multi-linguistic text analytics – Many companies offer 20 or so languages, but there is still a lot of room for growth—especially with more difficult languages.

Development of domain-specific modules – This is a quiet kind of development that could have a huge impact, especially if we get better at integrating the modules.

Behavior prediction – We have lots of ways of tracking what customers do and with social media analysis, we can now track what they say, but being able to predict what they will do is still difficult. This difficulty stems, in part, because it typically takes the combination of predictive analytics and text analytics.

Entity extraction will become a commodity – This has pretty much already happened, although disambiguation of unknown entities and fact extraction still represent some challenges.

Machine generated taxonomies – A number of vendors discussed this, along with a wizard to guide the human development. They are getting better, but that wizard still needs a lot of work.

Text analytics for SMEs – One vendor spokesperson talked about this more as a goal than a trend. A worthy goal, but given the complexity of language, I'm not sure. SMEs can use language, but text analytics requires talking about language—different skill. Still?

Text analytics assistants – The development of whole classes of text analytics–powered assistants to help people do their jobs smarter and easier.

New types and uses for taxonomies and ontologies – This came up in an interview with Sue Feldman in which she discussed what a breakthrough it is to shift, from having to specify everything upfront, to filter at the end using contexts to help. I see a part of this as new, simpler and more modular taxonomies/ontologies— not tasked with the whole job of information access but designed to work with multiple other components.

Text Analytics Arrives

We'll be covering many of these trends in much more detail in later chapters, but for now the big take away is, in my mind, the incredible potential for text analytics but at the same time the very real and difficult obstacles holding back the field.

Endnotes

1. Santayana, George. *The Life of Reason*. New York: Dover Publications, 1980. (Note: The actual quote is: "Those who cannot remember the past are condemned to repeat it.")

2. Grimes, Seth. "Text Analytics 2014: User Perspectives on Solutions and Providers." 2014. www.breakthroughanalysis.com/2014/04/11/text-analytics-2014/.

3. "Text Mining or Text Analytics." Decision Analyst. www.decisionanalyst.com/Database/TextMining.dai.

4. "Text Analytics: The Hurwitz Victory Index Report." Hurwitz & Associates, 2013. www.provalisresearch.com/Documents/HurwitzProvalis.pdf. (Note: This is a very good report and analysis of a number of text analytics vendors, but, as with all reports of this type, it is limited in the number of vendors that it covers.)

5. Saba, Walid. "Text Analytics and Semantic Technology—Myth vs. Reality." Agency Post. March 19, 2014. blog.hubspot.com/agency/text-analytics-and-semantic-technology-myth-vs-reality.

Text Analytics Smart Start

"A beginning is the time for taking the most delicate care that the balances are correct."

—Princess Irulan, *Manual of Muad'Dib*[1]

Getting Started with Text Analytics

After covering the basics of what text analytics is, why it's important to an organization and what kinds of benefits you can get by deciding to implement it within your organization, the next question is, how do you actually get started with text analytics?

Based on lessons from 10 years spent implementing a variety of text analytics initiatives and applications, I've come to the conclusion that the best way to start with text analytics is with a process I call *Smart Start*.

A Smart Start is essentially about creating a good foundation. This foundation consists of two parts—putting together the right team by doing the right research and initiating a software evaluation process that ensures a good selection for creating the semantic foundation upon which to build your application.

Just Buy It and Do It

So why don't we just go out and buy some text analytics software and get started on our first application? Bad idea! There is a whole lot you need to do before buying and implementing your software.

You might ask why such an involved and specific process is needed to get started with text analytics. Shouldn't it be just a matter of simply going out, buying the software, reading the manual, and getting started? You know—just like other software?

Unfortunately, it is not that simple—and there a whole lot of reasons why you need to have something like a Smart Start to get started in text analytics. First of all, text analytics is a bit weird, it's a bit academic, and it often seems not very practical. And on top of that, it's really difficult to do it right.

Very often I hear the standard question: "Well, how difficult can it be? It's not really rocket science." And the answer I always give: "No, it's not rocket science—it's way more difficult than rocket science!" After all, rocket science is just engineering and equations and building stuff that we know how to put together. When you're dealing with things as messy as language and meaning along with relevance and aboutness, it makes rocket science look like a kid's tinker toys set.

Once again, most organizations—and more importantly most decision-making executives—don't know what text analytics is or what it's for. Without this knowledge, even if the executive is convinced to go ahead and approve implementing text analytics, figuring out how to get started will likely be beyond everyone's comfort level and experience.

Enter the Smart Start approach. What this does is correct the unfortunately widely held (and false) model, which is that all you need is text analytics software, your subject matter experts … and you, too can successfully implement a text analytics initiative! This may work in a lot of situations and for a lot of types of software but not for text analytics. In fact, this "software + subject matter experts model" is behind the majority of failed initiatives, both within the enterprise and all of those early unsuccessful sentiment analysis attempts.

As discussed earlier, categorization is really the brains of text analytics, and categorization is a very different skill from actually knowing the subject matter. Subject matter experts know their material very well, and very often they know it so well that a great deal of their knowledge is implied or tacit knowledge—precisely the sort of thing that experts tend to fail to add to their categorization rules building. Their other frequent sin is assuming that everyone knows as much as they do.

Here's the kicker: Rule building itself is an esoteric skill that needs to be learned. It is something that a lot of people can learn, but not without sufficient training. Categorization rule building is part library science, part business analysis, part cognitive science, and part logical puzzle solving. It is not easy.

Another aspect of categorization rule building that most subject matter experts do not have experience in taking a taxonomy and developing the structure of that taxonomy and its associated rules. Then again, not too many people do.

Lastly, text analytics usually calls for an interdisciplinary team that most organizations don't have sitting around because they don't have sufficient experience in putting one together.

All these arguments are particularly true for enterprise text analytics and a lot of text analytics applications—and there are more ways to go wrong or at least fail to get full value than you can imagine.

Survey Says: Strategic Vision and Practical Application

At the Text Analytics World 2013 conference, I did a survey of attendees and potential attendees about text analytics within the enterprise.

There were two main things the survey revealed that were missing in most organizations: 1) a strategic vision of what text analytics can be in the enterprise, including what the business value of text analytics is, what problems could be solved with text analytics, and most importantly, how text analytics could impact the information overload that plagues all modern organizations; and 2) a real-life, functioning program that demonstrates the value of text analytics—in other words, a proof of concept that enables an enterprise buy-in.

Having an abstract strategic vision of text analytics is a necessary first step, but without an understanding of what text analytics is and with no functioning program to point to, it might seem that the only logical thing to do is to flip a coin and pick a vendor and hope they can help actually implement their software.

So, how can IT do its normal evaluation process based on scoring functions and features of the different software packages if no one understands text analytics software well enough to come up with a reasonable scoring judgment? The answer: Use a Smart Start methodology.

A Smart Start for your investment into text analytics involves developing a strategic vision of text analytics—what it can do in the organization along with a software evaluation process that builds on traditional software evaluation processes—but goes beyond and culminates with a proof of concept pilot between top contenders. The pilot accomplishes two things: First, it gives people in the organization a chance to gain a deep understanding and to develop the specific skills they will need to develop fully realized applications. Second, it provides that real life functioning program that is too often one of the missing pieces in an organization.

This may sound like an overly complex methodology for getting started, but on the one hand, it will increase the likelihood of success. And on the other, it can be done faster and easier than it might sound.

Where Are You Coming From?

Organizations can approach text analytics from a whole variety of starting points—and with a variety of initial ideas for applications. While these different starting points have a lot of implications for how that initial application or initiative is going to be done, the surprising thing is that there is a fairly standard methodology that can be applied in almost any case.

Some typical starting places include:

- An organization has heard that text analytics is the answer no matter what the question—as long as it has to do with unstructured text. And so they decide to undertake an enterprise information management (EIM) initiative. This is probably the absolute best way to start text analytics, and will normally lead to much higher value for the organization at a much lower cost. It's also probably the least likely in the United States, although according to a number of text analytics vendors that I spoke to, this approach resonates to a much greater degree in Europe.

- Jumping on the social media bandwagon is a much more common initial approach to text analytics. Using sentiment analysis, they want to know what customers think of them and their products. The more thoughtful organizations also want to monitor a variety of social media for more varied feedback, including early warning detection of problems and issues with their products.

- The continuing failure of enterprise search to deliver real results is another starting point for a lot of organizations. It usually comes up when they decide (maybe for the third time in ten years?) that they need a new search engine and have heard that text analytics just might be able to contribute something—like making the difference between success and another failure.

- The need to process and aggregate huge amounts of content is the starting point for a lot of organizations. This content might be external news sites or it may be documents that are submitted to them that they use to provide specific services.

- Specific initiatives within the organization that call for the use of text analytics is also another common starting point. These initiatives can be everything from improving the efficiency of legal reviews, developing an expertise location application for the KM department, or fraud detection.

- Finally, some companies are in the situation of having an existing text analytics application—anything from their enterprise search to a specific application like fraud detection—and they realize that text analytics can help in a whole variety of other areas within the organization. So they explore how to get more value from their initial implementation—and take a fresh look at their current text analytics software.

Even though the starting points are significantly different, they have certain elements in common. The first is the need to evaluate and select one or more text analytics software packages. Some of the details of that evaluation will be different depending on the starting point, but the overall process will be basically the same—or at least it should be.

The second thing that all of the starting points have in common is the need to understand the information environment in which the initiative is going to take place:

- What are the characteristics of the content that they will be dealing with?
- What information needs and behaviors will be part of that initiative?
- How does the technology fit in with their existing information technology?
- How can the analysis of unstructured text enhance specific business activities?

Based on the experience of the KAPS group and discussions with a variety of text analytics vendors, a best-practice methodology can be developed and applied to all of these different starting points.

Smart Start Methodology

"The path up and down is one and the same."

—Heraclitus[2]

In theory, organizations can and do approach text analytics from two extremes, though in the real world, the approach often combines some elements of each.

Deep Navel Gazing

One extreme is to begin with the development of a deep strategic vision of the information needs and behaviors within the organization—and what role text analytics can play throughout the organization. This approach treats text analytics as an infrastructure, or platform, for multiple applications. This approach is often associated with enterprise search and/or search-based applications.

The pluses are that you establish an infrastructure that will allow for faster and cheaper ongoing project development as the software utilization spreads throughout the enterprise. Another advantage of an infrastructure approach is that you are much more likely to avoid expensive mistakes by choosing the wrong technology, dead-end technology, or implementing the technology in a way that cannot be easily generalized to other applications.

A minus is that the first project will take longer to develop and, thus, involve something that most executives and organizations are not good at dealing with: delayed gratification. In addition, the first project will be more expensive. However, my experience has been that in the long run this approach will be much less expensive.

Blindly Blundering Along

The second approach is to simply start a project—often with a focus on a specific business goal, with text analytics seen as secondary. An initial project might be anything from a compliance application to new ways to take advantage of social media.

The pluses of starting with a small project are: 1) organizations can realize an immediate value and learn by doing, and 2) perhaps most important, it's much easier to get a management buy-in for a small, immediately targeted application than for a large-infrastructure, organization-wide initiative.

The minuses are the lack of a strategic vision to guide the development of additional applications, as well as the lack of a platform on which to build those applications. This means that potentially, the small targeted application will provide much less value to the organization in the long run—and increase the cost of any additional applications using text analytics software.

It can be very difficult to grow to the enterprise level from one small application without some attention and effort put into a strategic vision.

You Can Get There From Here

It might seem counterintuitive, but in many ways it doesn't matter which path you start from—you can achieve the best of both worlds with the right mindset. You can start building an enterprise infrastructure but at the same time create an application with an immediate payoff. Or, you can start with your one application but quickly develop a deeper vision as part of the application development.

However, without some sense of the strategic value of text analytics as a platform, it is possible to create that one, constrained application and get stuck there and fail to actualize the full potential of text analytics. On the other hand, it is also possible to do a strategic vision research project with the goal of transforming how information is handled that creates a pretty vision, though a vision with no hope of actually being implemented. The strategic vision joins countless other strategy papers that simply take up space.

The trick to avoiding both an empty strategy and a dead-end underperforming application is with the Smart Start process.

Smart Start Process: Research + Software Evaluation + Initial Project

The good news is that a Smart Start is a very adaptable methodology that can actually be incorporated into a small initial targeted project, or it can be part of a deep research project. So the scale of a Smart Start could be anywhere from two days to a week as preliminary work for an initial project on up to a three- or four-month deep research project to create a new foundation for better information access throughout the organization.

The research component can be anything from two people with a whiteboard mapping out information environments of an organization or what is needed for this particular application to a two-month research project involving multiple people from multiple departments throughout the enterprise. We will discuss the skills and roles that are needed for the selection team in the last section of this chapter.

The software evaluation process typically consists of two parts. The first is a fairly standard software evaluation process looking at features and capabilities of various vendors in the text analytics space. This should be done even if the organization has actually already purchased text analytics software simply to check on the current market to make sure that nothing new has been developed. This might be a four-week project or a more compressed two-week project.

The second and the most critical part of the evaluation is a proof of concept (POC), or a pilot. This can take anywhere from two weeks to three months.

We will discuss the software evaluation and POC process in the next chapter (Chapter 6). For now I want to focus on how important it is to get a deep understanding of the information environment in which text analytics will be developed. Every situation and every initial application will call for different scales and processes, but there are two main classes of text analytics initiatives: enterprise text analytics and social media analysis. These broad classes normally call for very different scales and processes. Let's start with a look at enterprise text analytics.

Enterprise Text Analytics

The starting point for enterprise text analytics is typically to develop an understanding of the information problems that the text analytics is being deployed to solve. What the problems are and how severe they are will determine a great deal about the initial approach.

The process that we used to develop this understanding is what we call a *knowledge audit* (but you can call it whatever resonates in your enterprise-speak) and consists of a series of research activities, including contextual and information interviews, content inventory and analysis, surveys, focus groups, ethnographic studies, and more (see Appendix A for a sample set of interview questions).

For specific applications (rather than an enterprise-wide initiative), a much more informal process can be used. Nevertheless, it is important to always start with a solid understanding of the information environment within which your company's text analytics will be developed.

The output of a knowledge audit is the development of a *preliminary knowledge map*. This map consists of a high level characterization of an organization's content, people, technology, and activity. The knowledge map contains the following:

- A *content catalog,* which is a high level characterization of the different types of content, any special issues or requirements for each type, publishers and publishing procedures, and any associated technologies such as content management software, databases, authoring tools, and collaboration software. It also contains a high-level topic or category model of the content along with a specification of any existing metadata and other infrastructure elements such as controlled vocabularies, taxonomies, and specialized lexicons.

- A *community catalog* of the various communities, users, and audiences within the enterprise. It includes formal and informal communities which are characterized according to their type such as communication or collaboration, their business and activity functions, their forms of internal and external communication channels, and their primary and secondary content repositories.

- An *information technology catalog* of information technologies such as search engines, categorization and taxonomy software, content management, portals, collaboration software, text and data mining, data analytics, learning management software, and a range of knowledge management platforms.

- A *business activity catalog* of the basic employee activities with a focus on the information component of those activities. This would also typically include all the stakeholders, from executive sponsors and content publishers to technical and business support personnel.

Social Media Applications

For social media applications, the research activities and output will be significantly different than for an enterprise text analytics initiative, but it is just as important to base any social media application on a deep research foundation.

The type and amount of research for social media applications will depend on the nature of the application, but in general it will be easier in many ways than for an enterprise applications. For example, it is normally easier to identify social communities since the community is the focus of their activity unlike in an enterprise setting where the focus is on business activities and communities are secondary.

As well, in the social media world the primary activity is basically communication within the community. In addition, the technology is relatively simple—blogs, Twitter, and forum technologies are well-established and ease-of-use is typically a major focus.

A major difference between social media environments and enterprise environments is the nature of the content. Social media content is radically different than most enterprise content, although as social media moves into the enterprise arena there is often the need to include social content in the enterprise content catalog. Twitter, blogs, and forums posts tend to be much shorter with much wilder spelling and syntax. This creates a set of problems that needs to be taken into consideration. For example, on one project we found 22 different spellings of the word customer in the first 2,000 posts—and that wasn't the worst offender.

On the other hand, the shortness of the post often makes it easier to categorize what an individual post is about. But posts are part of an active dialog, which means that identifying conversation threads is extremely important and often extremely difficult to do.

These threads can be within specific posts, or they can be between different posts by different people. An example of a thread within a single post is: "I bought an iPhone yesterday. It looks fantastic, but Jack thinks it is the wrong color for me. I've been on it almost nonstop all day today. All the calls sounded great." It is not easy to determine what the indefinite references are for "It"—especially the implied "It" of the last sentence.

Threads between posts that show up in social media and email can make it even more difficult to resolve the referent.

While the amount and focus of your initial research will vary, the essential first step for any text analytics initiative—whether a new search, a new sentiment analysis marketing project, adding new social media analysis to your competitive intelligence, or [fill in what you are contemplating]—is a heavy dose of research into the anticipated content, people, business activity, and related technologies.

Design of the Text Analytics Team

The last (but not least) issue we need to deal with before we get to the software evaluation part of a Smart Start is the make-up of the text analytics team. Who is going to do this research? Who will do the software evaluation and POC? And who will design and build the actual application? We will describe the design of an enterprise text analytics team in its entirety later in the book, but let's focus for now just on the team needed to make a good selection.

The Text Analytics Selection Team

As you might expect from what we have discussed so far about the nature of text analytics, the best team for selecting text analytics software is going to be an interdisciplinary team consisting of people from IT, the library, business groups, data analytics, and potentially an application-focused group (which could be anything from KM looking for an expertise location application to customer support looking for ways to improve their services and mine the rich text of customer support feedback).

IT

Among the traditional candidates, IT typically has experience with large software purchases—large both in the sense of expensive and complex, and also large in the sense of involving the entire enterprise. On the other hand, text analytics software is unlike other software and so their experience has to be expanded to deal with the unique features of text analytics software.

In addition, IT has experience with needs assessments, which is a critical part of all software selection and in particular for text analytics. However, there are unique features of the needs assessments for text analytics software that go beyond traditional needs assessments and extend into the realm of a knowledge audit or similar deep dive into content, content structure, and multiple applications.

So while it is critical to involve IT in the selection process, clearly they are unlikely to have all the necessary skills and experience to make a good decision. In some ways, asking IT to select text analytics software is like asking a construction company to select the design of your house.

In addition to their experience, IT has one other critical element which is they tend to be able to get budgets better than almost any other group. So let's invite IT to be part of the team!

Business Owners

Another traditional candidate—business owners—have critical experience along with a deep understanding of business and what kinds of activities need to be supported and enhanced. However, while business groups tend to understand the business, they typically don't understand information behaviors or semantics.

Having business groups on the team ensures that bottom-line business value will be paid attention to—and that decisions will not be made based on who has the coolest new technology. While this focus on business value is absolutely essential, at the same time, a focus on semantics is also needed.

Like IT, business groups very often have an easier time getting executive sponsorship, support, and budget. If real business value can be demonstrated using traditional value measures as well as the type of ROI arguments covered in Chapter 3, then the organization is more likely to get necessary budgets to select and buy text analytics software. So, let's invite them to be part of the team, too.

Libraries

A third traditional candidate that some organizations have is a library or other information professional group. The library has experience with understanding, developing, and using information structure, which is critical for success in text analytics. However, libraries don't often have a deeper understanding of how those information structures can be used in business or how they can deliver business value. They often don't have a technology background, either.

In many organizations, however, libraries do have expertise in working with search and information organization as part of an enterprise search group. Historically, this participation has been largely using taxonomies and other metadata tagging strategies to manually apply the structures to contents, which (as we will see in Chapter 10) has some major drawbacks. In addition, librarians and taxonomies tend to create structures that are useful for them and other experts, but not necessarily for basic business users.

Librarians and taxonomists aren't particularly adept at getting large budgets in most organizations, but they typically do have experience with a variety of search engines, taxonomy software, and potentially the integration issues involved in putting together an information solution. This experience makes them an invaluable part of the selection. We can invite them to be part of the team, too.

Data Analysts / Developers

Another group that has become increasingly important as text analytics is integrated into data-based analytic applications is data analysts or data scientists. These functions are very often found within IT or within other business application-focused areas. These groups tend to understand data as well as the really advanced analytics that you find in areas like predictive analytics and high-end analytic software that companies like SAS and IBM offer.

However, the focus is often mathematical and they tend to lack a deeper understanding of the complexities of language. This is just one reason that so many social media and sentiment analysis initiatives fail to deliver full value—they're great on data but not so good on language and context.

In addition to sharing IT's and the business groups' ability to get funding, they also add a significant dimension to any text analytics application. So we'll invite them to join the team as well.

The Best Discipline Is Interdisciplinary

Each group has needed skills, but no single group has all the skills, so the best solution is to put together a broad interdisciplinary team with members from IT and data analytics, business groups, a library, and other user groups. This team should be headed up by information professionals and ideally someone with experience in dealing with unstructured content.

If this type of experience does not exist within the organization, then it is probably a good idea to hire outside consultants to help with the process. These outside consultants very often perform many of the roles that the library group does but with the added experience of dealing with unstructured content in new and more flexible ways than is often done by library groups.

This type of broad interdisciplinary group is much more likely to make a good decision than any one group by itself. In addition, the experience of this interdisciplinary team working together will create a foundation for the eventual implementation of the software as well.

Summary

"The beginning is the most important part of the work."
—Plato, *The Republic*

As Plato reminds us, how you begin something is the most important step, and this is particularly true for something as complex and potentially powerful as text analytics. In other words, how you approach text analytics and envision its use will have a lot to do with how successful you are.

Here is how *not* to do it: You have heard that text analytics can do amazing things. Or more likely, you have heard that monitoring what people are saying about your company and its products is something that everyone, including your competitors, is doing and so you should, too. And so you go ask a friend to recommend something, or just Google "sentiment analysis vendors" and then you go out and buy one and just do it. You are clearly tempting fate, or the gods ... or whatever. Maybe you will be lucky and it won't be a disaster, but the likelihood of you finding or developing the best solution is, while higher than winning the lottery, still not very good.

The two critical ingredients for a successful text analytics initiative are one, having a well-articulated strategic vision of what you want and what text analytics can do for you, and two, getting the right software and using it properly to create an actual functioning initial application that can flesh out the details of that strategic vision and provide a foundation that you can build on. We will cover the second ingredient in the next chapter.

Before you go out and start software shopping, your first step—regardless of what you anticipate will be your first application—is to create a strategic vision. If that sounds too daunting or too corporate, then simply create a blueprint for what you want from text analytics.

This first step should start with an in-depth research and characterization of the anticipated content and content structure, the people (customers and/or employees) who will be served by this application, what associated technology you already have in place, and the business and information activities that the application will support.

Depending on the initial application, this research need not be a major project and the "strategic vision" might be a simple two-page description of what you want—and I recommend that you start by thinking big. Text analytics has so much potential and can be used to develop and/or enrich so many different kinds of applications that the biggest risk of not getting your money's worth is to think too small or too quick.

The motto that we have used for a number of years and for both enterprise clients and startup clients is:

Think Big—Start Small—Scale Fast!

One really important part of your initial research should be to think carefully about what text analytics skills will be needed as you develop your first and subsequent applications. Just as important is thinking about how to integrate those skills with your existing staff, such as your sales and marketing people.

The last critical element needed for a quick and smart start is the right design of the software selection team, which should be interdisciplinary and have representatives from IT, from one or more business areas, and information professionals.

In summary:

- Know what you are and what you want.
- Know what text analytics can and can't do.
- Know who you need on your team to do it right.
- Have the selection team in place.

Now you're ready to select your text analytics software and build a foundation for your first application!

Endnotes

1. *Frank Herbert's Dune.* Directed by David Kappes. Artisan Home Entertainment, 2002. Film.

2. Kirk, G. S., and J. E. Raven. *The Presocratic Philosophers: A Critical History with a Selection of Texts.* Cambridge, England: University Press, 1957.

CHAPTER **6**

Text Analytics Software Evaluation

"Self-knowledge is the highest form of knowledge."
—One or More of Those Early Greeks

"The unexamined life is not worth living."
—Plato, *Apology*

The Software Evaluation Process

As we discussed in the last chapter, the starting point for evaluating text analytics software is self-knowledge. The ancient Greeks considered self-knowledge as the highest form of knowledge and I strongly agree, and besides—it's fun using my History of Ideas degree for something.

Text analytics software is different from most types of software, which both explains why it is not yet ubiquitous across all industries as well as its unique power. As the primary difference is that it deals with language in all its complexity and messiness, it's no surprise that the method of evaluating the various text analytics software offerings and selecting the right one is unique among software selection processes.

Self-knowledge simply refers to the need for understanding the current information environment within an organization—and knowing exactly what you want.

One approach to developing the necessary self-knowledge to do text analytics is the research described in Chapter 5, where the result should be to develop *the* model for text analytics use in your enterprise. Even if the initial use of the software is for one specific application, developing this deeper self-knowledge is still the best approach to text analytics, given its capabilities as a platform or foundation for multiple applications.

Also, selecting the right software is more important in a field like text analytics than it is in other information areas, such as metadata management, taxonomy management, or taxonomy development (though taxonomy or metadata management can be a big plus—if necessary metadata and taxonomies can still be developed and maintained in spreadsheets).

However, there are no spreadsheets for semantics and text analytics, so if it's to be done at all, it needs to have sophisticated software to be done right. Thus it is very important to select the right software for your first immediate application as well as for long-term or infrastructure initiatives.

Varieties of Text Analytics Software

Text analytics software comes in a bewildering variety of shapes, sizes, combinations of capabilities, delivery modes, platforms, and just about every other thing you can imagine. Some are sold and labeled as "text analytics software," some as "text mining," and some are completely hidden inside other software.

We looked at this variety in Chapter 3 from a market perspective, but let's take another look from a purchasing perspective at some of the major variants:

Taxonomy management software, which, although the primary focus is to manage and develop taxonomies, very often includes some basic text analytics capabilities, particularly noun phrase extraction. In addition, taxonomy management is, or should be, an essential part of any text analytics software package, whether it is included in the text analytics component or added as a stand-alone capability.

Text mining software typically utilizes basic noun phrase and/or entity extraction, word counting, and statistical clustering as the primary text handling, and is supplemented by basic NLP capabilities such as understanding parts of speech and grammar. The primary focus, however, of text mining software is normally in terms of statistical and mathematical analytics, which are applied to fairly simple text processing capabilities. Be warned that the dividing line between text mining software and text analytics is somewhat fuzzy, so this is one area that should be looked at carefully when deciding on the best text analytics software for your organization.

Ontology management software often overlaps text analytics software in a number of areas as well. There are a number of vendors who focus almost exclusively on ontology management, due to the fact that maintaining complex ontological models can be a complex task. As with taxonomy management software, ontology management can be incorporated into text analytics, or it can be a stand-alone capability.

Sentiment analysis software was originally based on fairly simple text analytics capabilities, mostly extraction and the use of dictionaries of positive and negative terms. However, as these early sentiment analysis applications continued to disappoint and underperform, companies added more categorization-type capabilities to process sentiments and other expressions within text in more sophisticated ways by looking at the context surrounding these sentiment words. Today, the difference between general text analytics software and sentiment analysis software is mostly the type of built-in dictionaries, the language processing that the software utilizes, and the analytical front end—significant differences, but many companies offer both.

Embedded text analytics software can also be found in many enterprise search and/or content management software. Search engines like Coveo and Endeca have incorporated at least some text analytics capabilities for a number of years. Content management software is a natural fit—it is the best place to add categorization and metadata to documents as they are being published using a hybrid-model combination of software and human categorization. I used to think that that all content management software would have text analytics capabilities built-in by now, but the complexities of developing text analytics capabilities seem to have stalled that.

Another class of software with embedded text analytics is targeted application software like business intelligence or customer intelligence programs. While these programs depend on text analytics capabilities, there is rarely any explicit mention of their underlying capabilities—and very little capability of directly working with text analytics components:

Full-platform text analytics software offers a full-development environment that typically incorporates taxonomy or ontology management, noun phrase or entity extraction, and categorization along with other features, such as automatic summarization and automatic taxonomy generation through clustering. Development can be a combination of rules, training sets, and other techniques along with a testing environment that can be used to refine all capabilities, particularly categorization.

Open-source text analytics software offers a variety of different types of approaches to text analytics for companies that want to build their own software. Among the most widely used open-source text analytics software products are GATE, NLTK, R (used for text analytics development), and others.

Data and text analytics platforms combine high-end sophisticated data analysis, text mining, text analytics, advanced visualization, and in some cases, a little AI or other forms of machine learning. This is the very high end of the market in terms of capabilities (and often price).

Given the bewilderingly intricate software landscape, the complexity of dealing with language in all of its messiness, and the wide range of applications the software can be used for, it is not surprising that the process of evaluating which software to buy is also fairly involved.

At this point, let's assume that you have done the research described in Chapter 5 and you have put together your interdisciplinary selection team. You are now ready to begin the process of evaluating and selecting the best text analytics software for your company and/or project.

A Two-Stage Evaluation Process

The evaluation process described below is one that my company, the KAPS group, has used successfully for a number of clients. The basic process will likely be the same for most text analytics initiatives although some details will differ depending on the initial focus. The process consists of two major stages, an initial traditional software evaluation process and a second stage that consists of a short proof of concept (POC) or pilot project.

Text Analytics Evaluation: Stage One

The first stage consists of a traditional software evaluation—and that evaluation is used primarily as a filter to reduce the number of vendors down to two or three rather than actually select a vendor. The details of each stage and each filter are derived from your original research, although there are a number of standard questions and issues. Typically, we utilize three major filters.

Filter One: Generally Speaking

The first filter is general, basic company research into the strengths and reputations of the various vendors. This process may consist of getting expert opinions on the reputations of companies, either directly or by purchasing research from companies like Gartner and Forrester.

Factors to look at include the overall market strengths of each vendor, which platforms they are available on, and feedback from customers, if available. This should include both successful customers whose names can be collected from the vendors, and unsuccessful customers for which you will have to do your own research as vendors typically don't provide failure stories.

Another general consideration is overall company experience and stability. Going with a new startup can have a number of benefits, but not if the company is likely to go out of business in a couple of years, leaving you with a very expensive transition to a new vendor. This is particularly true in a young, volatile field like text analytics where companies come and go.

Another consideration is whether the company offers multiple products that need to be integrated or a single, fully integrated platform. A fully integrated platform has advantages, particularly for a company that doesn't have a strong IT capability. If good IT capabilities exist in your organization, then having multiple products or modules often gives more flexibility.

An important dimension to look at is the total cost of ownership, including both the initial price and ongoing support and need for ongoing development costs. This will also include the price and ease of the process of upgrading the software, because in a field like text analytics, companies are continually developing new features and capabilities. Some of these new features and capabilities are simple refinements, but in other cases they can involve whole new areas of functionality that the company either developed or obtained by buying another text analytics company.

Filter Two: The Fast Fantastic Feature Filter

A second filter includes an analysis of the software features and can include a standard feature scorecard. Again, the difference is using the scorecards to filter down to a minimum set of vendors. Some of the features to look for are standard basic features, such as:

- Operators – new, rename, delete, and merge for both taxonomy and text analytics features
- Other basic features – scope notes, spell check, and versioning
- Search – both taxonomy and text analytics rules

Other features include overall usability such as:

- Ease-of-use
- User documentation – user manuals, online help, and training and tutorials
- Visualization – of the taxonomy tree and/or file structure and of the test results

Advanced features include:

- Language support for whatever languages you will need
- Import-exports in formats such as XML OWL, SPARQL, and SKOS
- Mapping between taxonomies and categorization rules
- Having a fully developed API/SD and ease of integration
- Security, access rights, specifiable roles and workflows
- Scalability – many applications can involve tens of millions or hundreds of millions of documents
- Speed is always important – from compiling rules to analyzing hundreds of thousands to millions of documents
- Ability to quickly and easily test and validate categorization results
- Related to this is the overall configuration – how much improvement do you get by adding addition servers (especially since this is how they mostly deal with large document collections—add more servers)
- Connectors to multiple, diverse content sources and repositories and the related ability to process a wide range of document formats

The full set of features and, more importantly, the relative weight to give to each one is something that will vary depending on the initial application and is something that you should work out with your IT group.

Other general features include things like customizability and ease of customization in addition to out-of-the-box (OOB) features. Customization and OOB often end up being a trade-off, as very often the company with the strongest out-of-the-box offerings also tends to have the highest customization cost.

For example, some companies have developed a large complex semantic network capable of categorizing documents out-of-the-box with fairly high accuracy, but little granularity. This gives them an advantage and makes them look good in demos (another reason to do a full POC). The cost of customizing that semantic network can be very high and usually involves using the company's resources rather than your own, however, not all great OOB features carry a high customization cost.

Typically, looking at a traditional software evaluation of features capabilities involves two approaches.

The first approach is to look for the *lack* of (an) essential feature(s) that your organization will need as a filter to eliminate many of the companies right off, such as whether or not the vendor's technology is compatible with yours, and whether or not they are a good match for your overall scope and capabilities. This is an important filter, and one that looks at the lack of an essential ability to integrate with the company's existing technology and can be used to eliminate vendors whose offerings don't fit. Another example is that some companies may have good general categorization and/or entity extraction but lack the ability to easily develop sentiment analysis or other social media analysis. And yet another essential feature some companies may lack is language support for languages other than English, so if this is an issue for your organization, you can eliminate them, too.

The second is a standard scorecard approach, assigning scores to the various features you value most. For example, a feature that is often touted in vendor sales material is the ability to automatically generate a taxonomy. My own experience is that most of these automatic taxonomies are largely nonsense, however, they can sometimes be useful for generating new suggestions to incorporate into a taxonomy. The point is to use your team's experiences and insights to anticipate which features will be of the most value to your organization.

Filter Three: Demos Are Your Friend

After you've winnowed the vendors to a group of three to six by using the first two filters, you can then invite them to give you an in-depth demo of their product and capabilities. This demo might be a simple hour using the vendor's standard content. Or it might be more involved, with the vendor using your content along with some specific application features or scenarios that are important to you.

Many vendors are happy to do a standard out-of-the-box demo, but often want to charge for more involved demos. My company partners with a lot of text analytics vendors, but when it comes to charging for a demo, I tend to side with the customer. But it will depend on a lot of factors in your organization—how big you are, how important you anticipate text analytics will be to your organization, how many demos you want, and how unique your anticipated application is going to be—the more standard your application, the less likely the need for a lot of customization in the demo.

These demos can give you a more in-depth understanding of what the software is capable of, but they still won't answer the basic question of how well the software will work with your content and your scenarios. And more importantly, they won't give you a good idea of how much effort it will take on your part to develop the kinds of solutions you will need—or how to refine and maintain those solutions.

In other words, you're not done yet.

Does It Have to Be So Complicated?

At this point, a common question is, "Does it have to be so complicated?" And the answer is: Yes ... unless you're feeling lucky today.

One reason for doing this sort of complicated evaluation is that no one single company dominates the text analytics world. Different vendors have different strengths, and in different environments. For example, if your initial application involves millions of short, badly typed documents that you want to use to build a customer support or social media application, that will call for different strengths than if your initial application involves large, 200-page PDF documents that will be provided to the general public through a standard search function on your website.

And finding the right fit is also complicated by another factor—you! In other words, *you* have to map out the complex vendor landscape according to the uniqueness of your organization and your initial application. It helps to first answer the following questions:

- Are you a large organization that wants the absolutely most complete solution, and are you willing to pay a lot to have it developed by you or the vendor, professional services companies or a combination?
- Do you have a huge IT department (or one that consists of mostly IT), and do you want to build everything yourself?
- Do you have few IT resources or even worse, no library resources so you want to use a SaaS model? (I say worse in part because the language skills of information professionals are truly essential to the success of text analytics applications and those skills are often undervalued.)

The goal of this initial stage is to *reduce the number of vendors* to two or three, and to *create the depth of understanding* that makes the choice between those two or three vendors a good decision. However, deciding which vendor to buy based on just this standard evaluation is still very likely to cause problems—and could easily lead to a bad decision. And the worst part is that if it turns out to be the wrong (or at least not the best), you won't know it until you have spent months to years and hundreds of thousands to millions of dollars, not to mention the minds of dozens to hundreds of your employees—all for something that doesn't deliver what you want.

What is needed to avoid these kinds of disasters (large or small) is a second stage, consisting of a short POC.

Text Analytics Evaluation: Stage Two—Proof of Concept (POC)

Supposing the initial evaluation has reduced the chaotic landscape of text analytics software offerings to two top candidates, the best way to decide which of those candidates will really be superior is to carry out a short *proof of concept* project and/or an initial pilot project. We will discuss some of the general approaches and issues related to doing this sort of POC, and then describe two sample projects—a social media POC and an enterprise search pilot. Keep in mind, however, that every POC will be slightly different in its focus, the software features that are to be tested, and the internal resources of an organization—both in terms of people and in terms of content and content structure.

Initial Design of the Proof of Concept

The best way to prepare for a proof of concept or initial pilot project would be to conduct a knowledge audit, as described in Chapter 4. The deeper the initial research into the information environment of the organization, the better the results will likely be. However, very often, companies are not willing to undertake something this rigorous or involved.

Even if you're just looking at a single application, such as improving search or initiating a new social media analysis initiative, it's important to take as deep a look as possible in order to both make the best selection of text analytics software and also to develop the kind of strategic vision that will enable the enterprise to realize the full value of text analytics.

Regardless of the method and amount of effort, there are certain basic activities that you will need to do. The first is to develop your basic requirements—these will include general technical requirements and basic functionality requirements. But in addition, you should develop a set of user scenarios, or use cases. These use cases will vary depending on what the initial application is, but always remember the larger context—text analytics can do more than that first application.

The use cases or scenarios start with the broad application. This might include things like developing a better search engine for enterprise content, or it might be that one of the major players is the legal department, which is interested in enhancing their legal review process by semiautomating it using text analytics software. Within this broad context, you should dive more deeply into specific issues and translate specific use cases into a set of performance measures. These performance measures might include everything from indexing speed to minimum accuracy scores.

You should also map out the internal and external content that you will be working with since one of the key advantages of doing a POC is doing it with real content, not content that has been chosen by a vendor that might demonstrate the generic value of their software but not the real value of how it will work with your content.

Stage One—POC / Pilot Preparation

"In the fields of observation chance favors only the prepared mind."
—Louis Pasteur[1]

The POC, or pilot preparation, is basically a continuation of the initial research into text analytics and how your organization will use it. In this stage, there will be a shift in focus from a broad and complete characterization of your information environment to a deeper dive into the specific areas that the POC or pilot will cover. The selection of the major elements of the POC needs to be done carefully so that it covers all you need to know to make a purchasing or implementation decision while giving you a foundation for your first major application.

The first step is to select the use cases or user scenarios you're going to cover in the POC. These should be based on your broad analysis of your information needs. They should include characterizations of the different types and information needs of users. The scope of those information needs will vary depending on the initial focus. For example, if the first application is an enterprise-wide initiative, that will require a very broad characterization of information needs throughout the organization. On the other hand, if the first application is a social media initiative to track customer's comments about specific features of one line of your products, the information needs will be much more tightly defined.

Although these user scenarios will drive specific activities within each stage of the POC or pilot, there are a number of general steps that should be followed for pretty much any user scenario.

Content Is King

The first step is to do a preliminary analysis of your content. It is a good idea to do this analysis for both the overall content that might become part of your initial application and for the specific content that will be used in the POC. This analysis will produce an overall characterization of the content with specifics on such characteristics as total number of documents and the breakdown of documents by document types or formats. It should also look at document purpose—general communication, to establish company policy, announcements, etc.

This initial analysis should also include a look at the kinds of content structure available, including documents that have had significant amounts of metadata added such as title, author, and in particular subject keywords. It should also look at the special difficulties that wildly unstructured content, such as Twitter posts, will pose for a text analysis of those documents.

In addition to a characterization of the target content, discovering and characterizing existing content structure resources—such as taxonomies or controlled vocabularies—should be part of the preparation phase. This should include enterprise taxonomies and/or sentiment vocabularies of positive and negative terms that are available from sources outside the organization.

For an enterprise application, it should also include an analysis of any existing search terms if these are available. This should start with a standard search log analysis but should, time permitting, include a deeper analysis than just list of terms ranked by frequency. The analysis should dive into the categories of search terms—grouping them with clustering and/or human analysis. Analyzing how people search for content is essential in understanding how text analytics will be used for search—and it will impact how text analytics will be used in other applications, since search terms provide a window into the kind of information that is important in your organization.

Selection of POC / Pilot Training Content

In addition to an overall characterization of content, another essential step is in gathering specific test sets of content that will be used for both training the software and testing. The selection should reflect as much of the full range of characteristics of the complete content set that will be used in the initial applications as possible. However, it is important to select content that embodies specific issues that pose particular problems.

A typical scenario for categorization tasks would be to start with a taxonomy, or part of a taxonomy, or even simply a list of important categories.

This taxonomy may be conceptual for an enterprise application, or it may be a taxonomy of products and specific features that the organization wishes to track customer sentiment about. The next step is to select anywhere from 10 to 50 sample documents for each category in the case of large documents, or maybe a few thousand for smaller Twitter-type posts. These documents will become the initial training set that the software will use to do everything, from generating lists of frequent terms to automatically generating rules that can then be refined. On the other hand, for software that does not do automatic rules, these training sets can be used by information professionals to manually generate a starting set of rules.

The best way to select these documents, especially in the case of enterprise documents, is to ask your SMEs to select good examples for each category. Since this involves human categorization, it's also a good idea get more than one person for each area—as we've seen, humans are very good at categorization but not necessarily consistent categorization. In other words, people differ.

For social media training sets, very often it's possible to take the ratings of each post and use those for initial categorization. For example, on one project we had a few thousand posts about phones, their features, and the associated plans. The authors ranked their own overall judgment using one to five stars, five being the most positive. So we could take anything with a one- or two-star rating and count it as negative; a four or five was positive, a three neutral.

Even when it is not possible to get author-generated ratings, it still tends to be significantly easier to get initial training sets for sentiment analysis. The general consensus seems to be that it's easier to get started with sentiment analysis, but much harder to actually enhance or improve the results. For other types of social media monitoring, initial categorization might be carried out by specific SMEs, and in those cases it is particularly important to get input from multiple people.

Training Taxonomists / Text Analysts

Another important initial or preparatory activity is simply training taxonomists or text analysts on the specific software packages that will be tested in the POC and/or pilot. This is an extremely important part of the POC, since the goal is to test features of the software, not the capabilities of the specific text analysts doing the POC. This training has an added benefit, which is to give you an understanding of the ease-of-use of the software—in this case by seeing how difficult it is to train people.

There are many ways to staff the text analyst position for a POC. One model that the KAPS group has successfully employed in a number of different environments is to combine the general expertise of the text analysts in our (or your personal favorite) consulting group with internal resources that might include librarians or other content-focused employees. It is important to have people with experience in developing text analytics capabilities in order to get a true picture of the capabilities of the different software packages. In some cases our consultants have done all the text analysis work, but more often internal resources are included in the team and they supplement the consultants while learning from their experience.

In some cases, software companies will provide additional training to help carry out the POC/pilot, although many companies charge for this sort of training.

There are really two major dimensions—or levels—for this training. The first is simply learning the idiosyncrasies of each software package—how they handle all the various basic functions of text analytics as well as learning the categorization command language, which differs from software package to software package. This is similar to traditional software training, can be done relatively easily, and is usually offered by vendors.

The second dimension is much more complex and involves learning how to create good categorization rules—a skill that takes some time and effort to learn. For example, creating rules that will accurately categorize specific documents against a particular category is relatively straightforward, but developing rules that can accurately distinguish between two similar categories is much more difficult and tends to come from experience. These more complex rules also tend to use some of the more advanced operators in the language, such as DIST or SENTENCE. DIST is the number of words between two targets. It is used to treat words that are close to each other differently than words that merely appear in the same document. SENTENCE treats words differently if they are in the same sentence. These more sophisticated rules also tend to use negative evidence and the NOT operator.

For a sentiment analysis/social media application, very often the trick is developing rules that can handle things like multiple expressions within a single sentence, such as "I really would've loved that product if it had not been for that clunky user interface."

On the other hand, if your approach is to use training sets instead of rules, then you won't have to do as much training in the preparation phase, which seems like one of the advantages of a statistical rather than rules approach. However, in practice, going with training sets tends to shift the effort to the actual development phase, since refining categorization by refining the training set is a very complex skill that almost no one has.

The Initial Taxonomy

Another preliminary activity very often involves developing an initial taxonomy or categorization schema. In some cases, organizations have an existing taxonomy, but it is one that was developed for very specific indexing applications and is not very suitable for text analytics and categorization. In that case, the solution might be to select a smaller and simpler subset of this taxonomy. In other cases, it might involve generating a small taxonomic structure or list of categories that can often be provided by subject matter experts.

We will explore in another section the characteristics of the taxonomy that make it suitable for categorization, but for now some of the features to avoid include:

- A taxonomy that is too complex, such as one useful for indexing large documents sets with multiple and specific topics, like a pharmaceutical collection.

- Another common failing for taxonomies developed without text analytics in mind is using categories that are too similar and that have very few distinguishing characteristics within the documents. For example, a taxonomy might have information management, information strategy, and information technology. In terms of the vocabularies and the common concepts that are found in documents discussing information management and information strategy, there is an enormous amount of overlap and thus it is much more difficult to develop good categorization rules.

- Mixing document types with subject topics is another common mistake. Document type should be a separate facet from subject.

- Another issue with using existing taxonomies and/or taxonomies developed for other purposes is that these taxonomies very often do not reflect the major concepts found in your content. It can be the most beautiful and elegant taxonomy your library staff is capable of putting together (and yes, I agree a taxonomy can be a thing of beauty), but if you map it to your content and then discover significant numbers of taxonomy categories have virtually no content, then the taxonomy is a failure. Or it may be that, of your 100,000 documents, 90,000 fall into 10 categories, and the remaining 10,000 documents are spread thinly over 200 categories—a bad fit.

Multitasking Can Work—Sometimes

This may sound like an awful lot of work just to get ready for a POC or pilot, but keep two things in mind: First, it's not really all that much activity if it's spread out over the TA team and enterprise team. Second, and more importantly, this preliminary activity can be done while the initial software evaluation is being done.

A typical text analytics POC can be done in about four to six weeks, although the amount of total resources can vary dramatically, depending on the environment and the initial application. The basic POC should consist of at least two or three rounds of development—identifying and gathering appropriate content, developing categorization or sentiment rules, testing those rules against specific contents, and then refining the rules based on the results.

The main idea for doing a POC is that simply looking at features that come with the software and its ability to do categorization or extraction out-of-the-box is not enough to really make a good decision about which software to purchase. This is particularly true for understanding how that software will work in your environment, with your content, and with your scenarios or use cases. One of the key things to learn from the POC is the amount of effort it will take to go through one or more rounds of this develop-test-refine cycle.

Example Proof of Concept / Pilot Projects

To get a better idea of the elements of the POC, let's take a look at two projects that I worked on—one for Company A and another for Organization B. There were a number of differences in the two cases, but they also shared a number of characteristics. Of course, your POC will likely differ in some details, but the overall approach should be close to the same.

Company A—Customer Support and Sentiment Analysis

Company A was a telecommunications service provider that decided to look into text analytics to improve their customer support capabilities, although during the initial evaluation they realized there were a number of other capabilities that they wanted to look into, including sentiment analysis.

The project started with a standard software evaluation that led to the selection of six vendors, each of whom were invited to give a one-hour demo of their products. Four of the companies were invited back for additional discussions as they looked to be good candidates. Two of the candidates were eliminated because of specific capability gaps, leading to the choice of the top two companies. We then designed a POC bake-off for those two vendors.

The POC was set to run for four weeks, which meant that it had to be limited in scope. However, Company A wanted to look at a number of capabilities and so we limited the depth in each test to fit in with the time limitations. The POC was designed to look at four areas, one technical and three semantic. The technical dimension looked at two main issues: scale and integration with their existing software. The three semantic dimensions were categorization, sentiment analysis, and a third area of small exploratory tests of additional capabilities.

The technical dimension was carried out primarily by Company A's technical team, supported by the two vendors' technical teams and their documentation. Scale was an important issue since Company A needed to process up to 1 million documents a day. In addition, we looked at such elements as vendor viability, total cost of ownership, and integration issues. We also did a demo of the capabilities of the two vendors' higher-end analytic products that could be used to support and extend the basic text analytics capabilities.

The primary content for the POC was a set of customer support notes taken by Company A's customer support staff. These notes were taken while the support rep was on the phone dealing with customer calls, feverishly typing the notes while irate customers yelled in their ear, threatening to cancel their service if they didn't immediately fix their (badly expressed) problem. As you can imagine, this led to some amazingly bad spellings and syntax as well as general incoherence.

A secondary content set was taken from internet forum posts as people discussed various products and features. This was the content we used for the sentiment analysis part of the POC. It was also the content we used for a number of short tests of different capabilities, such as noun phrase extraction and event or action extraction.

The evaluation of the two text analytics vendors was done through a combination of accuracy scores and more general comparisons with human categorization. In addition, the final evaluation report included a section on usability done by our consultants.

We split our team into two groups, one for each vendor. Each team had one of our consultants, although occasionally that consultant was aided by one of our other consultants who had the needed specific experience. The client provided two or three part-time people for each team.

Company A had a taxonomy of customer call motivations and a second taxonomy that organized the type of interaction taken with the customer (see Figure 6.1). These taxonomies were used in the categorization evaluation, which took up about half of the four weeks. This is fairly normal as categorization is by far the most complex of text analytics capabilities.

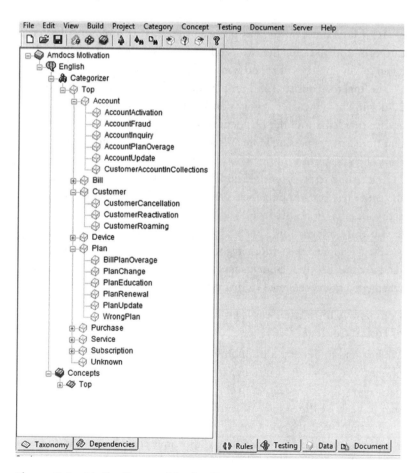

Figure 6.1   Motivation and Action Taxonomy

Company A Test Case One—Categorization of Customer Support Notes

We started the POC by setting up the content. The first step was to select 12 categories from their two taxonomies—motivation and interaction. We then had Company A's SME select two sets of documents: 50 good example documents for each category to be used for development and an additional 20 documents for each category that we would use for a final test.

The development process consisted of two rounds of rule development. The first round used half of the selected documents and we developed rules for each category until we reached 90% accuracy (both precision and recall). The second round added the remaining 25 documents per category and we repeated the development process until we were again at 90% accuracy.

At selected times during this process, we compared and normalized the categorization rules for the two vendors. We also tracked time and effort taken to develop the rules, and wrote up usability reports.

The final test consisted of three parts. First, we tested recall by taking the 20 documents for each category that had been categorized by their SMEs and counted the number of documents that were successfully matched, that is, received a passing score. We also asked testers to note any extreme cases of bad categorization.

The second test was for precision. We ran a test for each category against the entire test content documents and counted the number of wrong category files that were listed within the top 20.

The third test was for a much larger set of documents, uncategorized by SMEs. We applied the entire categorization taxonomy to this large content set, took the top 10 documents for each category, and had a tester evaluate whether or not it belonged to that category.

Company A Test Case Two—Sentiment Analysis of Forum Content

We first had to develop a taxonomy of products and features for different phones. We selected an internet forum in which the posters ranked the particular product or feature, using one to five stars. We took one to two stars as negative, three stars as neutral, and four to five stars as positive.

We then used the software to extract positive, negative, and neutral words and phrases. We then followed the same procedure as for categorization, which was a round 1 initial refinement of the rules, followed by a second round of refining the rules against new content.

The testing procedure is also basically the same as for categorization. In addition to accuracy scores, a key measure was the amount of time needed for a number of text analytics elements, including taxonomy development, rule generation, and various support and technical issues. We were particularly interested in the amount of effort it would take to refine rules, as this would give us a quantifiable measure of maintenance along with total cost of ownership (TCO).

We arrived at our overall results following two weeks spent primarily on categorization, the third week on sentiment tests and different entity extraction tests, and wrapping it up in the fourth week after analyzing, reviewing, discussing, and writing up the final evaluation.

The project ended with a final evaluation meeting of the entire team, both consultant and client, during which a final decision was made, and a product chosen. (You'll have to ask me privately which one ;-))

Organization B—Internal and External Search / Platform

Organization B was a government agency that wanted to enhance their search capabilities. The first use was for an external-facing website, and second was for their own internal search. They also wanted to explore the use of text analytics as a platform for a variety of applications, both internal- and external-facing. The project was much more formal than that for Company A, since they were looking at a variety of applications and, of course, they were a government agency.

The project followed the same initial evaluation process with an initial look at about 25 companies that offered some variation of text analytics, including companies whose text analytics were embedded in their search product and/or content management. The initial evaluation cut the number down to six, all of which are invited to submit an RFP or request for proposal. The six were then reduced to two leading candidates, based on general functionality as well as company viability, but in discussions around price, one of the two final candidates was eliminated.

In this case, with only one vendor making the cut, the POC/pilot was carried out with just them—interestingly, they were also one of the two finalists in the Company A project. The focus of the POC shifted from comparing two vendors to getting an in-depth analysis of what text analytics could do within their organization.

This POC was a five-week process designed to get an overall evaluation of text analytics within their agency and specifics about capabilities and development costs. There was considerable preliminary work done by the agency and our group to develop their taxonomy as well as select a good set of sample documents for each category.

The POC was developed around a complete set of 12 test cases designed to test a full range of text analytics capabilities. These included categorization tests (the most complex), which included different parts of their taxonomy and used two different sets of content. A final categorization test was done, using training sets instead of developing categorization rules. Many vendors claim they can get as good results with training sets as with rules, but in this case the results were so bad that only the first part of the test was carried out.

Other tests included using the clustering capability of the software in a search environment and for taxonomy building. The ability of the software to produce automatic summaries was also tested, but we didn't have time to do a complete test. The agency also tested various extraction capabilities and the ability of the software to identify personally identifiable information (PII), and the final test assessed taxonomy management capabilities of the software.

We made extensive use of an in-house group of indexers to add metadata to documents by hand. In this case, they seemed quite happy with the prospects of helping develop a semiautomatic capability that could put them out of a job (in reality, it would actually make their jobs simpler).

We followed the same basic pattern, using rounds of development and beginning with a small set of content before moving to increasingly larger sets of content. Since there were a number of indexers evaluating the results of specific categorization tests, we added another dimension: We observed them as they evaluated and asked for explanations of their decisions. This added a very valuable depth to the process. It also enabled us to track the amount of time it took for them to make their decisions, which varied from a few seconds to a few minutes, and gave us yet another handle into which categories might be problematic.

Another element that we tested and evaluated was the technical support from the vendor as various questions came up during the POC. This helped increase the comfort level for the organization to purchase the software.

An important part of the categorization test was to evaluate the software's capability of generating candidate rules automatically based on its analysis of sample documents. Our question: Was this a better starting point for rule-building, rather than asking SMEs to simply look at a few candidate documents, pick out some basic terms and then start building from there? Our conclusion: The automatic rules were *not* the best solution. In other cases with greater numbers of documents, the balance might have shifted.

Another test highlighted the need for good taxonomies. Testing the distinctness or "orthogonality" of various categories in the taxonomy, we were able to confirm that a number of these categories needed to be redefined and restructured—the amount of overlap between two or more categories was high enough to cause significant problems for categorization, either by the software or humans. Getting this kind of feedback on your organization's information resources is an extremely valuable outcome of doing this type of POC.

Entity extraction was tested for a number of types of entities that the search team had identified as good candidate facets for faceted navigation. These entity types included the standard person's name, location, address, and so on. It also included things like agency name, program name, weapons system, law name, and others. One of the successes of the POC/pilot was to show that it could populate large numbers of facets with a high degree of accuracy in a very short time.

Organization B—Results of the POC / Pilot

The five-week POC/pilot, using a combined team from our company and their agency, turned out to be a major success. It demonstrated the value of the particular text analytics software and, more importantly, the value of the various text analytics capabilities to the agency. At the same time, the pilot established the foundation on which the agency could continue to build and enabled the agency team to learn the skills needed.

General POC / Pilot Observations and Issues

The majority of time will be spent on auto-categorization, as this is the most complex of the different features you want to test in the POC, and is also the piece that makes all of the other features better and smarter. Major POC and/or pilot issues include such things as:

The quality of the content, which can vary dramatically in general and in how well the selected content works for auto-categorization and the other features. The content can also vary dramatically in size, with everything from Twitter size posts to large, formal 200-page PDFs. Developing tests that work with that variety of content is a difficult chore. And trying to normalize scores for that kind of variety can be very difficult.

The quality of the initial human categorization, because you are going to be testing the software against that initial human categorization. If not done well, the results may be skewed.

How to normalize among different test evaluators. Different humans categorize inconsistently within the group, and in fact, depending on what the test evaluators are exposed to, very often they are internally inconsistent and will categorize the same document differently the second time they see it.

The quality of the taxonomists involved, as they will often have a very wide range of experience in terms of their taxonomy experience, their experience with specific content, their experience with text analytics software, and their experience with understanding information needs and behaviors of users.

The quality of the existing taxonomy. This includes things like the general structure of the taxonomy—whether it's too flat or too deep for good categorization. As we discussed earlier, a taxonomy for text analytics is different than a taxonomy used for indexing or other related sorts of activities. Another issue is having overlapping or ambiguous categories. This is one of the key issues in developing good categorization rules. Having overlapping or nonorthogonal categories makes it very difficult to develop good rules.

The complexity of language and documents. This was an essential issue for categorization and/or sentiment. How are two words related to each other? What about near-synonyms (much harder than actual synonyms)? How does context change the meaning of words? Which one or two concepts are what the document is really about? And for sentiment, how do you deal with complex conditionals—and of course, sarcasm?

For the POC, all of these complexity issues raise multiple questions about the best way to evaluate how well the software—and your team—handles this complexity.

For entity extraction, there are three primary issues.

The first is simply scale. How much content exists and how many entities do you want to extract? It is relatively easy to extract, for example, all the names of people from a few hundred documents, but when you jump to millions of documents, the situation changes. This issue of scale impacts the issues discussed below as well.

The second issue is disambiguation. How do we distinguish between two words that are identical but mean different things, such as our standard example of Ford, which can be a car, a person, a company, or a way to cross a stream? This is where the auto-categorization feature of text analytics comes in, enabling you to develop rules that can look at the context around those entities to determine what's actually being referred to. For instance, if you see the word "pipeline" and it is surrounded by terms that refer to oil and gas that is a very different word from "pipeline" surrounded by pharmaceutical research or product-development terms.

The third issue is relevance, which will help you decide how to limit the entities you extract. Having a list of 10,000 names that show up in a document set does not really help anyone. Simple relevance is just like search, only easier—simply list the entities in order of most frequent mentions with a cutoff number. However, in real world applications, you may want to only extract entities that are relevant to a search query, which gets more difficult.

Perhaps the most important issue is making sure that *your POC gives you information about what comes after it.* In other words, you will need to have confidence in the software's ability to scale. What happens to performance when you go from 10,000 documents to millions of documents? Having at least one scale test in your POC is critical—and another critical feature is learning how to best move forward into production.

What If Your POC Fails?

This is very unlikely if done properly, but if it does fail, the best reaction will depend on the nature of the failure. Overall, I would look to a recent book, *Fail Better: Design Smart Mistakes and Succeed Sooner.*[4] The message of the book is, if the project is well designed, you can learn as much by failing as succeeding.

For example, suppose that you set as your goal to achieve 99% accuracy with only one half-time resource (don't be surprised if it fails). On the other hand, you might start with a more realistic set of goals, say 90% accuracy with two full-time resources, but you still fail to achieve that goal. In that case, if the POC is well designed, you should at least get a good idea of just what levels of accuracy and their required levels of effort you will need to succeed. In addition, a well-designed failure should identify the essential factors that were responsible for the failure.

The question then becomes, "Is this level of effort worth it for me?" I have yet to see a situation where it did not make business sense to go ahead with the effort, especially since the accuracy level can be adjusted in most cases. So if 90% costs too much, investigate what benefits your employees would get—or the quality of customer information your marketing department would get—at 85%.

But let's say that for whatever reason, an application absolutely required 95% accuracy and it only paid for a one-person resource, and there was no way to realistically achieve that. This means the benefit of your POC is reduced to one factor: At least you didn't buy the software and spend a lot of money implementing a doomed initiative.

We have discussed accuracy, relevance, precision, and recall with very precise numbers for each. The reality is that in the messy world of text, all these numbers need to be used very carefully, and the difference between 85% and 90% will be fuzzy in most environments.

Summary

Doing a Two-Step

In summary, the best way to select text analytics software is a two-part process: 1) a standard software evaluation that filters the full list of vendors down to two or three, and 2) a POC bake-off.

Such a process is needed because there is an enormous variety of software that qualifies as text analytics and there is even more variety in enterprise environments regarding potential uses for it. Not only is there a variety of vendors, but there is no single market leader for all possible situations: Different vendors have different strengths and weaknesses.

Solid Foundation: Strategic Vision

The starting point and the most essential foundation is to develop a strategic vision that will guide you through the process. You will need to decide whether to buy a dedicated package for your simple sentiment app (and then another for e-Discovery, and another for search, etc.). Or go for a broader (and usually, but not always more expensive) platform.

My experience is that a platform approach is usually better in the long run—and will cost way less. But every situation is different—small or large company, open source, build it yourself or buy and customize, buy as a service, what is the initial application—after all, it's rare that you just decided this morning that text analytics is the answer, now, what is the question? We will discuss this in more detail in the next chapter.

Match Your Feature Filters to Your Strategic Vision

As long as you have developed your strategic vision to a sufficient depth, this part is usually pretty straightforward. The key is weighting the various options and identifying the must-haves versus the nice-to-haves.

The Heart of the Process: POC

As we have seen, the most important part of the evaluation is to do a short POC, or pilot. This is best the way to make the best decision possible and avoid costly mistakes—both in the selection process and in your initial development.

In addition to providing the means for making the best decision, a POC creates the foundation for full-scale development, whether for your first application or the development of a full text analytics platform. This foundation can include:

- Build content structure resources – taxonomies, metadata standards, and design
- Develop the basic set of functionality – extraction, categorization, etc., including designing your basic approach to those features
- Build catalogs of entities – people, organizations, departments, etc.
- Train your people – software use and best practices for features like categorization and disambiguation of entities, etc.

Finally, a POC typically leads to a better understanding of what you need and what you can actually do. My experience is that you almost always develop new ideas out of a POC that leads to better implementation.

And now, you're ready for the next step—actual development.

Endnotes

1. "Louis Pasteur." Wikiquote. https://en.wikiquote.org/wiki/Louis_Pasteur.
2. Sastry, Anjali, and Kara Penn. *Fail Better: Design Smart Mistakes and Succeed Sooner.* Boston, Massachusetts: Harvard Business Review Press, 2014.

Text Analytics Development

CHAPTER 7

Enterprise Development

Now that you've done your research and selected a text analytics package, it's time to dive into the actual development of all of these incredible capabilities text analytics has. In this chapter, we are going to take a deep look into how to actually develop text analytics capabilities and applications.

The initial focus will be on *auto-categorization using a taxonomy*—this is not only one of the most difficult development processes but also one that is fundamental to almost every text analytics application. In addition, much of the development processes for this type of auto-categorization are the same for other types of text analytics development, including social media development covered in the next chapter. We'll also cover the development of noun phrase/entity extraction capabilities, which is much simpler but has a number of special design considerations.

The process, practices, and issues that I discuss in the next section are taken from my experience doing enterprise development with taxonomies and associated categorization rules. The essentials of categorization development are pretty much the same for almost any categorization project, but the details will differ.

Categorization Development Phases

There are three major phases in most text analytics categorization development projects:

- A preliminary phase of mostly materials gathering and creating the basic plan
- A development phase consisting of a number of development-refinement cycles
- An ongoing maintenance phase that includes governance

It is important that each phase be done well because failure in any one of those phases can lead to overall failure of the project. We'll take a look at some of the issues and best practices within each phase.

Preliminary Phase

The preliminary phase of a text analytics project is similar to any development project involving software. The differences are in the special issues that arise when dealing with text. This phase consists of three primary activities:

- Research – developing an in-depth understanding of the information environment within which development takes place

- Project planning – this is mostly standard project management but with one caveat: Always remember text is messy and tends to follow its own logic and timeline—in other words, a flexible project plan is a must

- Resource gathering – compiling the necessary resources needed for development, which can include content, content organization schemas, people, and whatever else you need

I will only deal with the first and last items above since I assume knowledge of good project planning is readily available.

Research begins with developing a high-level understanding of what is needed for development, what the overall information environment is, and an understanding of what the end application is designed to do. We typically try to develop a high-level knowledge map of the organization, but if the focus is on a single text analytics application, this research can be done with less depth and less time and effort.

The three critical areas to research are content and content structure, users and use cases, and existing information technology. Of these, information technology is the least important and the easiest to do, so we won't spend much time discussing it. A content inventory, along with any content structure resources (taxonomies, metadata, etc.) is relatively straightforward, but it is important to do a thorough job.

What is usually the most difficult to do is understand the users and what their information behaviors and needs are. This user analysis also typically includes looking at the business processes within which the text analytics application is intended to be used.

Let's take a deeper look at the big two: content and users.

Content Is King

The first major activity of this preliminary phase is analyzing the content and any existing content structures. Hopefully—if you've followed the advice in Chapters 5 and 6—you have already done most of this research.

However, it is often the case that for full-blown development efforts, some additional depth is needed.

Understanding the nature of the content is a necessary step that will guide a lot of the early development of categorization and also the design of any data extraction. Some of the basic analysis consists of simply looking at the size, variety, and basic characteristics of the content such as types of repositories and types of document formats.

In terms of size, two extremes that we've worked on were on the one hand, a collection of a few thousand documents each one of which was about a 200-page PDF formal business document, and on the other hand, an application in which there were hundreds of thousands to millions of customer support notes that averaged about a paragraph in length. Very different kinds of rules are needed in those two cases.

Additional considerations in this initial content analysis are the existence of any metadata associated with the documents. Do the documents have titles and/or authors? Are there other metadata elements such as date, format, and other standard Dublin Core metadata fields?

Other elements to look at are things such as how formal the documents are—for example, are there specific, well-defined sections in the documents? As we have noted, there is no such thing as a completely unstructured document and so one important question is, are there enough structures within the majority of documents to be used within categorization rules?

Some of the other high-level content analysis questions are more on the technical side, such as: Just how big is the document collection? How often is it indexed? And what kind of time limits are there for both searching and indexing documents?

Content Structure (Taxonomy) Is King II

Every text analytics development initiative that utilizes categorization needs to have some kind of structure on which to develop the categorization—typically a taxonomy or ontology. This structure can be anything from a flat list of 20 important concepts to a five- or six-level, many-thousand node formal taxonomy (such as Mesh).

A critical first step is looking at any existing content models. This includes formal taxonomies, existing metadata and metadata standards, and official vocabularies, such as glossaries or other types of controlled vocabularies. It also includes exploring search logs, looking for candidate terms for categorization. These resources are usually found within an organization or enterprise, but if not, it's very often possible to find vocabularies that cover important subject areas in public websites. These external vocabularies can be easily adapted to the specifics of the organization.

The important thing to remember is that you should never start from scratch—there are always some kinds of content models, vocabularies or taxonomies, either within your organization or publicly available.

Once you have some kind of starter taxonomy, the next step is to analyze the taxonomy as a tool for categorization. This is because categorization calls for specific characteristics in a taxonomy. In terms of overall structure, you typically want something more complex than a simple flat list but less complex than a Mesh-like taxonomy.

The good news is that it is becoming a kind of standard to build taxonomies of three levels with six to eight items per level/node. This means a taxonomy of about 200–500 nodes, which is relatively easy to develop rules for and relatively easy to maintain. The six-to-eight-items concept is based on cognitive science research that shows people can grasp that many items as single unit. More than that and most people have to scan the list sequentially, which limits the usefulness of an application with a user interface. There are—as with everything text analytics—lots of exceptions to this rule of thumb. One standard exception is when you are dealing with catalogs of parts and other "things."

Another general rule is that taxonomies are most useful for capturing conceptual relationships, while ontologies are better for objects and their relationships.

In addition to the overall structure or complexity of the taxonomy, another critical issue is how orthogonal—or exclusive—the categories are. Good orthogonal categories are important for any taxonomy but in particular for those developed for categorization. For example, trying to develop categorization rules that can distinguish between categories like information management and information strategy with high accuracy can be very difficult. In general, the more orthogonal the categories are, the easier it is to develop rules that can distinguish between those categories with very high accuracy.

Another major consideration in taxonomy design for categorization is the relationship of the rules between the levels of the taxonomy. There are basically three options:

1. Each taxonomy node has a rule associated with it.
2. A higher-level node is the sum of all the rules of its children's nodes.
3. A lower-level node is a combination of the higher-level rule and its own rule.

My experience has been that option one is the most common approach, but that is not something that is necessarily a best practice. At this stage, it does not seem that there is any one best way to structure the rules, although option one would tend to be more flexible and less brittle since it's not based on what can become complex relationships between the different taxonomy nodes. Also, some vendors don't seem to offer options two and three.

However, I would recommend these approaches be considered in an initial design of the taxonomy and the rule development. It will ultimately depend, as so much in text analytics does, on the nature of the content, the taxonomy, and the use cases and the application it is designed to support.

I really think that either a taxonomy or an ontology, with associated categorization, should have a different name to distinguish from models that just sit there looking pretty. How about a *catonomy*—a model of how people in an organization think about content—or a catology?

I don't want to keep writing taxonomy/ontology—or catonomy/catology—so I'm just going to use catonomy for both (catology sounds a little too much like scatology). I'll use taxonomy or ontology to refer to those structures themselves.

Understanding Users: Contextual and Information Interviews

In addition to a content map, another critical research activity is to dive down deeper into understanding users and use cases. Selecting representative users and their use cases is an extremely important task and typically requires someone with an intimate knowledge of the full range of potential users. However, while an internal expert knows the user population, they very often have gaps or blind spots, and no matter how expert a person is at predicting what users want and need; talking to actual users is always a good idea. They almost always surprise us.

We typically start with a series of interviews with users that are selected based on a knowledge of the organization that comes from internal resources and an understanding of how best to get a good representation of the full range of information needs and behaviors that usually comes from the external experts.

In addition we typically use two sets of interviews, starting with what we call *contextual interviews,* which are designed to provide a broader, more general knowledge of the information environment of the organization. The second set consists of *information interviews* in which we dive more specifically into individual information needs and behaviors. In practice, we very often combine the two interview templates, and then, based on the results of the initial question or two, decide whether to focus primarily on contextual issues or information issues. A sample combined interview templates is shown in Appendix A at the end of the book.

There's no set number of interviews needed for this research—it will vary dramatically depending on the size of the organization, and particularly on the existence of well-defined subcategories of users and subject areas. Other considerations include how deeply you want to go in this initial phase and how much will be developed later on. This is often driven more by economics than anything else, as no organization wants to pay high-priced consultants to do a lot of preliminary research that may not be used for some time.

The net result of these interviews should be an understanding of the context within which the text analytics development will take place. In addition to defining specific use cases that an initial application will have to support, these interviews also often uncover potential roadblocks and issues that need to be dealt with to achieve success. For example, in one interview, one person volunteered that a particular manager was very skeptical of the entire process and would need to be convinced. With this warning in hand, we were able to successfully convince him.

Development Process

Once you have done your basic research, it's time for the real fun—actually developing something that works. But first, there is a major design decision to be made: What kinds of categorization are you going to develop?

There is a broad range of categorization techniques, though they all fall into two major camps—rules-based and document-based. The question is, which one should you base your development on? This decision is often presented as a choice between the difficulty and tedium of developing rules versus simple and easy automatic categorization through documents.

As usual, the reality is more complex than that.

"Automatic" Categorization Rules

Both rules-based and document-based categorization start the same way, with the selection of what are usually called training sets of sample content. For some text analytics vendors, the selection of training sets is not only the starting point but the ending point as well. Their approach is to refine the training sets of documents to the point where they are getting good accuracy—both precision and recall—based on the software's analysis of the words and patterns in the training sets.

These vendors often refer to what they do as "automatic" categorization to distinguish it from rules-based categorization. Of course, it is not really automatic since it is humans that are selecting the training sets. But it looks good in marketing literature, and it is automatic in the sense that given the training sets, the software does produce a statistical signature that can be compared to the statistical signature of new documents. Perhaps a better name would be document categorization or training-set categorization.

My experience has been that this approach is not the best and very often only works for very simple taxonomies with very distinct categories and small, very distinct sets of documents. In other words, it makes for good demos. However, there is a great deal of incentive for companies to devote more and more research into enhancing the ability of the software to generate automatic rules based on the content alone. As we shall see, developing categorization rules using Boolean and advanced operators can be a time-consuming and resource-rich process.

However, to get any level of granularity beyond simple flat lists of topics, this technique does not work well in my experience. Selecting documents that are only about one topic and that can be distinguished from other documents that are about any related topic is a very difficult and arcane task. In addition, the software analysis tends to be a black box—and the only way that humans have to refine the rules is through selecting or deselecting additional training sets. This selection is done without knowing why the selections work or fail, which makes it rather difficult to improve their performance.

Another issue with using statistical signatures of sets of documents as your categorization rule is that these rules tend to be more brittle than categorization rules based on Boolean and advanced operators (described later). The problem is that content changes and as new documents are added they tend to include new vocabularies and new patterns of use. This is true regardless of the type of categorization, but good general rules tend to be more flexible—at least in my experience.

Developing these general categorization rules tends to require more initial development effort to get any kind of reasonable results. Categorization by training sets, on the other hand, can produce relatively reasonable results much more quickly. The problem is that when you try to refine the rules and go from relatively reasonable results (say about 60%–70% accuracy) to production level results (90%-plus), categorization by training sets tends to require much more effort than categorization by rules. And very often no amount of effort in selecting training sets can achieve 90%-plus accuracy.

As a reminder, this is one of the reasons that I often suggest to companies that when they are evaluating different text analytics software offerings, they do a short pilot with the leading two or three candidates rather than rely on demos and prepared material from the vendor. What looks good in a demo and early development can often be a very bad choice as you go to full production-level categorization.

Very often my experience has been that these automatically generated rules can be very good inputs and/or starting points for more sophisticated and explicit categorization rules. This is particularly true for software that generates a list of terms associated with the training set. These terms can then be used in building categorization rules.

However, in experiments, we have found that training sets tend to have different accuracy based on where in a taxonomy the rule is applied. At the top level of a taxonomy with very general concepts it is often possible to develop good document categorization rules. At the same time, if the taxonomy is sufficiently rich and complex (five or six or more levels, for example), then the lowest and most specific levels are so specific that fairly good automatic categorization can be developed.

The problem comes more often than not, in the intermediate levels, where concepts and documents share many characteristics. It can be very difficult to find training sets that distinguish documents and concepts at these intermediate levels with a high degree of accuracy.

One final advantage of categorization rules is that this capability can be used, not just for categorizing documents but for a variety of text-processing tasks from enriching fact extraction to disambiguating entity or noun phrase extraction. Basically, categorization rules can add intelligence and depth to virtually every text handling application.

Developing categorization rules with selected terms and Boolean/operator rules is not as heavily dependent on finding extremely good training sets for every category but has the added cost of human effort to develop the rules. Virtually in every project that I've worked on, developing these rules was considered the best approach and well worth the cost based on the enhanced accuracy and precision. However, looking just at the vendor space within text analytics, there certainly seems to be continuing interest in developing categorization by training sets.

Basic Development Process

Whether you decide to do rules-based categorization or categorization by training sets, the overall development process is roughly the same process, although the activity within each step will be different. The basic model for categorization development is:

1. Select sample content to be used as training sets or starting points—you will need some number of documents or examples for each category, anywhere from five to 50 per category for large documents and up to 2,000 for Twitter-sized posts.

2. Develop initial rules for each category, which will likely consist of a set of terms found within each category's training set.

3. Recall – test and refine these rules until they are correctly categorizing 90%–100% of the category's training set.

4. Test these rules against a larger set of content, for example, all the training sets for all the categories—this will almost certainly result in a major drop in recall accuracy.

5. Test and refine your rules against this larger set to improve both recall and precision:

    a. Recall – your rules are correctly categorizing 90% of your category's training sets.

    b. Precision – your rules are not categorizing the sample documents for the other categories.

6. Repeat this process with new sets of content until you reach a point where you're getting your target (90%-plus normally), and this accuracy does not drop off when you test it against a brand-new set of content.

7. Congratulations – you now have a mature categorization rule.

8. Repeat for all categories for which you are developing categorization.

It does require significant effort to develop these kinds of rules, but the surprising thing is with experience they can be developed relatively quickly. Depending on the complexity of the content, each category rule can take from a few hours to a couple of days to develop. We have developed full production level categorization for a taxonomy of 300 or 400 nodes in three months.

This basic process is one that we've used in a variety of different kinds of applications. There are a number of critical issues associated with a number of the steps in this development process. So let's take a closer look at the issues and best practices of some of those steps.

Selection of Content

One of the most critical steps is the selection of training sets. This is something that's best done with a combination of text analytics experience and internal resources who are familiar with all the content. Regardless of what form the final categorization rules take, all of them will need a good selection of training documents.

When developing categorization rules you typically want to have documents that are very good examples for each category. However, it is often also important to find near misses, that is, documents that share a lot of the characteristics and/or vocabulary of the good examples but belong to a different category. This is typically done later in the process when you're trying to refine the rules to a greater level of precision.

Developing sentiment analysis rules—with their simple good-bad-ugly categorization—calls for additional techniques. Even in this case you want to start with good examples of documents that, for example, deal with a taxonomy of products and the features that you're interested in. The next step is to find documents, sentences, or phrases that exemplify positive and negative sentiment. In some cases it may be sufficient to have a general collection of positive and negative statements, but in most cases there will be variations depending on the particular product or feature that you are interested in.

How many documents you need for training sets will vary dramatically depending on the nature of the content and the taxonomy. Generally, the more training documents that you can provide, the better—but this is very often a difficult task. We have found that somewhere between 20 and 50 documents for each category node is a good start.

When it comes to selecting content, however, another issue is getting good representative documents that reflect the complexity of the real world within which the application will be developed. This is a relatively simple task—as long as attention is paid to getting documents that represent the full range and avoiding any selection bias.

There is also the issue of human variability—that is, different people will categorize the same document in different ways and as we have seen, sometimes the same person will categorize the same document in different ways, depending on what they had for breakfast or what movie they saw last night. The best way to get around this variability is to have a number of subject matter experts categorizing your initial training set.

If it is impossible to get training sets selected by human experts, there is another technique which is simply to take the term of the category node, for example, "agriculture" and make that a rule which can then be applied against a collection of content in order to retrieve some documents that at least have that term in them (see the following screenshot). This is a slower process and not as good but can be used when it is impossible to get subject matter experts to select your initial documents.

A Good Trick: Category Name in the Filename

One technique that we've often used to help, both in the development and refinement of rules, is to incorporate the category name into the filenames for all the training set documents. This enables much easier evaluation of the results, by simply looking at the filenames instead of having to open each document in order to determine if it is a good fit. It also enables the use of nonexperts to do the evaluation of the category rule.

Cycles of Develop-Test-Refine

The heart of the development/refinement process is a series of *develop-test-refine* cycles. The basic process will be the same for almost any categorization development, although some of the details will differ. The process described in the next section is one that we've used in a number of projects—and should be able to be adapted to your project as well.

Categorization Rule Refinement Process

Developing categorization rules starts at the same place that automatic categorization or training set categorization does, which is a good set of training documents.

The first step is to look at the first few documents of a training set and scan those documents for words that look like they're good candidates and represent important terms or concepts that will be found in the documents that you would want to tag with that category node. This can be done even on a single document, but normally you would want to scan at least five or 10 documents.

Like with so many things in text analytics, the best approach here is to combine this human scanning effort with software that can analyze those documents and offer words that it finds that appear only in the training set. This is a feature that most text analytics software provides. However, the key step is in the human scanning effort, whether they are scanning raw documents or scanning the list of terms that the software offers. One of the fun benefits of scanning terms that the software offers is the occasional good laugh at the completely absurd term that the software thinks would be just fine as part of the categorization rule.

For example, this is a list of terms that were automatically generated by the software from a set of documents about agriculture:

benefits	growing	support
regulation	office	significant
critical	group	area
resources	consumer	Disease
produce	Workforce	products,
groups	BROWN	Forestry
requirement	small	

There are, of course, ways to work with these suggestions which will produce something much more useful, but you're still going to get some pretty strange results with a completely "automatic" approach.

The next step is to take those terms that have been found in the documents and create a categorization rule that consists simply of the list of those terms. As you generate the list of terms it is good practice to just automatically add variants of those terms that you expect to be in the documents as well including simple plurals. You now have a simple categorization rule:

```
food industry
bovine spongiform encephalopathy
mad cow disease
meat
ingredient@
```

```
food companies
recalls
food products
sandwiches
bread
plant species
soybean crop
increased production costs
soybean production
soybean
fungicides
breeding
*agriculture@
*Agriculture
```

The next step is to apply the rule against a complete training set, if you have one, or if not, against some subset of new content. You may go through a number of cycles with this process until you get to the point where the rule is correctly categorizing 80%–90% or more of the training set. This early phase is focused primarily on recall, but once that is done you're ready for the next cycle.

It is very often possible to develop a rule that simply consists of a series of these key terms and get up to 90% accuracy when the rule is applied to the starting training set. However, the next step is to apply the rule to a larger set of content, including content that is not an example of that category, and even better, is an example of categories that are somewhat similar to the one you're testing.

The typical result when you first apply your key term rule to this new content is that it will categorize a large number of documents that are false hits, that is, that don't belong and should not be tagged with that category. So the next stage is to look at the documents that are false hits and see why they're being returned and try to refine your rule so that they're not returned.

This is very often the stage in which you need to go beyond rules that simply consist of sets of key terms and start developing more sophisticated categorization rules that use the kind of operators that most text analytics software provides. For example, you may get a false hit because the document uses one or more of those same terms but uses them either in different ways or has other terms around it that can indicate that this term should not be counted.

One frequent use of this technique is to ignore terms that are systemic, rather than real content. In the example below, the first rule states that you should look for the word "agriculture," but not if it is within the phrase "Department of Agriculture" or the phrase "Committee on Agriculture."

```
(OR,
(START_200,
(NOTIN,"agriculture@", "Department of
  Agriculture"),
(NOTIN,"agriculture@", "Committee on
  Agriculture,")),
(START_100,(NOTIN,"food@", "Food and Drug
  Administration")),
(START_100, "crop@"),
(START_100, "livestock@"),
(START_100, "farm@"),
(START_100, "animal@"),
(START_100, "food safety"),
(START_100, "USDA"),
(START_100, "agricultural")
)
```

In the following example, the idea is to distinguish between mentions of the word "battery" that refer to phone batteries, and specific problems such as a low charge from mentions of the word "battery" that refer to car or boat batteries. In the real world, there might be dozens of words that mean the same thing as "phone" or "car"—and these variations can be stored in vocabulary resources in order to keep the logic of the rule relatively simple and easy to understand.

```
(DIST_5, "battery", (OR, "low", "charge",
  "[phone]"),
(AND,
(NOT, (DIST_5, "battery", (OR, "[car]",
  "[boat]"))
))
```

So in our example, we are now able to distinguish between documents that simply have the target word "battery" and documents where "battery" is near words indicating a meaning or usage other than the one we are looking for.

Recall-Precision Cycles

The next stage is to refine the rules with more precise terms and advanced sophisticated rules, then test them against larger sets and start tracking the *recall-precision* scores that you're getting. This refinement of the rules and testing accuracy scores can continue until you get to an agreed-upon accuracy for that particular category node.

Once you've reached the point of your target accuracy against your initial set of documents, the next step is to bring in a whole new set of content and test your rules against the new content. Typically what happens is your accuracy goes way down with the new content. And so you repeat the process above until you get your target accuracy with the new content. The next step, of course, is to repeat the process with new content.

This process gets repeated until you reach the point where *the new content is not causing a significant drop in accuracy*—at that point you have a mature complete categorization rule. Congratulations!

Yes, it sounds complicated—and it is. But it is relatively easy to learn (I almost always train internal resources as I develop these rules), and it can take as little as a few hours to develop a mature categorization rule.

One big development design question is, should you take one category rule all the way from the messy and chaotic gutter to the Nirvana of a mature categorization rule, or should you try to work on multiple categories at the same time? Unfortunately, there is no hard and fast rule. It will largely depend on your content and target applications. If the content is relatively uniform between categories, then bringing one category node to completion is probably the best tactic. However, something like an intranet or enterprise taxonomy where the content can be radically different would likely call for exploring multiple categories and lower levels before trying to achieve "perfection."

One of the key design considerations is whether or not it's possible to develop a standard template that can then be applied to all categories in the taxonomy. In general, this is a very good practice if the content is sufficiently uniform. In the example below, we were dealing with relatively uniform PubMed content and so we developed a template with the following form:

```
(OR,
_/article/title:"[arthritis]",
(AND, _/article/mesh:"[arthritis]",_/article/
  abstract:"[arthritis]"),
(MINOC_2, _/article/abstract:"[arthritis]"),
(START_500, (MINOC_2,"[arthritis]")))
```

This rule was developed for one disease—arthritis—and then we used the same template for all the other diseases with the only difference being the vocabulary associated with each disease. In this rule, "[arthritis]" is a variable that points to a list of terms associated with arthritis. These terms can go way beyond simple synonyms and include a variety of things, such as:

```
arthritis,
Osteoarthritis,
"rheumatoid arthritis",
polyarticular,
jra,
"Journal of Rheumatology",
Rheumatology,
```

This rule also exemplifies two other best practices. First, the different components of the rule can be weighted differently to give a much more sophisticated relevance ranking. In this rule, the first part looks for any arthritis word in the title—this is ranked the highest. The next part of the rule is:

```
(AND, _/article/mesh:"[arthritis]",_/article/
  abstract:"[arthritis]"),
```

This states that if you find any arthritis word in the abstract of the document AND a section for keywords, then count it—and this gets the second-highest ranking. The remainder of the rule looks at situations where you find at least two arthritis words in the abstract or in the first 500 words of the article. These are significant but rated lower.

The second-best practice is something that is based on the realization that so-called unstructured documents are really semistructured, and good categorization rules can take advantage of what structure there is in the document. In this case, there was a great deal of structure with, for example, most documents having an abstract section. However, it turned out that the abstract was designated by a number of different terms in the different science journals that were captured in a variable:

```
Abstract,
ABSTRACT,
Introduction,
Background,
Summary,
Background:,
Aim,
SUMMARY,
```

In this particular case, because the documents were relatively highly structured, we were actually able to achieve close to 100% accuracy. With less structured documents and more variation between the content associated with each taxonomy node, these results will likely be lower and it will be important to set a realistic target accuracy. One mistake to avoid is aiming for such a high level of accuracy that it will take entirely too much time and effort to get there.

It should be clear from this description that these kinds of categorization rules are never actually finished but can always be improved. This indicates the importance of an ongoing maintenance refinement plan, but practically speaking once you reach your target accuracy the catonomy is ready to be applied to enterprise search or whatever the first application is.

Testing: Relevance Ranking and Scoring

In order to refine your categorization rules, you need to be able to test those rules and get accuracy scores for recall and precision. So virtually all text analytics software has a test function in which the rules (one by one or all at once) are applied to a designated set of test documents. The software calculates a "relevancy" score for each document for each rule. Most software also allows developers to set specific pass/fail scores. The software then returns the results in a ranked list, like the one shown in Figure 7.1.

Basic Testing Process

The display in Figure 7.1 also demonstrates the technique I mentioned earlier of incorporating a category name in the file name—the big advantage

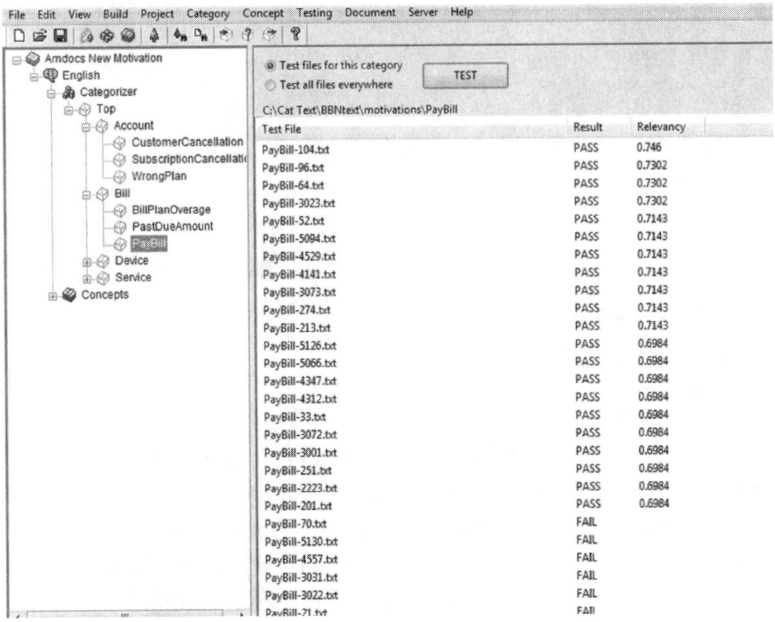

Figure 7.1   Test Results Screen

is that anyone can simply scan the results and calculate a total score for a basic test. This display is a typical one when you are working on increasing recall, that is, how many files that were categorized by humans as belonging to the category. The refinement process is to look at the files that were categorized as belonging to the category—for example "PayBill" by human SMEs—but were not categorized as such by the rule. A developer would then explore each file for words or phrases or other indicators and incorporate them into the rule until the rule achieve the target accuracy. At that point, recall would be in the 90%-plus range.

The display in Figure 7.2 is a standard type of display for refining the precision of the rule, that is, how many false hits did the software generate. Here the refinement process is to look at each false hit to determine why it was falsely categorized and determine how the rule needs to be changed to exclude those files. Again, the technique of incorporating the category name in the file name makes this go much faster.

Of course, some files will be categorized as belonging to more than one category and it may turn out that when a file with a different category name, BillIncludesProrates for example, also fits with the target category

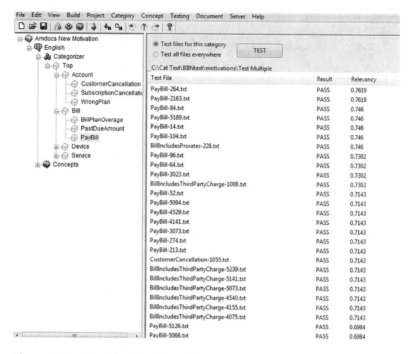

Figure 7.2   Precision Test Results

(in this case, PayBill). In which case, it may be that the rule is OK, but the scoring could be adjusted.

So, for example, in Figure 7.3, the rule might be adjusted by discounting the word "bill" when it appears with words like "explained." Another way to refine the rule might be to put in logic that says to categorize the document as "PayBill" if it has these words, UNLESS it scores higher on another category. What options are available will depend on the software.

The relevancy scores on the right in Figures 7.1 and 7.2 are quite similar to the relevancy scores you get with search engines. The big difference is that these scores are actually pretty relevant—because they can take in a variety of factors—from where in the documents words appear to contextual clues, such as what words appear in proximity or within the same sentence, which can be used to weight words more positively or eliminate them entirely. In addition, these kinds of rules can use a whole range of words that are in the same subject area as the target word, even though they would never show up in a synonym list.

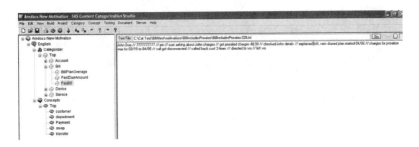

Figure 7.3   Rule Refinement

Compare this with the simplistic counting the number of times the target word appears in a document and assuming that is somehow indicative. When you think about it, what does it mean to say that a particular document is "more" about a particular topic such as "agriculture" simply because the word "agriculture" appears more often in the document?

Even if we go beyond simply counting the number of times a search term appears in a document with weighting (title counts more, etc.) and adding synonyms, it is still pretty meaningless to say that document X is more likely to be the target document the searchers are looking for simply because that one word appears more often.

When I train people within an organization to develop these kinds of rules, it is often during the testing process that you can see the light go off as they realize how significant these relevancy scores are. And when they see the relevancy scores go up with the addition of new terms and the negation of terms that bring back false hits, they also understand the power of text analytics categorization compared with traditional relevancy scores.

Summary: Surprise—It's Not That Difficult—and Can Even Be Fun!

We'll get a better idea of how much effort is involved in this process in Chapter 9 where we discuss actual use cases taken from example projects. I know this sounds extremely complex and difficult to do but surprisingly enough it is not all that difficult. It does call for a certain amount of experience in picking out terms that not only are important for particular concepts or categories but also can function as terms that will distinguish that category from all others.

Luckily, the software can continue to provide feedback—and people can learn what works and what doesn't.

Maintenance / Governance: All is Flux[1]

The last development phase for text analytics initiatives is ongoing maintenance and refinement of the categorization rules and associated resources such as a taxonomy and other metadata elements. This is a phase that very often does not get enough attention but is absolutely critical to overall success since rules go out of date as content changes—even if they are developed with good broad logic. Taxonomies, metadata values, and categorization rules are all living, breathing entities that require periodic evaluations and updates.

So the development of a good maintenance and governance plan is essential. This plan will include policies and procedures, covering roles, update processes, testing plans, communication—within the team and with business groups, and most of all, feedback on the functioning of the application or sets of applications. The scale of the plan and staffing the plan will be significantly less than the process we will describe for single applications, but the functions are basically the same. It's just that your governance team might be a couple of part-timers.

Since a catonomy is a model of how people in the organization think about content, to keep it up to date requires not just a central text analytics team but input from all groups within the organization. One of the primary challenges in maintaining a catonomy is to capture the individual variations in how people describe their documents—and at the same time, developing a common structure that can become a foundation for communication and a whole range of applications.

Each organization will likely have its own special requirements, but some common elements to consider include:

- Taxonomy governance. Who controls the overall structure and particular nodes of the taxonomy and who provides input into it? One example I've seen is to give different departments governance over the part of the taxonomy that falls within their subject matter expertise. On the other hand, as we've seen, there is usually a need for taxonomy expertise as well as subject matter expertise.

- Metadata schemas. The best practice is to have a single enterprise-wide metadata standard to avoid duplication and conflicting implementations. This is often not feasible, but at least a governance group can provide the means to coordinate various metadata schemas.

- Information structures. These can include controlled vocabularies, thesauri, and other lexical resources.
- Implementation methods. These include editorial rules for applying a taxonomy as well as software that implements the taxonomy for applications such as search and other applications.
- What is the process for change including access to the software? You might not want to have everyone able to change any taxonomy node or rule—unless you have a very unusual set of employees.
- What kinds of changes do you expect and do you need to develop and assign different roles for different types of changes? For example, if you have a template solution like the biotech example, which consists of uniform rule templates with lots of variation in vocabulary, you should specify who can change a template and who can merely change a vocabulary term.
- A policy for how to resolve disagreements over those changes, including specifiable criteria (where they are applicable).
- Communication methods, covering everything from suggestions for changes to updates for the business groups that include why some changes might be important. In some cases, this might include communication to and from users.
- Style guide specifications might be important or they might be seen as silly nitpicking—it depends on your culture and the specific applications. This is something that is often important to taxonomists/librarians but rarely considered by social media projects like voice of the customer. Likewise, metadata standards and associated tagging policies are very important to enterprise search–focused applications but not to a whole range of social media or other user-focused applications.

Governance Activities

The full range of activities of the various maintenance/governance groups will vary depending on the organization, but some of the basic activities could include such tasks as:

- Creating, acquiring, and evaluating taxonomies
- Maintaining metadata standards and vocabularies and overseeing the application

- Socializing the benefits of text analytics, taxonomy, and metadata
- Input into information technology design and decisions— search, content management, portals, etc.
- Evaluating metadata quality and facilitating author metadata
- Analyzing the results of metadata and how communities are using it
- Research metadata and category theory and user-centric metadata

If the central group is part of a larger knowledge management (KM) approach, their tasks might also include:

- Facilitating knowledge flow
- Facilitating projects and KM project teams
- Facilitating knowledge capture in meetings, best practices
- Designing and running KM forums, education, and innovation fairs
- Working with content experts to develop training and incorporating intelligence into applications
- Answering online questions and facilitating online discussions
- Supporting innovation and knowledge creation in communities

For a very good discussion of the related issues of maintenance and governance of taxonomies, see Heather Hedden's book *The Accidental Taxonomist*.[2]

Maintenance and governance can be particularly difficult in some dimensions like roles and communication because of the need for interdisciplinary teams in a text analytics application. But this is also precisely why it is so important—not figuring out who does what and how they can and should communicate with each other can doom an otherwise perfect text analytics initiative.

The elements of governance described below are based on an infrastructure approach which will be a good idea for almost everyone, even if you think all you need is a quick and dirty sentiment project. However, if you insist on not doing it right (or you really are a small company just starting out), you can take and adapt or apply what makes sense in your environment.

The Governance Team: A Model

The best way to handle the underlying dichotomy of the need for central standards and individual variations is to establish a distributed model that includes a variety of roles, processes, and software as part of a governance team. One example model is presented below—there will obviously be a lot of individual company variations—so adapt as ye will.

At the top is an *executive committee*. This committee should be relatively small and consist of policy makers. Typically this committee would be chaired by an executive with some text analytics and/or information management experience. One good candidate, if you have him/her, is the head of a knowledge management group. Other members might include IT, other business unit executives who have an interest in information and text analytics, or librarians if you have them.

Two key activities of this group are to set policy and to provide executive support and sponsorship.

A second level is a *steering committee,* which is larger than the executive committee and discusses and drives implementation of the policy set by the executive committee. The steering committee would typically get reports from the groups below them, discuss the implications and prepare recommendations for the executive committee.

The third level of the model is a *catonomy group*, which is a central group of half- to full-time text analysts and taxonomy architects responsible for the actual work on developing and maintaining the taxonomy, associated text analytics rules, and other semantic elements. They report up to the steering committee and are also a clearing house for communication with subject matter experts and indirectly, individual authors.

The fourth level is an *SME council*, a council or less formal group of subject matter experts (SMEs) that represent the various groups within the organization and who have either deep expertise of the subject matter of their group or a special interest in information structure such as database administrators or designers. The SMEs provide expert input into the validity and suitability of terms within the taxonomy for their subject area and also act as a conduit for broader input from individual authors within their group. They rarely have the expertise to evaluate the text analytics rules directly but can provide expert feedback on the output of those rules.

The fifth level, *authors-publishers*, is the least defined and includes virtually all authors who publish into the enterprise content management system as well as selected authors who generate important content within another system, such as a dedicated knowledge management application. This level also includes users of text analytics–based applications, like search and a KM expertise location application.

The Governance Team: Partners

In addition to the text analytics dedicated governance team, another essential part of governance is dealing with special partners such as IT and various business groups. Text analytics obviously requires significant IT involvement, but it also requires something outside the normal range of IT—namely language and meaning and all of its complexity. It is important that IT recognizes that text analytics applications are a different breed and require special treatment.

The few times that I have seen an unsuccessful text analytics initiative, the common element is an IT group that refuses to recognize the special problems that software designed to deal with meaning has to successfully manage and build upon.

The relationship with business is less likely to develop serious issues—except where business does not recognize the value and special problems that text analytics initiatives entail. If that occurs, it is normally the fault of the text analytics team. Gaining, building, and maintaining the understanding of business leaders is one of the main tasks of the text analytics team.

The best way to develop and deepen that understanding will, of course, vary from organization to organization—and it will be up to you to determine what works best in your environment. Not to be too glib, but buying and reading this book should give you all the arguments you need. However, it is, as always with text analytics, important to deal with the fundamental disjunction between business concerns and the complexity of language and meaning.

It is relatively easy to get support for the specific applications—after all who could be opposed to finding information better and faster, mining the internet for customer comments and expressed sentiment about your company and/or products, or any of the other applications described in the next section of this book. The trick is to manage expectations about the complexity of developing those applications. It won't do you any good to get business support for your new sentiment analysis application if they don't also know that it will require some significant development to get beyond simply producing reports that throw up a bunch of negative and positive words.

Catonomy Feedback: Feed the Plan

Feedback is probably the most often overlooked component of a maintenance plan, but it is one of the most essential. This feedback should be obtained from as a large and diverse a set of resources as possible. You need to get feedback on a variety of elements:

- The accuracy of your categorization
- Identification of internal taxonomy trouble spots, for example, which categories don't make sense to some audiences or which categories are missing
- Identification of trouble spots that arise when people try to use the taxonomy to tag documents
- The overall understandability and suitability of your categorization rules, and so on

A good place to start is with the users of those applications. You should set up a mechanism for them to report any issues with all the text analytics elements including any catonomy issues as well as evaluating the output from those elements. Issues can range from general usability to the suitability of specific terms to suggestions for missing terms (or the obverse—terms that no longer belong).

One simple mechanism would be to put a link on the main screens of all text analytics applications. This link could be routed to both a designated SME for a particular area of the taxonomy or other content structure and to a central group of taxonomy/text analytics architects.

However, I also recommend that the text analytics group periodically undertake a more proactive initiative to uncover any issues and problems with the text analytics components of the application. This is particularly true for applications that use external content where you don't have a publishing process you can utilize for feedback. One option would be to conduct surveys or usability sessions on a regular basis. Of course, you need to balance the amount of feedback you can get with not wanting to ask too much time and effort from users.

A method that takes up less time from users is to utilize software that can monitor how the application is being used (particularly in respect to rules and taxonomic structures) and generate reports on such variables as how long or frequently people use different application functions and number of downloads. Specific applications can also track how often users are successful in completing various tasks.

Another source of feedback is from the authors who are publishing into the ECM. They use the application to tag documents and you should include easy ways for them to communicate with SME's and text analytics architects about the suitability of the elements of the application such as the taxonomy—whether it has missing terms, bad labels, and so on.

In addition, there should be regular meetings of the SME council or sub-groups to share feedback they are getting from the users and authors as well as their own experience. These groups might meet periodically to discuss current issues and brainstorm on possible solutions, orchestrating work sessions to specifically improve parts of the application—categorization rules, taxonomy, etc.

In very large organizations with a dedicated enterprise text analytics approach, the governance team may be an essential part of the formal organization of your enterprise. Although even in that case, the total number of people dedicated to text analytics governance will likely be fairly small. It is important to remember that most of these roles will be very part-time. And in the case of a small company doing primarily social media analysis, all of these roles may be filled by two or three people.

You don't need a lot of people spending a lot of time on governance and maintenance, but if you ignore this key part of any text analytics initiative, you'll likely fail in the long run.

Entity / Noun Phrase Extraction

The capability of entity/noun phrase extraction is orders of magnitude easier than categorization which is probably why some vendors focus almost exclusively on it and why it is often the first (and sometimes only) text analytics application that organizations undertake.

Simple Judgments Are Easy and Fun (Mostly)

First, in entity extraction, you don't have to make complex judgments about what a document is about, all you have to do is find items of specific classes or types. In many cases, this is simply a matter of text matching—if the text "Department of Transportation" appears, then capture it and list it along with other organization names.

Even at this simple level, however, there is some additional work that needs to be done. The basic question is to determine if that entity is important enough to capture, since in many environments with large documents, it does not make sense to capture every entity as our standard 200-page PDF might include hundreds or even thousands of names. This determination is a kind of "relevance ranking," although much simpler and easier than trying to make a complex judgment about what a document is about.

Although even this simple relevance ranking needs to go beyond simple frequency, you may very well want to extract any names mentioned more than three times, but very often a name that is mentioned only once can also be important enough to extract.

Also, there is one case where frequently mentioned names need to be discounted, which is the example we discussed earlier where the entity mentioned is part of systematic text—like having "Department of Agriculture" as part of a heading or other repeating systemic text.

Buy, Don't Build

A second advantage is that for entities, unlike categorization, there are multiple entity catalogs and/or building blocks available to buy. Most text analytics vendors offer prebuilt entity catalogs for such entity types as states, cities, addresses, organizations, and more. In addition, they often offer prebuilt simple sets of rules such as regular expressions rules for things like phone numbers and social security numbers.

Even if these prebuilt entity catalogs are missing important entities only found in your environment, the process of refining the catalogs to cover your particular industry or area is usually pretty straightforward. It usually only requires adding your entities to the catalogs, unless the catalog is in some esoteric proprietary format, in which case you might have to convert your text or Excel catalog to their format. Although a better solution is probably to find a new vendor that plays well with others and uses XML or some other standard.

Beg, Borrow, or Steal

A third advantage is that even if you can't simply buy an entity catalog from a vendor, there are usually multiple existing resources that can be used to quickly build your own specialized entity catalog. For example, your HR database can be the basis for a "people" entity catalog. There are also multiple industry catalogs of people and organizations for many industries.

In these cases, there might be a need to write a script to convert these resources into a format that your text analytics software can use, but those formats are usually simple XML, so it should not be very difficult. Just make sure you remember to add all the variants, abbreviations, and acronyms that apply.

Known Unknowns and Unknown Unknowns

The entity extraction examples we've discussed so far are all of one type—known entities where you know or can specify the entities you are interested in. These are the easiest type of entities to extract, but there is another class of entities that are often more important and/or are used in different kinds of applications: unknown entities.

Suppose you want to extract all the locations in a set of documents but there is no handy, simple catalog that is granular enough, that is, you're not just interested in states and cities, but you want all sorts of locales—and even specific buildings. Another example is that you want all mentions of people regardless of whether they work for your organization.

In these cases, you will have to build rules that are very much like categorization rules. Figure 7.4 shows one vendor's entity catalog. The left side shows the various entities that come prepackaged with the software. The right side shows a set of rules for extracting locations of all types. The highlighted area shows some simple rules. The first rule: INITCAP INITCAP LOCSUFF says that if you see two words that both start with a capital letter and are followed by any of the text specified as "LOCSUFF," then count it as a location.

Figure 7.4   Unknown Entity Rules

Figure 7.5   Unknown Entity Rule—Detail 1

Figure 7.5 shows the kind of text in "LOCSUFF."

So if you see two words that begin with a capital letter followed by some-thing like "harbor" or "headquarters," then it is probably a location. The second rule says if you see one of the text items below (LOCPRF) followed by a word that begins with a capital letter, then it is probably a location.

You can combine various elements to develop a full range of rules. One feature of these two examples is that they are a combination of known items and unknown patterns. This is typical for the entity catalogs that you can purchase from text analytics vendors. You can also develop your own rules or more commonly, start with a vendor catalog and add to and/or refine both the rules and the text items.

Building these rules is basically the same process as developing categori-zation rules but easier. In both cases, you use sample documents and input from SMEs to develop draft rules and then test and refine against larger sets of documents.

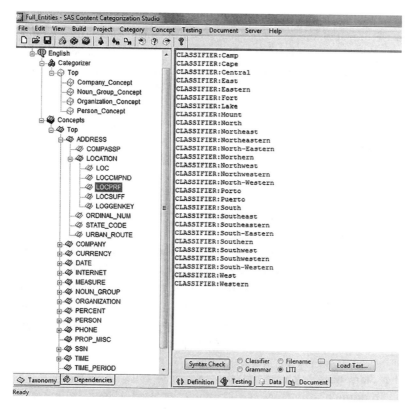

Figure 7.6 Unknown Entity Rule—Detail 2

The tradeoff with developing rules for unknown entities is that you can develop much broader and more flexible capabilities (and in some cases there is no substitute since there is no source for all items), but they also tend to be significantly less accurate. Where the balance is for your organization will depend on the application.

Life Can Be Complex, Even for Entities

While it might be (relatively) easy to extract entities from unstructured text, when you go to develop applications utilizing entity extraction, things get more complicated. There are at least two major issues that complicate life for extraction applications. Both of these issues involve the idea of context. In many cases, it is not simply a matter of identifying the entity itself but also taking into account how the context around those words changes the meaning.

Context is one of the most important concepts in understanding language. It is something that humans use all the time to grasp the meaning of a phrase or sentence—and it is something that is fundamentally difficult to teach to computers. It is often the difference between a sophisticated understanding of language and the understanding that a new learner exhibits (either a child or someone learning a second language).

One text analytics vendor went so far as to rename its text analytics development software, Contextual Analysis. In the interest of full disclosure (and to brag a little), I was instrumental in coming up with that name.

Ambiguity

The first contextual issue is disambiguation which we discussed earlier. There are two types of disambiguation. The first is the classic case of a single word with multiple meanings, such as Ford. As we indicated, we know that we have to build rules to distinguish these multiple meanings—Ford is a car, a company, a person and, according to the OED, "a shallow in a river or other body of water where a man or beast may cross by wading," "a tract of shallow water," and "to cross or wade."[3] As you can see by the date in the footnote, I have an old edition from school days—which might also account for the vestiges of sexism in their definition, since I assume they didn't really intend to imply that women did not cross streams.

To distinguish these several meanings, we need to look at the words around "Ford" for clues—looking for words having to do with cars, company information, personal names or titles, and finally an idyllic frolic in nature, or perhaps more sinisterly, drowning or some lesser water-based mishap. The last case is easy, but for cars, companies and people, the vocabularies can overlap and the rules need to be a bit more sophisticated. This might sound like a relatively contained problem but something close to 40% of English words have more than one meaning.

The other case is where two or more different words mean the same thing such as "nosh, gobble, scarf, devour, grub, chow down, gorge," and finally for the historically minded, "gormandize" all mean "to eat."[4] This type of case is usually dealt with through simple dictionaries and it is more of an application design issue of whether to merge the various meanings or list each separately.

Whose Entity Is It? Or, Fact Extraction

The other complexity issue for entity extraction also needs to look at the context around the entity, but in this case, it can be a much more complex context. In this case, the task is to not just find a single entity but to find a set of entities that "belong" to each other. This is what is commonly called "fact extraction" that we discussed in Chapter 2. Fact extraction normally tries to extract two entities and their relationship. For example, you might extract two company names and the relationship between them, such as one company is a supplier to another.

However, in some cases what you're interested in extracting is a single entity and characterizing what kind of entity it is by looking at the context around the entity.

For example, it is easy to build a regular expression that will capture any phone number in a document, but for many applications, the important issue is whose phone number it is. We worked on one project where the goal was to pull out sets of related entities, such as the name of an architect along with the associated information of address and phone number. When the document was well formed, this was easy—four or more items on separate lines immediately following the name. Of course, it is never that easy in real-life documents.

The development process we followed was much more like categorization development than simple entity extraction. So for example, we started with a simple date extraction and then developed rules to distinguish dates that were official bid dates from all the other dates mentioned in the document. These other dates might include random dates but also other official dates, such as meeting dates or walk-through dates.

These rules also required solving complex coreference issues. The application must capture threads of references, such as a paragraph that mentions an architect's name and a sentence or three later, say something like, "and their phone number is XXX-XXX-XXXX." In some case, the "their" is obvious but not always. And while it is obvious to a human mind, software still needs to be given rules to capture the obvious.

Entities Need Categorization

What these examples of the complexity of entity extraction point out is that—to do entity extraction really well—you are required to build categorization-type rules and take advantage of the categorization capability of the software. This particularly true for unknown entities. So while a software vendor who only provides extraction capabilities will almost certainly be cheaper (and it will be easier to build your initial entity catalogs with their software), if the quality and precision of the extraction is important you should make sure the software can handle these contextual complexity issues.

This was brought home to me in a project in which the client had already tried to do this type of advanced extraction with a different vendor. That project was never able to achieve a level of accuracy that the client needed, but by using the techniques described here we were able to actually surpass the accuracy levels needed.

Endnotes

1. Kirk, G. S., and J. E. Raven. *The Presocratic Philosophers: A Critical History with a Selection of Texts*. Cambridge, England: University Press, 1957. (Note: One of the favorites of young philosophy students that some of us never outgrew.)

2. Hedden, Heather. *The Accidental Taxonomist,* Second Edition. Medford, N.J.: Information Today, 2016.

3. *Oxford English Dictionary*. Oxford, England: Oxford University Press, 1971.

4. "Synonyms and Antonyms of Words." Thesaurus.com.

CHAPTER **8**

Social Media Development

The second big area of text analytics development is *social media analysis*. Social media analysis encompasses a broad variety of applications, content, and approaches. However, there are certain characteristics that are shared by most activity in this area that are significantly different from enterprise text analytics development, as summarized in Table 8.1.

Table 8.1   Enterprise vs. Social Media Analysis

Features	Enterprise	Social
Scale	Tens of thousands to millions of documents	Billions of documents
Speed	Slow—few new documents, often weekly schedule	Fast—millions of new documents a day
Documents	Broad variety of types, often large—tend to hundreds of pages	Mostly small paragraph sized posts
Document Streams	Relatively formal, stand-alone or formal references to other documents	Conversations— meaning found in the interaction of posts
Publishing process	Relatively formal, ability to control the process	No control
Publishing process	Access to authors	No access to authors

There are other differences, but for text analytics development these are probably the most critical as there are a number of implications of these differences for the types of applications and approaches.

For development, one major implication is that the best balance between "automatic" and "human-mediated" development tilts more towards the automatic side. However, as we shall see, the best solutions still tend to be hybrid.

Within social media, there are two major types of applications and development. The first is sentiment analysis, in which the task is to capture

185

and characterize sentiments expressed in these billions of small (and usually badly written) posts. The second area is probably best characterized as general social media analysis.

General social media analysis started with customer intelligence and business intelligence applications that were mostly about data, such as tracking the behavior of customers and competitors. It was only later that text analytics was added.

In sentiment analysis—where the focus was always on text—most applications attempted to tie the sentiment expressed in text to customer and competitor behaviors.

We will look at examples from both social media analysis and sentiment analysis. In terms of development, however, both of these areas and enterprise text analytics development tend to (or should) use roughly the same approach, as shown below.

The basic model for social media development is the same as for categorization development, described in Chapter 7:

1. Select sample content to be used as training sets or starting points. You will need some number of documents or examples for each category—anywhere from five to 2,000 per category.

2. Develop initial rules for each category which will likely consist of a set of terms found within each category's training set.

3. Recall – test and refine these rules until they are correctly categorizing 90%–100% of the category's training set.

4. Test these rules against a larger set of content, for example, all the training sets for all the categories. This will almost certainly result in a major drop in recall accuracy.

5. Test and refine your rules against this larger set to improve both recall and precision:
   a. Recall – your rules are correctly categorizing 90% of your category's training sets.
   b. Precision – your rules are *not* categorizing the sample documents for the other categories.

6. Repeat this process with new sets of content until you reach a point where you're getting your target (normally 90%-plus)—and this accuracy does not drop off when you test it against a brand-new set of content.

7. Congratulations! You now have a mature categorization rule.

8. Repeat this process for all categories for which you are developing categorization.

There are, however, a number of significant differences which we will discuss as we dive more deeply into these two areas of social media and sentiment analysis.

Sentiment Analysis Development

While enterprise search was one of the first application areas for text analytics, the first true explosion of interest in text analytics was fueled by sentiment analysis. The promise of being able to track and analyze what that most precious of commodities—customers—were saying about your company and products had companies scrambling to institute their voice of the customer program. It also led to an explosion of companies that offered only sentiment analysis.

Everyone was happy, but there was one problem—*it didn't work!* The accuracy of these early efforts was barely above chance. It turned out that doing sentiment analysis—and doing it well—was pretty difficult. In fact, in my experience, it is almost as difficult as doing categorization, although with a different set of problems. The reason that it didn't work is because the wrong approach was taken to development.

I have made that claim in other places in the book, but it is not only borne out by my experience—it is also a conclusion shared by other writers on sentiment analysis.

Learn History or Repeat It

There is a very good book by Bing Liu that covers the history of sentiment analysis development approaches and has a good summary of its current problems and issues.[1] It focuses on academic research, but the main themes and the historical track applies to commercial development as well.

The first frenzied outburst of activity was based on the simple technique of viewing documents as "bags of words" and applying standard statistical methods, such as SVM, or support vector machines, where every word was represented by a vector, the length of which corresponded to the frequency. Early experiments were done at the document level.

There were a few problems—documents are the wrong level, bags of words ignored a variety of structural elements of online discourse, and

SVM was nowhere near powerful enough. But other than that, it worked just fine.

And so the inevitable happened—a giant hype—bubble of activity and expectations followed, not by just a "trough of disillusion" but an outburst of ridicule and major loss of faith in the whole idea.

After the Bubble

Luckily not everyone was deterred by the failure and the ridicule after the bubble—not to mention the underlying and overwhelming value of opening up whole new ways to understand customers. Thus, companies continued to innovate, academics continued their research, and things got better. At least somewhat.

First, document-level sentiment was abandoned and sentence-level sentiment mostly followed—after all, sentences can be quite complex as they express multiple and conflicting sentiments. What became the focus and best practice was to do what is called *aspect sentiment*—that is, products (or entities) and their features or properties. This shift made identifying sentiment easier, and also more valuable, but added quite a bit of complexity to the overall process compared with the "bag of words" and SVM approach.

The next stage of sentiment analysis witnessed companies and researchers experimenting with a variety of techniques and approaches including machine learning (supervised learning), topic modeling, developing more advanced lexicons of sentiment words and phrases, and incorporating domain knowledge.

We will discuss these approaches in more detail, including the still-significant number of unresolved problems, but first let's look at an example of a sentiment project that we did in 2010—it usually helps to have some concrete examples to add some specificity to the discussion.

Sentiment Project: Loving / Hating Your Phone

The sentiment project was a combination research-and-development project, in which we were tasked with developing ways to characterize and capture positive and negative sentiment expressed in an online forum devoted to a wide range of different phones, models, and plans. Members could post whatever they wanted to talk about and although the focus was supposed to be telephones, there typically was a great deal of personal storytelling, multiple asides, and "that reminds me of" banter. All of this not only made for a lot of fun reading but also made the sentiment analysis task much harder.

This project included an evaluation of categorization and entity extraction capabilities, which probably made it easier to realize that the best approach to sentiment was "all of the above" and how best to integrate the different approaches. The broad nature of the project also helped make clear that sentiment analysis is a combination of entity extraction and categorization, with the categorization part having a number of unique elements.

The Development Approach

As with enterprise development, the overall approach consists of the same three phases:

1. Research into content, content structures, users and use cases, and the overall information environment
2. Development, consisting of cycles of develop-test-refine
3. Maintenance and governance of the various elements of the solution

There are, however, significant differences due to the unique characteristics of social media content as well as the specific applications. So let's take a look at some of these development activities in this particular project.

Research

As we do with almost all our projects, we began with research into the information environment—looking at the overall strategy, users and information behaviors, and in particular, content and content structures. In this case, the users were analysts rather than end users, and this meant more focus on the whole process of data analysis after the text analysis was done. It also meant more focus on the usability of the analytical front end.

The research was much less formal than for a typical enterprise initiative and consisted mostly of a series of meetings. The client had actually already done a great deal of that research since they had an actual application in mind.

Taxonomy

As with most text analytics developments, one major early step was to develop a taxonomy of products and features, as shown on the left side of Figure 8.2. This was considerably easier than a conceptual taxonomy and consisted of a simple two-level structure, with specific phones as the top level and specific features of those phones as the second level.

While the product-feature taxonomy was simple, what was not simple was developing rules to identify particular posts that discussed the different features. There are quite a few ways to describe features, such as "ease-of-use." What we did was start with simple synonyms or closely-related terms, such as "easy to use," "not difficult/hard to use," etc. We expanded those rules using much the same techniques that we used for subject categorization.

Selecting Content / Initial Categorization

After the initial research and taxonomy design work, the next big step was to select content for the initial development. The content we used came from a number of forums, in which a variety of phones were rated and users were invited to post both general comments on the phones and also two specific fields: "what is good" and "what is bad," regarding the phones. In addition, users were asked to give a numerical rating of one to five for the phone.

Having a numerical rating made the selection of positive, negative, and neutral content much easier. We took all the ones and twos as negative, three as neutral, and fours and fives as positive. Even with the advantage of numerical ratings, we still did some manual evaluation of the posts but nothing like the amount we would have had to do without them.

In planning for a sentiment analysis project, you should make sure you have enough time and resources assigned to the preliminary analysis of content. As well, one of the standard techniques that we followed was to select an initial training set of documents that was used to develop the initial sentiment rules, along with a larger set of testing documents used to test and refine those rules.

Polarity Keywords

After the content was selected, the next step was to develop a general set of positive and negative words and phrases. The approach we used was to employ both a general dictionary of both positive and negative words (and phrases) and then apply it to the corpus of forum posts. This enabled us to not only get the quick start that a general dictionary provides but also to capture the specific terms that people use to apply to phones, which is very different from phrases used for cars or computers. According to Liu, this is one of the issues still bedeviling sentiment analysis.[2]

The screen in Figure 8.1 shows some of the early positive sentiment terms. Each phrase was also given a weight or base sentiment score.

File Edit View Build Help

	Type	Rule Body	Weight
1	CLASSIFIER	Love	571.168823
2	CLASSIFIER	perfect	554.977051
3	CLASSIFIER	Everything What	540.653564
4	CLASSIFIER	Great phone	456.850250
5	CLASSIFIER	Bold	436.059143
6	CLASSIFIER	absolutely	425.183502
7	CLASSIFIER	play	417.922546
8	CLASSIFIER	enjoy	378.247620
9	CLASSIFIER	Ease	341.318673
10	CLASSIFIER	Epic	317.266754
11	CLASSIFIER	capability	300.256378
12	CLASSIFIER	provide	284.848877
13	CLASSIFIER	resolution	281.419312
14	CLASSIFIER	game	276.496918
15	CLASSIFIER	early	270.315948
16	CLASSIFIER	fantastic	246.460388
17	CLASSIFIER	smart phone	230.356652
18	CLASSIFIER	GREAT	226.663498
19	CLASSIFIER	simply	216.668961
20	CLASSIFIER	heavy	216.503418
21	CLASSIFIER	great camera	213.931763
22	CLASSIFIER	Awesome	202.554428
23	CLASSIFIER	crisp	202.026886
24	CLASSIFIER	responsive	185.685974
25	CLASSIFIER	satisfy	178.718628
26	CLASSIFIER	best buy	174.286530
27	CLASSIFIER	impress	168.587479
28	CLASSIFIER	only complaint	164.763321
29	CLASSIFIER	solid	163.051529
30	CLASSIFIER	lol	159.533585

Training Corpora — Statistical Model — Polarity Keywords — Keywords — Tonal Keyword — Positive — Negative — Neutral — Product — Test

Figure 8.1   Sentiment Terms 1

This initial and broad extraction of terms provides a good jumpstart for developing sentiment analysis, but as you can see by scanning the list of words, it also produces a great deal of noise—words that don't really express sentiment such as "provide," descriptive words that may imply a positive sentiment such as "solid," positive sentiment words (that look good by themselves but may very well express the opposite depending on how they are used in sentences), and finally, words and phrases that are pretty straightforward, such as "GREAT."

This kind of automatic generation of positive and negative words is, on the one hand, a really essential way to get started without a lot of manual effort. On the other hand—and as this list shows—automatic is *never* good enough.

After we developed those rules using the standard method of successive testing and refining cycles, we were ready to identify candidate sentiment terms and phrases associated with those features. An example of a cleaned-up list of terms can be seen in Figure 8.2, showing negative terms for features.

In addition to capturing various kinds of negative terms—by capturing full phrases in the context around these negative terms—we were able to also identify specific issues that could be incorporated into the initial

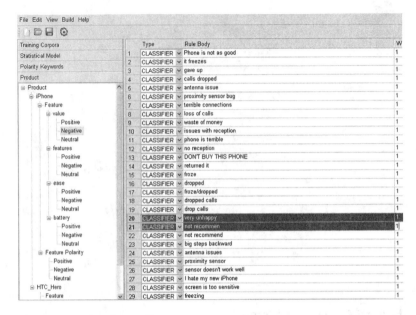

File Edit View Build Help

	Type	Rule Body	W
1	CLASSIFIER	Phone is not as good	1
2	CLASSIFIER	it freezes	1
3	CLASSIFIER	gave up	1
4	CLASSIFIER	calls dropped	1
5	CLASSIFIER	antenna issue	1
6	CLASSIFIER	proximity sensor bug	1
7	CLASSIFIER	terrible connections	1
8	CLASSIFIER	loss of calls	1
9	CLASSIFIER	waste of money	1
10	CLASSIFIER	issues with reception	1
11	CLASSIFIER	phone is terrible	1
12	CLASSIFIER	no reception	1
13	CLASSIFIER	DON'T BUY THIS PHONE	1
14	CLASSIFIER	returned it	1
15	CLASSIFIER	froze	1
16	CLASSIFIER	dropped	1
17	CLASSIFIER	froze/dropped	1
18	CLASSIFIER	dropped calls	1
19	CLASSIFIER	drop calls	1
20	CLASSIFIER	very unhappy	1
21	CLASSIFIER	not recommen	1
22	CLASSIFIER	not recommend	1
23	CLASSIFIER	big steps backward	1
24	CLASSIFIER	antenna issues	1
25	CLASSIFIER	proximity sensor	1
26	CLASSIFIER	sensor doesn't work well	1
27	CLASSIFIER	I hate my new iPhone	1
28	CLASSIFIER	screen is too sensitive	1
29	CLASSIFIER	freezing	1

Training Corpora
Statistical Model
Polarity Keywords
Product
⊟ Product
  ⊟ iPhone
    ⊟ Feature
      ⊟ value
          Positive
          Negative
          Neutral
      ⊟ features
          Positive
          Negative
          Neutral
      ⊟ ease
          Positive
          Negative
          Neutral
      ⊟ battery
          Positive
          Negative
          Neutral
    ⊟ Feature Polarity
        Positive
        Negative
        Neutral
  ⊟ HTC_Hero
      Feature

Figure 8.2   Sentiment Terms 2

application but could also be a part of an early-warning application of potential problems. An example is the phrase "antenna issues."

What we did in this case was to generalize the rule for antenna issues. First, we generalized the text phrases to include text that meant the same thing as "antenna." As with most text analytics development, this involved more than simple dictionary synonyms. It required input from their SMEs to include esoteric or slang words for "antenna" as well as specific product names for specific antennas. We also generalized the rule by developing broad synonyms for the term "issues," which ranged from the mundane to some truly colorful and creative phrases.

A second process was to characterize specific issues under the general term such as "flimsy" or "bad reception." Ultimately, this would evolve into a two-level taxonomy of types of issues, which was much more useful than just tracking issues alone.

As an aside, looking at negative terms was a lot more fun and everyone agreed that the negative phrases exhibited a lot more creativity.

We then continued to refine the rules and the set of properties that we wanted to track. In addition to terms and their weights, we also developed more sophisticated rules, such as the rule in Figure 8.3 that looks for any word meaning "best" within five words of any term meaning "screen."

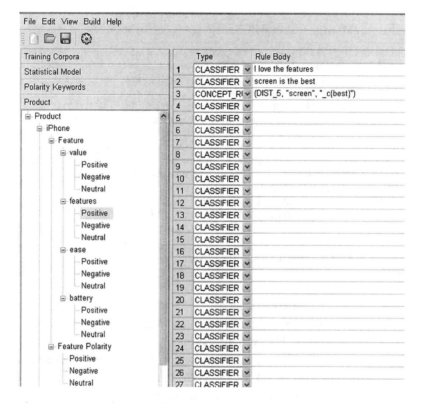

Figure 8.3   Sentiment Rules

We used the same process that we used in enterprise categorization (described in Chapter 7) for refining the rules until we were getting good results with an initial test set of posts. We then tested those rules against a new set of content and continued to refine the rules until they were getting good results with entirely new content.

All Kinds of Complexity

The actual testing process was more manual and more complex than concept categorization and involved using both SMEs and our own team. In addition, the content was in many ways more complicated than subject or concept categorization. Some of sources of this complexity can be seen in the example in Figure 8.4.

This example demonstrates a number of issues with sentiment analysis, the first issue being rather strong evidence against trying to do

This is a cute little phone with a nice qwerty keyboard. It makes phone calls and sends text messages. It also goes to the internet, but the access is very limited. Most of the mobile websites I tried to open were incompatible. And forget about Opera Mini, it does not run on this phone. Get the $50 monthly plan for unlimited minutes if you want to use its very basic internet service. Otherwise, it is too expensive. The cost for internet access is the same as a phone call, it is charged by the minute. If you check your emaill everyday and take 10 minutes to do so, it will cost you $1 per day. That is, $30 a month. Only a plan with ulimited minutes makes it worthwhile . The camera takes pictures and videos. The stills are OK, but the video quality is very low. The video images are extremely blurry, almost snowy. You can make out who or what is in the video, but cannot see any of the details. What's great about it: ☐ MAKING CALLS, TEXTING, LOW MONTHLY RATES What's not so great: ☐ LIMITED AND COSTLY INTERNET, LOW VIDEO QUALITY

Figure 8.4   Sentiment Document Example

"document-level" sentiment analysis. This post was rated negative (getting a "one" or a "two"), but it clearly contains a variety of judgments, both positive and negative about various features.

Another issue is coreference. In the sentences, "The camera takes pictures and videos. The stills are OK, but the video quality is very low." The software needs to "understand" that "stills" refers to "camera" and "pictures."

In addition, the sentence is a "but" sentence that contains two judgments— one *sort of* positive—the other negative.

Finally, this example shows the need for domain knowledge and exemplifies the situation where a straight factual statement is used to convey sentiment in the sentence, "The video images are extremely blurry, almost snowy." And, "You can make out who or what is in the video but cannot see any of the details."

The first sentence requires the knowledge that "blurry" and "snowy" are undesirable qualities for a phone camera. Seems obvious to us, but we need to tell the software. The second sentence is even more difficult as "cannot see any of the details" also needs to be flagged as a negative—and one that can be expressed in a variety of ways. The subject matter expertise required can get much more specific and extensive, especially for products with complex electronics. Is heavy good or bad? Is dense good or bad? It depends on the context.

In some ways, sentiment analysis can be even more difficult than subject categorization, but on the other hand, it is possible to get value from sentiment analysis without solving all these complex situations. So in the example above, shown in Figure 8.4 we can capture some negative sentiment "it is too expensive" even if we miss "cannot see any of the details."

One last example of some of the complexity of sentiment analysis in this case, is that the users had a tendency to tell little stories full of interesting (to them and their family) details with any sentiment expressions pretty well buried:

> I bought this phone after my old Samsung Propel stopped working. I text a lot, and a full keyboard was important to me. My sister had gotten this phone a few days before I had. She is in love with it. I only have one complaint though, what bothers me is that when you respond to a text, after the text is send, the old one stays up and you have to go back and close it in order to see the next text you will be receiving. I am not yet used to this, but I am sure that I will be soon enough. I really like the camera too. It is a better quality than my old phone. I was also expecting the touch screen to be jumpy and really difficult to use, but it was very solid. I really like this phone so far What's great about it? A: QWERTY keyboard and good picture quality What's not so great? A: messages don't close automatically.

In addition to the difficulty of finding the sentiment buried within the story, there are a number of other issues in this post. One is the sentence, "She is in love with it." This sounds like a very positive sentiment, but we must be careful since it refers to a third person. In this case, the poster seems to agree, but in other cases we saw statements like this followed by something like, "But I don't agree."

A second issue is in the statement, "I only have one complaint though," which has a negative word, "complaint," which is a minor complaint and the actual description of the complaint is so long that it would be extremely difficult to capture in a rule. And in fact, having only one complaint is very often positive.

A third issue is the counter-factual statement, "I was also expecting the touch screen to be jumpy and really difficult to use, but it was very solid." If you just have a rule that looks for "touch screen" within a few words of negatives like "jumpy" or "difficult to use," then this comes out as negative, when it is really positive.

Finally, there is the quite positive, "I really like this phone so far," toward the end of the post. This is something else that is often the case—namely, that the most important phrases are either near the beginning or near the end.

Ancient Greek to the Rescue

I first became aware of the power of "first and last" when I took courses in Ancient Greek in college as my language requirement (another of those eminently impractical choices I made). In ancient Greek, there is no systematic word order, and so they used word order for emphasis and other aesthetic impacts. For example, the opening line of the Iliad is usually translated as "Sing Goddess of the accursed wrath of Achilles, son of Peleus." But in Greek, it is actually, "Wrath sing Goddess of son of Peleus Achilles accursed." This is because the two most important words are "wrath" and "accursed," so one is first and the other last. I'm glad I don't have to do sentiment analysis in ancient Greek.

General Points

A couple of general points about this project. First, while the difficulty of developing rules to handle the variety of expressions and their associated issues should be very apparent, the alternative of statistics-based sentiment was so poor that even the vendor suggested we only play with it or use it to generate ideas. This is what we did, and after getting some pretty strange results, we concluded that the rules approach was worth the effort.

Lastly, we did not try to develop a more complex emotion taxonomy, but if I were to do the project today, I would look at doing both an appraisal taxonomy (described in Chapter 7) for more complex sentiment phrases. I would also develop a simple taxonomy of emotions, with finer distinctions than just positive or negative, such as joy, sadness, fear, anger, surprise, and disgust. In addition, I would look at more complex emotions such as pride or embarrassment, or situational emotions like confusion or skepticism.

Emotion taxonomies, like taxonomies or products and features, are relatively simple. What is not simple is the almost infinite ways those emotions can be expressed in language.

Social Media Project

Not all social media analysis is restricted to a focus on sentiment analysis. One of the exciting things about this whole area is the incredible variety of applications that people have been or will be developing. For example, another project (described in part in a number of places herein) that we worked on was focused primarily on gathering other kinds of customer information, although it also included a small sentiment component as well.

This project also demonstrates there are other rich sources besides the standard social media conversation sites like Facebook or Twitter. In this case, it was a kind of indirect social media application, and although it was generated within the enterprise, it shares most of the characteristics of social media analysis. Also, the source was ultimately from customers, even if filtered through customer support reps.

The analysis was focused on billions of customer support notes that were coming in at a rate of millions per day. These customer support notes were typed up by customer support reps taking these notes in real time with real customers screaming in their ear about all their issues. In this case, the application was also for the telephone industry.

In addition to the scale of the amount of content and the rate of new posts, these customer support notes shared a number of other character-istics with traditional social media source: They were short, cryptic notes filled with incredibly creative spelling and syntax as well as personal jargon, group jargon, and the official jargon.

We won't go into as much detail as we did in the last section—the over-all development process was basically the same as both sentiment analysis development as well as enterprise development.

Research

As usual, the project started with initial research into the content and con-tent structure, the full range of use cases, and a look at the business and technological environment. The difference in this case was that we did a lot less research and the research was mostly high-level discussions with their experts.

Content

Even though ultimately the application would be dealing with billions of notes, the initial content selected for development and testing was in the thousands. These posts had all been categorized by customer support reps and others in the organization. One issue with human categorization is its variability, so we had to normalize among the different human cataloguers to achieve greater initial accuracy and consistency.

Taxonomy

In this case, the client had already created two complete taxonomies and the beginnings of a third. The reason they already had a taxonomy was that they had tried to develop this application prior to bringing us in using a different technology and different development techniques. Their basic development technique was to rely on "automatic" categorization, or more accurately, categorization by document. This project was another example of why I find that categorization by document or training set is not strong enough to develop advanced applications.

The two initial taxonomies described the different motivations, that is, the reasons why customers were calling customer support, and secondly, one for actions which described the outcome of the call in the action taken by the customer support rep. Part of the taxonomy can be seen in Figure 8.5, a screen capture taken early in the project.

In addition to the taxonomy, you can also see some of the variation that we found in the first 2,000 documents, in this case, the word "transfer." The reason there are so many variations is that this is a critical action that the support reps take at the end of a call.

The taxonomy started as a reasonably small list, to which we added the second level to enable reporting of groups of categories. There were a couple of issues, the first that a number of categories were not truly orthogonal, or exclusive. For example, there was a great deal of overlap conceptually and in terms of the vocabulary among all of the categories having to do with billing—AbnormalFee, BillGreaterThanLast, BillIncludes, and ChargeDispute. This made it difficult to achieve much above 80% accuracy.

Another issue that impacted the accuracy was that many of the calls were about more than one thing. This is a very common problem when dealing with any kind of overall categorization of a document or a note.

Develop-Test-Refine

The primary task was to develop rules to categorize what the calls were about. We started with about 2,000 documents for each category, taking 200 documents from each category and developing an initial set of rules, after which we continued to refine them until they achieved the desired accuracy.

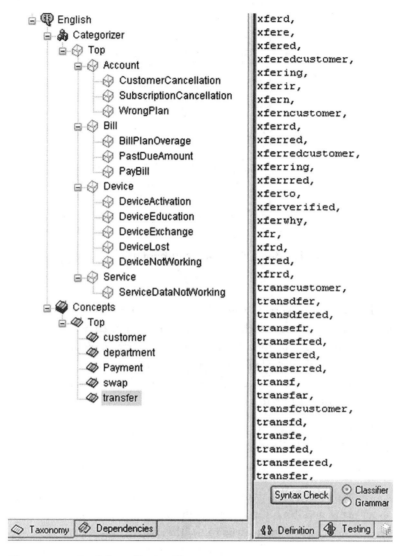

Figure 8.5   Social Media Spelling

Once the rules were categorizing the 200 documents correctly, we then brought in the full set of 2,000 documents for each category and continued to refine the rules until they achieved the target accuracy for the larger set.

The refining process followed the standard model of first developing rules based on very frequent terms found in the notes. Early rules might look something like what's shown in Figure 8.6.

```
English
  Categorizer
    Top
      Account
        CustomerCancellation
        SubscriptionCancellation
        WrongPlan
      Bill
        BillPlanOverage
        PastDueAmount
        PayBill
      Device
        DeviceActivation
        DeviceEducation
        DeviceExchange
        DeviceLost
        DeviceNotWorking
      Service
        ServiceDataNotWorking
  Concepts
    Top
      customer
      department
      Payment
      swap
      transfer
```

```
"change plan",
"chagne plan",

(DIST_7,
(OR, "plan0", "ptn s", "ptns", "3100 lien","pp", "pland", "plan.", "plans",
"anything data"),
(OR, "chagne", "change", "changes*", "changed", "changing", "chaned", "chng",
"chnge", "moved", "check", "cange", "chage", "chnage", "asking", "question*")
),

(DIST_7, (OR, "should", "switched", "placed", "called about", "put on",
"asking", "order", "inq", "inquire", "swu", "wanted to know what", "add?"),
(OR, "everything data 450","data3000", "data 3000", "data 450", "int connect",
"everything data", "ed450", "international", "talk 900", "ed1500", "unl messaging",
"talk 450", "talk 700", "intl plan")
),

"wrong plan",
"wrong pp",
"plan error",
"plan inquiry",
"customer took plan",
"better plan",
"lower plans", "lower plan",
"cheaper plan",
"plan analysis",
"rate plan",
"upgrade their lines",
"current price plan",
"change plan*",
"what price plans",
"old plan",
"add/remove"
```

Figure 8.6   Social Media Rule Development 1

Typically, the next steps would be to try to gather as many terms as possible, and add logic about where different words appeared in relation to the note and/or in relation to each other. Then finally, we developed a template with a separation of the logic of the rule from the actual vocabularies.

The end result would be to take a large messy rule, such as the one above, and turn it into this rule:

```
(OR,
(DIST_7, "[plans]", "[wrong]")
)
```

This rule just looks at any of the words indicating that the note was about plans, and if it finds words that mean "wrong" in some sense within seven words of the plans, then count it. The simple rule could produce very high accuracy, because all the notes about the wrong plan had very distinct vocabularies. As you can see in the first version, the variables [plans] and [wrong] can contain a lot more than simple synonyms. WrongPlan was the easiest and simplest rule to develop.

On the other hand, the most complex rule was the one for SubscriptionCancellation:

```
(OR,
(DIST_7, "[customer]", (NOTIN, "[cancel]",
  "cancellation on ban:")),
```

```
(DIST_7, (NOTIN, "[cancel]", "cancellation on
  ban:"), (OR, "[called]", "[customer]", "[wants]",
  "[cancel-what-sub]", "[cancel-related]")),
(DIST_5, (NOTIN, "[cancel]", "cancellation on
  ban:"), "[called]")
)
```

We won't go into detail about the meaning of this rule, but I'll leave that up to the reader to see if they have seen enough of these examples to figure it out—try it, it could be fun! :-)

One of the keys of the rule was to discount systemic text, in this case, "cancellation on ban:"—this phrase appeared in the majority of notes. Cancellation rules were the most complex, not only because of the systemic text, but also because they wanted to distinguish canceling a subscription versus canceling a service—not to mention the vocabulary of the two cases overlapped a great deal.

It typically took about eight hours to develop a rule, which for this project usually consisted of two people working three hours each, followed by a couple of hours spent merging the two results.

The goal of the categorization rules was to improve the accuracy of the categorization of new calls and to reduce the time and effort that individual customer support reps had to spend categorizing the note. As usual, the best solution was this hybrid of categorization and human effort.

However, the plan was also to use these rules to automatically categorize hundreds of millions of previous notes. This was so the client could utilize this incredibly rich source of content to mine for insights based on overall statistics and trends of, for example, changes in frequencies of specific types of calls. While the statistical analysis tends to get the most press, ultimately, the statistics are only as good as the categorization.

Unknown Issues

In addition to categorizing notes against a taxonomy of known call motivations, we also developed rules to look for previously unknown issues. As you might expect, this is a lot more difficult and found us combining both data and text analysis. The data was a list of products and known issues, for which the information was put into a simple taxonomy like the simplified version shown in Figure 8.7.

The rule for unknown issues basically looked for text indicating there was a problem, which could be anything from "the problem is" to

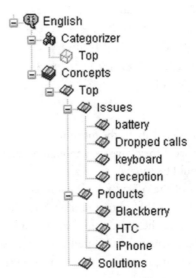

Figure 8.7   Social Media Unknown Issues

discussions of specific features along with a range of problem terms and/or negative sentiment terms. This is where we incorporated sentiment analysis along with the categorization rules developed for motivations, actions, and issues.

Common Method with Differences

As you can see from these two examples and the ones discussed in Chapter 10, most text analytics development follows a very basic common method. At the same time, each application, each information environment, and each set of content will have differences that need to be taken into account during the development process.

This combination of common method and individual differences is behind a basic best practice for text analytics development which is to combine the expertise of text analysts, building on the common method, with subject matter expertise to characterize and capture all the individual differences within each environment.

Issues, We've Got Lots and Lots of Issues

In looking at our experience with sentiment analysis (and reading Liu's book on the subject as well as other descriptions), it is very clear that sentiment analysis, while able to deliver value, is plagued by a variety of issues that people are still struggling with. Many of these issues are also applicable to general social media analysis.

In his summary, Bing Liu put it this way:

> ... sentiment analysis is very challenging technically ... None of the sub-problems have been solved satisfactorily ...

The main reason is that this is a natural language processing task, and natural language processing has no easy tasks. Another reason may be due to our popular ways of doing research. And yet another: "We probably relied too much on machine learning."[3]

I agree with this completely. And I also agree that significant progress has been made, though we still have a long way to go and continuing progress will largely depend on which approaches we focus on—and whether enough people, both in academia and in business, heed the warning about too much reliance on machine learning.

So what are these issues or sub-problems that have yet to be solved? They include the following:

- How to identify subjective sentences, that is, sentences that express a subjective sentiment or opinion
- How to identify objective phrases that express or imply opinions
- How to recognize and correctly process conditional sentences
- How to recognize sarcasm (good luck with that one)
- How to do sentiment analysis in multiple languages
- How to get the best of both easy-to-develop generic sentiment dictionaries and specific dictionaries that reflect the actual usage of a particular application and particular content
- How to interpret "but" clauses, distinguishing ones that reflect two different opinions from those in which one clause negates the other
- How to do good coreference identification
- How to do good disambiguation of entities and features
- How to incorporate relevant domain knowledge that either expresses a sentiment or is needed to correctly interpret the sentiment

Quite a list—and one that will keep academic and business researchers busy for years.

Solving some of these issues will be relatively straightforward, but overall solutions will likely require the development of specific modules and at the same time building better ways of integrating all the various modules into more sophisticated solutions.

Modules might include new general dictionaries of sentiment words and a growing number of subject or industry dictionaries as well as standard ways of customizing those dictionaries to match specific corpus. Other modules might include new techniques for processing conditional sentences with new machine learning techniques as well as training human editors or librarians in how to prune and customize the machine learning output.

One major problem in this area is that most machine learning techniques "produce no human understandable results."[4] This makes it very difficult to incorporate human subject matter expertise into refining the performance of these rules. What's needed are new ways to present the results of machine learning as well as additional training for the human experts.

Another problem is that too often, any use of manual effort by editors or librarians is seen as a sign of failure on the part of the software, or at best considered a primitive solution that will be replaced by automatic solutions when the software gets good enough.

The real danger with this attitude is that people will accept low-performing solutions because they are automatic (even though the selection of training contents is human mediated). We've seen this happen in another area, enterprise search, where companies buy one "automatic" search engine after another instead of investing in human metadata taggers and/or taxonomy developers. So an exclusive reliance on automatic sentiment analysis will likely have the same outcome as it has for enterprise search—the overwhelmingly dominant attitude toward performance as "sentiment sucks."

One of the surprising things about text analytics is the prevalence of this attitude toward automatic solutions. You don't see that "automatic is best" attitude in many other fields. Imagine if your HR software didn't just support better screening and analysis of resumes, but was tasked with making the final hire and/or fire decisions—automatically! So why do people think text analytics should be able to do without human judgment?

Rather, the right approach is to develop better and better machine-based algorithmic capabilities AND better and better human techniques and training AND better and better ways to integrate all of the above into complete and smart solutions—solutions that are hybrid solutions of machine and human.

Endnotes

1. Liu, Bing. *Sentiment Analysis and Opinion Mining.* San Rafael, Calif.: Morgan & Claypool, 2012.

2. Ibid, page 88.

3. Ibid, page 134.

4. Ibid, page 134.

CHAPTER 9

Development: Best Practices and Case Studies

In Chapters 7 and 8, we discussed the general process of text analytics development in the enterprise and social media. In this chapter, I'm going to describe a number of specific development projects to try to add a level of detail and real-world application development.

In these real-world case studies, I will also describe what we uncovered as best (and worst) practices in hopes that you can learn what works and how to avoid the mistakes that we made. Whether it is better to focus on what works rather than mistakes, I'll leave up to you, but I have to admit it is more fun describing what didn't work (although in one case in particular, the memories are still a bit painful).

Achieving New Inx(s)ights into the News

The first case study was for a web-based news aggregator in which we used an early text analytics software package from Inxight called Smart Discovery (see Chapter 4 for more on their role in the history of text analytics).

The application was creating a series of daily newsletters that were then sold to various associations. The original process was that editors were manually creating these newsletters every day.

The content was being scraped from over 800 internet news sources, which meant that there was some variation in the quality of the writing, but most of the content was fairly well written by professional news people. The volume of stories was fairly low as this was an early application—about 5,000 stories a day.

I found that news stories written by professionals almost always produce better results than the sort of documents you find within organizations, or currently on social media or Twitter sources—because they know how to write good opening sentences. Although lately I've been seeing two different schools of news stories openings: 1) good high-level description sentences (great for capturing summaries), and 2) opening with a small, highly detailed story about some aspect of the overall article, followed by those good summary sentences. So we now have to build rules to distinguish two different styles. More on that in the future.

Because of the range of subject areas, the project required the development of a number of taxonomies including healthcare, travel, media, education, general business, and consumer goods. The goal of the project was not to come up with fully automatic categorization of stories but rather a hybrid combination of editors and automation. The job of the software was to do an initial categorization of the 5,000 stories, then present the provisionally categorized stories to the editors. This hybrid solution meant that recall was much more important than precision—the one thing the editors did not want was to miss an important story.

Working with the editors and a team from the KAPS Group of three people, we developed taxonomies and categorization rules for eight subject areas. The entire project took about five months. The process we in followed each area was the same as described below. During this process, we also trained their people so they could maintain the catonomy while developing new subject areas.

At one point we tried a feature many text analytics packages have—an automatic taxonomy generation feature. In this feature, the software is pointed at a collection of stories and analyzes those stories using various clustering of co-occurring terms to try to come up with a taxonomy structure. Right now, a number of companies are trying to enhance this feature with a lot of standard taxonomy structures and advanced mathematical and statistical clustering, but at the time the results were very strange and not at all usable. While the new "automatic taxonomy" features have gotten better, they are still no substitute for a good taxonomist, but at least they are beginning to be a more useful tool in the hybrid software-taxonomist model.

It was good for two things though: 1) every once in a while, it would suggest a new term that the editors hadn't thought of, and 2) the more common use of providing a good laugh for the entire team at the truly bizarre taxonomy suggestions.

What we used instead was an initial high-level taxonomy that came from the editors and was based in part on the existing sections within the newsletters (but which they expanded based on their experience in the field). They provided this taxonomy to the taxonomists within the KAPS Group, who analyzed it based on good taxonomy design principles, specifically taxonomy design for auto-categorization.

After the taxonomy had gone through this initial refinement process, the next step was to put together multiple test collections and start the process of developing categorization rules. In this case, since we had content that had already been categorized, we were able to put together test collections that included good stories, bad stories, and stories that were close misses, which in turn enabled us to develop much more refined rules.

We used the basic refinement process described in Chapter 7 that began with the KAPS Group text analysts doing a number of rounds of recall and precision cycles, where we would develop rules with very good recall. Once we were getting 90%-plus, we would add new content that had not been categorized as belonging to that category and work on improving precision, that is, reduce the number of false hits. The goal was to enhance precision without losing much in the way of recall. After a number of rounds of this process, we then began a more formal scoring process in which the editors would review the results with actual daily content. Based on their review, we would then do additional rounds of refinements. Typically, we would run through two or three rounds of this process until the rules were achieving in the 80%–90% accuracy range.

This entire process took about four weeks for each taxonomy and set of categorization rules. The graphic in Figure 9.1 shows part of the healthcare taxonomy using the star tree functionality of the Smart Discovery product. This visualization of taxonomies works very well for taxonomies in the three to four level/few hundred node scale of taxonomies. However, if the number of taxonomy nodes gets much higher, then the usefulness of this sort of visualization drops off.

In addition to using the star tree to move around within the taxonomy, it also supported clicking down to lower levels, such as shown in Figure 9.2.

Finally, you could double-click into the category and see the underlying categorization rules, such as the one in Figure 9.3 that shows a number of the kinds of additions that you can make to rules beyond simple lists of terms—these include filtering on certain sources as well as setting category thresholds and other rule components. Of course, actual production rules were much more complex than this one, but since they are proprietary, you'll have to use your imagination.

This was a very successful project with everyone happy with the outcome. Categorization rules resulted in better newsletters. The big advantage in terms of the quality of stories was that the categorization rules very often found stories that human editors would have missed, either because of a

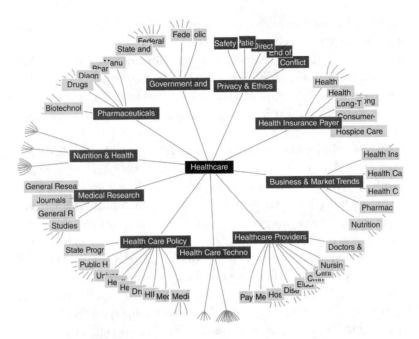

Figure 9.1   Inxight Star Tree

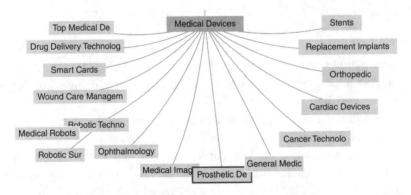

Figure 9.2   Inxight Star Tree Level 2

misleading title or an unusual source. Another advantage was that editors didn't suffer from category fatigue from looking at very similar sets of stories.

The biggest advantage, however, was in time savings. Before this project editors were taking on average about four hours a day to produce a single newsletter. Using auto-categorization to filter the stories enabled them to reduce the time from four hours to 20 minutes—an enormous saving.

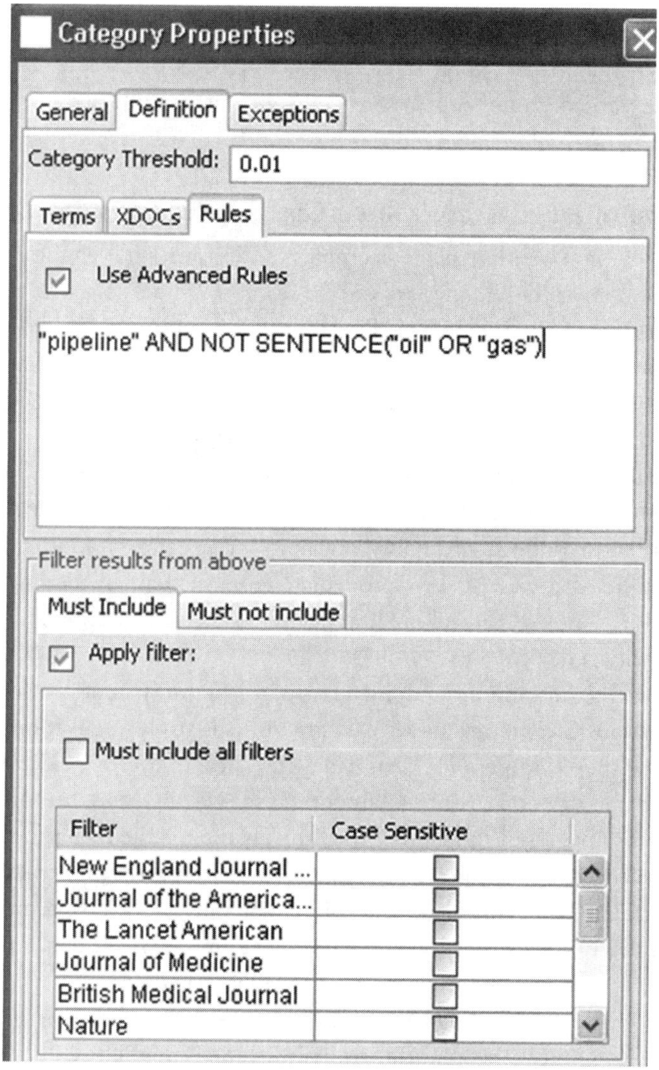

Figure 9.3   Inxight Star Tree Detail

Of course, the more significant issue is, what do you do with all that extra time? The simple and (almost always) less valuable answer is to reduce staff and costs. The other—and usually better—answer is to use the extra time to enhance your capabilities by adding additional products—either by simply adding more newsletters or adding a whole new range of applications or services.

Lessons Learned

This was the first text analytics development project that we worked on—and we learned a number of lessons that continue to guide my thinking on text analytics projects.

Taxonomy and Categorization: Can This Relationship Last?

The first lesson was that there's a complex relationship between the depth of the taxonomy and the complexity of the categorization rules. At a very high level, such as with a topic like "healthcare," it is fairly easy to write a categorization rule that doesn't need a lot of sophisticated logic but does tend to include a large vocabulary. At a low level, say a level-three concept like "prosthetic device," it is also fairly easy to write a categorization rule that takes advantage of the specificity of the node. This level node is also likely to be the kind of node that refers to specific things as opposed to concepts.

The most difficult taxonomy nodes to write categorization rules for were nodes that were at the intermediate level, such as "medical devices," which are a mix of general medical device characteristics and lists of specific medical devices.

However, an even more difficult type of taxonomy node to write categorization rules for are nodes that are difficult to distinguish one from another, that is, those nodes that had a great deal of overlap. Good taxonomy design turns out to be very important for writing good categorization rules. In most cases, the more formal the taxonomy, the better the results of the categorization rules. In this case, "formal" largely refers to having a specifiable rule for distinguishing children of a particular taxonomy node. What did not work at all were browse taxonomies, which tend to throw together a variety of concepts that are broadly related.

Of course, this finding came out of broad news applications and may not hold in other areas. But the surprising thing is that it actually has held in our experience for a number of different applications. One exception to that rule is described below in the use case of the good taxonomy.

The Best Rules: It All Depends

Another conclusion is that there is no simple best answer to taxonomy structure or the format of the specific rules, but rather, it depends on the application. For example, in this case recall was much more important than precision, since the editors were reviewing the results. One implication of this is that every text analytics project needs some custom development. This does not mean that a project cannot build on previous work done in other areas, but that the uniqueness of the environment or the contents or the specific use cases mean that every job does need some custom development.

Taxonomy Nodes: Aggregate vs. Independent?

Another interesting issue involving taxonomy structure has to do with aggregate versus independent nodes. Aggregate nodes are the sum of all the children of that node. For example, in the screenshot in Figure 9.2, documents that would be tagged "medical devices" were simply all the documents that were tagged with any one of the children of "medical devices," such as "smart cards" and "cancer technologies." There was no actual categorization rule associated with medical devices in general. On the other hand, for independent nodes, each node had its own categorization rule.

What we found was that in some cases, aggregate nodes worked better with the example of "medical devices," but in other cases, independent nodes worked best. In those, we would develop a rule for the parent node that referred to very general documents, and then the children would refer to specific items under that. As in the example above, one key issue was that aggregate taxonomy nodes worked best with things rather than concepts.

A third option was to develop rules in which the parent categorization rules are designed to capture all the documents that had anything to do with a particular area and use that as a filter so that all the children first had to fit the general rule and then add specifics to define children. This differs from the general rule (find only documents that only have general terms) in that it finds all topic-related documents. In this particular case, we mostly used independent rules and a general rule for the parent node, but in subsequent projects, we have used aggregate nodes quite successfully.

Mixed Marriages Work Best

Some of the other lessons learned in this project (and which we perhaps didn't appreciate as much as we should have at the time) was that the combination of SMEs and taxonomy professionals is a great way to do text analytics. In this case, we were blessed with the wonderful situation of having editors who knew their subject areas but also had some taxonomy experience combined with the taxonomy professionals in the KAPS Group. Having this combination is probably one of the main reasons that we are able to do each catonomy in that four-week period.

Let's Work Together

Another lesson was that the best way to approach text analytics is by combining a variety of features, rather than asking any single feature to do all the work. For example, we ended up using both entity extraction and categorization rules. Entity extraction was used simply to generate additional metadata, such as pulling out people names or medical device names, but it was also used as input into a categorization rule. In some cases, we found that simple lists of terms were more than sufficient, but in other cases, we needed to develop more sophisticated Boolean rules. Finding the right combination of all these features required the combination of subject matter expertise and good language skills.

We also found that this combination approach was the best way to build text analytics–based search applications. Trying to have the taxonomy—even with categorization rules—do all the work of finding information led to taxonomies and categorization rules that were very brittle and difficult to maintain as new content was incorporated into the application. It was much better to have smaller taxonomies, rarely going below third or fourth level, with more flexible categorization rules combined with other means of finding information, such as a faceted navigation front end using other metadata such as author, date, organization, document type, and so on.

Find Similar Doesn't

Substituting the arcane skill of selecting documents that would function as a kind of "find similar feature" (something that doesn't work well for search engines, either) resulted not only in rules unable to distinguish concepts at a very granular level but also left us with no real understanding of what worked and what didn't—the standard black-box problem in text analytics. And so finally, this project is where we came to the strongly held conclusion that trying to develop categorization rules based entirely on training sets of selected documents was not a very good idea. In fact, it was by far the worst approach of any that we tried.

A Tale of Two Taxonomies

The next case studies take a look at two projects that were very similar and yet one was a major success and the other was a major failure. In other words—in almost the words of Dickens—it was the best of catonomies, it was the worst of catonomies.

Both projects were for large organizations with a great deal of scientific and engineering information and vocabularies, and both projects followed the same methodology described in Chapter 7:

- Starting with initial meetings and project planning
- Developing a high-level knowledge map of content, people, and technology
- Contextual (broad background information) and information interviews (specific information needs and behaviors)
- Content analysis
- Developing a draft taxonomy and refining it based on validation interviews
- Developing categorization and entity extraction rules
- Finally, developing integration and governance plans

Two almost-identical projects, and yet one failed and the other succeeded—so what went right and what went wrong? No one likes talking about their failures, but hopefully you (and we) can learn some lessons from those failures. One of the interesting things about both the success story and the failure is the success and failure factors were mostly *not* related to the actual text analytics development—they were mostly about how the projects approached this development. Let's take a closer look at the two projects.

Success = Multiple Projects + Approaches + Deep Integration

The successful project was for a large company that specialized in science and engineering consulting. It was actually a number of projects carried out over about six months, but the initial motivation was to develop an expertise location application. There were four major components: 1) a research effort, 2) a taxonomy development project, 3) a text analytics evaluation process, and finally, 4) the expertise location pilot.

Research

The research effort, which is really the foundation of the project, began with a knowledge audit of the organization's information environment. This was supplemented by specific research efforts, such as the feasibility of using existing external taxonomies and an analysis of how the taxonomy and document tagging would work within their environment and what benefits they could anticipate. These research efforts led to a set of recommendations and best practices tailored specifically to this organization.

Taxonomy Development

The taxonomy development efforts involved creating a large enterprise taxonomy—not to describe the organization but to cover all of the scientific and engineering disciplines that they offered consulting services for. We developed a broad taxonomy that covered all of those disciplines, then did a deep-development dive into two areas: healthcare and chemistry. The idea was that we would develop a framework, and in the process, train their internal resources to continue the development after our consultants were gone.

In addition to the taxonomy development, we also carried out a small manual metadata-tagging process that was used to get a better idea of the best approach for tagging documents.

Software Evaluation

The software evaluation process looked at the full range of options for both taxonomy management and text analytics (recall the overall process is described in full in Chapter 5). In this case, the project included an analysis of about 5,000 resumes used to describe their internal expertise, and also a comparison of manual and software-aided tagging.

Expertise Location Application

The last part was an actual expertise location pilot to develop a framework for an expertise location application and explore the issues involved in that effort.

The solution that we came up with involved developing a large taxonomy of scientific subjects or disciplines with categorization rules for each node as has become standard. As consultants, our job was to develop the broad taxonomy and formulate complete categorization rules for one subject area, in the process training internal resources to complete the other areas of the taxonomy with categorization rules. This approach has a two-fold advantage—we had more resources to develop the project faster—and the client got a trained set of resources.

In addition to the scientific and engineering taxonomy, we also designed and developed a number of specific facets that would become part of search front end. Some of these facets were ones that have become more or less standard, such as "organization" and "content type." In addition, during the taxonomy development, we identified a number of facets that reflected the way the intended audience looked for information that were common across the different disciplines. These included facets such as "methods" and "materials," and the full set of facets are shown in the following list with examples of levels two and three:

- Organization → Division → Group
- Clients → Federal → EPA
- Facilities → Division → Location → Building X
- Content Type → Knowledge Asset → Proposals
- Instruments → Environmental Testing → Ocean Analysis → Vehicle
- Methods → Social → Population Study
- Materials → Compounds → Chemicals

Success Factors and Best Practices

Some of the success factors and best practices are common to any good project, but I'll try to focus on the ones that are specific to text analytics projects.

Project Location / Owners

One of the first factors that helped make this project a success was *who the project owner was*. In this case, it was a knowledge management department that had been given the task to enhance information access within the organization and build applications, such as locating expertise within the organization. Since the knowledge management department had a history of working with other areas, it was natural to include a variety of business groups, as well as IT-based groups like records management. This turned out to be a very good choice for ownership of the project.

One of the most important success factors was that the knowledge management department involved the library in the project from the beginning. One of the things that has become very clear in text analytics projects is that library science is an absolutely critical part of the entire process. It is very difficult to succeed if an organization does not have some library expertise within the organization. This does not mean that a full-fledged library is needed, since this is something that very few small companies are currently able/or willing to fund. There are quite a few ways to bring in library expertise.

For example, the project described in the first case study in this chapter, the "library expertise" was actually provided by teams of editors having the responsibility for creating a publication for their specific subject areas. Their experience in putting together and structuring these publications turned out to be a great resource in getting started with building a taxonomy. They also were able to provide expert feedback on the categorization rules that we developed for the taxonomy.

Within an enterprise environment, and very often when an information project or a text analytics project is launched by an IT group, budgets tend to overestimate the need for technology and underestimate the need for language and categorization skills.

Flexible Project Plan

For this project, both the knowledge management department and the library understood that dealing with language—especially within a broad context of improving access to information—is not something that can typically follow rigid schedules. This understanding meant that there was a great deal of support for developing a flexible project plan.

It is very difficult to force a text analytics project, or any language-based project, to rigid schedules. First of all, development is an iterative process as we've seen above—and it has no well-defined endpoint. Achieving success or simply a mature application is often a sliding scale rather than a simple either/or. It is not "Does the program work or not?"

In addition, progress tends not to be linear but rather fits a kind of punctuated equilibrium model, i.e., slow cumulative progress punctuated by breakthroughs that can literally jump accuracy from 30% to 80% in a matter of minutes.

This does not mean that project plans and schedules are not important, but it does mean that they have to be approached with the flexibility not found in a lot of other projects.

Successful Interviews

A strategic interviewing approach contributed significantly to the success of the project. We began with contextual interviews to understand the overall information needs and behaviors of various groups within the company. These interviews gave us a deep understanding of the overall information environment, which was the foundation for developing an overall information strategy that included where taxonomy and text analytics would play an important role.

These contextual interviews were followed up by a series of information interviews, which focused primarily on the one deep area: chemistry. These information interviews enabled us to understand more deeply what kinds of elements would actually help them find information as well as fleshing out important concepts that needed to go into the taxonomy.

The optimum number of interviews and best selection of people for interviews is something that will vary from project to project and company to company. The design of the information interviews is typically developed during the contextual interviews. In this project, we did 15 information interviews with people, ranging from management to consultants to support people.

A Good Draft Taxonomy and Ongoing Refinement

Developing a good draft taxonomy was also a critical step, along with having the support to do an extended process of refinement for that taxonomy. Again, the library was critical not only in helping this process but also in helping create an understanding throughout the rest of the organization of the importance of doing this extended refinement.

While the information interviews were an important input into the taxonomy development, good taxonomies typically grow from a variety of sources. This included looking at existing external taxonomies related to their subject areas, or in some cases simply using a good textbook as a starting point. For this project, we had to develop the taxonomy before we had text analytics software in place, but in subsequent projects, using text analytics software to help develop the taxonomy has also been an important addition.

Integration of External and Internal Resources

Creating a good team that integrates external consultants with internal resources is essential for success and typically consists of a variety of approaches.

The first step is making sure that there are enough internal resources for the project and that those internal resources are the right ones. The "right ones" will, of course, vary from project to project, and selecting them is one of the important steps in creating an initial project plan. Normally, however, the right ones include a good mix of technical and linguistic/library expertise.

In addition to assigning the right ones, it's important that the internal resources are actually assigned to the project, and their work is not something that is expected to be done in their "spare time." In other words, don't make it extra work—that usually means they won't do as good a job, and they will be resentful of the entire project. That does not make for a happy, functioning team.

One of the most critical parts of creating a well-integrated team is good communication. In the case of a text analytics project, a key element is being able to translate the external expertise in text analytics and taxonomy to the internal team and translate the subject matter expert's knowledge of their field to the external team.

Again, there is no one technique that works in all cases. The most important thing is to realize that there is a great deal of effort needed to ensure this communication. One technique that we used on this project was to develop a *benefits document*—this detailed and explained the benefits that the project intended to bring to the organization. This document was then used to help generate and maintain support for the project.

The benefits document also explained what we needed to do for a successful project. Having this understanding on the part of the internal team is critical, not just to get resource, but enthusiastic resources who wanted to work on the project.

Learn by Doing

Very few organizations have resources trained on the job in text analytics. A library staff may very well have some taxonomy experience and understand organizing information, but developing a good taxonomy that is designed to work with good categorization rules is something that can realistically only be learned by on-the-job training. No one wants to pay consultants to maintain a complex taxonomy with built-in categorization rules—and to be honest, lots of us consultants would probably get bored with the maintenance tasks.

So one of the key activities was for us to incorporate internal resources (in this case mostly from the library) into our team. Then, we'd have them participate at greater and greater levels as the project proceeded, all the way up until it came time to pass the project over entirely to them—and *that* was done only when we all agreed they were ready. In short, I've found there is really no substitute for this learn-by-doing approach in text analytics.

Failure = Wrong Approach / Mindset + Lack of Integration

"The fear of failure can poison learning by creating aversions to the kinds of experimentation and risk-taking that characterize striving, or by diminishing performance under pressure."[1]

—*Make It Stick: The Science of Successful Learning*

No one likes to talk about failures, but as the quote above indicates, without the risk of failure, it is hard to achieve breakthrough successes—as long as one learns from those failures. Although in the case of this unsuccessful project, the failure was not by striving too high, but rather everything that could be done wrong *was* done wrong (but it was a great learning experience).

The project was also for a large company that wanted to develop a large science and engineering taxonomy, which was to be used to develop a text analytics application to improve enterprise search. We tried to follow the same process as in the successful project, where the major elements of the project were essentially the same, but the outcome was dramatically different.

We followed the same basic outline of steps starting with research, interviews, and developing a taxonomy of scientific disciplines, particularly geology. As in the first project, we also developed facets to enhance an enterprise search application:

- Organization → Division → Group
- Process → Drill Well → File Test Plan
- Assets → Platforms → Platform A
- Content Type → Communication → Presentations

So what went wrong? The answer is, of course, *everything!* Well, *almost* everything …

Broad Environmental and Project Issues
The Wrong Project Owner

The first problem was the project owner was a group in IT who had just bought a new records management software and wanted to conquer the world with it—in other words, "sell" everyone in the organization on using the software. It was a solution in search of a problem, and we never really got beyond this fundamental issue.

The primary focus became how to use the records management software to enhance the taxonomy, text analytics tagging, and enterprise search—which is a rather backward way of looking at it.

Lack of a Library

Even though there were internal library staff, they were not invited to join the project. This lack of library science was a major problem, both in terms of developing a taxonomy and also developing a good information access solution. One of the critical problems was, without a library staff, the difficulty of merging their internal expertise and our taxonomy and text analytics expertise was extremely difficult to overcome.

This also meant that while there was a general understanding of the value of the taxonomy, there was no understanding of the complexity and scope of trying to develop a large enterprise-wide catonomy.

Underbudgeted and Understaffed

This lack of an understanding was a major contributor to the entire project being underbudgeted and understaffed. This, of course, is a hard sell for an outside consulting group like us to make as your clients often simply assume that we were overstating the case and trying to pad the project. The lack of resources severely hampered what could be accomplished in the project, but a lack of understanding was the greater problem, which continued to plague us throughout the whole project.

Project Mindset Is the Wrong Set

The other broad environment issue: The internal group's mindset—and thus their approach—was that this was simply one more project. What we were building was more of a semantic infrastructure, an enterprise taxonomy, and a text analytics tagging capability designed to support a variety of projects, starting with enterprise search and then building on that foundation. One impact of this project mindset was that we were continually rushing to meet artificial deadlines, which is something that simply does not work when dealing with language and semantics.

This project mindset and/or corporate culture also tended to denigrate the importance of integration across different units within their organization as well as integrating our efforts with their internal teams.

The project mindset also led to a situation where following the project plan was more important than getting good results. And, when the inevitable conflict between a punctuated equilibrium model of text analytics collided with the project plan, the result was a loss of faith in the entire project by the project leader and consequently the records management team.

Research Issues

Insufficient Research

The main issue with the research that we did was there simply was not enough of it, particularly the context and information interviews. Why didn't we do more research? Probably lots of reasons, starting with the lack of buy-in by the project owner that any research was really needed. Related to that was a great deal of resistance on the part of the people that were to be interviewed. And of course, the almighty project plan couldn't fit more in.

Ultimately, however, the reason is that I was unable to convince the project owner of the need for more and better (see next point) research.

Wrong Research

Not only did we not do enough research, but very often we also ended up talking to the wrong people who had no real stake in the project and thus no real interest in helping. They were the opposite of enthusiastic participation—the very definition of deal-breakers.

They also tended to be the wrong job function. Since this was a records management project, we were given access to people in the records management team but not actual end users. So what we got were the records management team's ideas about what end users might want or should want. And as we've seen time and time again, IT or management teams' ideas about what end users want are almost always woefully inadequate.

There is no substitution for talking to end users—they always have a way of surprising us. That lesson was brought home to me in a very early project for a biotech company where we were designing an intranet portal for a sales team. After a great deal of effort went into the design of the portal, we did a survey of end users and discovered that the design of the portal made no difference because the salespeople didn't want to use the intranet at all. They wanted something they could listen to as they drove between sales calls.

Users don't always know what is best for them, but they almost always tell you things that you need to know—and they are more often right about what is best for themselves than not.

Misunderstood Research

In addition to not enough research and the wrong kind of research, the very nature of the research that we did was basically misunderstood. In discussions after the research was done, I discovered that the project lead expected a kind of tinker-toy connection between interviews and the taxonomy. So, for example, interviewing person X would lead to (a) specific taxonomy node(s) being added. Since none of the people we interviewed were taxonomists, we could hardly expect them to simply suggest specific nodes for the taxonomy.

The interviews that we were doing were designed to understand more about how the taxonomy and text analytics would help people do their jobs. In hindsight, this misunderstanding basically doomed the project before it really began.

Design Issues

Bad Facet Design—General

The design issues were primarily around the facet designs for the enterprise search application which was the first and primary application for the taxonomy and text analytics development. The only really thing wrong with the facet design was we did not have not enough facets, we had the wrong set of facets—and those facets were ill defined. But other than that, they were fine.

Faceted navigation works best when you provide a variety of different ways for users to find information, based on what they already know about what they're looking for. Having just four facets did not really support enough variety of different user perspectives or a variety of search use cases.

Bad Facet Design—Ill-Defined Facets

In addition, having only four facets meant that they ended up being *ill-defined facets*—that is, they ended up with too complex an internal structure for the facet. For example, the concept of process is extremely complex, and includes dozens of different kinds of processes. What this really meant was that instead of one taxonomy and four facets, we essentially had three taxonomies and two facets ("organization" and "content type").

Bad Facet Design—Wrong Type of Facet

The last problem was that this was simply the wrong set of facets that reflected how the project lead thought about the business, rather than designing a system for improving information access. Basically, process and assets refer to business processes but not to the information which needs to be accessed during those business processes. In other words, this was more of a model of the business, rather than the information within the business.

Also, facets work best when they are very orthogonal, which normally means they are very one-dimensional. The power of facets comes from the intersection of one-dimensional simple facets—not from a facet with a complex internal structure.

Risk Factors

Lack of Understanding

The main issue was a lack of understanding on the part of the project lead and the team that he put together. Even though they seemed to value the project, there was a great deal of resistance based on this misunderstanding. The problem wasn't a complete lack of understanding—it was more subtle. For example, rather than not understanding a specific conclusion, there would be a reinterpretation of that conclusion and particularly of the relative importance of specific recommendations.

Lack of Access to Content and the Right People

Another problem was getting access to the necessary content and the right people. Like the situation with a lack of understanding, it was not that we did not have access to content and people—we simply didn't have the right kind of access or the right amount.

Our access to the content was limited by not having any guidance as to the nature of the content in how people were using it to find information. This was a direct result of not doing enough information and contextual interviews.

Our access to people was limited by what I call the enthusiasm factor, which shows up in interviews when people come to the interview because they were told to but had no real interest in the project or in the process of the interview. The worst example of this was someone who came in 15 minutes late, then sat in their office with their laptop open during the entire interview, doing their email while they gave desultory one-word answers. We might as well have shut down and gone home.

Communication, Communication, Communication

The combination of the lack of communication and miscommunication doomed this project from the start. One major factor in the miscommunication was not having either a library staff or staff with a content focus involved in the project. As noted above, the best solution for large organizations that have a library is to have them involved in the project. For smaller organizations, this role can be played by a number of functions within the organization, from IT to training and to business roles—as long as they have a user focus. In other words, as long as they have some experience and/or interest in understanding how users utilize information in their jobs and how they look for information, they can be helpful.

While there was a great deal of shared responsibility for these various failure factors and in particular the lack of communication, ultimately the responsibility was mine. Quite honestly, I was not able to translate the essential taxonomy and text analytics ideas to the records management group. I hope I've learned to speak IT and business better today—and having that experience certainly motivated me to work on it.

Summary

What I found interesting was that the project failed not because of any of the information issues around the complexity of the taxonomy or the complexity of text analytics categorization rules but rather for the same reason so many projects fail—bad project management, lack of understanding, and a lack of communication.

Endnote

1. Brown, Peter C., Henry Roediger, and Mark McDaniel. *Make It Stick: The Science of Successful Learning*. Dreamscape Media, 2014.

Text
Analytics
Applications

CHAPTER 10

Text Analytics Applications—Search

There are really three major areas for applications of text analytics: enterprise search, text analytics–based applications, and social media. We'll take a look at text analytics–based apps in Chapter 11 and social media in Chapter 12. In this chapter, we'll look at how text analytics is changing search—from a chronic underperforming problem to something that actually *doesn't suck.*

Since before Google changed everything for internet search, enterprise search has been struggling to solve the fundamental problem of finding information within the enterprise. Unfortunately, unlike Google, enterprise search seems to be stuck. There have been very few advances in enterprise search, other than in the purely technical dimension.

It seems like every year or two, search vendors unveil the next generation search tool with the requisite new breakthrough features. However, when you look at what those features are, they are almost all technical advances: the new search engine is faster, the new search engine has a whole new architecture, the new search engine can now index even more types of documents. Thus, enterprise search is now faster than ever and able to index more content than ever—we just can't use it to find anything!

So what is wrong with enterprise search? The short answer is *pretty much everything!* First of all, it is the wrong technology. Basic search engines take a document and strip out all the things that humans use to figure out the meaning of the document, like section headings and summaries and titles, and create an inverted index of every single word in the documents, which strips out any remaining context. Yes, better search engines aren't quite so extreme and they do retain some context, just not any real meaning. And once they have stripped out all the meaningful elements, they try to make sense of the document by applying mathematics to what is a linguistic artifact.

Secondly, the really fundamental issue is that technology is *not* the answer. As we will see, it is part of the answer but not enough by itself. What's needed is to really deal with all the linguistic elements, semantics, and context in all of its variety.

The Enterprise Search Dance

So we have the situation that as companies focus on technology, they get stuck in an enterprise search dance, which we've described before, but goes like this: employees complain that they can't find anything, so IT goes out and buys a new search engine. Things get better for a little while (largely because they haven't yet integrated all the content and partially just because it's new), but then the complaints start growing, the content continues to grow and the refrain "enterprise search sucks" starts to be heard more and more. And so anywhere from two to five years later, IT goes out and tries to solve the problem by buying another new and shiny search engine with all those wonderful new technical advances. And the cycle begins again.

It doesn't work! It will never work!

A Rising Chorus of Complaints

Despite all the advances in search engines—and particularly the attempts to improve relevance ranking—the complaints and the overall dissatisfaction with search are, at best, not improving. And this is not just the opinion of one cranky ex-taxonomist, now text analyst.

There was a good survey done in 2011, by Smartlogic and MindMetre,[1] of over 2,000 managers and directors in the United States, United Kingdom, France, and Germany. There were some interesting variations among the countries, but two results from that survey highlight the current dissatisfaction with enterprise search:

- 52% of respondents say they cannot find the information they are seeking within an acceptable amount of time (two minutes or less).

- 27% say that it takes more than four minutes to find what they are looking for.

The World of Stupid Chicken Scratches

Why won't it work? Because search engines are stupid! And humans have better things to do than try to improve the performance of the stupid search engine. They have jobs to do and businesses to run, and even if you ask them to help "educate" the search engine (like adding metadata and such), they won't.

The fundamental problem with your standard stupid search engine is that documents deal in language, but search engines deal in meaningless chicken scratches. Imagine trying to understand what a document is about in a language that you've never seen before. This is basically what search engines are trying to do, for example: *Fjnaiouh fjalke [qmntgyh nneoidgh nnnveig mmsweeovgp mmert].*

That is essentially what a sentence looks like to a search engine. It's true that we've gotten very clever about trying to give a search engine some intelligence in dealing with these chicken scratches. We've developed ways for the search engine to count plurals and singulars as the same chicken scratch and even told the search engine that "fredgty" and "gerdgty" are the same chicken scratch (synonyms). We've also developed rules, so that when the search engine sees a chicken scratch in a title, it should give it added mathematical weight.

But in essence, all the search engine can do is count up the number of chicken scratches and related chicken scratches and sometimes apply an overall mathematical pattern of chicken scratches in order to try to determine the meaning of a document. We call this *relevance ranking*— and its performance is pathetic. Not surprising! It has nothing to do with meaning.

What About Google?

At this point in the discussion someone always brings up: "But what about Google? They figured it out, so why can't we do the same thing inside the enterprise?" This is a good question that has a number of answers. First, information behavior within the enterprise tends to be very different from internet searches. In the enterprise, we are not looking for a website that might or might not contain the answer to our question, we are looking for THE document—the official HR policy, or the new document that refers to a new technique and is published by the team working on the new database rollout.

But the deeper answer is that Google, in fact, developed very clever ways of adding meaning by incorporating human judgment into their software in two ways. The first, which really did change everything, is their link/PageRank algorithm, in which relevance is defined not by the most chicken scratches that match the chicken scratch of the search but by the links within and to the document. Then, they add up all the links, which are really human judgments, that is, links are indicators of the importance of the document. They were able to improve the performance of search dramatically. And they have been building on that improvement ever since.

Of course, another clever thing about the PageRank algorithm is that what it really is returning is the most popular answer, the website that everyone else is linking to. So it's not too surprising that if you return the most popular answer, your performance will be popular.

The second way that Google is adding meaning is something that we do in enterprise search, but we simply don't have the money or the resources of Google to make it work as well. This is what we call "best bets," and Google does it by hiring thousands of editors to look at search terms in order to decide which set of documents and/or websites are the most likely answer that people are looking for.

Great, But ...

Unfortunately, within the enterprise the PageRank algorithm doesn't work. First, as mentioned, users tend to look for different things than on internet searches. But more importantly the link algorithm requires millions and millions of links to produce good results. Also, documents within the enterprise don't have the same structure as internet websites particularly in their use of links.

As far as implementing the second Google tactic, best bets, so far most enterprises have not carried this out in any systematic way. And even among search gurus, best bets tend to be seen as a kind of old-school and not very powerful. Considering that most enterprises either don't do any analysis of their search logs or only use the logs to identify the top very popular searches, it seems unlikely that they will go out and hire teams of editors to match search queries with documents. This is especially unlikely, since according to a number of studies in the US, the average number of resources assigned to search has been estimated at between 0.5 and 1.5 persons.

Instituting a powerful best bets is certainly better than another expensive round in the enterprise search dance, but it does have problems with scale. It also tends to be a limited solution in that the focus is on popular search queries, not those very difficult and esoteric searches that cost so much time.

So, why not just simply buy the Google search appliance for the enterprise? The answer is that unfortunately, its performance within the enterprise is no better than any standard plain-vanilla search engine—in other words pretty pathetic. This is primarily because the PageRank algorithm does not work in an enterprise environment, and in most installations, it is simply turned off.

The Automatic Solution

But what about some automatic, Google-like clever new search engine approach that can finally solve the poor performance of enterprise search? In other words, is there a search engine that is so good and so advanced that all you have to do is point the search engine to a collection of documents and it will analyze them, organize them into a taxonomy, and provide a great user search experience? Perhaps someday, but not today.

However, there are a number of companies that are quite willing to make that claim or similar ones. They use a variety of techniques such as NLP, semantic indexing, advanced statistical processing of document training sets, and more. The problem is that, for other than carefully chosen content and queries (used mostly for sales demos), these automatic solutions don't work.

One way to see how far automatic indexing solutions are from reality is to look at a "find similar" function of most search engines. And ask yourself: How well does this "find similar" work? And the answer is that it doesn't; although sometimes it can be a good tool for exploring content that might be related in some fashion or other, its track record for finding specific documents continues to be pretty abysmal.

Out-of-the-Box Meaning

There are some advances being made in trying to develop an out-of-the-box search functionality. While they are not quite ready to revolutionize search, they do provide an interesting and valuable capability. One example is an approach taken by the Italian text analytics and search company, Expert System. They have developed a large semantic network that not only captures relationships between terms like taxonomy but also includes the capability to apply it to documents.

A semantic network is a general technique going back to the nineteenth century philosopher Charles Pierce, which can be used to model a number of different kinds of relationships. One type is more of an ontology, such as the example shown in Figure 10.1.

Another type is a lexical semantic network, such as WordNet. A lexical semantic network is similar to a taxonomy but includes more types of relationships. It is this type of semantic network that is being used by Expert System and other companies to improve search.

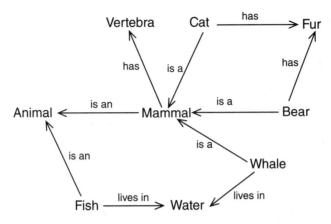

Figure 10.1   Semantic Network

Having a large, advanced semantic network as a starting point is a major advance over starting from scratch, but within the enterprise it usually can only function as a starting point. At this stage, the semantic networks that have been developed are, by necessity, a general tool that works well at a high level but does not have the specificity needed to support search within the enterprise.

For example, we were evaluating a particular semantic network for a client project and without any training or any input from us, the semantic network was able to identify documents as being about "telecommunications," which is an impressive accomplishment. However, since this company was a telecommunications company and virtually all the documents were about telecommunications, the out-of-the-box functionality was not really very useful without a significant amount of additional development. As noted however, having this out-of-the-box functionality does provide a starting point on which to build—at least in some cases.

Another approach comes from a company called Luminoso, which has developed an extremely large knowledgebase with truly advanced reasoning built in. The goal, according to CEO Catherine Havasi, is to develop a program that is capable of a basic level of common sense. As of this writing, they have achieved a kind of common sense knowledge of the world that is roughly equivalent to that of a four- to five-year-old.[2]

While this is not developed enough to really help with enterprise search, it is a very promising avenue of research, and the team at Luminoso has some very interesting case studies[3]—stay tuned!

Automatic "Solutions" Are the Problem, Not the Solution

As of today, there are no automatic solutions, despite what some companies say. In fact, this is one of the problems plaguing enterprise search—the notion that if our IT departments and programmers are clever enough, they should be able to develop an enterprise search that simply works. While this image may make life easier for salesmen trying to sell software without having to bring up all that messy language stuff and taxonomies and metadata, it has set the whole field of enterprise search back a decade. Part of the problem is you have IT-centric salesmen, selling to IT departments, speaking the same language and operating from the same assumptions—but none of them "speaks" semantics or meaning—and so the enterprise search dance continues.

In fact, putting IT in charge of enterprise search is a classic case of "the tail wagging the dog." Now I don't want you to get the idea that I'm anti-IT—some of my best friends are in IT ;-)—and in fact, I used to work in IT as a programmer developing educational software (and before that, I got started by designing and programming two computer games, but that's another story).

The issue is that—in too many organizations—there is a pronounced imbalance. IT, or information technology, has been either redefined as data technology, or instead of a healthy and productive integration of the two parts (information and technology), you have an overwhelming emphasis on one part—and it looks more like information technology.

IT is actually an essential part of a successful enterprise search system, but it's just that technology is not THE answer for improving enterprise search. One of the most successful enterprise search projects that I ever worked on was my first consulting project, which involved developing a new corporate intranet and implementing a new search engine along with a new metadata standard. The unique factor in this project was that a corporate library was given control of the intranet and search (unfortunately, this is still rare in the corporate world). In fact, in a company political battle (that as a consultant I remained happily ignorant of), someone in IT ousted the CIO, and among the many "changes for the better," the intranet was taken from the library and given to IT. And it was never the same.

What's Wrong with Enterprise Search—Other Voices

It is not just me that thinks that enterprise search is broken. For example, there is a very good article written by a company on the failures of enterprise search, called "Search Technologies: The Glass Box Approach to Enterprise Search,"[4] in which they discuss many factors behind the failure of enterprise search and recognize that lack of technology is *not* the problem. They see the problem as having more to do with the overall approach to enterprise search.

They see one basic problem as simply the growth in content—"if you double the size of the data set, it will become twice as hard for users to find what they seek." As we will discuss later, the problem is actually worse since a lot of that new content is duplicates—or near-duplicates—of existing content, which makes finding the right document even more difficult.

They cite some of the same factors that contribute to this failure of enterprise search that we've covered elsewhere, such as "the belief in plug-and-play" and the overselling of the black-box approach, which claims that their technology is so good that search will work this time. And if you believe that, have I got a bridge to sell you!

A Partial Solution—Facets and Metadata

The authors of the "Glass Box Approach" article see faceted search as the most exciting new direction for search. A conclusion that I strongly agree with—and I also agree with their statement that "All the important features of successful enterprise search systems are dependent on data quality." What they mean by *data* quality is really *metadata* quality. While faceted search is not all that new (Marti Hearst has been exploring and touting it for a couple of decades), it is still new enough to too many companies.

The solution that they offer consists of two main components—faceted search, or as they call it, search navigators—and the quality of the metadata behind that search.

This is a very good article, particularly when discussing the sorts of approaches that don't work as well as the emphasis on metadata and faceted search. However, one absolutely essential area they don't deal with is how you actually get all that good, high-quality metadata in the first place. This is where text analytics can play a critical role, but before we describe the role of text analytics, we need to take a little bit deeper look at faceted navigation, or faceted search.

Essentials of Faceted Navigation

A complete discussion of facets and faceted navigation is outside the scope of this book, but there are a number of essential characteristics to keep in mind about faceted navigation and how text analytics plays a role. Marti Hearst at UC Berkeley has probably done more to develop and promote the idea of faceted navigation than anyone, and you can see her work at the Flamenco Project,[5] or see the article I wrote in 2007.[6] Faceted navigation has become a standard for eCommerce and other product-focused websites, especially those offering multiple products, like Amazon or Home Depot. But it has not had the same impact within the enterprise—although text analytics can change all that.

Facets Are Filters

One thing to remember is that facets are essentially filters for narrowing down a search-result set. For example, you can filter by a date range, or only include certain document types or only include documents that are from a particular department. While having a set of good filters dramatically improves the usability of search interfaces, they are not some sort of automatic solution and require work on the part of users.

Facets Are Not Categories

One essential point is that facets are *not* categories. Categories are what a document is about, and even for large documents, there are a limited number of categories that you want to characterize as being what the document is about. On the other hand, facets are essentially contained within a document—and there can be any number of them.

Facets Are Orthogonal

Facets are (or should be) *orthogonal*. That is, facets should be defined to be *mutually exclusive*. It is this orthogonal nature that gives facets so much power and makes them easy to use—*an event is not a person is not a document is not a place*. If facets are defined without this orthogonal nature, they can get very confusing.

Facets Have Flavors

Facets can have a variety of structures and individual units. While this may seem like it would make them difficult to use, the reality is that it tends not to—again, as long as facets are defined properly. Facets can be structured by numerical ranges (for example, price), by location (which can be structured either geographically or from big to small units), alphabetically, or even hierarchically. In tests from Marti Hearst's research, people intuitively knew how to use the different organization schemes. After all, you would not expect locations to be organized by the year they were first discovered!

Facets Need Friends

Facets are designed to be used in combination with each other and with the subject area. The basic idea behind facets is not simply to drill down in one facet but instead make selections from a variety of facets. This is, in fact, what gives them their power and their ease-of-use. By making two or three simple choices, users are able to construct what is in essence a complex search query. We know from long, sad experience that users still do not want to construct complex search queries from scratch, but they will gladly make a few simple choices and create a query such as "wine where color equals red, price equals excessive, location equals California, and sentiment equals snotty."

Advantages of Faceted Navigation

It is these essentials which give faceted navigation its great advantages. One general advantage is that facets can be developed before the query, and then the query is used to select which elements to expose, or the whole thing can be done dynamically at search query time. Faceted navigation also has a number of specific advantages.

Facets Are Intuitive

First, facets are intuitive, that is, it's easy to guess what is behind each door—as long as they are properly designed. The key is to have a simple internal organization of the facets so that every choice is simple. Choosing price ranges or locations are choices that virtually everyone can make easily. In addition, using facets is kind of like playing 20 Questions: Is it bigger than a breadbox?—and we all know how to play 20 Questions.

Facets Are Dynamic

Second, facets allow for a dynamic selection of dimensions. You don't have to build a structure to represent all the different possible choices, but rather you can allow users to dynamically interact with the user interface. This supports multiple perspectives, backgrounds, and interests.

Facets Are Economical

Third, there are systematic advantages in using facets, the chief one being that there are fewer elements in a set of facets than there are in other types of organizations. For example, having four facets with 10 choices per facet gives you 10,000 possible combinations. Making simple choices between four facets is orders of magnitude simpler than trying to scroll down through a 10,000-node taxonomy.

Facets Are Flexible

Fourth, facets are flexible in that they can be combined with other navigation elements. The most common and powerful is often a subject matter taxonomy, but it can be combined with other elements as well.

Facet Design General Issues

There are also a number of general facet design issues that impact the use of text analytics to power faceted navigation.

Democracy and Dominance

One basic design question is, what is the right combination of facets? For example, should there be one dominant dimension, such as subject area, or should there be equal facets? Of course, dominance and equality can be expressed in different ways. A dominant facet may simply take up more screen real estate, or it may be just centrally located. Or it may be that there is a browse topics component using standard browse taxonomies, combined with filtering by facets (usually located on the periphery of the screen), and then a search box as well.

The Right Number of Facets

A related design question is the number of facets. Again, there is no single answer that can be applied, although there are certain extremes that should be avoided. But more often than not, the answer will come from usability testing with your users. Although I think we can safely say that 20 or 30 facets is way more than any regular user will ever want. And as we saw in Chapter 9, it is possible to have too few facets—the problem in that case was the imbalance between the extremely large size of the content set as well as the large and varied user population—and a very limited number of facets.

The Right Number of Entities

Another design decision is the number of entities or units that you want to expose within individual facets. The more entities, the more complex the task is to choose within each facet. Unfortunately, there is no standard number for all facets, but rather the numbers will depend on the nature of the facet as well as usability testing to reflect audience needs. For example, on one project that I'm working on as I write this, the client has a facet of construction materials that has thousands of items. In that case, the solution is to organize the materials into a taxonomy based on their materials catalogs—one that would be very difficult for a novice to transverse but child's play for the experienced users that the application is designed to support.

Tools, Not Models

There is also a question of the type of facets. Again, as we saw in Chapter 9 on development best practices, using facets that had more to do with business processes than the information needs and behaviors within those processes can lead to a bad set of facets. In other words, facets should not be used to create a model of the business itself, rather they are tools to help find information while carrying out those business processes.

The Simple Life

An additional design decision has to do with the question of internal structure of the facet—here we know from experience that the simpler the internal structure, the easier it is to use facets.

A Different Type of Relevance

Lastly, there is a critical design decision in which text analytics plays an important role which is related to the entire concept of relevance ranking. In this case, rather than trying to rank the relevance of particular documents against a search query, the relevance ranking is used to determine the threshold for extracting entities from documents. For example, if one facet is "people," and the document set consists of relatively large, relatively academic content, then you very likely would not want to expose every single mention of every person in every document.

Rather, there should be a threshold and relevance score to only expose significant mentions of people. For example, if a document has a significant number of footnotes that cite other works it is likely that you would not want to list every person mentioned in every footnote in a 100-page document. Setting these kinds of thresholds can be done with a variety of rules, for example, ignore footnotes or count them more heavily depending on the content. It can also be done with standard relevance ranking by counting of the number of mentions and other categorization like rules, such as counting names in titles and other important sections of the documents more highly.

Text Analytics and Faceted Navigation

While faceted navigation has become the new standard model for eCommerce and product-focused websites, the story inside the enterprise is very different. The most common situations in the enterprise are either no facets or a very simple set—"date," "people," and "organizations." The latter two are mainly the result of search engines incorporating basic "people" and "organization" catalogs.

The success of faceted navigation in eCommerce sites is due to one major factor—they are starting with rich catalogs of products and their features. These catalogs provided both the basic facet design and the necessary metadata to feed the facets. As noted, facets work best with a rich enough set of mutually exclusive facets.

It's hard to get examples of enterprise implementations (firewalls and all), but you can get an idea of the difference by comparing general news websites that use facets (but don't have a catalog), and one of the early implementations of facets done by Marti Hearst (using a catalog of the Getty art collection), shown in Figure 10.2.

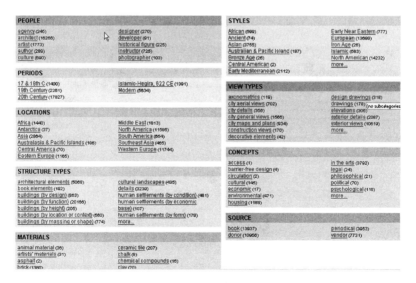

Figure 10.2   Faceted Navigation—Getty

This rich set of facets enables the user to interact with the collection with an almost unlimited number of combinations—and all these combinations mean very precise results. The news site pictured in Figure 10.3, on the other hand, while it has more facets than most, doesn't come close to the number found in a catalog-driven site.

The reason for the difference is, of course, that news sites are based on unstructured information rather than a data catalog. And the situation is even worse for enterprise information.

This raises two questions: Can enterprise search make an effective use of faceted navigation and thus produce a superior search experience? And if not, why have I spent so much time talking about faceted navigation?

As you might guess, the answer to the first question is *yes*—although it is a qualified yes. It is qualified, because while I don't have complete figures on the success of faceted navigation within the enterprise, my sense (and experience) is that it is not making a big impact—yet. However, there is a way to make it work and transform enterprise search from its current sad state to something that actually works—text analytics!

And the answer to the second question is twofold. First, it is important to remember that faceted navigation needs to be designed and developed carefully, especially for unstructured enterprise information. Second, the key component for getting faceted navigation for enterprise information to really work is using text analytics.

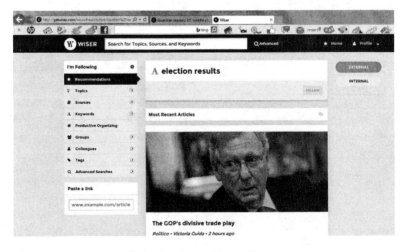

Figure 10.3   Faceted Navigation—News Site

What catalogs provide is the necessary structure to build rich, faceted navigation. Unfortunately, there are no catalogs for enterprise information, but the equivalent can be produced. What catalogs provide is essentially metadata—dates, location, multiple types of products, etc. And good faceted navigation requires a lot of metadata—something that has restricted its use within the enterprise.

And this is how text analytics can rescue search—text analytics is the best way to generate the large amount of metadata necessary for good faceted navigation.

Text analytics can be used to develop good faceted navigation and search systems in a variety of ways but particularly in two ways. First, it can provide a cost-effective way to generate all that metadata and enhance the quality of the metadata. Second, even though having a number of facets with which to filter search results is a great advance, there still needs to be a good solution to the fairest facet of all: "subject."

Metadata Is the Answer?

Actually we've known for many years that adding metadata to unstructured content is one way in which enterprise search can work—if it is actually done and done well. The problem is that most metadata that's been added to content hasn't really helped in terms of findability. Establishing the Dublin Core[7] as an enterprise metadata standard has been touted as one way to enhance search, but the reality is the Dublin Core has been more useful for archiving and indexing content than for improving search.

Other than using "title" and "author" to help find documents, most of the Dublin Core is not used for search. The one field, "subject," is *the* field/tag that should be used to enhance search, but performance is limited by two factors.

One factor is, if the "subject" field is filled with simple keywords generated by authors, the results are very poor. The problem is that keywords don't scale—they work well for small pilots or situations where you have a small number of documents, but once you try to grow the collection of keywords, they become almost as complex as the documents themselves.

People tried a number of things to improve the performance of keywords, including Thomas Vander Wal's folksonomies,[8] but an organically grown collection of keywords, even if authors are willing to spend the time to improve that collection, ends up being way too disorganized to find information at the specific levels needed in the enterprise. And folksonomies in SharePoint 2010 are not *really* folksonomies—they lack the key components of a community of authors all tagging together and improving through their interactions. So, the SharePoint 2010 folksono-mies are just collections of keywords.

The other factor—and the alternative for the "subject" tag—is to use a taxonomy. This is something that a lot of us, including my company, tried for a number of years, and while I think we improved things and man-aged to develop some very beautiful (to us language geeks) taxonomies, there are two big issues with a taxonomy-based solution. First, it takes a lot of effort to develop good taxonomies, and almost as much effort to continually refine them to keep them current. This was particularly true in the early days when taxonomies were built by librarians who were used to creating (and using) very large taxonomies or library catalogs.

Developing smaller subject taxonomies that work with other facets helps somewhat, but regardless of the size of the taxonomy, there is still the second issue—there is a fundamental gap between the taxonomies and the collection of documents. In other words, trying to apply a taxonomy to a collection of documents is a very complex and time-consuming task—and the results are often not very good.

SharePoint 2010—Part of the Solution

Microsoft did a great job with SharePoint 2010—in particular by add-ing taxonomy support and metadata tagging, which is a big step in the right direction. Integrating SharePoint 2010 with the FAST search engine is also a good step towards creating the type of semantic infrastructure platform that we will discuss in Part 5: Enterprise Text Analytics as a Platform. However, this platform is still missing a very critical piece—a text analytics piece.

What Microsoft, as a software company, did was provide the technical integration needed for a semantic infrastructure platform, but their han-dling of the dimension of meaning is severely lacking. What they've done is to create a platform with the ability to add taxonomies and keyword tag-ging but without really supporting the key issues involved in either.

For example, on page 108 of the book, *How to Do Everything: Microsoft SharePoint 2010,*[10] there is this description:

> There are two types of taxonomy available in SharePoint server 2010:
>
> - *Managed.* This is a centrally managed and controlled tagging system. The benefit is that the tags can be guaranteed to fit into a rigid taxonomy. However, this

type of system needs to be properly planned and built before users can start applying tags.

- *Social tagging (a.k.a. folksonomy)*. This is a loose system that can lead to varied results. On the positive side, people are free to use a taxonomy that makes sense to them, and because people define their own terms, they may find items easier. However, issues are likely to arise where slightly different terms are used to tag items that really should all have the same tags.

For anyone who has dealt with the development and application of taxonomies for enterprise search, this statement is a nightmare of misunderstandings—of both the nature of taxonomies and the issues involved in using them to enhance search. It doesn't take a rigid taxonomy geek to shudder at the characterization of social tagging or keyword tagging as a taxonomy. Sticking an "-onomy" at the end of a word does not mean it suddenly has an organizational structure.

The lack of understanding of the nature of the taxonomy is seen in other parts of the same chapter, including the characterization of an "open taxonomy" as a folksonomy. It seems pretty clear that the term "open taxonomy" is a contradiction in terms. The confusion, as well as an underlying attitude towards structure, is also seen in page 116 of *How to Do Everything:* "I've heard people wonder aloud whether anyone but a library scientist or a taxonomist will complain."

This was in response to why Microsoft didn't try to add ontologies (misusing and misunderstanding word "ontology"). As a recovering taxonomist, yes, I will complain—and so will anyone who really wants to use taxonomies and tagging to improve search. I'm afraid that with this attitude, the real complaints will come from users who still won't be able to find anything.

Following this misunderstanding is one that's even worse: "Managed keywords (or just "keywords") are used for user-focused tagging ... this type of open tagging is called a "folksonomy" because it's created by people instead of laid out by the organization." I'm afraid this also misuses the term "folksonomy." Folksonomies are more than just simply a collection of keywords and I find the equivalence of keywords and managed keywords to be very telling.

Folksonomies, in the original concept anyway, referred to a process where users would work together to improve each other's tags. It's not a concept that ever actually went very far, so maybe it doesn't matter if we call keywords folksonomies. And the last time I checked, organizations consist mostly of people, but the people-versus-organizations mindset is a telling one here as well.

The real problem is not those geeky librarians with their abstract complaints, but rather that keywords, managed keywords, folksonomies, open taxonomies, and so on do very little—if anything—to improve the quality of search.

The last complaint I have about the way that SharePoint 2010 instituted tagging is that it's more of an afterthought (tagging and notes field and/or in the properties sheet) than a process that is well integrated into their publishing workflow.

The good news is that a number of text analytics companies have developed a more in-depth integration of text analytics and SharePoint 2010.

If it sounds like I'm being too hard on IT and SharePoint 2010, it's because I'm truly amazed that people with a background in software development and/or programming feel comfortable making pronouncements about something, in this case, taxonomies and metadata, that they clearly have had no experience with. So, please, if I start writing about the best approach for developing Java code or the latest software design ideas— ignore everything that I say!

OK, end of rant. And I have to say that the rest of the book is very good, and provides a lot of guidance for learning SharePoint 2010.

Text Analytics to the Rescue

So if keywords/folksonomies don't really work, and taxonomies are too expensive and too rigid (not really sure about that last point), then what *is* the solution?

The basic answer is that by integrating text analytics with content management and/or SharePoint 2010/2013 and a search engine, a high-quality and economical solution can be developed. This can be done in a number of ways—one answer is using text analytics to develop better and smaller taxonomies, and the second answer can be found in that wonderful London Underground sign and warning: Mind the Gap.

The Fairest Facet of Them All—Subject

"Subject" is still the one thing that people know that they are looking for more than any other metadata or facet value. And it is still the most difficult to develop. In my experience, the only feasible way of getting good value out of a "subject" facet is with that element that the SharePoint 2010 author seems to have a great deal of difficulty with—a taxonomy. Free-form keywords simply don't work very well, but that does not mean that organizations are condemned to hiring teams of taxonomists to develop and maintain multithousand-node taxonomies.

Simple and Faceted Taxonomies

First of all, if text analytics is used to generate faceted metadata and to help categorize documents, then the need for a giant enterprise taxonomy is largely eliminated. One implication—or side effect—of having a faceted navigation capability is that the taxonomy no longer needs to do most or all of the organizational work to enable people to find their documents. Instead of browsing down a gigantic complex taxonomy to find your documents, faceted navigation enables users to make a few simple choices instead.

Also, if the taxonomy is developed with faceted navigation in mind, it can be designed as a number of facets rather than a large single taxonomy. For example, in the case of the engineering and consulting use case we discussed in Chapter 9, what we did was to realize that there were a number of facets that cut across a number of different subject areas and could be pulled out and made their own facet—these included "methods," "facilities," and "material." This made the taxonomy easier to develop and much easier to use.

Semiautomatic Taxonomies

The second way text analytics can help is to reduce the cost and effort in developing a taxonomy by doing so semiautomatically. Text analytics—specifically text mining—can be used to analyze the documents to which the taxonomy will be applied. One simple method is to use the text mining capability to pull out the most frequent terms within different subsets of documents. Human taxonomists can then quickly scan those lists for concepts that are particularly important for the taxonomy.

We used this method on a project for a highly technical taxonomy that had been developed 10 years before, but had not been maintained. To update the taxonomy, we explored all the documents that had been published since the last update of the taxonomy. The primary focus was on documents that didn't fit into the old taxonomy. Another focus was categories that witnessed a great deal of new activity, including new technologies and approaches.

In addition to simple text mining approaches, it is also possible to apply simple categorization rules to focus the text mining on more specific areas.

As is often the case with text analytics, an iterative and hybrid approach is best. For example, a librarian and/or subject matter experts could select documents that represented new topics that were not in the old taxonomy. The software would then analyze those documents and use the categorization rules to find other related documents. Then, the software can analyze those documents for the most frequent terms and present those to the librarians/taxonomists.

This process is typically enhanced with the use of the text analytics clustering capability, where the software can find clusters of co-occurring terms and present those as candidate taxonomy concepts, or nodes. It is important to remember that these clusters are suggestions that need to be evaluated by human taxonomists—despite the advances being made in so-called automatic taxonomies. It only takes a couple of experiments to realize that an "automatic" taxonomy is good for two things—exploratory suggestions and a great mechanism for raising the spirits of tired taxonomists with some truly hilarious nonsensical clusters.

The net result of applying this variety of text analytics techniques was a relatively short and inexpensive process to update a highly volatile taxonomy. In addition, the quality of the taxonomy that came out of this process is often considerably better than what can be done with a simple human taxonomist's effort.

Mind the Gap

Even with smaller and more modular taxonomies, better taxonomies, and easier, cheaper ways to develop taxonomies, the really fundamental problem with taxonomies is that there is a giant gap between the taxonomy and the documents to which it needs to be applied.

There are a number of ways that people have tried to bridge the gap, but none of them have been particularly successful. Basically, tagging documents with a taxonomy is difficult and expensive, regardless of the solution that you try. The two basic approaches are to use a staff of information professionals (librarians or editors), or distributed authors/subject matter experts.

Librarians have one big advantage, which is that they tend to take an enterprise-level perspective, whereas individual subject matter experts tend to focus on their own field. Librarians also have a great deal of experience with categorization and information organization in general. Authors, on the other hand, know their own area better than librarians tend to, and they are a distributed resource.

Using a small group of librarians or editors creates a very narrow bottleneck through which all documents have to pass. This works fine if you have a small number of very high-value documents. The problem is that people want to use taxonomies to tag all the documents in an organization, and in that case the cost becomes prohibitive. In addition, librarians may very well be experts in categorization but not necessarily experts in the particular subject area. Or, it may be that they don't understand the business processes to the kind of depth that you need to get really good tagging—the kind of tagging that actually helps users find information.

On the other hand, authors are experts in their subject matter—and usually also the business processes—but they're very often terrible at categorization. The problems of asking authors to tag documents are very well known and continue to plague organizations. The first issue is inconsistency between different authors—and even with the same author. Different authors will very often tag the same document with very different tags, depending on their own perspective and/or their own experience. In fact, it's been shown that a single author will tag the same document differently, depending on what they been exposed to between the first tag and the second. This is a concept called "intertwingleness."[10]

In addition, choosing tags from a complex taxonomy is a very difficult and complex task, which is rarely done well if the authors have not had training specifically for categorization. Being an expert in something does not mean that you're also an expert in categorizing that document for someone else's use, particularly someone who is not an expert. This is an entirely different skill that most authors don't have.

Finally, authors have shown a great deal of resistance to tagging—either passive resistance or active resistance. Authors can be very creative in finding ways to avoid having to tag documents, even if it is the official governance policy that "thou shalt tag!" (their answer is usually they shalt *not* tag.) Or the resistance may be passive, with the well-known story/strategy of an author tagging documents with three or four keywords in their first month on the job and then tagging every single document they ever write for the next 10 years with those same three keywords—because it's much easier to do that than try to actually think up what words actually can be used to find this document.

A Hybrid Solution

There is a solution, but it is not what some software companies in the text analytics space will tell you (which is just buy their software, point it at your content, and it will automatically categorize all their documents, automatically create a new taxonomy, automatically wash your dishes, automatically clear up your acne, and so on). If the salesperson comes to your organization and tells you this or any variant, run screaming from the room as fast as you can—there is no such thing as a fully automatic solution.

So how do we "mind the gap," in other words, how do we solve the gap between taxonomies and documents? The answer: We use an automatic–human hybrid tagging strategy employing text analytics.

There are a great many ways to implement a hybrid tagging strategy, and most organizations will likely develop more than one model. A manual-automatic hybrid is really a spectrum running from attempts at fully automatic to fully manual human tagging, with both ends of the spectrum being something to mostly avoid, except in special cases.

The basics of a hybrid solution are fairly straightforward, even if there are a variety of implementation strategies. For example, it may make sense to have different strategies for different types of documents. For very high-value documents, it may make sense to go all out with a full hybrid solution, but for other documents, it may make sense to go much more automatic.

We can distinguish three basic cases (with lots of variants) that call for different strategies:

- New internal content: new internal documents that are being published in a content management system
- Mass tagging: large collections of existing documents that need to be integrated into a content repository that might include both internal and external documents
- Dynamic tagging: external documents that are only processed at search time

New Documents in a Content Management System / SharePoint

This is probably the best situation and one in which a hybrid solution is particularly powerful. The basic model is this:

- An author writes a document and submits it to the content management system, which performs its usual workflow processing of that document.

- Then, a text analytics component (which can be fully integrated into the content management software or can simply be called by it) takes the document and processes it. The text analytics component analyzes the document and categorizes it as primarily about topic A, with perhaps some secondary topics as well. In addition, it pulls out a range of metadata elements using a combination of rules and entity extraction to populate metadata fields, such as "people," "organizations," or other facets.

- The software then presents the results of this analysis to the author, who can quickly scan the categorization and metadata suggestions made by the text analytics software and respond by either simply approving the results, or in some cases, changing some of the suggested values.

- This fully tagged document then gets published in the content management system and is ready for the search engine to take advantage of all the additional tags and structure.

There are a number of advantages to this hybrid model. The first is, instead of asking authors to make a very cognitively difficult set of decisions about the categorization of the document (and at the same time avoid the tedium of pulling out and populating additional metadata fields), authors are presented with a much simpler cognitive task, which is to react to the suggested categorization and metadata. This is something that is much easier to get authors to do than asking them to add all this metadata themselves.

It also produces much more consistent categorization and metadata. Until we get full AI, humans will continue to be much better at categorization—better in every way, except for that little matter of consistency. Therefore, a hybrid system taking advantage of the intelligence of the human and the consistency of text analytics categorization gives organizations the best of both worlds.

But even with this much simpler task there will be situations where authors just automatically say *yes* to the suggested metadata. This is not ideal, but there is at least the advantage of automatic tagging, which, if the system is set up right, will be getting better and better as the system is used more and more.

There might even be a side benefit in which authors get additional training in what constitutes good metadata by being exposed to good categorization and consistent metadata. On the other hand, in the case where the categorization isn't that good, another advantage is that by giving authors the opportunity to change values, this can be used to provide feedback that can in turn be used to improve categorization rules and metadata extraction.

Mass Tagging

Mass tagging is a variation of this hybrid model when there is a large number of legacy documents that need to be tagged. In this case, a small team of librarians, editors, or SMEs can use this same hybrid model to quickly go through tens of thousands of documents in a very short time. This is a situation where it would make sense to analyze the documents and distinguish the high-value documents that need a full metadata set from the lower-value documents that might only get a "subject" tag.

Closely related to the case of legacy documents are documents that are external to the organization, but need to be integrated with internal content. This situation may also arise when there is no content management system but simply large content repositories consisting of internal content, external content, or both. In this case, depending on the size and complexity of the content, it might make sense to use the same model of a small number of librarians or editors, or it may make sense to distribute the task among larger numbers of subject matter experts.

The important point is that without the text analytics components analyzing the documents and making metadata suggestions, the amount of effort required to tag large collections of documents is simply too large for most organizations. In addition, as noted, the quality of the metadata in most of those cases is usually very poor.

Dynamic Tagging

The third case, dynamic tagging, is where the documents will never end up in a content repository or content management system. This situation might include Twitter posts or other small text documents, like customer support notes, email, or large internet content sets. In this case, a potential solution would be to incorporate text analytics capabilities directly into the search engine to dynamically categorize and tag search results sets.

In this case the only solution is automatic tagging, which will give much less accurate results, but with very little human effort—at tagging time. The effort will primarily be by text analysts, taxonomists, and SMEs prior to tagging time. In other words, this type of automatic categorization and metadata generation will require the development of very advanced and sophisticated categorization and extraction rules.

One advantage of building these advanced rules is that they can also be used by the search engine to produce much better relevance ranking based not just on simple frequency counts or simple location rules (such as *words in the title count more*), but on much more sophisticated categorization and extraction rules (see Chapter 7 for more details).

In one sense, this case is really a matter of developing a search engine that can compete with commercially available search engines which considering the success of internet search engines like Google and Bing will only make sense in very specific situations. The more esoteric the content and vocabulary in the content, the more likely this solution will make sense. Also, if the types of searches are very formal and/or highly restricted, then it might make sense to put the effort into developing a custom-search capability.

Flocks of Facets

To fill the fairest facet of all—"subject"—full categorization capabilities and taxonomies are required. For all the other facets, the task is much simpler, although even here categorization has a part to play. To fill facets such as "people," "organization," or more specialized ones like "methods" or "materials," the basic text analytics capability that is used is noun phrase or entity extraction.

As we saw in Chapter 7, entity extraction is done primarily with dictionaries of entities and their various spellings for known entity extraction—or with rules to find unnamed entities. Entity extraction can be applied to an almost unlimited number of types of entities, or in our current focus, facets. Another advantage of entity extraction for filling facets is that it can be done both prior to search and at search results time.

This relative ease-of-use is one reason why this area has taken off faster than other text analytics capabilities. It is also why a large number of companies decided to focus almost exclusively on entity extraction. This makes a great deal of business sense, but it does have one serious flaw—you need an auto-categorization capability in order to deal with the whole issue of disambiguation.

For example, as discussed in Chapter 7, being able to recognize the word "Ford" is only a start. The question is, is it Ford the person, Ford the car, Ford the company, or describing a way to cross the stream? Disambiguating these different meanings requires the ability to look at the context around those words and determine if the sentence or paragraph contains car words, people words, company words, or perhaps nature hike words. Even this is often not enough as you have to develop more sophisticated rules to handle the situation where a sentence may be talking about the car but is surrounded by company words.

So while it is relatively easy to get moderately accurate results with just straight entity extraction, getting much better results requires a combination of categorization-type rules along with entity extraction rules. Another issue is setting thresholds to only extract entities that are significant, rather than extracting every entity in every document.

Tag Clouds

In addition to extracting metadata out of the documents and applying the taxonomy to those documents with good categorization rules, another feature that is often added to good faceted navigation is tag clouds or clusters of keywords that the software finds dynamically at the time of the search. These clusters or tag clouds are useful tools for the discovery and exploration of new information—even if they are not particularly useful for finding specific documents.

For example, tag clouds represent the frequency of words in the document or set of documents, as shown in Figure 10.4.

Closing the Loop—Feedback

I find it ironic that the two elements of search that offer the most promise for improving the quality of search—text analytics and feedback—are also the most neglected. With text analytics itself, hopefully that neglect is

Figure 10.4   Tag Cloud

beginning to end. As for putting energy and effort into getting really good feedback on the quality of your search and search results, it still amazes me that so many organizations will spend hundreds of thousands of dollars on search technology, then neglect to hire one part-time person to track usage and get feedback from the users of that technology.

Even when organizations do get feedback, it too often consists primarily of a search results analysis that identifies the top 10 most popular searches. And they think that adding depth to this analysis is primarily a matter of extending the top 10 to perhaps the top 100 or 1,000.

There is a great deal that can and should be done in terms of search results analysis that can dramatically improve search performance independently of text analytics, but text analytics adds a level of analysis and intelligence and automation (or at least semiautomation) to the process.

Actually, text analytics can provide a means for getting feedback even before the search experience. As we mentioned above, the first opportunity for feedback about the elements that go into search that make it better, that is, taxonomies and metadata, can be gathered at publication time if an organization uses a hybrid model, as described above.

As authors look at the results of text analytics' categorization of their document and extracting metadata to fill all those facets, they can provide direct feedback on the quality of that categorization and extracted metadata, which can then be used to improve the rules. Authors can not only pinpoint problem areas in the taxonomy or categorization rules or metadata extraction rules, but they can also provide suggestions that can be incorporated into any improvements.

It is also possible to design search results screen such that users can also provide feedback directly into the quality of the categorization and faceted metadata. This is much trickier to design well, but can take advantage of the reactions of large numbers of users. The feedback tends to be much broader and more difficult to interpret, but there is so much of it that it still makes sense to incorporate it into any search results screen.

The last way that text analytics can enhance feedback is with search log analysis. Search logs are essentially inverted indexes of the most common search queries. As noted, most search log analysis consists of reports on the top 10, 100, or a 1,000 search queries, with perhaps some additional work to group alternate spellings and even synonyms. Smart companies will at least use these popularity reports to develop best bets. Unfortunately—and too often—companies will simply track their most frequent queries and not do anything with the information besides generate some pretty and mostly worthless reports.

With the addition of text analytics, however, it is possible to cluster and categorize those search queries against a taxonomy and thus gain a level of analytical intelligence. Knowing that a list of words represents the 10 most frequent queries can be somewhat useful, but knowing how the 10,000 most frequent queries map into each area of the taxonomy can provide a level of detail that is orders of magnitude more useful.

Beyond Documents

So far we've been talking about the categorization of documents and/or extracting entities from documents. Since we are very often looking for specific documents, this is a natural approach for a search application. However, just as we saw in the case of social media analysis, documents are sometimes not the best unit to focus on. For search, text analytics can be applied to both larger and smaller units—corpus of documents and sections of documents. What this involves is basically categorization and/ or analysis by corpus, by page, by section—or even sentences and phrases.

Think Big: Corpus

A *corpus of documents* can be defined by such characteristics as the publisher (HR, IT, marketing), by function (training, research, policy), by subject (top levels of a taxonomy), or even dynamically as the entire set of documents returned in a search results set. Corpus of documents can differ in a variety of ways—and by using text analytics, we can use those differences to improve search.

Vocabulary

The simplest difference is *vocabulary*. Documents published by HR will have very different vocabularies than those published by IT. In some cases, the differences will simply be reflected in a taxonomy and/or categorization rules, but in other cases, the two groups will use the same word to mean different things. Some of these differences can be handled by contextual rules like the "pipeline" example, that is, look to see if HR or IT words show up in the same sentence or paragraph.

However, some differences may be more subtle. For example, you might have a resume for an IT position that has lots of both IT and HR vocabularies. Using a text analytics characterization of a mix of IT and HR and resume-type vocabularies could support treating documents differently, such as identifying resume documents and putting them in a facet. This would improve the results for both the user looking for IT resumes (so the results list would not include a lot of technical IT documents) and for the IT user looking just for those technical documents by removing the HR resume documents.

Characterizing the overall vocabulary of different document corpus can be done with both categorization type rules and/or with statistical patterns. Probably the best results would be the integration of both rules and patterns—integration usually is.

This technique can also be used to develop a variety of other applications in addition to search. We will look at some of these applications in the next chapter.

Size

Another characteristic of corpus of documents is their *size,* which in some cases, can be handled on a document level and in other cases, on a corpus level. A number of search relevance-ranking methods already takes size into account, and with text analytics, you can add more explicit and sophisticated handling.

For example, one corpus might be our standard set of PDF documents that average around 200 pages and are intended for the general public. These documents will require very different handling from a corpus of Twitter posts and/or customer support notes having an average length of a couple of sentences.

Generality and Complexity

Another interesting approach is to use text mining techniques to add new ways of looking at the characteristics of documents or document sets, such as the *level of generality* of the terms or concepts within that document or corpus. The levels of generality of the corpus of documents is something that should be reflected in the nature of a taxonomy that is applied to that document corpus. In addition, the level of generality of concepts can and should influence the type of categorization rules that are built.

One way that search might use the generality level of documents is to simply make generality a facet and allow the user to select a level of specificity that they are interested in—the novice more likely to find what they are looking for in general documents and the expert more likely interested in more specific documents.

A related concept is the *textual complexity* of a document or corpus. A textual complexity score would include things like the average length of words, sentences (and number of clauses), paragraphs, and the number of clauses. This score could be used with a generality score, or on its own.

Small Is Beautiful: Sections and Less

Even though different documents by different authors might use different words to define sections within a documents, there are often enough similarities in how people define sections and the roles that those sections play in the structure of the document to develop systematic rules to help understand what documents are about.

As we discussed earlier, when looking at documents, it's important to remember that so-called unstructured documents are not really unstructured. Rather, they have a variety of structures, some well-formed and others barely hinted at. But these kinds of structures are exactly what humans use in forming judgments about the content of documents. And so one use of text analytics looks below the level of the document and develops rules that can capture this structure, for example, segmenting a document into sections.

As the example in Chapter 7 described, for one project we developed categorization-like rules that could first be used to define what constituted a section in a document, and then incorporated those sections into the rules that influenced the overall relevance ranking of words in the document.

The screen in Figure 10.5 shows an early version of the rule that looked for sections that function as an abstract—even if they were not labeled as such. In

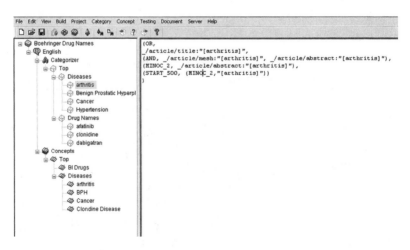

Figure 10.5   Section Categorization Rule

essence, these sections functioned as a kind of metasection in that they would typically either summarize the overall documents and/or describe certain key elements of the document, such as methods. The rule looked like this:

```
(START_2000, (AND,
(OR, _/article:"[Abstract]", _/
   article:"[Methods]"),
(OR, _/article:"clinical trial*", _/
   article:"humans",
(NOT,
(DIST_5,
(OR,_/article:"approved", _/article:"use", _/
   article:"animals"),
```

What this rule basically says is that if this article has sections—like abstract or methods within the first 2,000 words—and within those sections, there are words that refer to clinical trials or included words associated with humans, then count it as a hit and give it a very high relevancy score—UNLESS those sections had words that indicated that it dealt with animals, or that it dealt primarily with the description of the drug as approved, safe, or how it was used.

These are the kind of sophisticated rules that can be built relatively easily and that greatly enhance the ability to both discover structure within so-called unstructured content and to incorporate those structures into rules. In this particular case, we were able to achieve nearly 100% accuracy characterizing whether these documents dealt with human clinical trials of specific drugs. This is the level of sophistication that you need to enable search to work and make search work as a platform for a whole new generation of applications.

Another use of the ability of text analytics to capture sections of documents is that entire documents are very rarely about only one major concept. Just looking at the document level, this is usually handled by listing the top two or three concepts with some minor concepts, but if we look below the level of the document, you may find that it makes sense to categorize individual sections. How this will show up in the search results lists is something that we can speculate about and/or experiment with. For example, instead of a link to a document in response to a search query, we could return a link to the most relevant sections of the document. Alternatively, we could generate a relevance score for each section and combine them based on different weights per section.

Another possibility would be to develop a document viewer that, instead of simply showing the full text of the document, could show a summary that consisted of a title, an overall subject, a series of sections of the document, and major entities. For each section, it could show the primary subject and secondary subjects for each section. It could also show the major entities of each section. Each section could have its own set of facets.

Related to the idea of sections is capturing and combining important pieces of information as a single, complex entity. This could be used to extract that information or it could be used to influence relevance ranking—especially if it were combined with a section relevancy rank. An example of these types of complex entities can be seen in the Figure 10.6 screen.

In this example, we were extracting a wide range of complex data, which could then be used for multiple applications. Some of that data included the area of a building, how many stories it had, how many stories were underground, and so on. The rule to the right states that if you see

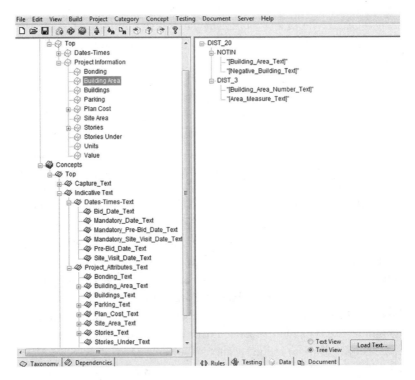

Figure 10.6   Complex Entity Rule

text that tells you it has to do with an area of a building—with the actual number following within three words (to accommodate different writing styles)—but not within a phrase, that indicated it was part of a different type of description.

What we were doing was capturing complex data in unstructured text—a kind of superentity extraction. An even more advanced capture would be to capture the name of a person in one section, then find and extract that person's salary from another section, and finally, find their address in an appendix. And once the data was captured, it could be integrated into any kind of data analysis application.

The next stage would be to use this analysis to return not a link but the answer to a query, but that is for the future—or is it?

Wait a Minute—Isn't That Overkill?

OK, this might sound like a lot of effort, and a lot of money, and involve a lot of unfamiliar things, like taxonomies and auto-categorization (and for which no expertise exists in your enterprise), and…I guess that's what's meant by overkill. This is especially true for smaller organizations, where the idea for enterprise search is to grab some cheap or free search engine and fire it up, index some documents, and go for it.

To be honest, the answer is that not all organizations are prime targets for this text analytics based approach. However, the surprising thing is how many organizations could benefit—in large part because there are all sorts of options to cut costs and effort while getting expert help.

The answer to the objection that this is too expensive is the easiest one to make. First, take a look at the numbers in Chapter 3—having a search that works only 30% better than your current one can save your organization over $6 million a year per 1,000 employees. So even for a company of 100 employees, that's still $600,000 a year to fund search—including buying and implementing some text analytics software—and still come out ahead.

Also, there are a lot of lower-cost text analytics options available. But don't go so low that you don't get the functionality needed to do good categorization and extraction.

Regarding the objection that your organization doesn't have a librarian or text analyst, or someone with language or categorization experience, and that hiring someone is expensive, the answer is also easy—just hire my company to get you started and train your people in how to build on the initial foundation!

OK, I'm somewhat kidding, but the reality is that there are options here as well. There are a number of consulting companies that can provide the needed expertise, ranging from single consultants to large, professional consulting firms. In addition, many—if not most—text analytics vendors have some professional services resources, or can point you to those resources.

Lastly, it is important to remember that once you have established the kind of text analytics foundation needed to implement this type of advanced search, you now have the foundation to develop a whole range of search-based or text analytics–based applications (more on those applications in the next chapter). These applications can be developed for little additional cost while providing enormous benefits in all kinds of ways, from e-Discovery, to legal review, to social media applications—and even to something you haven't thought of yet.

For a better approach, however, take a look at the last part of the book, where we discuss how to establish a text analytics capability within your organization.

Summary

To sum it up, enterprise search has been pretty pathetic for a very long time. It seems to me that it is past time to try a new approach to making it work—and text analytics is the essential component of that new approach. Pursuing a technology-only solution will never work (until we get full AI ... and maybe not even then) because search engines deal in chicken scratches, not meaning.

There is no "Google for the enterprise," so the various attempts to add general intelligence for searching through the development of semantic networks or knowledge bases—while fascinating and a step in the right direction—don't work in the enterprise environment and its specialized, very specific vocabularies without significant customization.

Another step in the right direction is faceted navigation and the addition of more and more metadata to add more structure to our unstructured documents. This comes with two caveats—first, it is important to do faceted navigation well and with the right designs, based on content and understanding the user's needs. We've been getting good at that in some environments but not so much within the enterprise. The second caveat is that most organizations don't have a good strategy for how to add all the metadata needed to make faceted navigation work effectively. This is particularly true for that most difficult of metadata—the subject of a document.

With its support for taxonomies and folksonomies, SharePoint 2010 looks like a step in the right direction—but it fails on two key points. First, folksonomies don't really help much, particularly as implemented in SharePoint where they are just a fancy word for author-generated metadata—something that has failed to significantly improve search for a long time. Second, while it is a good thing to support taxonomies, it would be much better if SharePoint supported the development of taxonomies, and even more importantly, had some way to bridge the gap between taxonomies and documents.

The best solution? Use text analytics initially to help develop dynamic and faceted taxonomies, then follow up by using a variety of text analytics–based methods to 1) generate the large amount of metadata that faceted navigation needs, and 2) apply the subject taxonomies to all enterprise documents. Text analytics can be used to tag documents in a variety of ways, from fully automatic tagging (legacy untagged documents or external documents) to a hybrid model of the software suggesting tags, and on to human authors in a content management system. These methods lead to both a more economical tagging process and higher-quality metadata tags.

In addition to semiautomatic tagging, text analytics can be used to add a whole new level of intelligence to search, with such techniques as using corpus-level metadata, adding additional levels of structure to unstructured text (via techniques like dynamically capturing section information), and extracting more complex data that can be used to do everything from enhance relevance ranking to finding specific answers within the documents—not just returning a list of links to documents.

Finally, once enterprise search is established on a text analytics foundation, there is an enormous added benefit. The text analytics foundation that enables a smart search can also be used to create an ever-growing number of smarter and smarter search-based/text analytics–based applications. We will explore that world of smart applications, or InfoApps, in the next chapter.

Endnotes

1. "Mind the Search Gap." MindMetre Research & Smartlogic, 2011.

2. Havasi, Catherine. "Who's Doing Common-Sense Reasoning and Why It Matters." TechCrunch. August 9, 2014. www.techcrunch.com/2014/08/09/guide-to-common-sense-reasoning-whos-doing-it-and-why-it-matters/.

3. Please see www.luminoso.com/resources/ for webinars and case studies.

4. "The Glass Box Approach to Enterprise Search." Searchtechnologies.com, 2015, accessed December 30, 2015. www.searchtechnologies.com/public/GlassBox.pdf.

5. Please access the Flamenco Project at flamenco.berkeley.edu/index.html. (Note: It appears that there has not been much publishing activity since 2009, which may be indicative of how faceted navigation is somewhat stalled and/or there's not a lot of new input into the theory and design of facets.)

6. Reamy, Tom. "Facets for Enterprise Content." Kapsgroup.com. 2007. www.kapsgroup .com/presentations/Facets for Enterprise Content.doc.

7. "DCMI Home: Dublin Core® Metadata Initiative (DCMI)." Dublincore.org, 2015.

8. Vander Wal, Thomas. "Folksonomy." Vanderwal.net. 2007. www.vanderwal.net/ folksonomy.html.

9. Cawood, Stephen. *How to Do Everything: Microsoft SharePoint 2010*. New York: McGraw-Hill Osborne Media, 2010.

10. Morville, Peter. *Intertwingled: Information Changes Everything*. 2015. (Note: Ted Nelson originated the term *intertwingled*.)

CHAPTER 11

Text Analytics Applications—InfoApps

I happen to be one of those strange people who actually enjoy doing text analytics, but I have to admit that as many analysts and others have said, text analytics by itself is pretty useless. The incredible benefits that text analytics can drive are only realized by developing applications. On the other hand, what a truly amazing variety and range of applications can be built using text analytics!

The number and variety of applications utilizing text analytics continues to grow at an incredible pace, as organizations find ever-better ways to use that previously underused resource: unstructured text. In this chapter, rather than dive too deeply into any one application, I will try to convey a sense of this ever-growing number of applications—and hopefully spark some ideas for you and your organization to explore.

These applications can be very broadly categorized into enterprise text analytics applications and social media text analytics applications, but the reality is that the two areas are merging and overlapping more and more. Nevertheless, we will use that breakdown as a rough guide—with lots of caveats and qualifications.

Enterprise Text Analytics Applications

While enterprise search remains the single most important type of enterprise text analytics application, there seems to be a shift, with more and more focus on using text analytics for direct business value and cost cutting, rather than the productivity enhancements that enterprise search represents. Companies are realizing that enhancing information access is a means, not an end in itself. Of course, this also makes it much easier to justify the expense of text analytics and to make a better ROI case.

It was Sue Feldman at International Data Corporation (IDC) who coined the phrase *search-based applications*, or SBAs, to describe a range of new applications that included things like e-Discovery and a variety of dashboard, workbench, and portal type applications—all of which use search engines to access unstructured text. She has since abandoned that phrase in favor of *InfoApps*—which I think is much better terminology.

One issue that I have with SBAs is that the phrase puts the focus on the underlying technology rather than on the more important semantic side. For example, the Wikipedia article[1] on search-based applications talks about the key for SBA being that search engines provide two essentials: scalability and ad hoc access to multiple heterogeneous sources. I agree that these are essentials to have, but without text analytics or semantics, they still won't provide much value. In other words, search engine capabilities of fast indexing of multiple content types are necessary conditions, but they are not sufficient conditions to really develop advanced applications and provide access, not just to the content repositories but to the meaning within that content.

Having extremely fast access to multiple sources is critical for all of these applications, but the technical issues of providing access to different formats, such as PDF and Word documents, are minor compared to the complexity of integrating those different content repositories at the semantic level.

I agree that InfoApps is a much better term than search-based applications, but in some ways a more accurate description would be text analytics–based applications, or TABA, but that's a bit of a mouthful and nowhere near as catchy and easy to remember as InfoApps. So I'll stick with InfoApps for now, but the important thing to remember is that these applications depend more on text analytics than on search—as we saw in the last chapter, search by itself still struggles to provide meaningful access to all that content.

I do have to admit, however, that calling them text-based applications is a bit of a reach as well, since there are so many different elements that go into the success of these applications—particularly the variety of advanced data analytics that have been developed. The key point from a text analytics perspective is that those advanced data analytics can't be applied to unstructured text without text analytics.

Another key point is that all these applications basically require an approach fed by multiple methods. These multiple methods can include things like using additional system metadata about document types, authors combined with HR data, or repository level metadata—in fact, this may include structuring our content repositories in different ways, along with developing rules that use document types and formats as well as author-added metadata.

So now let's take a look at some of these applications.

Business Intelligence (BI)

Business intelligence (BI) is, of course, not a single application but a whole set of applications that organizations use to gather and analyze data and information from a wide variety of sources in order to discover actionable trends. Uses include identifying problems in products before they reach a critical stage—or using behavior prediction to reduce customer churn. It is a growing field, with revenues of $13.1 billion in 2012.

It consists of multiple techniques and approaches and includes a number of social media based applications. People in BI recognized early on that integration of sources was an important element, and so they combined both internal and external data.

BI techniques include a whole variety of analytic processing techniques, predictive analytics, a variety of reporting techniques, and heavy use of data mining. Describing and discussing these techniques is well beyond the scope of this book, and there are already a number of good books on the field.

But from our text analytics perspective, the critical trend is that very early, people in BI realized there was an incredible amount of important intelligence hidden in unstructured content. Initial attempts to add unstructured text to BI focused on simply adding metadata, such as title, author, date, publisher, etc. This was quickly followed by the desire to add a deeper analysis of all this textual information.

One very good book that discusses the initial attempts to add unstructured text to BI is *Tapping into Unstructured Data* by Bill Inmon and Anthony Nesavich,[2] which I recommend. Of course, I do find it interesting that people in the field of BI always talk about unstructured data—but there seems to be a great deal of resistance to using the word "text." Could it be due to something from early childhood?

Of course, the first thing that happened when people began to try to add unstructured content to BI is they ran into all the well-known problems of dealing with messy text. The early applications avoided a lot of the issues with text by focusing on text mining and NLP with an emphasis on what could be done "automatically."

Inmon and Nesavich list a variety of basic text-handling capabilities that were incorporated into BI applications including synonyms, stemming, stop words, multiple spellings, and other similar basic text-handling capabilities. These basic text-handling functions can usually be done with dictionaries and related resources.

What I found interesting was they also included three other capabilities that are probably an order of magnitude more complex than those basic ones. These three capabilities all require more fully developed text analytics approaches, including categorization and extraction rules:

- Extracting themes from documents (apparently through clustering)
- Determining the relevance of the document
- Document consolidation, where documents that hold like information are consolidated into a single document

Even clustering for themes or topics typically requires a significant amount of refinement, unless the application is content with finding a very few interesting themes or topics. Clustering is based primarily on simply counting the number of co-occurring terms. While there have been advances in the various mathematical algorithms underlying clustering, the performance is still dramatically worse than what you get with categorization rules.

As far as determining the relevance of the document, we've been trying to do that in search for the last 20 years without much success—unless you add the full range of text analytics capabilities, including auto-categorization.

Document consolidation requires some fairly sophisticated text analytics rules to resolve coreference, as well as ultimately determining what each individual document is "about"—in other words, categorization once again.

It is possible to do all three of these tasks without incorporating the full suite of text analytics capabilities, but the results will most likely continue to disappoint.

The good news is that the possibilities for incorporating more sophisticated text analytics into BI applications are increasingly becoming clear to more and more companies. Inmon and Nesavich recognize that right now, there is very little overlap or connection between the two worlds of structured data and unstructured information. They go on to extol readers to imagine the possibilities if the two worlds could connect in a meaningful way.

And the answer is that they are beginning to connect more and more—and the possibilities are truly amazing. For example, Inmon and Nesavich state that there are no rules for the content of unstructured systems, but as we've seen in earlier chapters, unstructured text is not really unstructured, but rather it is semistructured. We are getting better and better at understanding that partial or more organic structure, and as we saw in Chapters 7 and 10, we are getting better and better at developing rules to capture and utilize that semistructure.

As has been the case so often, the best way to improve BI applications is an interdisciplinary collaboration between BI analysts and text analysts. The first thing that deep-text analytics brings is a capability of developing extraction rules for unknown items, products, names, companies, and so forth. As we saw, this is done with the development of extraction rules that take the context of these noun phrases or entities into account. In addition, these extraction rules can be developed in a way to disambiguate terms that are spelled the same but have different meanings (swing as a thing you sit one and swing as a type of music) and eliminate this source of error.

The next thing that a full text analytics approach brings is the whole suite of capabilities that we call auto-categorization, but which really is simply a way to add analytical capabilities into our rules for handling unstructured/semistructured text. Categorization is the piece that can tell you what the document is about, what themes are in the documents, and also which themes are significant and which ones aren't.

If we look at some common BI applications, we can see what this capability can mean. One standard application is to identify problems in products before they reach a critical stage. This requires a deep contextual analysis of things, like technician comments or call center logs, to find not only directly stated problems and indirectly stated problems but also the ones that can't be done with simple dictionaries and pattern matching.

Another good example that we looked at in Chapter 8 is behavior prediction or reducing customer churn. The text analytics piece can be used to not only detect sentiment, such as whether they are happy or unhappy with your product but also the likelihood that they will actually cancel their account. For example, in the case cited in Chapter 8, we developed rules to characterize tech support notes (a great source for both BI and CI) as bargaining versus real cancellation threats. Bargaining posts had phrases like: "Do X or I'll cancel," where the "or" indicates that they really want something from you. It is this added dimension of deeper meaning and intelligence that is the strength of text analytics.

It is important to remember that to develop applications that take full advantage of the depth that text analytics brings, you need a combined, integrated approach with multiple roles and multiple techniques. BI applications should have roles for business users, IT, product people, cutomer-facing people, and lastly, text analysts whether recovering librarians or flexible data analysts.

Integrating all those different types of people with their different languages and different senses of value is no easy task, but it is essential in order to create really advanced applications.

Another component that has to be successfully integrated for the best applications would be techniques that use radically different ways of analyzing text—and consequently are practiced by people with very different kinds of skills as well as languages. Not just languages like SQL or C++ but much deeper linguistic differences—and even deeper cultural differences. If you don't believe me, try this experiment—go to a conference that is designed for business if you're IT, or one designed for IT if you're business—or either if you're a text/language person—and try to make sense of what they are saying. Or, take the cheaper route and just sit down at one of "their" tables.

You will be lucky to understand a tenth of what they are saying. Not only will they be speaking in foreign tongues, they will seem alien in other ways. One side says, "They just start trying things without any plans or thought for consequences," while the other says, "They take forever to do the simplest tasks and they have to ask permission for everything."

Then there is the issue of technical integration—in this case, how to combine structured and unstructured data, text, images, and simple text mining and full text analytics capabilities. There are many, many ways for this integration to happen. For example, you can combine text mining and text analytics to develop capabilities: text mining to build a taxonomy, which text analytics then uses to analyze or categorize documents/tweets/notes, etc. Or you might use the full categorization capabilities to enhance data extraction from that text—disambiguating data and looking at the context around each data element.

Or it might be at the application level, such as combining textual patterns discovered with text mining with using a text analytics deep dive into the documents to add section patterns to word clusters, or combining data elements from a database query with textual extraction of additional information about that person/company/product from blog posts—which are not in the database.

In summary, what we are seeing is a full integration of text mining and text analytics, data analytics being fed by text analytics, data and unstructured text, and external and internal information. And we are not stuck with simply imagining the possibilities, but we can actually see how this is happening today.

e-Discovery, Legal Discovery, Public Disclosure

e-Discovery, in which attorneys have to produce all the relevant documents for particular legal cases is something that used to be done almost by hand using simple search engine techniques but now is one of the well-established areas of text analytics applications. In addition to the development of new techniques in text analytics, the other main driver for semiautomated text analytics based approaches is that the number of requests continues to grow at a rapid rate and, of course, the amount of information continues to double every few years.

This application area really is an example of search-based applications (SBAs), as attorneys typically use a search front end (now supplemented by text analytics) to find all the relevant documents. For search in general, the usual dynamic is to find the right balance between precision and recall, but in e-Discovery that balance is totally skewed towards recall. The goal is normally to get as close to 100% recall as possible with precision—particularly false positives—being handled by human judgment of the attorneys.

There have been a number of technological and semantic approaches developed over the last few years in text analytics in general, as well as a number of vendors that developed document management systems specifically designed for e-Discovery, including Recommind, kCura, and Symantec. Document management systems—used to store and tag documents before searching front ends—are applied to those documents to cut down on the human effort.

However, the standard approach is still a hybrid of machine and human—a primary goal of the software being to reduce the number of documents requiring attorney review while maintaining close to 100% recall. Search-based front ends and text analytics–based back ends are used to present the information in ways that also improve the quality of the review process—in part by organizing content by topic, domain, and other categories or facets.

The basic development process for e-Discovery applications is essentially the same as it is for most text analytics applications. The starting point for SMEs, in this case attorneys, is selecting training sets of hundreds or even thousands of documents that in their estimation are good examples of particular topic areas. The range of topics is typically less complex than for enterprise applications with full taxonomies. This usually means it is easier to start with larger sets of training documents.

A large number of training sets also makes sense when the full size of the target document set is taken into consideration—very often in the tens of millions, possibly hundreds of millions of documents.

Most of the early e-Discovery applications used training sets to develop machine learning–based auto-categorization, but now more companies are exploring the development of text analytics auto-categorization rules. Whichever method is chosen, the next step is this now-familiar process: rounds of review and refinement of that categorization capability until the accuracy hits the target. With nearly 100% recall as the target, this very often involves longer—and more—rounds of review and refinement.

It is interesting that most articles that cover e-Discovery applications identify the major issues as the huge scale (hundreds of millions of documents) as well as the variety of native formats that have to be handled by the software. I find this interesting, because these issues are entirely technical and, in fact, are relatively easy to solve. The real issues have to do with our old friend semantics and messy language … here, the progress has been a lot slower.

Some of the semantic issues include disambiguation, in other words, understanding the context around words to determine the actual meanings. The other big issue is getting the software to organize the results by topic so that attorneys can interact with the document collections in more sophisticated and productive ways. These topics can be generated by clustering, which tends to be more automatic with lower human effort required—as well as the corresponding lower levels of accuracy. Or they can be generated through categorization rules which are semi-automatic, require somewhat more human effort but offer much higher accuracy, which in this case means much fewer false positives for attorneys to wade through.

One interesting area that people are working on now is how to prioritize documents by the level of risk, which can be a complex decision based on a variety of factors. Therefore, companies are typically using multiple methods, including predictive coding, both machine learning and categorization, keyword searching or more powerful faceted navigation, and developing the facility for grouping documents by variety of criteria.

As in so many areas of text analytics, integration is an important issue. This is both for integrating different approaches within text analytics, and also because e-Discovery typically involves multiple departments—IT, legal, and various business areas—which require both technical and organizational integration.

There is great potential for major savings using these techniques. For example, as cited in Chapter 3, one company was faced with the task of trying to filter 1.6 million documents down to a set that attorneys could reasonably scan while not losing any essential documents. They estimated that for this one project, they saved $2 million using these text analytics techniques.

Text Analytics–Assisted Review

e-Discovery applications are actually just one example of a broad range of applications in which text analytics can provide the means to review large document collections. It is, however, by far the most well-known, most developed, and not coincidentally, the most profitable example.

But the reality is that text analytics can be used to review and/or search any large collection of semistructured text. The applications range from simply being able to search these collections to finding the answers to specific questions, to much more involved and formal processes that more closely resemble e-Discovery applications. In other words, the potential applications are almost limitless.

An example of a more formal type of application is a project that my group helped set up in 2014, in which the application was to analyze millions of emails in order to find indications in the text that the client is due a payment and/or discounts. In addition to the emails, they also had to analyze the attachments, which often contained the best indicators. Their clients were large retailers, like Walmart and Home Depot, and the emails might be from, or may just mention, thousands of vendors that did business with the client company.

Besides scanning the unstructured text in the emails and attachments, they also had a number of SQL databases that contained information used to help guide their analysis.

In this case, the amount of money that can be recovered through this process more than pays for a good-sized team of analysts reviewing millions of emails. They started by developing a completely homegrown solution but were looking to both upgrade their search engine and add better text analytics capabilities, especially categorization and noun phrase extraction.

Their homegrown solution included a very basic (and cheap) search engine and a collection of stored queries. To give you an idea of the performance levels, the typical scenario was to set up a search, hit "run," go have lunch, then come back and hope that the search was done. While they demonstrated good creativity to minimize the impact of such a slow search, what would happen if the search needed to be rerun? How many lunches or extended coffee breaks can you take in one day? This was a rather severe limit to their solution. The amazing thing was they could show a profit—even with this slow and mostly manual solution.

A much better solution, based on a new, faster search engine and a better, more flexible text analytics platform, however, could lead to much greater profit. This platform was not only faster and smarter, but it also enabled the development of new capabilities and applications.

To develop the basic solution platform, they needed a much deeper characterization of key elements in the text—just like sentiment analysis needed a deeper characterization of what constituted positive and negative indicators. In this case, however, the analysis dealt with much more complex indicators than simple sentiment analysis applications.

Some of the elements of the solution included:

- Remove duplicates, not just based on title or sender but content as well.
- Capture and incorporate different vocabularies associated with different clients.
- Develop models that capture the even more varied vocabularies for each vendor, because what indicates a missed claim will vary by vendor, specific events, and other contexts.
- Support different types of audits, including all emails or targeted collections looking for specific types of promotions or projects.
- Incorporate information from an accounts payable database.
- Capture specific components of claims, such as people who signed, any mentions of money, etc., then categorize the context around those money mentions and ignore the majority of them, along with specific types of events.
- Look for text that indicates the email should be ignored, such as systematic text that indicates that it is a form email.
- Apply a basic, problem-indicator text vocabulary, along with variations for the changing claims of different types.

A major part of the solution is an analytical front end that allows an analyst to interactively explore preliminary results to ensure they find every claim. In this case, as with many hybrid (human and machine) text analytics applications, recall was much more important than precision. The key was to use text analytics to greatly reduce the human labor.

In this case, recall was doubly important because the client, say a Walmart or similar, would give the same set of emails to three or four competing companies and compare the results. If one company found a claim that the others didn't, there was a bonus—and a penalty if they missed a claim that others found. Now, if we could just figure out a way to incorporate that into enterprise search engines, perhaps we'd see an exponential leap in accuracy ;-)

This analytical front end was a kind of smart summarization, which allowed the analyst to preview emails in a variety of ways. For example, the software might extract and present a list of all the vendors or all the promotions in a set of emails.

The output of all this analysis is a claim with a package of evidence for the claim, along with supporting and related documents—both other emails and documents/information from other sources, such as databases and things like promotional literature.

In addition to vastly improving their performance and profit, once there was a text analytics platform in place, they could explore developing new applications—for instance collecting a wide range of information about specific projects, promotions, and contracts. This information could then be integrated into a number of applications.

Even more exciting was the possibility of not just having the software find specific entities like project names, numbers, and claims, but having it find sets of related facts—connecting people with promotions, addresses, or other facts, along with building whole new kinds of applications.

Financial Services Fraud Detection

Financial services companies are adding text analytics to traditional anti–money laundering techniques, both to improve their fraud detection and add a new dimension to the analysis. Generally, structured data is used to answer the *what* questions, while a text analytics analysis of unstructured text answers the *why* questions.

The potential uses and applications here are many and varied, but they tend to be relatively straightforward parts of the broader applications focusing on structured data. However, as discussed in earlier chapters, there is a technique that was developed by a professor at the University of Texas that was a brilliant use of text analytics/text mining, and it turned a lot of the traditional techniques on their heads. I highly recommend his book *The Secret Life of Pronouns*.[3]

What he did in his research was focus on all the words that everyone else in the field has been taught to pull out and disregard. They are called *stop words* and they include pronouns, articles, prepositions, conjunctions, and others. From the text mining perspective, people spent significant amount of time figuring out ways to get rid of the stop words, but from the psychology perspective, it turns out that these words have a number of characteristics that make them very interesting to use when analyzing text.

Dr. Pennebaker calls these words *function words*—and it turns out that their interesting characteristics include:

- They are used at a very high rate.
- They are short and hard to detect.
- They're very social.
- They are even processed in the brain differently than content words.

These characteristics suggest, at least to some researchers like Dr. Pennebaker, that it would be very interesting to explore the patterns associated with these function words. This is just what he did, and some of the things he discovered are fascinating.

He figured out how to use the patterns of function words to determine such characteristics as the sex and age of the person writing. It was also possible to tell the power status of the person writing, relative to whom he was writing to. So the same writer would have a different profile of function words, depending on whether he was writing the email to someone with more power than him or to someone with less power.

Dr. Pennebaker's techniques are also able to characterize a number of other personality traits of individuals and entire groups by analyzing these patterns. This kind of analysis could be used in a whole range of applications, particularly social media applications. But in the context of fraud, one very fascinating result was that he could characterize emails that contained a significant amount of lies. This pattern could then be used in a fraud detection application.

I had the pleasure of having a number of conversations with Dr. Pennebaker when I invited him to be the keynote speaker at Text Analytics World, which as I've mentioned before I chair. I also had the chance to download the greatest example of fraud in text that we have—the Enron emails—and try out some of the techniques. Some of the main characteristics of emails with lies in them include:

- Overall, they have fewer and shorter words.
- They have fewer conjunctions.
- They have more positive emotion words (something we should keep in mind for sentiment analysis applications).
- They had more use of the words: "if, any, those, he, she, they, you."
- On the other hand, they have significantly fewer uses of the word "I."
- They have more social and causal words.

We won't go into detail about the findings, but I highly recommend that you take a look at this book and the research behind it.

However, about the best that he got in terms of accuracy was about 76%, which is fine for some applications, though it would be nice if we could improve it. And, as with so many things in text analytics, the way to improve it is to incorporate additional text analytics capabilities, such as disambiguation and categorization into the analysis as well as utilizing other types of data analytics. For almost all applications, integration of multiple methods is almost always the best answer.

Expertise Analysis

Another application that is similar in that it uses both text mining and text analytics functionality is expertise analysis. This type of analysis tends to focus more on the text analytics side; at least that's what my company—the KAPS Group—did when we did a number of projects in this area.

One application that we worked on was an expertise location initiative for a knowledge management group in a large scientific and engineering consulting company. For this particular application, we started with well-developed and well-written resumes that individual expert consultants were charged with maintaining, then we were able to supplement that effort with an expertise analysis of the documents they published within the enterprise, as well as external publications.

The first step was to develop a taxonomy of the scientific and engineering subjects that characterized the company focus. This was used to automatically catalog the expertise of every consultant in the company, so if a manager needed an expert in biochemistry and genetics for a project, they could find every consultant with that combination. Or, they might need someone with DNA extraction and purification experience—and also experience with particular techniques in polymerase chain reaction (yes, we got that specific).

However, there is another type of expertise characterization, based not on a taxonomy of subjects but on an analysis of the language used in documents created by individuals and/or communities.

Experts use different language than nonexperts. What studies in expertise have shown is that experts chunk concepts at a different level than nonexperts, and they tend to think more in terms of process rather than subject area. These differences can be captured in categorization rules and/or text mining clusters that can then be used to characterize the expertise of individual authors, communities, documents, and sets of documents.

Once you are able to accurately characterize the expertise level of people in documents, there are a whole variety of applications that can be built on this foundation. In areas like business and customer intelligence—as well as voice of the customer—it can be used to add a new dimension in which it's possible to distinguish what experts are saying about your product, or about products in general from what nonexperts are saying. This can be extremely important in some cases.

Applying expertise analysis to communities within the organization *and* customers enables companies to develop much better models of how communication flows within these communities, along with a deeper characterization of customers.

Another area where this type of expertise analysis can be used is in the area of security and threat detection. For example, if people within a small group are talking about building bombs or biological threats, it can be very important to determine whether they're really experts ... or just simply blowing off steam.

AI Headhunters

A related area is using software to screen job applicants. There was a recent article in the *New Scientist* (one of my favorite journals if you haven't guessed), titled "The AI Headhunters," which described the rising use of AI recruitment software to scan resumes and reject any that don't fit a specified criteria. The article discusses the limits and drawbacks to the approach, for instance, the resume uses different words that don't match the software's set of keywords. One human headhunter was cited as saying "potentially outstanding candidates are being unfairly ruled out by some systems."[4]

However, I don't think the major problem is using software to screen applicants, it's just that they are doing it badly by only using keywords.

What they need is a more fully developed set of text analytics categorization-type rules that can look at the context around those words. They could also benefit from some more words and types of contexts.

Drowning in Duplicates

Another text analytics application that uses search-based techniques is identifying and enabling removal of duplicate documents. This may not sound very sexy, and it may not sound very significant in terms of the cost of doing business, but companies can save millions of dollars by removing duplicates from their unstructured content repositories.

The savings are primarily in terms of productivity savings and/or improvements in information quality. Productivity savings are primarily search-time savings, as having multiple or even dozens of virtual duplicate documents showing up in a search results list clutters the entire experience—and that makes it doubly difficult to find the one documents that users are looking for.

Just as important is the quality of information, because deciding which is the best document among 10 almost identical documents is something that is extremely difficult to do and can waste enormous amount of time. Even worse, if the user selects the wrong document, it could lead to bad business decisions, and in turn, even more time and money wasted.

Finding duplicate documents can be done with a standard search-based "find similar" function, in which the software creates a statistical signature of the document and uses that to look for other documents that are extremely close. Unfortunately, just as it is for search, this approach rarely has the accuracy needed. In most cases, companies will need to develop more sophisticated rules to define duplicates.

These rules need not be overly complex, and could even include rules that compare titles and first and last paragraphs along with some randomly selected paragraph(s) within the documents. Or, for more important documents, it may be worthwhile to create more complex rules.

It is not just for search that the removal of duplicate/near-duplicate documents is valuable. Virtually every application that utilizes semistructured text can benefit by removing duplicates from any significantly-sized content repository.

Essay Evaluation Software

Like social media, essay evaluation is an application area that has already gone through a hype, boom, and bust cycle and is just now beginning to develop a level of maturity.

Early essay evaluation software used simple text mining–type techniques, where they simply tracked things like the length of the sentence and the number of multisyllabic words. Some students, being somewhat smart, figured out they could game system just by throwing in as many big words as they could, regardless of the meaning.

As techniques were developed to detect this sort of gaming, those techniques were combined with general improvements such that essay evaluation software is now a useful technique. However, like the legal review application example, this is an area that also typically involves a hybrid solution, with the text analytics analyzing essays and then passing on the results to a human. I would still hesitate at this stage to base a student's grade on an "automatic" essay evaluation.

One area showing real promise is taking the type of expertise analysis described above and combining it with traditional essay evaluation software to get a more sophisticated picture of the knowledge of the essay writer.

Automatic Summaries

A related application of text analytics that a number of companies are exploring is to use summarization-like features to automate news summaries.

For example, Forbes is using a company called Narrative Science to write reports on corporate earnings.[5] Narrative Science also created an application to write summaries of information about 52,000 schools in a database. Some of these applications use predeveloped templates and simply stick data into the appropriate place. However, some of the robot reporters have been used to write summaries of sporting events, for which a test group of 30 readers could not tell the difference between human and machine generated stories. The readers found the automated articles "trustworthy and informative, albeit a bit boring."

Another company, Automated Insights, builds robot reporters that create small summaries that are recaps of events. By automating the process, the company can write millions of pieces of content that can then be targeted to very small audiences, such as a recap of someone's fantasy football team's performance.

If the software continues to improve and is able to write more interesting stories, this could have an enormous impact, as the human brain seems designed to pay more attention to stories and narratives than other types of summaries. Also, if this were done well, we could then turn around and use those techniques to improve summaries for search results.

Other companies doing this kind of summarization include TextTeaser, Cruxbot, and Summly, which was purchased in March 2013 by Yahoo for a reported $30 million.

Rich Summarization / Smart Extraction

A different type of summarization application is something called *rich summarization*, which is based on advanced entity and fact extraction.

Rich summarization extracts multiple data elements and combines them into a snapshot of the larger document. Some of the data elements are standards, such as title and author, but most of the data elements are extracted from within the document itself—not from metadata about the document. These data elements can include a variety of people, organizations, significant dates, and a whole range of other significant data. It may or may not include the kind of summarization of the topic of the document described in the previous example.

To get an idea of the kinds of things that might go into a rich summarization, let's take another look at a project we worked on during late 2013 through early 2014.

The client was a company that received up to 700,000 proposals a year, with each proposal ranging from 50 to 2,000 pages. They would create a summary of all the essential information for each proposal and make that summary available to their clients, such that there would only be a three- to five-page summary packed with all the essential information of the 2,000-page monster for clients to read. They initially began this service by manually extracting all the information from each proposal, but that had obvious drawbacks and limits, so we were brought in to help develop a semiautomatic summarization capability using text analytics.

By switching to text analytics, they were able to achieve what is probably by now the familiar range of benefits: save time and money, institute more flexible hiring of staff, and build new products that they can then offer to their clients.

The initial project took about four months, used a combination of our resources and theirs, and was followed by a number of months of extended development by their team.

Text analytics, using both categorization and noun phrase extraction, was used to develop three essential parts of this rich summary. The first was to create a section structure to every document, based on a combination of construction codes and various text headings. The section structures could then be used to enhance the remaining two elements in a couple of ways.

```
RCD Indexing 20130905 1330                      (AND,
  English
    Categorizer                                   (OR,
      Top                                           (ORD,"[SectionHeaderTags]","[Division00_RegEx]","[TechnicalSpecPhrases]",
        Index_01000-01500 (01000)                     (ORDDIST_3,"[SectionBodyPart]","[SectionBodyDesc]"
        Index_01600-01900 (01600)                   )
        Index_BidDocument (00000C)                  ),
        Index_BlankPage (Delete)
        Index_CoverPage                             (OR,"[Division00_RegEx]","[TechnicalSpecPhrases]",
        Index_DrawingList                             (ORDDIST_3,"[SectionBodyPart]","[SectionBodyDesc]"
        Index_EndOfSection                          )
        Index_MiscellaneousBid                    )
        Index_TableOfContents (00000B)          ))
        Index_TechnicalSpec
    Concepts
      Top
        Common_Sections
          BlankPage
          CoverPage
          CSIRegExCodes
            Division00_RegEx
            Division01A_RegEx
            Division01B_RegEx
            TechnicalSpec_RegEx
          CSISectionBody
            SectionBodyDesc
            SectionBodyPart
          EndOfSection
          ReferencedSections
          SectionHeaderTags
          TableOfContents
        SectionPhrases
```

Figure 11.1   Automated Table of Contents

The second part was to create an automated table of contents based on the section structure and other key data elements. Figure 11.1 shows the variety of section types and rules used to generate the automated table of contents.

Once the structural elements were developed, the next and more complex step was to develop rules to extract all the key data elements out of the various kinds of proposals. These key data elements included:

- Bid dates and times
- Names, addresses, and phone numbers of key personnel, such as architect or designer
- A variety of project attributes, such as cost and invitation number
- Additional attributes, such as whether and where parking was part of the project

This might seem like a fairly standard entity-extraction application, pulling out people names and other data elements. However, in this case the essential part was not to simply find people's names, addresses, and phone numbers, but specific people's information. For example, we needed to identify who the architect for the project was along with their key information. So, some of the extractions could use standard techniques, such as those in Figures 11.2 and 11.3.

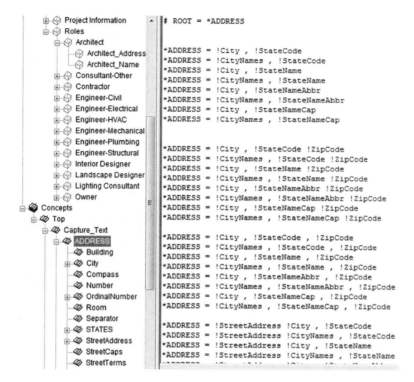

Figure 11.2   Basic Entity Extraction

Address was the single most complicated data element to extract because of the huge variety in the ways that addresses can be described. There were a whole variety of ways of describing street addresses, as well as some addresses that had no street address. Phone numbers, on the other hand, were relatively simple, although even in documents filled with numbers, there were a number of special cases.

Currently, many text analytics vendors provide extraction catalogs to do standard elements like address, date, generic people, and others. In most cases, these generic extraction catalogs do require additional customization, but they are still a great time saver.

In addition to fairly straightforward data extraction methods like those described in Chapter 7, we then had to add categorization type rules to determine whether a particular address belonged to an architect, a designer, or other key person, whether it was the address of the actual project or some other nonessential address hidden somewhere in the document.

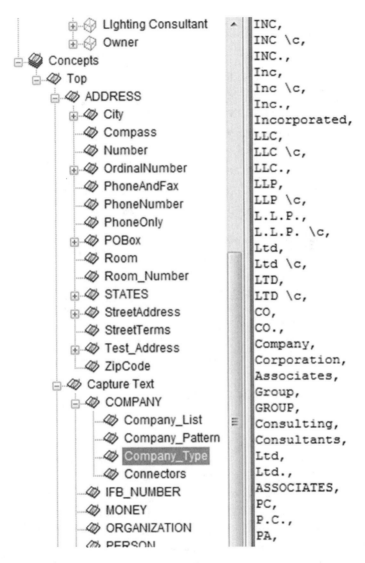

Figure 11.3   Entity Extraction Detail

This project is one of the examples that brought home to me the need for advanced categorization-type rules to do really good data extraction.

The output from the text analytics development, as is often the case, first went into a hybrid application that the client's employees could use to dramatically speed up the process of creating this rich summarization. In other words, a hybrid solution is still almost always the best one. The payoff was huge—instead of having to scan through hundreds or thousands of pages, the analysts had a neat, simple summary that they could use to guide their efforts, or in some cases, simply acknowledge that the automated answer was correct.

Once the automated rich summarizations were developed, they could be used as part of the client service to their customers. In addition, these kinds of rich summarizations could ultimately be incorporated into a search application.

Summary

As you can see from just this partial list, the number and variety of text analytics–based applications is huge, and it is growing every day. There is a really staggering amount of money that companies can save with text analytics. There is also an almost unlimited number of ways that text analytics can create value—and spur the creation of new companies with new types of services and products.

And in the words of one of those movies, whose title I forget, "You ain't seen nothing yet."

For some of these yet-to-be-invented products and services, we'll have to wait a year or three, but in the meantime, there is another whole type of text analytics applications that we haven't discussed in depth yet—social media applications. And that is the subject of the next chapter.

Endnotes

1. "Search-based Application." Wikipedia. https://en.wikipedia.org/wiki/Search-based _application.

2. Inmon, William H., and Anthony Nesavich. *Tapping into Unstructured Data: Integrating Unstructured Data and Textual Analytics into Business Intelligence.* Upper Saddle River, NJ: Prentice Hall, 2008.

3. Pennebaker, James W. *The Secret Life of Pronouns: What Our Words Say about Us.* New York: Bloomsbury Press, 2011.

4. "The AI Headhunters." *New Scientist,* October 31, 2015.

5. "Rise of Robot Reporters: When Software Writes the News." *New Scientist,* March 26, 2014.

CHAPTER **12**

Text Analytics Applications—
Social Media

Social media applications utilizing sentiment analysis and other text analytics capabilities have become an area of major growth in the last few years. These applications, while using a number of the same text analytics capabilities that are used in enterprise applications, have some very different characteristics and typically require different strategies and techniques.

Many of these differences come from a focus on customers rather than employees, and a lot of the differences come from the target of the analysis. Trying to extract sentiment or emotion from the wildly chaotic content found in social media posts, blogs, and Twitter is very different from trying to characterize the subject and/or extract entities from formal business documents.

These differences have led many companies to jump on the social media analysis bandwagon, then go out and buy one of the many social media analysis software offerings that have sprung up in the last couple of years with little real thought into what they want to achieve or how to approach it—and little or no interest in the rest of text analytics.

My experience has been that companies can get better results, for both social media applications and various enterprise applications by looking at ways to integrate the two, rather than keep them entirely separate. But regardless of how you approach the two types of applications, there is no denying that social media text analytics is the current hot topic in the field.

General Social Media—Basic Characteristics

There are many differences between the typical social media and enterprise environments; however, there are four basic characteristics that serve as the main drivers for shaping the social media market and application design.

Bigger Is Better—Mostly

The first characteristic is the *enormous scale of text* found in social media. People and industry analysts (who are almost people ;-)) like to talk about information overload within the enterprise, but social media information dwarfs enterprise information. Consequently, new techniques and technologies—such as text analytics, text mining, and to some extent, big data—are required. Text analytics is not a nice-to-have when looking at social media—*it is a must-have.*

The large scale also places more emphasis on automatic solutions, which really means that most of the human effort and creativity goes into the pre-application development phase, rather than at application time. However, even in the application phase, there are often good hybrid solutions, as we will discuss later in the chapter.

Poor Quality of Text

A second major characteristic of social media is (often) the incredibly poor quality of the text found there. Some purists among English professors may lament the state of writing found within the typical enterprise, but it is orders of magnitude better than what you find in Twitter and other social media. Poor quality includes poor spelling, mangled syntax, a high level of incoherence—and what makes it even harder to analyze is the shortness of the typical "document," which provides little context.

Conversations: Talk to Me and Everyone Else

The third characteristic is that social media is typically expressed in *conversations* (in some cases, multiple conversations), not documents carefully prepared for publication for specific or general audiences.

This means that the timescale is also radically different, as published documents may take days, weeks, or even months to write, and are expected to live for months or years. In a conversation, the posts typically take seconds, or at the most minutes to write, and thus responses are often immediate or very close to it.

This makes conversations much harder to track and harder to understand than published documents. We need to understand, for example, who is talking, who they are talking to, what they are talking about, and the nature of those comments. To do this, we need to develop better ways to track conversations, and while there has been significant work in this area, it remains a difficult problem—we need to figure out who the "he" is in the "he said-she said" blurb posted five messages earlier.

We also need much more sophisticated topic categories. The categories need to be more granular to characterize what people are talking about, and more flexible categories to capture the fluid and dynamic nature of conversations.

This need for more sophisticated categories is true for factual topics, such as the latest screen size of the new iPhone, and also when trying to capture sentiment beyond the simple "are they saying nice things about us?" The simple positive, negative, and neutral categories of early sentiment analysis are now being replaced by more sophisticated "taxonomies" of emotions and techniques, such as appraisal taxonomies.

Direct Business Value: The Social Bottom Line

The fourth characteristic is that it is often possible to tie social media to *direct business value*, rather than the productivity gains exhibited in enterprise text analytics applications, such as reducing the amount of time people have to search. And yet, according to a number of authors, companies are struggling to measure the ROI from social media analysis. Everybody knows that it's there, but it's very often difficult to directly measure. There are lots of specific or anecdotal stories of finding issues with the new keyboard in time to avoid significant manufacturing losses, but in general, measuring the ROI for social media analysis program remains difficult to do.

Even though it is often possible to capture these specific stories with direct bottom-line impact, a lot of social media initiatives are also about creating awareness—of the company, of new products, and so forth. Awareness can be very difficult to quantify—one consulting company offers a complete set of 50 KPIs (or key performance indicators), which kind of tells you that they haven't quite figured it out yet.

These characteristics, along with the overall difficulty of analyzing social media, have already led to an initial wave of disillusionment. This disillusionment, fed by the fact that it's actually pretty easy to analyze social media at a superficial level, led to a whole host of inflated claims for the early applications. The reality is that analyzing things like Twitter crowds requires a combination of psychology, marketing (is this redundant?), sociology, cognitive science, and because it is expressed in text, sophisticated text analysis.

All of this sounds very complex and outside the normal realm of a lot of businesses, but all that complexity seems worth it, as companies realize that social media has incredible potential for developing new applications and new insights into that most precious of commodities: *customers*.

Home on the Range of Social Media Applications

So, enough about *general* social media (wasn't he a famous Civil War hero?)—let's take a look at some of the specific applications of social media text analysis in the next few sections.

Customer Relationship Management (CRM)

While I was reviewing articles and overviews of various trends in CRM, or customer relationship management, I found there was quite a bit on data along with the importance of contact centers, cloud contact center infrastructure, and predictive analytics but absolutely nothing on text analytics. In fact, it was hard to find any mention of text at all. In one article, there was actually a mention of wanting better search than simple keyword-based search for sentiment, but that was quickly dropped, and the focus went back to technology and data.

What was interesting was the sheer amount of discussion around the need and desire for tracking everything the customer does—including capturing all the data related to interactions that customers have with the company—but there was no mention whatsoever about tracking the most important information of all: *what customers are saying about your company and products.*

It seems that CRM, at least in terms of the software and technology offered by various vendors, exists largely in a silo, separate from all the exciting new work being done in customer sentiment, voice of the customer, and social media in general. However, once you leave the realm of CRM software vendors and look at what companies are doing, the situation looks significantly better. For example, a number of companies are trying to incorporate text analysis into their customer relationship management program.

One company, Sony,[1] is using text mining/text analytics to process both email and chat to improve their customer relationships. They estimate they are monitoring about 4.8 million messages a year, and within those, there are about 25,000 unique issues that they want to incorporate into their CRM program.

The methods they use are quite similar to the process described in Chapter 8, specifically the telecommunications company example, where the first step would be to develop a taxonomy of issues. Their current taxonomy has 25 top-level categories, 113 sub-level categories, and 400 of what they call symptoms or issues. This taxonomy is used to categorize about 25,000 unique issues a year.

The first thing they discovered was that the amount of information in social media was orders of magnitude more than what they been dealing with, and so required sophisticated text mining/text analytics software. The process they followed was similar to one that we've done with a number of companies and consisted of five steps:

1. Collect all social media information.

2. Have human experts categorize that information to identify what was relevant to their company and their set of issues.

3. Clean up data and filter out any duplicates along with simple spam identification, then sort the information into conversations.

4. Process the cleaned-up information with a variety of industry- and client-specific taxonomies to develop a set of potential issue descriptions.

5. Finally—and as is often is the case with text analytics— have a manual assessment done by members of the issues- tracking team.

This analysis of various external social media sources was actually a later development in their use of text analysis. Sony began—as they recommend other companies should do—with a simple text analysis of the standard open comments field in a variety of surveys. Their current process also incorporates a basic sentiment analysis, using just simple positive, negative, and neutral valuations.

What this kind of application provides is a much deeper understanding of customers, and specifically why customers rate products the way they do. This is an example of a key use of text analytics, which is that it adds the whole dimension of "why" in addition to the simple "what" that can be gathered from tracking customer behavior and data.

In Sony's case, they used the analysis of unstructured text in various social media to, for example, change the severity rating of different issues. They did this using their text analysis, combining it with their internal expertise to rank severity along a number of scales, and when they did, they could characterize severity according to customer reaction, rather than an internal scale based more on a product definition (for instance, whether it involved important parts, or parts which are difficult to fix). This customer-based severity characterization was also fed with sentiment analysis, such as distinguishing an everyday rant from an anguished scream.

Another huge advantage was that text analytics enabled them to add a new, deeper level of granularity. This, in turn, enabled the discovery and analysis of more actionable information.

For example, instead of capturing the information that a new product had a large negative sentiment rating, they could track what the specific issues were—such as issues related to routers, hotspots, battery life, mobile data, and so on. One example of the power of going more granular was, within a few days of analyzing social media discussions of a new product, they identified a problem with the keyboard. The problem was that the coating of the keypad was peeling off, and it was due to a manufacturing error. Problem identified and quickly fixed—and before word spread of an embarrassing glitch that could create a widespread negative image.

Sony estimated that their basic cost savings were in the hundreds of thousands of dollars, and that was just in warranty costs. Big additional savings (although harder to measure) came through avoiding brand damage and the consequent loss of potential future sales.

They estimated that they achieved a 75% reduction in time spent for large analytics projects, while at the same time obtaining more accurate results. They also routinely found that they could reduce the response time from an entire day (way too slow in today's business and social environment) to an hour or less.

In summary, text analytics is being added to CRM projects in a growing number of companies. It is part of an overall trend to look at interactions with customers and potential customers in a variety of ways, then integrating the results into a more sophisticated level of understanding. Data captured by CRM software is being integrated with social media analysis, sentiment analysis, and voice of the customer initiatives. More on that in the next part.

Voice of the Customer (VOC)

The largest class of social media applications is voice of the customer, or VOC. Companies have had successful VOC programs long before the development of advanced text analytics–based features. These programs were largely data-driven and included tracking customer behavior, analyzing customer survey responses, and in some cases, doing some manual text analysis of the open question portions of the survey.

Social media applications of text analytics include a variety of different approaches, different areas of focus, and, of course, different acronyms, but the vast majority of these applications basically revolve around gathering and analyzing customer feedback (direct or indirect) regarding their feelings and experiences with the company's products and/or services. Direct monitoring is usually in the form of customer surveys, while indirect monitoring typically involves general social media channels such as Facebook, Twitter, and various blogs and other sources.

However, with the explosion of information in general and especially in social media, current VOC programs are typically based on text analytics and/or text mining capabilities. At this point, there is way too much text to even think about doing it manually. Most early text handling capabilities used simple text mining word counting and automatic theme detection, based on clustering and simple term frequency. Currently, the trend is to add more text analytics capabilities to improve the overall intelligence of the applications.

The basic goal of VOC programs is to better understand and act on what customers say they want (even if that is sometimes not what they really want). Some of the specific goals of VOC programs include:

- Getting early warnings about potential customer issues, such as problems with products and services
- Identifying opportunities for new product and service sales or new feature improvements
- Enabling companies to find and understand correlations between promotional campaigns and customer reactions, including but not limited to sales
- Discovering business or competitor intelligence of all types

VOC platforms typically include:

- Basic text-handling capabilities – multiple formats, basic syntax and parts of speech, etc.
- Text analytics/text mining to identify relevant topics and what customers are saying about those topics – what they like, what they don't like, what they really hate, etc.
- Sentiment analysis capabilities to capture the variety of customer comments
- Text analytics/text mining/sentiment to categorize customer comments, expressed in a variety of ways, where the categorization can be done either with clusters, or even better

(and more typically), with a taxonomy of product/services features and potential issues

- An analytical platform enabling statistical analysis of aggregated results of the initial text analytics processing

What Text Analytics Adds to VOC

The first and probably most important kind of benefit that text analytics can bring to VOC is the whole dimension of why people behave the way they do and say the things they do. Early VOC programs basically monitored what people were doing, which can be very valuable, but text analytics enables companies to monitor what people are saying—and that provides another whole dimension of analysis and insight.

It is not enough to know that the customer is unhappy, without understanding why they are unhappy and what specifically they are unhappy about. It is this detailed level of understanding that enables companies to choose the best actions to take.

It is also the text analytics component that enables such capabilities as the early warning detection of issues and problems with products and services mentioned above.

How to Get Started

Most companies and analysts suggest starting small and don't bother trying to analyze the entire social media universe. Starting small provides you with some immediate benefits, including learning the expertise needed to eventually deal with the complexity and scale of broad social media monitoring along with the ability to dive more deeply into specific situations.

For many companies, the starting point is using text analytics on the open-text responses within their existing customer surveys. Another good way to start is by analyzing posts on your own social media pages.

Success Factors

One key for success is utilizing more advanced text analytics capabilities. Simple text mining, counting and clustering can provide some value, but without more sophisticated text analytics capabilities, such as categorization to a simple taxonomy, companies are in danger of missing essential messages.

As I've emphasized throughout this book, integration is also a major factor in getting full value out of unstructured text. The first level is simply to integrate the results of text analytics processing with existing survey data, as well as more general CRM and ERP, or enterprise resource planning, data. In addition, it is considered best practice to integrate across a whole variety of sources of text and data, as well as integrate your VOC program with other marketing and sales programs.

Future Trends

In June of 2014, Forrester published a report[2] on voice of the customer programs that is a great summary of where VOC is and where it seems to be headed.

The key takeaways are:

- VOC programs are vital for improving customer experience. Many companies have started down this path, but they need to devote more resources to realize the full potential.

- VOC programs are good at gathering feedback, but most have serious shortcomings when it comes to analyzing that feedback and driving actions from the insights they generate.

- VOC programs must become embedded in the way companies do business. For example, currently:
  o Only 40% use VOC insights to inform CX design decisions.
  o Only 35% say that employees embrace the program.
  o Only 34% said they had adequate resources.

In a lot of ways, this report highlights how nascent VOC programs still are. For example, about three out of four companies don't know—or don't track—what the ROI of their VOC programs is, and most companies don't have more than one or two employees dedicated to a VOC program. This is in spite of the generally perceived benefits:

- Lower customer attrition

- Higher and more stable revenue

- Lower cost of services

The Forrester report does go on to discuss the future plans of the surveyed companies to enhance their VOC programs. Most of the enhancements have to do with the overall design of the program—better integration with company processes, better sharing of information, and better education about the value of the program.

It is also interesting that surveys are still the dominant means of gathering feedback—and only 29% use general social media. So despite all the excitement and press (hype?) about social media analysis, the reality is that it is still in an early stage.

One big issue from my perspective is that a great deal of the unstructured customer feedback is not really used, so even though they collect the unstructured text, they don't analyze it. And even where this text is analyzed, it is normally done with the "automatic" features of text mining, when what it really needs is more advanced text analytics capabilities.

When companies talk about improving the actual analysis, it is mostly about getting a new technology and/or a new vendor. It seems unlikely that companies will invest in developing their own text analytics capabilities just for a VOC program and honestly, it probably doesn't make sense to do so. However, if it is building one application on an existing text analytics platform (technology and deep linguistics/semantics), then it makes much more sense.

The other area for improvements is for VOC vendors to improve their own text analytics capabilities by using more advanced language/categorization approaches. The issue in that approach is the amount of customization needed to adequately incorporate the specialized languages within each enterprise. However, as we have seen in chapters on development, it is possible to build general logic and ranking rules that only need to have a quick vocabulary addition, which is something that can be semiautomated.

One thing is clear: there is a lot of room for improvement, both in business processes and text analytics capabilities. I recommend that you check with Forrester's VOC report for other features/needs for successful VOC programs.

The Filtered / Augmented Voice of the Customer

In addition to tracking and analyzing the voice of the customer as expressed on Twitter, Facebook and such, another great source combines the direct capture of customer feedback with that captured by customer support teams. This approach has a number of advantages over just monitoring the wild world of Twitter, et al.

One advantage is that it enables customer support employees to identify problems, well ahead of the customer, and fix issues before they become a problem.

Another big value of these programs is that the information from customers is not always accurate and is often slanted. In addition, customers sometimes don't know what it is that bothers them, so it becomes important to augment the customer's voice with the voice of someone with a great deal of expertise in the company's products and services.

As Leonard Klie says in the journal, *Customer Relationship Management:*

> Employees on the front lines are ideally positioned to recognize patterns based on a conversation with the many customers who call them every day. Not only can they identify common issues but they can also assess how important those issues are to customers, help understand what's causing them, and provide insight into how customers would like those issues corrected.[3]

The article goes on to discuss a number of the issues involved in setting up these programs, including who owns them. The best solution, as we've often seen, is cross departmental, but the main issue from a text analytics perspective is the enormous scale of contact center interactions.

For example, the author cites that the company, Best Buy, deals with around 1 billion interactions with customers each year. The US Postal Service faces an even bigger challenge, with its 700,000 employees spread out over 40,000 locations—as well as a customer base that includes the entire US population.

Given the scale, the only realistic way to approach generating useful insights is with the use of text analytics. In response, a number of companies have developed full-blown enterprise feedback solutions that combine VOC and VOE, or voice of the employee programs, which provide not only the text analytics capability, but a general analytical front end as well.

In addition to giant retailers like Best Buy and government agencies, other industries that have been early adopters include travel, hospitality, telecommunications, financial services, and high-tech.

From the text analytics perspective, as noted earlier, trying to capture and analyze text from customer support representatives has a number of challenges. Chief among them, is the creative spelling, syntax, and grammar that are typically exemplified in their notes.

For example, in the following notes, we have a couple of samples of customer support notes that we worked with on a project in 2013:

> Note 1: n anon-rc/na/valda m taylor/pin/909-555-1212/ci request for pa/ask for partial pyment/cx said none/cx wants to extnd until may 1 for the $111.61/nocol made/acct not delinquent/assure no servce intrptions/cx yes noi/ir-yes r n i a

Note 2: John Doe ivr cld to pa for $303.79 for 5/1/2010 advsd $224.65 for 5/4/2010 processed as per jo777779 donecustomer passed authentication with the following information: authenticated in the ivr.

Some of this is code that the software can easily be trained to recognize, but others are personal codes of the support rep, and some are just wild typing. In fact, on this project, during the early development phase, we identified 40 different spellings of the word "transfer" in just the first 2,000 posts we examined.

To make sense of these kinds of notes—and to develop a framework that enables companies to do some in-depth analytics—requires significant work in terms of developing taxonomies of products and issues, textual analysis to capture all the variations in "word" usage, and developing sophisticated enough categorization to provide useful insights. Look at Chapter 8 for more information about the best way to do this.

There is a major school within the text analytics community that finds the idea of taxonomies abhorrent and the idea that humans should be involved in this kind of analysis equally absurd and primitive. Taxonomies? We don't need no stinking taxonomies! We want software to do all that—either automatic taxonomies or just good old clustering of frequently co-occurring terms.

As you may have gathered, I am not part of that school. And one of my favorite examples to use to show the limits of that approach is this project and these rapid-fire typing exercises. Imagine the kinds of clusters you would get with this almost random spelling and syntax—and in many cases, not even any consistent word breaks. You may be able to cluster some of the pieces, but how are you going to tell the clustering engine that cx and customer (and cust and ct and none/cx), and up to 100 other variations are all the same word?

One way, of course, is a catalog/dictionary. One that has to be developed, usually using semiautomated approaches, and then maintained. If you're going to do that, why not just go a bit further and organize the dictionary into a simple taxonomy?

Once you have developed this platform, there are a range of other applications that can be built to support and enhance a variety of the customer support objectives. These include:

- A semiautomated and cleaned up summary of the last call from this customer

- Detection – recurring problems, categorized by subject, customer, client, product, product parts, or even by representative
- Analytics – evaluate and track the effectiveness of each representative
- Evaluation of effectiveness – particular policies, programs, and even specific actions taken, including unintended consequences
- Detection of recurring or immediate problems – high rate of failure, etc.
- Fraud detection – recurring, gaming the system
- Competitive intelligence – calls to switch from brand X to Y in a particular region
- Tracking of calls – correlate (numbers, patterns) with marketing activities, promos, competitive campaigns, rate increases and other activities
- Training – evaluate its effectiveness
- Subscriber mood – before and after a call, and why
- Pattern matching of initial motivation to subsequent actions – optimize responses and develop proactive steps

Sentiment Analysis

Sentiment analysis is both a basic functionality of text analytics and a rapidly growing application area. Like so much of text analytics, sentiment analysis is really a platform for a broad variety of applications.

Early Approaches

As an application area, it is also often referred to as opinion analysis and it actually predates text analytics, since an initial application was to analyze customer survey responses manually. Needless to say, manual analysis was severely restricted and often would simply take a few random samples and hope they were representative.

The application area took off with the development of text analytics, and specifically "automated" sentiment analysis. Then, it became possible to analyze larger and larger amounts of text—something that was needed even before the explosion of social media.

These early applications were characterized by two fundamental approaches. The first is that they primarily analyzed direct or explicit documents, such as product and movie reviews. Reviews are much easier to analyze, since their primary purpose is to express sentiment or an opinion. In addition, the statements within these documents are also largely direct expressions of emotions or opinions.

The second major characteristic of these early applications was that they employed very simplistic text analytics techniques. They were applied to entire documents—and even a document as short and direct as a product review was too long and expressed too many different sentiments. In addition, and as noted earlier, they used the basic "bag of words" approach, which simply looked at all the words in the document as basic units, while ignoring all the complex and structural relationships between words. This approach not only misses the larger textual grouping of phrase, sentence, and paragraph, it also misses the more complex meaning-based relationships, such as when a phrase or sentence refers back to earlier expressions.

The amazing thing is that even with these basic, simplistic approaches, the emerging field of sentiment analysis generated a huge amount of excitement and expectations. With the rise of social media driving a bandwagon phenomenon as well as the promise and potential of this relatively direct access to that most precious of commodities—customers—the high level of enthusiasm is not really surprising.

The problem, of course, as we discussed in Chapter 8, is that the performance of these early applications was very poor, and in many cases the results were barely above chance. So, if your only concern was whether something was positive or negative, you could flip a coin and get almost as good a result.

The basic problem with these early approaches is simply that they did not deal with the complexity found within social media and other sources. First of all, documents are way too complex a unit as they express multiple sentiments and opinions. Also, in many ways, emotional utterances are more complex than simple factual statements—or rather, it is a different type of complexity altogether.

Factual and conceptual analysis deals with the complexity of the subject matter. Sentiment or emotional analysis deals with the complexity of expression. While emotions are generally much simpler than concepts, these simple emotions can be expressed in an almost infinite number of ways. And so the problem is in building models or categorization rules that recognize that these few hundred thousand expressions are all really saying almost the same thing: "This thing sucks." But some of them are saying, "This thing really sucks," and "This thing really, really sucks," and so on.

Positive Trends

Once this initial hype and inevitable disillusionment passed, there emerged three trends that have been driving the field to its current more mature and more useful state.

The first trend has been to narrow the focus of the target, from documents to paragraphs and sentences, and from sentences to phrases, and to combine that with adding more detail to the target by focusing on more specific aspects of a product or service. Rather than ask, "Is this document/post positive or negative about our product?" the new approach is to ask, "Is this phrase extremely positive or negative about the screen size of our product?" and "Is this phrase part of a sentence that contains words/phrases that change the meaning of the phrase with reversals or qualifiers?"

The second trend has been to expand from direct and explicit statements to more indirect and implicit expressions of sentiment and emotions. Instead of reviews, target content is the much wilder medium of social media, blogs, and Twitter. As people realized the potential contained within these implicit statements and started to develop text analytics capabilities to mine this rich source, they also quickly realized that their existing techniques ("bags of words" and dictionaries of positive and negative words) were completely inadequate in this new medium.

This realization led to the third and most critical trend, which is adding depth and sophistication to the basic sentiment analysis techniques. These techniques, discussed in Chapter 8, include more sophisticated rules, ways to deal with things like counterfactuals, and the development of appraisal taxonomies that can model a more complex use of language. One important use has been not just to identify the polarity (positive or negative) of the statements but to characterize the intensity of the emotion within that statement.

In addition to more sophisticated techniques, the applications themselves began to exhibit much more sophistication, like a deeper understanding of the different types of customers and types of social media writers or posters. One technique has been to identify which posters can be characterized as major influencers by tracking the spread of their posts and ideas through the social media environment. This is largely about a data-driven evaluation of influence with the text analytics component providing a more sophisticated characterization of the topics that they are influential about.

Types of Applications

So what type of applications are these three trends leading to? The answer is just about anything you can imagine, and the possibilities are nearly infinite! While most of the initial applications focused on analyzing real, potential, or imagined customers, the potential targets of applications are expanding exponentially.

Let's take a look at some of the areas for these (almost) infinite applications of sentiment analysis.

Customer Applications

Sentiment analysis is a major part of voice of the customer applications that we described in the previous section.

The basic role of sentiment analysis, within voice of the customer applications, is to spot unhappy customers, capture just how unhappy they are, and determine what they are unhappy about. However, another application is to actually try to find happy customers both to figure out what exactly is making them happy, as well as potential ways to use these happy customers to help promote a company's products.

Also, it is not just products and services, but sentiment analysis can be applied to things like reactions to a new company's strategy, a new marketing campaign, new features, and even new names for products. This kind of analysis could fall under a broader topic, such as brand management.

Voice of the Voter

One interesting application is what Seth Grimes calls "voice of the voter," in which sentiment analysis is used to analyze voters' reactions to specific messages, events, or blunders. So, in addition to customers, sentiment analysis can be used for other groups of people.

It can also be used to analyze how well a damage control effort is working, or to make decisions, such as whether it is time to change a message, or even if it is the right time to drop out of a particular race. It is hard to imagine any political campaign basing their decision solely on social media analysis, but again, like so many text analytics applications, it is something that can be used in conjunction with other types of analysis.

Voice of the Market

One potential application that some investment companies are looking at is using social media to forecast market movement or to spot new specific opportunities in the market. Predicting general market movement always strikes me as something akin to astrology, but getting early warnings of a serious problem with the company's products or services, or a potential scandal in the making, could give investors a slight edge in anticipating a downward trend from that company's stock.

Deep Psychology Applications

One intriguing application that I recently saw was the idea of characterizing a user's overall personality as either negative or positive, and using that to sell specific products or services. For example, someone with a negative personality would likely be more amenable to buying extra protection for particular product. Or, a company could use characterizations of people as positive or negative to tailor their sales message such that it resonates with the personality.

In addition, just as we are now going beyond simple positive-negative sentiment, it should be possible to characterize personalities in more complex ways. Marketing and advertising have been working on this for quite a while, but with social media and sentiment analysis, there are new possibilities to apply the traditional techniques to a much larger audience, in addition to fine tuning these techniques to make them much more effective.

This area seems to still be in its infancy, but I wouldn't be surprised to see it grow in the near future.

Political Personalities

I came across an interesting article, titled "Your Brain on Politics: the Cognitive Neuroscience of Liberals and Conservatives,"[4] that discussed the differences between liberals and conservatives at a cognitive science level. It turns out that liberals have a more active *anterior cingulate cortex,* or ACC—an area of the brain associated with being open to new experiences—while conservatives have a more active amygdala, which is associated with strong emotional reactions. The article went on to cite the results that conservatives have a stronger reaction to images associated with the emotion of disgust.

This propensity could be used to track and characterize people as liberal or conservative as well as frame arguments and ads—something that is going on all the time now—but the advent of sentiment analysis and social media opens up all sorts of new possibilities.

In addition, sentiment analysis of personalities can be combined with other types of analysis, such as that found in Dr. James Pennebaker's *The Secret Life of Pronouns.*[5] Dr. Pennebaker analyzed the patterns of what he calls "function words" (pronouns, articles, prepositions, etc.) and discovered that he could accurately determine the writer's age, gender, and personality.

As we noted above, the possibilities for sentiment analysis fueled applications are practically endless—and a little bit scary.

Acting Up—Behavior Prediction

Another text analytics application is not only determining what customers are saying but also analyzing what kinds of behaviors they might indulge in—for example, that project that we worked on for a telecommunications customer service application, where the goal was to distinguish customers who were likely to cancel an entire account from those customers who were simply unhappy about something, or wanted to get something. Distinguishing real threats enabled the company to take timely preventative action.

What Are You Talking About?

In determining the meaning of words having many variations, the first step in building the application was to determine what the customer support notes were about. This involved building a simple, one-dimensional taxonomy (called a list ;-)). In fact, the application actually used two lists—one for actions that the customer support rep took at the end of the call—that was the one that contained the 40 variations of the word "transfer" mentioned earlier, and the other was motivations, that is, why were the customers calling?

Here is a list of the transfer "spellings"—about 117 in all:

xfer,	xferredcustomer,
xferd,	xferring,
xfere,	xferrred,
xfered,	xferto,
xferedcustomer,	xferverified,
xfering,	xferwhy,
xferir,	xfr,
xfern,	xfrd,
xferncustomer,	xfred,
xferrd,	xfrrd,
xferred,	transcustomer,

transdfer,

transdfered,

transefr,

transefred,

transered,

transerred,

transf,

transfar,

transfcustomer,

transfd,

transfe,

transfed,

transfeered,

transfer,

transfercall,

transfere,

transfered,

transfereed,

transfererd,

transfering,

transferit,

transfern,

transferna,

transferr,

transferrd,

transferre,

transferred,

transferreed,

transferring,

transferrred,

transfers,

transferto,

transfertransfer,

transferv,

transfery,

transferyes,

transff,

transffer,

transffered,

transfferred,

transffrd,

transfr,

transfrd,

transfre,

transfred,

transfreed,

transfrrd,

transfrred,

trasfer,

trasferd,

trasfered,

trasfering,

trasferred,

trasfner,

trasnefr,

trasnf,

trasnfe,

trasnfer,

trasnferd,

trasnfered,

trasnferred,

trasnferring,

txfer,

txfered,

txfering,

txferred,

txfr,

txfred,

Are You Motivated?

Motivations included basic things, like calling about a lost device, or that the device had stopped working, or other complaints, such as that the current bill was higher than their last, or that their bill contained an abnormal fee. The one that we were most interested in was customer cancellation.

As it turned out, calling about a bill being higher than the last was the most difficult to identify. We figured out that the issue had to do with the comparative nature of the call—it shared all the basic vocabulary of asking about bills, but differed only in the use of a few words having to do with more or less—words that are shared with quite a few of the other motivations.

For the cancellation calls, the complicating issue was that they wanted to distinguish between customers who were calling to cancel one of their accounts (something that happened a lot as customers tried to find the best plan) and customers who were calling to cancel service completely. In the latter case, it meant that they were leaving and going to a competitor.

It is the ability to add this level of specificity that an advanced text analytics capability show its true value. Using simple text mining that looks just for cancellation words was not able to distinguish the two cases.

This was a hybrid application, that is, the text analytics categorization was sent to a human operator who checked the results for accuracy. Prior to this application, the company checked each note manually by reading the entire note, then making a relatively complex judgement. They did this to be able to track the motivations of customers and to look for spikes in certain types of calls and other patterns. These other patterns could alert them to emerging problems in both their products and services.

As with most hybrid applications, one key was to focus on *recall*—that is, find all the cases, even if it means some false positives. This works because the human operator can quickly discard those false positives.

Some early testing resulted in the Figure 12.1 list.

The basic application we worked on was to semiautomate this process, and the savings were twofold. First, the actual process of reviewing notes was orders of magnitude faster, since the cognitive task of evaluating the correctness of a suggested categorization is much simpler than reading the full note and picking from one of 30 motivations (and they often overlapped, or the calls were about two motivations).

Second, as the automatic categorization got better, they could shift to mostly spot checking—say every 10 notes, then every 100 notes. The goal was not to achieve completely automated categorization, but to improve

Test File	Result	Relevanc
C:\BBNNewText\CustomerReactivation\CustomerReactivation_9.67...	PASS	0.6181
C:\BBNNewText\BillRateIncrease\BillRateIncrease_9.68524731E8.txt	PASS	0.6181
C:\BBNNewText\BillRateIncrease\BillRateIncrease_9.68054177E8.txt	PASS	0.6181
BillGreaterThanLast_9.67727626E8.txt	PASS	0.6181
BillGreaterThanLast_9.67585642E8.txt	PASS	0.6181
BillGreaterThanLast_9.67583772E8.txt	PASS	0.6181
BillGreaterThanLast_9.67580228E8.txt	PASS	0.6181
BillGreaterThanLast_9.67571434E8.txt	PASS	0.6181
BillGreaterThanLast_9.67570529E8.txt	PASS	0.6181
BillGreaterThanLast_9.67570421E8.txt	PASS	0.6181
BillGreaterThanLast_9.67569121E8.txt	PASS	0.6181
BillGreaterThanLast_9.67559181E8.txt	PASS	0.6181
BillGreaterThanLast_9.67554681E8.txt	PASS	0.6181
BillGreaterThanLast_9.6758604E8.txt	PASS	0.5556
BillGreaterThanLast_9.6758541E8.txt	PASS	0.5556
BillGreaterThanLast_9.67573326E8.txt	PASS	0.5556
BillGreaterThanLast_9.67569323E8.txt	PASS	0.5556
BillGreaterThanLast_9.67562116E8.txt	PASS	0.5556
BillGreaterThanLast_9.67556972E8.txt	PASS	0.5556
BillGreaterThanLast_9.67551886E8.txt	PASS	0.5556
BillGreaterThanLast_9.67547547E8.txt	PASS	0.5556
C:\BBNNewText\WrongPlan\WrongPlan_9.67990923E8.txt	PASS	0.5
C:\BBNNewText\WrongPlan\WrongPlan_9.67583158E8.txt	PASS	0.5
C:\BBNNewText\SubscriptionCancellation\SubscriptionCancellation...	PASS	0.5
C:\BBNNewText\SubscriptionCancellation\SubscriptionCancellation...	PASS	0.5
C:\BBNNewText\SubscriptionCancellation\SubscriptionCancellation...	PASS	0.5
C:\BBNNewText\SubscriptionCancellation\SubscriptionCancellation...	PASS	0.5
C:\BBNNewText\SubscriptionCancellation\SubscriptionCancellation...	PASS	0.5
C:\BBNNewText\SubscriptionCancellation\SubscriptionCancellation...	PASS	0.5
C:\BBNNewText\SubscriptionCancellation\SubscriptionCancellation...	PASS	0.5
C:\BBNNewText\SubscriptionCancellation\SubscriptionCancellation...	PASS	0.5
C:\BBNNewText\SubscriptionCancellation\SubscriptionCancellation...	PASS	0.5
C:\BBNNewText\SubscriptionCancellation\SubscriptionCancellation...	PASS	0.5
C:\BBNNewText\SubscriptionCancellation\SubscriptionCancellation...	PASS	0.5
C:\BBNNewText\SubscriptionCancellation\SubscriptionCancellation...	PASS	0.5
C:\BBNNewText\SubscriptionCancellation\SubscriptionCancellation...	PASS	0.5
C:\BBNNewText\SubscriptionCancellation\SubscriptionCancellation...	PASS	0.5
C:\BBNNewText\SubscriptionCancellation\SubscriptionCancellation...	PASS	0.5

Figure 12.1   Early Categorization Results

the quality of the categorization by utilizing the best qualities of human and automatic.

Just being able to improve the accuracy and speed of the analytical process has the potential to save millions of dollars in direct costs, as well as improving the accuracy of their analysis.

Categorization Rules Rule!

The next step was to build on the basic categorization, with the ability to flag a customer calling to cancel their account so the support rep could take appropriate action. If you know that someone is really likely to cancel, then it makes sense to treat them differently, including offering them special deals and prices—but you don't want to offer those same costly deals and prices to someone who is not really canceling their account.

So here is the basic rule that we developed to distinguish customers calling to cancel an entire account, versus those bargaining to get something:

```
(START_20, (AND,  (DIST_7," [cancel]",
  "[cancel-what-cust]"),
(NOT,(DIST_10, "[cancel]", (OR, "[one-line]",
  "[restore]", "[if]")))))
```

Makes for fun reading, right? What this rule basically says is:

- START_20 – Only count words that are in the first 20 words of the note (this was designed to eliminate a lot of noise that seemed to show up near the end of the customer support notes).

- DIST_7,"[cancel]", "[cancel-what-cust]") – This says look for words that indicate that the customer is calling to cancel, but only count them if they appear within seven words of words that indicate that the customer is talking about their entire account. This includes words like "account" or "service." The words for cancel include the usual wildly creative variations:

cancel,	cna,
cancellation,	cnacel,
cancellation*,	cnacelled,
canc,	cnam,
canceld,	cnat,
calcellations,	cncel,
cancelation*,	cncl,
cancelation*,	cncle,
cancell,	cnel,
cancellatioin,	cnl,
cancellatiom,	cxl,
cancl,	cxld,
canclation,	cxpd,
clld,	close,
cn,	deact,

- NOT,(DIST_10, "[cancel]", (OR, "[one-line]", "[restore]", "[if]")))))) – This says don't count those cancel-type words, if they appear within 10 words of words that indicate they are calling about just one line, or calling to actually restore a line that had been canceled—something that used many of the same words as calling to cancel.

- And the heart of the rule – Don't count these words if they appear within 10 words of "if" words. These are words that indicate that the customer is really only threatening to cancel in order to get something. In other words, they are bargaining words. They want something, either for the company to stop doing something or to give the customer something.

For example: "customer called to say he will *cancel his account if* the does not stop receiving a call from the ad agency."

That note indicates that what the customer really wants is to stop receiving calls from the ad agency. Another example: "cci and *is upset that he has the asl charge and wants it off* or is going to *cancel* his acct."

In that second example, the customer wants a new charge taken off—and is backing up the complaint with a threat to cancel.

In both of these examples, what's really going on is *bargaining*—customers are saying they will cancel the entire account unless they get something. From the customer rep's point of view, it's very important to distinguish these kinds of calls from calls where the customer really is only calling to cancel their account. The actions that the customer support rep will take, and who they might transfer the call to, depend on whether this is a real threat or a bargain.

To do a full capture of all the ways customers might express bargaining goes beyond just a list of bargaining words or even multiple phrases. But what the rule can do is capture a broad range of candidates for special treatment before passing them on to a human analyst.

What made developing this kind of sophisticated application really difficult is the variability of human judgement. It is particularly difficult to develop semiautomatic rules when people tell you very different things about what a note is all about. People are very good at quickly categorizing a document or note, but their consistency is highly suspect.

Regardless of the difficulties in developing applications that rest on this type of advanced text analytics, the payoff is huge. You simply cannot develop something like a behavior-prediction application based on the text (especially this chaotic type of text) with simple sentiment word counting. On the other hand, you can build a behavior-prediction application not using text at all—just using traditional behavior monitoring and predictive analytics.

But just imagine what you can do when you combine traditional behavior-prediction programs with the kind of deep-text analytics capabilities that we did in this project! The possibilities endlessly multiply and enrich.

With the right foundation, the future can be amazing!

Endnotes

1. Hagelin, Olle. LT Accelerate, 2014: "The Voice of the Customer X 650 Million at Sony Mobile." Interview by Seth Grimes.

2. Schmidt-Subramanian, Maxie. "The State of Voice of the Customer Programs: It's Time to Act." Forrester Research. June 20, 2014.

3. Klie, Leonard. *Customer Relationship Management*, September, 2014. 43-45.

4. Kuszewski, Andrea. "Your Brain on Politics: The Cognitive Neuroscience of Liberals and Conservatives." *Discover Magazine,* September 7, 2011.

5. Pennebaker, James W. *The Secret Life of Pronouns: What Our Words Say about Us.* New York: Bloomsbury Press, 2011.

PART 5

Enterprise Text Analytics as a Platform

CHAPTER 13

Text Analytics as a Platform

So far, through the first four parts of the book, we have covered what text analytics is, the value that it brings to organizations, how to get started with text analytics, how to develop applications, and what those applications can be. Throughout, we have maintained that the best approach to text analytics is to view it as an infrastructure or platform for multiple applications.

In this section, I want to take a deeper look at what that might mean, and how organizations might go about doing it. In the process, I will take a somewhat speculative look at establishing a text analytics group within the enterprise.

This chapter and the approach are described in places throughout the book, but I will try to bring them together in an overall model of text analytics in the enterprise.

Text Analytics in the Enterprise

First, let's take a look at what the various options are for text analytics in the enterprise. In Chapters 5 and 6, we looked at the situation in which an organization decides to buy text analytics software and we looked at it essentially in isolation. But the reality is, as usual, much more complex. In some cases, for example, an organization may already have one, two, or even three text analytics software packages. Also, buying and developing your own text analytics software and applications is not the only path to adding text analytics capabilities to the organization.

And so there are, as always, a lot of different options and which one is best for your organization is something that you will have to decide. But, in general, there are three options for adding text analytics capabilities to an organization. These options are more of the spectrum than fully independent options.

Three Options: Finding Your Place on the Spectrum

Text Analytics? We Don't Need No Stinking Text Analytics!

The first option is simply to not have or develop any internal text analytics capability. This can be done in two ways aside from just simply ignoring text analytics entirely. One is to outsource your text analytics applications. This is a model that a number of text analytics vendors are offering. It is an option that is particularly attractive to smaller companies that are only interested in a voice of the customer application. This option seems an easy way to get started, but it has many limits.

It might make sense to go with a cloud-based option, but inevitably, as social media continues to grow and the creativity of companies continues to find new ways to explore and utilize all that social media, companies will be faced with the need/desire for more than just a voice of the customer application. And for text analytics enterprise applications, the need for additional internal text analytics capabilities is even more pronounced.

Finally, even if you go with this model, you will most likely need some internal text analytics team to work with the vendor to refine profiles, interpret the results, and work with business units to maximize the utility of the various applications.

Halfway House

Another option is also to just buy text analytics–based applications, which are maintained by your IT group, or by the text analytics vendor. In this option, you have more control over the functioning of the application, but lack any major internal development capabilities.

This approach is halfway between no internal text analytics capabilities within the enterprise and a full text analytics team that is involved in everything from initial development to ongoing refinement of base capabilities to working with users to improve each application. In many cases, the vendor also provides some professional services to help implement each application.

You will likely also have a dedicated team of analysts, who are using one or more applications and are slightly involved in providing feedback to IT and/or an outside vendor. This team (anywhere from one half-time resource to a full analytical team of three to five people) is involved in using the software, but don't do any development.

Full House—Enterprise Text Analytics Team (ETA)

The third option is to develop that full text analytics team for doing development and refinement. This approach builds on the Smart Start process (described in Chapters 4 and 5), and so it should come as no surprise that this is the approach that I think is going to be the best—for most organizations.

The ETA team typically partners with IT in a number of ways, and might also have IT developers and programmers on the team. On the other hand, the ETA team might be a couple of people in the corporate library, who work with IT and business to create a suite of text analytics applications and develop the taxonomies/information organization essential for successful text analytics capabilities.

Strategic Vision of (and in) Text Analytics

But that leaves the Big Question: what is the right answer for your organization? Or more importantly, how do you come up with your strategic vision of the right answer for your organization?

The best method to decide what the right answer is, is to base your decision on a solid research foundation into your information environment and the use of unstructured text that we described in Chapter 5. Regardless of your final decision, it should be guided by an overall strategy of text analytics in your organization.

This is true even if you decide that you are going to go with a project-oriented approach. Outsourcing text analytics applications or deciding on a series of quick tactical projects can be successful, but only if there is some overall strategy guiding them.

Also, at a minimum, organizations need to base their decision of which option is best on a fully developed understanding of what text analytics can do for them. Otherwise, they are just guessing blindly and that can easily lead to many false steps and dead ends.

Of course, if the decision is to go with an enterprise text analytics approach, then this deep understanding of text analytics is even more essential.

Best Approach: Strategic or Tactical / Platform or Project?

"Concepts without percepts are empty, percepts without concepts are blind."

—Immanuel Kant, *Critique of Pure Reason*

Having a fully articulated text analytics strategy does not mean that you are tied to a deep, strategic platform approach—your best strategy might be to (strategically) decide on a tactical project approach.

What is important is to base your decisions on a deep understanding of text analytics in your organization, and one of the most critical decisions is what your overall approach should be. Should you focus on a strategic approach that emphasizes the infrastructure and integration of information, or should you think tactically and just get that new application out, then worry about the big picture later?

As with most dichotomies, the answer is almost never either/or, but what the right balance really is. Or to paraphrase one of my favorite philosophers, Immanuel Kant, "Strategy without applications is empty, applications without strategy are blind."

In the United States, and particularly within certain industries and types of applications (web, cloud, tech, etc.), the balance seems to be almost entirely on the tactical/project side. Whether this is overall a good thing or not I'll leave to industry and social pundits to debate, but in the case of text analytics, the answer is much more straightforward: We need to emphasize strategy and infrastructure.

Yes, it is true that too much emphasis and time spent on strategy can lead to a kind of paralysis and so nothing of any value gets done. And projects do have one main advantage in that they can bring in immediate value, which always looks good on accounting spreadsheets that emphasize cash flow above all else. But the dangers of mindlessly launching one information project after another—and watching them fail to deliver real solutions—are all too real.

This is particularly true in a field like text analytics, in part because text analytics software can be used to develop/support/implement such a wide variety of applications. And even more importantly, text analytics enables the deeper and more sophisticated use of information across the enterprise and within each application—but only if the right infrastructure is put in place. In other words, text analytics is really a platform technology.

Projects Produce—Yes, But

It is certainly possible to approach text analytics with a tactical/project mindset. But if so, the danger of failed, or more likely underachieving projects, is very real. The following scenario is too often how many companies do text analytics.

First, the marketing department decides they want to do a social media–based marketing project. So they go out and look at text analytics software that is used primarily for social media analysis, buy the software, try to figure out how to use it, follow some examples of other companies, assign a couple of part-time people to the actual text analytics development, launch—and then wonder why it didn't work as well as they had hoped.

And then another group in the company wants to do a business intelligence application, so they go out and repeat the same project steps—and very likely end up buying a different software package and having to build everything from scratch.

And then, perhaps the enterprise search team has heard that text analytics can improve their search, so they go out and do an enterprise search project, repeating all the same steps, but making the usual mistake of expecting the software to do it all, while neglecting to develop the semantic components that might give search a chance.

And so now the company has three different text analytics packages, three different application initiatives—none of which have taken advantage of the work in the other two—and wind up all the poorer for it, with none of the applications talking to each other very well. Finally, none of the projects were done with a broad enough context to deeply understand the scope of information access problems throughout the enterprise—or even in their limited application—and there is no central team that can share best practices and resources.

The one advantage of doing this tactical/project approach is that each one of those projects can be done faster and cheaper than if they were slowed down by all that strategy stuff. Of course, if you add up the costs of all three projects, each one starting from scratch, typically the overall time and cost will be much, much higher. Short term profits and long term losses—sound familiar?

Infrastructure / Platform Is a Good (Best?) Solution

A much better approach, in my experience, is an infrastructure or platform approach. And yes, I'm probably prejudiced since I help companies develop these infrastructure platforms, but I think the case can be made for many more organizations adopting this approach. And, if you take a good look at how such an approach could work in your organization, you may be pleasantly surprised at both the power of the solution as well as the economics. The scale of the solution can vary dramatically to fit a variety of different-sized organizations and different budgets.

The Best of All Possible Worlds

Actually, it is possible to get the best of both a strategic and a tactical approach, an infrastructure and a project approach. The way to do this is summed up in the slogan that I've used on a number of projects:

Think Big—Start Small—Scale Fast

We first considered this slogan back on page 120, in Chapter 5. What it basically means is that you need to start with a broad strategic vision, then select a small but important first project to implement that vision, and then use the strategic vision along with the resources developed in that first project to quickly develop a whole range of text analytics applications.

And if the development of the infrastructure components (taxonomies, a TA team of developers and analysts, technical platform, corporate policies, etc.) is done as part of an initial text analytics project—such as search or social media analysis—then that development may add 10% to the cost of that initial project, but it will also mean that every additional project can be done for half the price and get twice the value. Of course those numbers are somewhat arbitrary and unproven, but based on my experience with a variety of enterprise of all sizes and industry sectors, it's a good rough guideline.

And while this may seem like a very complex solution, the intractable nature of the problem of unstructured information should tell us that something more than just simply doing another project, whether its search or social media, or whatever, is going to be the solution.

So let's take a closer look at what you get for less than you think, and why an infrastructure approach is (normally) the best way to go.

After a Few Thousand Failures, It's Time for a Change

One simple answer is that a tactical/project approach has been tried and has failed for decades to deal with the fundamental issue of information overload (enterprise and social). Clearly, some new approach is needed if we're ever going to come to grips with the basic overload problems facing enterprises in the information age.

For example, enterprise search will never solve information overload. In fact, these days, when you read their literature, they are not even trying. When you look at new product announcements or new enhancement announcements from search engines, what you see is a lot of talk about indexing speed and enhanced ability to federate across multiple information repositories. In other words, they are getting better at adding more information to the information overload—not at making information more findable.

If you look at content management software, you see the same situation. Basically, their announced improvements have to do with storing content in ways that enable companies to manage storing their content but not actually making that content usable or findable.

It may seem that the situation with social media applications is somewhat different, and there was certainly a huge rush to throw together tactical/projects of all sorts, all trying to figure out what customers were saying. These early projects did, in fact, capture some expressions of customer sentiment. This is perhaps one of the reasons why it became such a hot area in text analytics—that and the promise of immediate and direct benefits, as opposed to the productivity benefits of most enterprise applications.

However, when it came to creating real business value from those early sentiment captures and diving more deeply into what customers were really saying, these projects tended to come up short. Over the last few years, there has been a backlash against sentiment analysis and some of the social media applications, precisely because they were done too simplistically and quickly without enough depth and strategy.

For example, in a recent survey by Seth Grimes, a text analytics industry analyst, one question was: "What guidance do you have for others who are evaluating text/contents analytics?" Most of the comments had to do with the need for a deeper understanding of what companies actually want out of social media applications. Some of those comments follow:

- First, identify key benefits.
- Identify specific problems you need to solve first.
- Evaluate your content and your need for precision first.

The abysmal record of failing year after year to solve information overload, or to get the most out of social media, is in part because of this "project" mindset. Solving information overload requires an *infrastructure mindset*—looking at the entire lifecycle of information and all the processes that go into creating, storing, using—and especially structuring—information. There are no magic bullets, no new "automatic" technology. And I promise not to get up on my soapbox and repeat that more than a few times in this chapter.

It's Alive—and Growing!

Another powerful argument for ETA, or enterprise text analytics, is that the amount of unstructured content continues to increase at an ever-growing rate. Current estimates are that unstructured content contains 90% of all the important business information. That is up from the traditional 80%—mostly because of social media content. I'm not sure how they measure that, but it's safe to say that it is a huge amount.

Right now, that content is being used in very, very limited ways. It's not that companies are not getting any value at all from that content, it is that they are getting much less than they could. In fact, the staggering amounts of unstructured information, as we have been hearing for years, is more of a problem than a solution.

Compare that with the situation with another hot topic, Big Data. Here, "bigness" is a virtue and not a problem, so why not for Big Text, which is much, *much* bigger than Big Data? And the answer is that Big Data has structure, organization, and consequently, well-known and well-developed methods for utilizing all that bigness.

So how do we add structure and methods for utilizing all this Big Text? The simple answer is—text analytics! Text analytics not only gives enterprises the ability to add structure to so-called unstructured text but also enables the development of methods that support applications able to incorporate semistructured text.

In other words, text analytics gives us the ability to, just like Big Data, turn bigness into an asset, not an information-overload problem.

In addition to adding structure to unstructured text, text analytics can also extract more and more data out of unstructured text, using entity or noun phrase extraction along with the even more valuable fact extraction. Once extracted, this data can be added to Big Data, and so Big Text can make Big Data even bigger—and more valuable.

It's Everywhere! It's Everywhere!

The platform—or infrastructure—approach is the best approach, in part because that unstructured content is everywhere. It's not in any one department, nor is it only needed for any one application. In addition, it is found both within the organization and increasingly, outside the enterprise. It is needed throughout the organization in every department and in every application.

So, the specific content might be different in different parts of the enterprise, but the technology and techniques for getting value out of all that text are common across departments. What this means is that we can either develop an infrastructure approach that takes advantage of those common elements, or we can have a bunch of unintegrated projects duplicating effort and achieving maximum inefficiency.

Having a central, enterprise text analytics team enables the skills and resources developed for one project (say, enterprise search) to be used in additional projects, such as enhancing e-Discovery projects.

In addition, having a dedicated team of experienced text analysts (both development and analytical) will likely lead to higher-quality results. Too often, a project approach means that each project will have to staff those functions within the project team—and normally this means with people having little experience.

Importance of Integration

Since unstructured text is everywhere and there are common text handling issues and methods in every department, the need for integration becomes even more important in maximizing the value to be obtained from that text.

Enterprise text analytics enables enterprises not only to integrate text from all over the enterprise but also to develop applications that integrate both unstructured text and structured data. For example, a health care application can not only capture important insights in unstructured content like doctor's notes,[1] but even better, it could integrate a variety of other sources of information. For example, it could combine those unstructured notes with other hospital, or external research documents and other data sources.

Value of Unstructured Text

Very often the most important insights can be found in unstructured text, rather than just the data. For example, in a recent article by Craig Rhinehart in *KMWorld*, he states, "Healthcare data is not as precise. In fact, the most valuable data is often unstructured notes recorded from patient and doctor visits or encounters." He goes on to cite cases, such as 74% of critical heart values were found in notes, compared with 2% from structured data.

Integrating all these sources enables maximum synergies that can both deepen our knowledge of the various medical situations, and also catch a whole range of missing connections—connections between people, between diseases and drugs, etc. This type of integration also opens up new avenues for application-level synergies.

Quality Counts

The ultimate answer, however, is simply that a strategic, enterprise approach produces much higher quality products and results. This is particularly true for something as complex as text analytics, where it's very easy to get lost in the complexity of language or get lost in the euphoria of imagined value—and social media applications seem particularly susceptible to this overblown hype.

One thing that is normally missing from project-oriented approaches is someone with a deep understanding of language and the organization of concepts. It was often possible to find this expertise in the library, but now it seems like most companies have been cutting back in this area.

One common mistake that many companies make is to underestimate the need for these language skills. And so the project ends up taking five to ten times longer than planned, because someone in business or IT thinks, "How hard can this language stuff be, it's not rocket science?"

I'm always amazed how often I hear this—and how often I repeat one of my favorite conference talk lines—"No, it's not rocket science, it's much harder than rocket science. Rocket science is math and engineering, and there are specific answers, but language is messy and creative, and there are few if any yes/no answers."

Of course, you are free to hire an external text analyst/developer (I'm more than happy to help), but that can be very expensive, especially since many, if not most, text analytics applications require some ongoing maintenance of those linguistic elements.

While an emphasis on language and meaning and taxonomies might seem foreign to many enterprises, it is a necessary counterpoint to the all-too-frequent focus on software as THE solution to all information problems. Instead of trying to solve information overload by rushing out and buying yet another new technology, or jumping on a social media bandwagon without a clear idea of what will actually create business value, a much better approach is to start by focusing on your overall strategy, and second on the addition of intelligence and depth to your ability to deal with unstructured content.

Good News

However, the good news is that more and more organizations are coming to recognize that an infrastructure approach is needed. For example, companies are looking at enterprise search, not just as a search engine but as a platform for a range of search-based applications, or InfoApps. This is a step in the right direction, but as we have seen, search itself is dependent on good metadata—and therefore a well-developed text analytics platform.

A great deal of the resistance to a platform or infrastructure approach is probably more cultural than intellectual or practical. In the US, and especially in places like Northern California, the culture is one of superfast technology with little sympathy for the need for infrastructure—or the complexity of language. Of course, that mindset tends to ignore how much of the startup culture rests on a well-developed technical infrastructure.

However, even here (I live in the San Francisco Bay Area), things are changing. There was a great story about one of the giants of our high-tech, high-speed culture, Mark Zuckerberg. It was at the occasion of his donating $120 million to Bay Area schools (thank you), and he was quoted as saying that at Facebook, the original motto: "Move fast and break things" had been replaced with "Move fast with a stable infrastructure."[2] Sounds good to me.

However, it is not just a technical infrastructure that is needed but also a semantic infrastructure—using enterprise text analytics. It is ETA that enables the development of an infrastructure based not just on technical networks, but on social networks—and not just on a network that moves packets of the containers of information around, but on a network of meaning—a semantic network.

This is a new kind of infrastructure—one for the future—and one that takes information and meaning seriously.

A Text Analytics Infrastructure Approach

However, a big question remains, which is: What would such an infrastructure look like, and how would you go about building it?

As you can imagine, the answer to that question is not simple or short, and we'll take the next two chapters to answer it. What I will describe is a full-platform/infrastructure solution. However, as with all things in text analytics, actual solutions and implementations can vary significantly.

In your implementation, you may find that you will only use parts of the solution described here, or you may use all the parts and add a number of your own. But, even if you decided on option one (outsource it all), you should still find some useful ideas and concepts that you can adapt to your environment.

Even so, my experience has led me to the conclusion that the best way to approach text analytics is the establishment of a new approach, which I've mentioned before, and refer to as *enterprise text analytics* (ETA).

Endnotes

1. Rhinehart, Craig. "Making Healthcare Cognitive." *KM World*, December 31, 2014.
2. "Zuckerberg, Wife Gift $120M to CA Schools" *San Francisco Chronicle*, May 31, 2014.

Enterprise Text Analytics— Elements

Enterprise Text Analytics (ETA)—What Is It?

Enterprise text analytics (ETA) is the development, maintenance, refinement, and application of the semantic infrastructure of the enterprise.

There are basically two key elements to enterprise text analytics: 1) an enterprise text analytics team, and 2) a semantic infrastructure. We'll explore both of these ideas in detail throughout the rest of the chapter, but since the idea of a semantic infrastructure is probably rather foreign to most readers, let's do a quick introduction to the idea.

Semantic Infrastructure: The Heart of ETA

Basically, a *semantic infrastructure* consists of *all the elements needed to deal with the dimension of meaning across the entire enterprise.* And I am using the word "semantic" in its original meaning, not the one that got hijacked by the semantic web—although semantic web[1] technology and approaches can be included in a semantic infrastructure.

The semantic infrastructure is the element that supports the integration of an enterprise's content at the meaning level. Without some way of integrating content based on meaning, we are stuck with simply integrating a bunch of chicken scratches, not concepts. Meaning makes the world go round, and for now, text analytics is what adds the ability to take advantage of all that meaning.

A powerful example of what you are left with—without dealing with meaning—was brought home to me as I researched a similar concept to ETA—in this case, a book on enterprise information management (EIM). When reading about current approaches to EIM, it quickly becomes apparent that EIM has almost nothing to do with meaning. What they are talking about is not actually information, but almost exclusively about the containers of information—documents. It should probably be renamed enterprise information container management (EICM)—but that's not quite as catchy.

For example, one section discussed the major challenges in EIM as: fragmentation, security, governance, and the "three Vs"—velocity, variety, and volume. These are all significant challenges, but none of them have much to do with the real challenge facing information utilization in the enterprise (utilization, meaning the systems we use to manage, find, and apply information).

I imagine that in the future this will seem very primitive and mindless—dumb information management. I mean no disrespect to the intelligence and hard work that goes into these EIM systems, but just dumb in the sense of not being able to deal with the meaning of that information.

OK, so we have an idea of what a semantic infrastructure can do, but what is it? A semantic infrastructure not only consists of the basic structural and semantic elements of information content but also includes the semantic components of an enterprise's communities and the associated information technologies and information policy. We will go into detail about how these models work and how they are developed, but for now, a brief description will hopefully make the idea a bit more concrete.

So a description of a semantic infrastructure might include:

1. A map of all the content, both within and outside the organization that is needed for optimal utilization of the organization's information. This map should capture not just the amount and type of content and the various content repositories, but how it will/could be used.

2. A map of the content models associated with that content, including metadata, taxonomies, ontologies, and other resources. Some of these content models tend to live completely within an application, and so have to be ferreted out while some are clearly enterprise- or department-wide resources—like an enterprise taxonomy. Some of these models are relatively static, like an enterprise taxonomy, and some are dynamic, such as clustering or the ability to add sections to documents based on categorization rules.

3. A map of the current information technology of the organization, including enterprise or strategic software like enterprise search engines and content management systems, BI and CI technology, and, of course, text analytics.

4. A complete description of the various information lifecycles within the organization, including the creation of content, approval processes and tagging processes, publishing, and finally, the consumption of information. This also includes what is perhaps the most important element of an information lifecycle within an organization and one of the most neglected—a distributed feedback mechanism that allows people to provide the kind of feedback that will improve all the other elements, from tag values to publishing procedures to the selection of technology.

5. In addition, a critical piece is a map of the people and communities within your organization (and those outside that play critical roles), along with a focus on the information needs and behaviors of those people and communities. For example, the map would include the different information behaviors and needs of the various roles and functions within the organization—sales, technical support, researchers, and management—all have different requirements.

6. An up-to-date description of policies and procedures that directly impact the use of information within the organization. These policies may directly govern certain aspects of information, such as a policy describing what metadata needs to be associated with what content, or these policies may have indirect implications for information, such as security or governance.

With that brief description in mind, let us take a deeper look at the first key element for enterprise text analytics—the ETA team.

Enterprise Text Analytics Department

OK, it might be a bit of a fantasy, but I'd like to use a kind of thought experiment and describe what an ETA department might look like. The model is mostly based on my experience with large organizations (government, biopharma, and the like). Using this model allows us to explore what ETA can do, how best to do it, and what skills and functions are needed to carry it off successfully.

Even though it is based on a large organizational model, it still applies to small organizations and companies. The function, skills, and make-up of the team will essentially be the same, whether the enterprise is 100,000 employees spread over 25 campuses, or a company with 100 employees in a single building. The difference will be in the scale, but the basic elements and functions will be mostly the same. So even if your company is too small for an ETA department, you will still have to deal with the same issues that an ETA department would. In other words, your ETA department might be one person and a number of partners/collaborators.

Of course, if your company is 10 to 20 people in a startup, you probably don't need text analytics at all—yet. But if you are planning on growing quickly, or your company produces a product or service that deals with large quantities of unstructured text, stay tuned—don't skip to the next chapter just yet. There should be some valuable ideas that you can use—you'll just have to adapt them to a smaller environment.

On the other hand, if you are part of one of those large, complex organizations, you might want to consider making this thought experiment a reality—at some level at least. As we discussed earlier, taking an infrastructure approach to text analytics is probably the best way for most enterprises to get the most out of text analytics. Unstructured text is everywhere—and it crosses departmental boundaries—and so an interdisciplinary central team is probably the best way to add depth and intelligence to every aspect of text analytics, from research into the latest techniques to the development of applications founded on something more substantial than "I heard we should have a VOC program."

To describe this hypothetical ETA department, we'll look at the following areas:

- The organizational location of the ETA team
- ETA team – what skills do they need?
- Technology – internal and external to the team
- Functions – basic and services

Location of the ETA Team

The location of the ETA department and how it will be staffed is the easy question to answer—it depends. It depends on the current organization of the company, and on the current culture of the company; it could also depend on the size of the organization. For example, a large pharmaceutical company would be more likely to have a dedicated department that has a major place within the organization, while a small insurance company might have a small central group that partners with other parts of the organization. And the company that sells widgets or beans may have a single person and various part-time functions making up the central team.

Having said that, there are a couple of general considerations. The first issue is to find the right structure for your company between the two extremes of having a single ETA department that has all the needed elements within the department, or having a small dedicated core of people who work with other groups for a number of critical capabilities. These critical capabilities include IT (programming, general software, etc.) and business subject matter expertise.

The central group should always partner with other cross organizational units as well as specific departments. The cross organizational units include library, IT, HR, corporate communication, and training departments. These groups are natural partners for a central semantic infrastructure team.

Given that—even for a hypothetical thought experiment—it seems highly unlikely that an organization will start out with a super-size department in a brand new area, I assume most companies will start with a small core team, and as they grow in importance and scope (and I assume they will) determine how, if and when to incorporate these support activities within the growing ETA department. (OK, I'm dreaming a bit.)

The second issue involves the organizational location of ETA—will it be in IT, or some other group? One place that I have seen result in success is to locate an enterprise text analytics effort within a knowledge management, or KM group. There are a number of schools of KM, and as long as the KM group is not one of those doctrinaire anti-technology schools, or one that insists on the radical division of knowledge and information, then locating ETA within a KM department takes advantage of the various synergies that exist between KM and ETA.

A KM department is a natural fit, in part because text analytics can be used to support a number of KM initiatives, such as expertise location. And the KM group can add a depth and dynamism to dealing with information/knowledge with concepts such as tacit knowledge.

It is not so important where to locate text analytics, as long as certain pitfalls are avoided. The best approach to text analytics is a fundamentally interdisciplinary one, so the real question is this: How is it best to support an interdepartmental collaboration?

Location: The Cloud?

In the last couple of years, cloud-based services and products have become more popular, so the questions is, could something as fundamental as ETA be located in the cloud? And, as expected, the answer is *yes and no*.

Locating an enterprise-wide text analytics capability in the cloud has some distinct advantages. Instead of trying to add or develop new resources and skills to your enterprise, you could utilize the skills and software of an established firm that had developed these skills and enhanced their software, so you don't have to. For example, the company Clarabridge has been offering sentiment analysis in the cloud for a number of years. They take your content and apply their software and expertise to produce reports tailored to your specific needs. Could this model be generalized to the enterprise's entire text analytics needs?

The short answer is "not yet." The longer answer is that some parts of an ETA "department" could be located in the cloud. There will be a lot of security issues needing to be addressed, but assuming that is done, much of an ETA could be located in the cloud.

The software is one obvious candidate as long as it can be set up with access to all the necessary content. The text analytics development skills could also be located in the cloud using one company's established experience. However, figuring out all the different kinds of text analytics applications that could benefit your enterprise is something that requires some knowledge to be located with your enterprise.

This also implies that the vendor needs certain additional skills. One skill becomes particularly important—the skill of interviewing/working with your enterprise's subject matter experts.

Right now, I don't know of any company that offers to host an enterprise-wide text analytics capability, or even can host the development of some of the advanced applications that we discussed in Chapter 11. But stay tuned—I won't be surprised to see more offerings in this area.

One issue that came up for a company that I work with is that the cloud-based company's software was using machine learning techniques and was not able to achieve a high enough accuracy to be useful. The problem is that "automatic" solutions simply can't get a high enough accuracy for many enterprise applications—and there is no generic solution. As we have noted, text analytics typically requires a significant amount of customization—and that means understanding the uniqueness of each enterprise.

What this customization requires is some internal text analytics expertise to work with the vendor's text analytics experts. A cloud-based solution would not require as much internal resources, but some level of text analytics skill is still a necessary capability for the enterprise—in other words, you still want a text analytics "department" with a particular set of skills. Even if the vendor provides the text analytics development skills, much better results can be obtained if there is a strong knowledge of those development skills within the enterprise. This development skills can enable the enterprise to work with the vendor's developers, and the combination of the internal and external will usually provide better applications.

Text Analytics Skill Requirements

An enterprise text analytics department will need a wide variety of skills, either on the team or through obtaining the services of one of their partner groups. However, regardless of how the group is staffed, there will be a need for one particular set of skills—those skills that are needed to actually develop text analytics capabilities. Unfortunately, this is a still mostly undefined area. Currently, there is not enough experience in companies, or even in academia to answer the question of what skills are needed.

For example, as we saw in the chapter on ROI, one reason that text analytics hasn't grown faster and become more established is that there is no academic foundation or training ground for text analytics. The only area of text analytics that you can find in academia is text mining— and text mining is normally taught in computer science with a mathematics connection.

What you won't find in academia is conneeting text analytics with linguistics, with business language use, or even more importantly, cognitive science. So perhaps you linguistic majors should take a look at adding text analytics to broaden your employment possibilities.

Text Analytics Skill Requirements: How to Obtain Them

Also, most companies don't have the skills in-house as they start out. So the main question, besides what actual skills are needed, is how to get those skills. Without any existing training mechanism, there are two avenues. The first is to ask a text analytics vendor to train your people. In fact, this type of training is offered by most vendors. There is a problem with this training, though: it is almost exclusively *software* training; that is, it emphasizes how to use the functions of the software. This is valuable, but it's not enough. Such training doesn't teach people how to deal with all the complex language issues involved in text analytics.

Also, too many text analytics companies prefer to sell their software as basically automatic—all you need is their software, your SMEs, and you're somehow golden. As a partner to many of these companies, I'm somewhat loath to contradict one of their main sales pitches, but the reality that

I've seen is that this method does not get you to where you need to be. It might get you there if the SMEs are good at learning new skills, including the ability to put themselves in the mindset of a nonexpert, but too often with this approach, companies get stuck at a low level of performance and blame the software.

The second avenue, learning or training by doing with expert guidance, is described in Chapter 6. This not only trains your people in the software but also gives them experience with the language issues. I admit I'm prejudiced since my company offers this type of service, but to me the method seems vastly superior to anything else. I have seen too many people struggle to produce anything beyond very simple, and thus not very useful categorization and/or entity extraction. And then they blame it on the software—if not on the whole idea of text analytics itself.

Without this deeper knowledge, it will be very difficult for your ETA team either to develop the semantic infrastructure for text analytics or to work with others in the company to develop sophisticated applications utilizing text analytics. One project I'm exploring to build on this book is a basic and advanced course in text analytics.

Text Analytics Skill Requirements: Who to Train

On a personal level, I find my own background to be ideally suited for text analytics, but it's not a background or academic career that I could suggest that anyone else follow. I was a very stereotypical professional student, with the equivalence of an undergraduate degree in English, philosophy, and finally the history of ideas, which is the degree I finally (and reluctantly) graduated with and what I also got a master's (and ABD) in. In addition, there were major research efforts in artificial intelligence and cognitive science, with language and library science thrown in for good measure.

So, aside from looking for professional students with an AI and cognitive science interest, who are the best candidates for training in text analytics?

Some of My Best Friends Are Librarians

Finding the right people to be trained in text analytics is not always easy. However, for my consulting company, the KAPS group, the vast majority of people that I've hired as consultants have had a library science background. Library science is certainly the closest to an academic field that prepares people for text analytics work. However, not all librarians have a good background, or the linguistic focus needed for text analytics.

The librarians that make the best text analysts are reference librarians. Reference librarians have, among other skills, experience in dealing with users and trying to interpret what they want. This is invaluable experience for text analytics.

In addition, librarians tend to have experience in cataloging or categorizing—also essential for text analytics success. However, cataloging complete books against a typical or traditional library science catalog structure is quite different from categorizing business documents against a specialized business taxonomy—or sentiments against an emotion taxonomy.

In addition, this cataloging experience doesn't cover one of the other major skill areas for text analytics which is the development of automated categorization rules which require a much more flexible understanding of categorization in general. In addition, rule writing requires learning to write good queries and/or good problem-solving techniques.

What I have found is that the best starting place for finding a good text analyst is a librarian, with either specific background skills and/or a wide background of skills and experience. In practice, however, successful text analysis requires a lot of learning by doing, particularly the problem-solving aspects of text analytics. In addition, the kinds of categorization rules that are needed for most applications call for a deep understanding of the practical dimensions of language, and particularly business language.

In almost every case, the librarians that I employ on projects need additional training and experience in order to do text analytics well. They need this additional training in two major areas: 1) going beyond traditional library science and learning how to model and utilize day-to-day use of language, particularly social and business language, which are much messier and less structured than many librarians are used to dealing with, and 2) learning to use text analytics software which is outside their normal realm of experience and, depending on the vendor, can be quite complex.

Learning the basics of the software is required, but even more importantly, learning the categorization language that the different software packages provide. Learning the syntax of what is essentially a simple programming language is the first step. But the more important and more difficult step is learning how to use the different operators to create good categorization rules.

In a conversation with a colleague who has been doing text analytics even longer than I have, he described a project in which he tried to train 10 librarians to do text analytics, and only two of them became proficient enough to be used on the project.

Anyone Can Do It

Many text analytics vendors like to say that all you need to do good text analytics is their software and your SMEs. I have argued against this position at conferences and in articles (and earlier in this book), but to be honest, there is an element of truth to the claim.

I agree that almost any job function or background can be trained to do text analytics—if they get the right kind of training and they have the right kind of mindset. Just as you never know who can turn out to be an infrastructure champion (as I'll describe in Chapter 15), so you never know who can turn out to be a good text analyst.

For example, in addition to consultants with a library science background that I've used on my team, and people that we've trained within various clients, they have come from a variety of backgrounds—librarians, KM, IT, database developers, trainers, and even people in marketing (although not sales).

We've had a lot of experience with providing the right kind of training to a variety of job functions, but it is still largely trial and error to find someone with the right mindset. There are lots of clues, such as liking to do crossword puzzles (logic and language), but no infallible test.

This is actually another advantage of doing a short pilot/POC when selecting text analytics software—or even just starting your first text analytics project—not only can you use the POC to train your resources but also discover which ones really don't quite fit.

Text Analytics Partners and Contributors

If you have them, looking for someone with a library science background is still probably the best place to start. However, given the interdisciplinary nature of text analytics, there are a number of other skills and/or fields that can contribute to text analytics—both ideas and people. Let's take a look at some of them.

Cognitive Science: A Real Revolution

Text analytics can also greatly benefit from an understanding of cognitive science, particularly the study of how people think and how they write. Cognitive science is a field that is perhaps one of the most exciting areas on the planet today. We have learned more about the human brain and how it works in the last 20 years than we have in the last 20,000.

Another academic field that is potentially useful for text analytics is anthropology and/or cognitive anthropology. One of the things that we typically do when we go into an organization for a project in text analytics is a sort of anthropological study of the different groups or tribes within the organization. These tribes go by the esoteric names of things, like HR or IT or customer support. What we found is that each tribe has its own culture and its own language, and that if we are going to be successful, we need to understand those tribal languages and customs in order to develop a powerful new means for these different groups to communicate with each other.

It's about Language

Language studies are something that also can play a major role in text analytics. For example, as we discussed earlier, studying the business language of all the varying tribes within modern organizations can uncover what we would call natural level categories within each of those different tribes. This kind of deep language study is needed to go beyond basic, very abstract systems and develop the means whereby the different tribes can communicate.

But of course, communicating between tribes is only one aspect of communication within the modern organization. In addition, each tribe tends to develop a language for internal use that is filled with acronyms, and what seems like meaningless jargon to everyone outside the tribe, but which they call key concepts and are used to speed up communication within the group or tribe.

Communication is about more than just a theoretical knowledge of language, and so another natural partner for text analytics would be corporate communications. They may be focused more on getting the company's message out to the world and to employees, but they often have—or can learn—a deep appreciation for communication issues and approaches.

Training the Trainers to Train to Do

Another corporate group that can and should be providing skills for ETA, or partnering with ETA, are training groups. They have the cross community perspective and experience with the company's information world that make them good candidates—at the very least for providing input into text analytics development and in many cases, they can be trained as developers.

In addition, they can be used to develop training material on text analytics development itself, as well as on text analytics–based applications. Some of my company's more successful projects have been when we were brought into a company by the training group.

Oh Yes, and IT as Well

Language and categorization are not the only important skills text analysts need; they require sophisticated software as well. And text analysts need to have, at least, certain facility using software, even if they don't need deep computer science skills. As we've seen, text analytics requires an overall interdisciplinary approach, and in the case of computer science skills, most of that can be provided by IT for a lot of situations.

What is required is that the IT department understands that text analytics requires a *different kind* of software and/or a *different use* of software than what is traditional in most business IT environments. One of the biggest dangers to a successful text analytics projects is a misunderstanding about what the software can do, what the software needs to, and what has to be done by humans.

It Helps to Know What You Are Talking About

The final skill dimension that I want to discuss is simply the topic of what subject matter expertise is needed to do good text analytics. As noted above, the notion that text analytics can be done by simply buying some software and asking your subject matter experts to develop categorization rules is a model that can work, but there are dangers in using SMEs.

First of all, SMEs are *themselves* typically members of one of those tribes within an organization. While this enables them to understand the specialized language that their tribe uses to communicate amongst themselves, it makes them not very suitable for developing ways to communicate with members of other tribes within the organization. Anyone who's ever overheard a conversation by two experts in the field, in which they are not experts, knows the difficulty in understanding their jargon-laden speech.

However, having some subject matter expertise is definitely a plus when trying to do text analytics for particular areas. A decade or two ago, this was an area that could be easily and amply filled by corporate librarians, but unfortunately most enterprises have been reducing the number of librarians, who, in turn, are being largely replaced by software. Perhaps the growing importance of text analytics will provide sufficient motivation to turn back the tide on this particular trend. In an information age, we need more information professionals, not fewer.

In addition to having subject matter expertise in the field within which the organization operates, corporate librarians also tend to have experience and skills in dealing with the multiple tribes within an organization. This type of cross tribal communication is an essential piece to a successful text analytics initiative.

Mathematics and Data Are Your Friends

So far I have been focused on the need to deal with the complexity and messiness of language, in part because it has been somewhat neglected in early applications. These applications were primarily in text mining and basically looked at unstructured text as a source for data-word counting and entity extraction.

Another reason for not focusing on text mining is that it has been covered quite well in books like *The Text Mining Handbook*,[2] numerous articles and how-to books.

However, more and more applications are being developed that integrate text analytics and text mining, so it is important to include people with the mathematical expertise to do in-depth statistical analysis. This is particularly true for social media applications, such as voice of the customer, sentiment analysis tracking, and others.

Another important and mathematically heavy area that can be integrated with text analytics is the whole field of predictive analytics. As with many of the areas we been discussing, the relationship of predictive analytics and text analytics is two-way—each enriches the other.

Finally, it is important to remember that, while we tend to strongly distinguish unstructured text from structured data, the reality is that a good text analytics team needs a good data analytics team with database designers, application developers and DBAs. The data analytics team need not be part of the same team as the text analytics people, but cooperation between the two is essential for the intelligent use of information in the enterprise.

ETA Technology

I know that I may have sounded a bit harsh when talking about IT, but that is only because too often, technology is presented as the solution, and too often IT makes decisions about something that is outside their expertise. But other than that, I love IT!

Seriously, technology is an essential part of text analytics and is one of the foundations of enterprise text analytics. Without the advances in information technology of the last 20 years, text analytics would not be possible.

The specific technology decisions will obviously be different for a full-blown ETA department than for a simple text analytics initiative, but the basic elements are still essentially similar. Which path you choose will definitely impact which text analytics package you choose, but whichever one is chosen will still be a part of a larger technology environment. And how the text analytics software integrates into that environment is something that should be carefully assessed.

On the other hand, the actual technology behind most TA software is pretty simple—any good IT department should be able to install it and keep it running with a minimum of effort and no special training. The only real exception is when the text analytics development environment is part of an enterprise software package, like those from SAS, IBM, and SAP, but then if you are buying and implementing that sort of software, you will presumably already put together a dedicated IT team.

We will cover the main technology areas that are particularly important for ETA. There may well be more for some organizations. The four are: 1) text analytics development software, 2) enterprise search, 3) enterprise content management, and finally, 4) a whole range of software that has text analytics—or more likely text mining—capabilities embedded.

Text Analytics Software

As we saw in Chapter 4, there is a big variety of types of text analytics software. The most important type for the ETA group is full-development software, which has the platform needed to develop the basic capabilities of text analytics—entity extraction, sentiment analysis, text mining, and especially auto-categorization.

One big question for the ETA group is whether this development platform is a stand-alone package, or is part of a larger enterprise software, such as the enterprise software from SAS, IBM, and SAP. These enterprise packages typically include a much more complete text mining development environment as well as multiple-application capabilities.

Even for the stand-alone development platforms, integration with other software, including text mining development, is going to be necessary for a complete set of ETA tools. The good news is that this type of integration is relatively easy.

Enterprise Search

The next critical software for ETA is enterprise search. Most organizations already have some type of enterprise search, and so there are two questions about the best way to proceed. The first is, does the addition of full text analytics capabilities imply the need for a more powerful search engine that can take full advantage of text analytics? The answer here will have more to do with the search engine's capabilities of supporting the development of search-based or text analytics–based applications than the dedicated search functionality.

The second question is whether or not you need a search engine at all, since some of the text analytics software has built-in search functionality. For example, one vendor, Expert System, has been selling itself as a search engine in Europe, and only changed their focus to text analytics development when they moved more into the US market.

As with text analytics and other enterprise data analytics packages, a key is integration of text analytics and search. And just as in that case, the integration is relativity easy, being accomplished at a basic level with simple XML. Deeper integration is also possible with a modest amount of programming effort.

Having text analytics driving search makes the development of the current best practice in search—faceted navigation—much easier and much more powerful as we shall see in Chapter 10.

Enterprise Content Management

The next important software is enterprise content management—this is the most logical place to use text analytics capabilities to add all the metadata needed to implement faceted navigation, as well as provide the structure and intelligence that are needed for applications of all kinds.

One common and powerful use case is the hybrid tagging scheme described in more detail in Chapter 10, but the basic idea is to incorporate text analytics, entity extraction, and auto-categorization to analyze a document as it is being published into the content management repository, offering a potential subject(s) tag, as well as a full range of facet metadata, such as "organization" or "people," or more esoteric facets like "methods" or "materials." At that point, the system can either simply add the metadata tags to the document or present the results to an author, who can accept the suggested tags or override particular tags with their own suggestion.

Content management is also the logical place to combine the text analytics–generated metadata with system metadata, such as "publisher" or "date." If the organization doesn't have an enterprise content management capability, or more likely for widely distributed organizations, they have multiple local content management, the ETA team could generate the metadata itself. This can be done either within a content management system of their own, or they can develop the capability of automatic tagging or dynamic tagging at search time.

The role of the ETA team is primarily to create the text analytics capabilities used to generate all that metadata, but they would likely be involved in other information management activities, such as the adoption of metadata standards, or other information policy.

SharePoint—Class by Itself

And then there is SharePoint—part content management, part collaboration software, part filing/directory software—and all Microsoft, with all the good and bad that implies. The good, among other things, includes SharePoint's support for taxonomy and folksonomies. As we have seen, taxonomies are essential for well-designed text analytics. Folksonomies, on the other hand, are not much good for much of anything except as input into creating something useful, like a taxonomy or a "best bets" for search.

The bad is that while taxonomies are included in SharePoint 2013, the support has nothing to do with creating and/or applying taxonomies. This is where text analytics comes in—both as a tool to help create the taxonomy and as a tool to apply the taxonomy through auto or semiauto tagging. With text analytics, SharePoint 2013 can fulfill its claim of real support of and for taxonomy.

Of course, because it is Microsoft, the other good news is that most, if not all, TA vendors offer SharePoint integration. There is significant variation in how complete that integration is, especially without some customization, and this is another reason to be diligent in your initial TA evaluation. This is particularly true, since the majority of TA vendors are working to add deeper SharePoint integration.

Embedded Text Analytics Application Software

The fourth technology encompasses the whole variety of applications that utilize text analytics capabilities. This includes a whole range of customer and company analytics such as business intelligence, customer intelligence, CRM, customer experience management, and other similarly named software. It also includes broad enterprise analytics offered by companies like SAS and Verint.

This type of software mostly uses text mining and/or NLP and other techniques that are positioned as being automatic, rather than rules-based text analytics. The usual claim is that the software automatically uncovers subjects or themes in the content.

Depending on how the ETA team is defined and staffed, this software would fall under their purview (though usually owned by the business group), or is something that might be integrated with the text analytics developed by the ETA team.

The issue of how best to integrate text analytics and text mining is an extremely important one, and one for which various approaches have been tried, but for now, one basic relationship is that text analytics can be used to add additional structure to content that the text mining software could take advantage of. In that case, text analytics could provide multiple ways to slice and dice the data that an analytical software could use in its analysis of the unstructured text.

This is a technology area that can consist of mostly stand-alone commercial software supported by IT and owned by various business groups, or it may feature software that is developed in-house, in part by the ETA team. For example, fraud detection is something that is offered by some vendors but for some environments it may make sense for the company to use its text analytics platform to build their own fraud detection capabilities, utilizing resources developed by the ETA team for other related applications.

A third option would be for the ETA team to work with the output of the commercial software to improve its accuracy since that seems to be an issue for many (or all) of the automatic solutions.

Enterprise Text Analytics Services

Just as the overall makeup of the enterprise text analytics team and its location will vary depending on a variety of factors, from size to industry to corporate culture, so will the range of services they can offer. One option that a number of companies are exploring is to outsource many of these services as a number of text analytics vendors are offering cloud-based capabilities.

This will be a basic design question that each organization will have to answer—how much of the ETA team should be in located within the enterprise, and how much can be located in the cloud? As with most things to do with text analytics, there is no one-size-fits-all. In the current environment, particularly in the United States, the danger is trying to outsource too much of this.

Development Services: The basic function of the ETA team is to develop the elements of a semantic infrastructure. The ETA team should develop resources, such as extraction catalogs and categorization taxonomies for the overall enterprise, and potentially specific department variations. Typically, the ETA team would work with other groups to develop a suite of text analytics resources.

In addition, it is important to remember that a semantic infrastructure, like any other infrastructure, is something that is never finished, but needs ongoing care and feeding—maintenance, refinement based on new potential applications, and feedback from users. The maintenance and governance of these semantic resources should be an essential part of any enterprise information management effort.

Application Development: In addition to developing enterprise text analytics resources, another basic function would be for the text analytics development group to add text analytics features to a range of projects, some of which might be labeled specifically as text analytics projects, such as search or social media projects, but could also include any project that had, or could have, a major unstructured text component.

One advantage to having an ETA team with existing text analytics resources and catalogs is that each project does not have to start their development effort from scratch, but can adapt existing resources, which is usually much more efficient and economical.

Another advantage of having an ETA team is that the text analytics development within those new projects can take advantage of the expertise and experience of the ETA team, both in terms of using text analytics software (which is too often too complex) and more importantly, experience in dealing with the messy linguistic elements of text analytics.

Education: Another function of the ETA team is to educate the organization in how best to use text analytics and promote the use of text analytics throughout the organization. One factor that potentially has been slowing down the use of text analytics is that many business groups don't know how adding structure to unstructured text can open up all kinds of new applications, as well as simply making life easier by doing useful things, like cleaning up duplicate or near-duplicate text.

This education function is not limited to simply describing what text analytics can do for other departments, but looking specifically at existing content, internal and external communities, and in some cases whole new types of applications, generating detailed ideas that individual departments can incorporate into their plans.

Research Services: The first research task for an ETA team is to research the overall text analytics space. This normally starts with the research that goes into selecting text analytics software and continues with researching the integration of text analytics software with the related technologies described in Part 2. In addition, the ETA team would be expected to keep up with the latest developments in text analytics and related software, as well as what new and exciting application possibilities that other companies are doing with text analytics.

This research should also include frequent and regular consultations with other groups throughout the enterprise to discover how text analytics can help those groups with their current unstructured text issues and problems. In addition to fixing problems, the ETA team can also consult with these enterprise groups about the development of new kinds of applications fueled by text analytics, opening their eyes and minds to a whole range of possibilities.

What my company often does is to combine the research needed to select the best text analytics software, with a broad organization-wide research into an "as complete as possible" characterization of information behaviors and needs throughout the enterprise, with a combination of interviews and surveys as described in Chapter 5. With this kind of broad foundation, it becomes a relatively simple task to keep your internal research efforts up to date.

Is All This Really Necessary?

No, it is not really necessary. You can continue to not only underutilize 90% of your company's information, but also to view all that (potentially) valuable information as a problem called information overload, rather than as a foundation for a whole new generation of applications.

However, if you want to really get value from all that unstructured text, then yes, all this is necessary. That does not mean you have to develop a new large, text analytics department, but it does mean you should think through all these questions of staff, location, and skills when designing your approach to text analytics.

The basic answer is that an ETA team, regardless of the level of formality, adds quality to all projects utilizing unstructured text. So why the difficulty in getting organizations to realize the value of this approach?

It seems to me that one fundamental reason is all this language and concept theory stuff seems so un-businesslike. What do things like parts of speech, natural level concepts, and good categorization rules have to do with business? It all seems so academic and impractical.

And there is an element of truth to that accusation. But the reality is that in the new world of information-rich business, you do actually have to pay attention to—information! And in the case of so-called unstructured information, that means paying attention to language—in all its messy and creative richness.

While it may seem un-businesslike, the example of data analytics provides a good comparison. We think of databases and data analytics as fundamental to business, but think back a few (OK, quite a few) years, when concepts like programming in SQL also seemed very strange and un-businesslike. And they were. After all, learning to write queries like the one following is pretty far removed from basic business:

```
SELECT odate, SUM (amt)
    FROM Orders a
    GROUP BY odae
    HAVING SUM (amt) >
    (SELECT 2000.00 + MAX(amt)
    FROM Orders b
    WHERE a.odate = b.odate);
```

But we've gotten used to them, and we've developed a whole industry along with a standard set of jobs around those concepts.

Therefore, I predict that in a few years, language concept—like natural level categories and the finer points of categorization theory and practice—will become as basic to the functioning of enterprises as SQL and database design are today.

To carry our data analytics/text analytics comparison a step further, imagine having all those databases, without hiring a DBA and other data analytics specialists. So, the fact that doing text analytics right requires some staff and training should not be that surprising.

Summary: Creating Your ETA

This chapter has introduced a number of concepts that are likely to be unfamiliar to most readers, but which I hope will become more familiar to more and more people in the not-too-distant future.

So, to summarize, we've explored the concept of a semantic infrastructure as the focus of our ETA department/team. A semantic infrastructure includes all the content and content models (metadata, taxonomies, etc.), and the care and feeding of this semantic infrastructure includes looking at an enterprise's communities and their communication, as well as all the associated information technologies, policies, and applications. And yes, it sounds like a lot, but remember the real essential focus is on the dimension of meaning—and it is this dimension that is where text analytics (enterprise or not) adds its greatest value.

The rest of the chapter described a hypothetical ETA department, looking at its place in the enterprise, skill requirements to staff our department, the technology dimension of TA software and related technology, and finally, the types of services that the ETA department can offer, from developing resources, to adding semantics to applications, to education and research.

And if you do all this, you, too, can solve all your information-related problems, create fantastic new applications that will revolutionize everything, easily create a new seamless and powerful information organization for both internal and external content, bake some great new kinds of bread, and solve climate change.

Sound too good to be true? Of course, but the really amazing part is how much of that seeming hyperbole is (or can be) true.

So, are we likely to start seeing a new addition to the organizational structure of most businesses and other enterprises—namely the ETA Department with a staff of 10 or so dedicated employees and connections, with virtually every other department in the organization?

What do *you* think?

OK, it might take awhile, but really, if we live in an information age, if information is an essential part of everything that contemporary enterprises do, if most organizations feel completely overwhelmed by the scale and complexity of all that unstructured text, then maybe we ought to give it some serious thought. At least consider an ETA team, if not a department.

Endnotes

1. There is some hope that we can rescue the meaning of semantic. A conference that I speak at often used to call itself "Semantic Technology," but changed its name to "Smart Data." Now, if we can just get rid of "semantic web."

2. Feldman, Ronen, and James Sanger. *The Text Mining Handbook: Advanced Approaches in Analyzing Unstructured Data*. Cambridge: Cambridge University Press, 2007.

CHAPTER **15**

Developing ETA—Semantic Infrastructure

The primary task of the ETA team is the development of a semantic infrastructure that will provide the foundation for utilizing unstructured text—both enterprise and social—with a depth and intelligence that can not only solve information overload but also open up an incredible variety of new and exciting applications. This infrastructure consists of both a set of semantic resource and a new and more powerful set of text analytics techniques. These techniques can be used create the semantic resources and apply them to various problems and opportunities.

The two basic components of a semantic infrastructure are *content* and *communities*—the *what* and the *who* of communication. Let's take a look at what the ETA team does in both of these arenas.

Content and Content Models

Text analytics is dependent on both the actual text content and on the various models of the structure of that content. As noted, text analytics solutions normally have to be highly customized for different content sets—both for subject matter and content format. Biology and technology have very different vocabularies. The logic that works for Tweets usually doesn't work for blogs, much less a 100-page business strategy paper.

Content Map: What You Have and Why

When preparing to develop a semantic infrastructure, a good first step is to create a complete and detailed content map of the entire organization. A content map includes both unstructured and structured information and both internal content and the external content that is used within the organization. The external content can include not only basic social media content but also older more professionally written content, from science journals to news websites.

347

In addition to simply listing all the content and content repositories, the map should include the different types of contents and content repositories and a variety of descriptors of that content. Exactly how the content is described in the content map will vary, depending on the organization and their initial focus.

Some of the standard content descriptors might include the following:

- Content format: Word, PDF, blog posts, online forums, notes fields within various applications, Twitter and other social media, websites, etc.

- Amount of content: will impact technical needs (indexing speed, etc.)

- Content use: policy, communication, technical support, education-training, etc.

- Repositories: personal file folders, SharePoint, blogs, online forums, news, scientific literature, email, notes (technical support or contact centers), social media, websites, intranet, shared drives, content management stores, engineering drawings (CADD files, business documents), organizational charts, official descriptions

Very often it's also a good idea to characterize the general value of the content, for example—*high value, medium value,* and *low value.* Characterizing the value of the contents can enable you to develop a multitier approach, specifically how much effort to put into structuring that content and making it more findable and/or useful. However, it is probably a good idea not to get too specific when characterizing the value of content—wars have been started for less.

In addition to simply mapping out what your current content and content resources/structures are, a content map can also be used to pinpoint what additional content and/or content resources will be needed for specific applications.

Content Models: Metadata—The Bones That Hold Content Together

An essential part of a content map is to also map the current metadata fields and current tagging process and/or policy. Metadata fields will typically include the standards such as title, author, date, etc., as well as a variety of application-specific fields, like materials or methods. I'm always amazed at how many organizations don't consider metadata important enough to do this. To them, I say: Imagine trying to develop all your database applications without a standard, well-defined set of database fields.

Some of this metadata is often generated automatically, but for many fields, including the most important (subject), or standard facets (people, organizations, etc.), tagging is often done by humans. For these metadata elements, it is important to describe the current governance/policy, for instance, who tags documents and what the standard values are for different fields.

Of course, this governance/policy will dramatically change with the addition of semiautomatic tagging using text analytics software. In fact, this will be an essential part of any plan to transition into text analytics–based tagging, as the new system will want to incorporate as much as possible from the old, including retraining taggers and incorporating the current semantic resources into the new plan.

Many organizations do have metadata standards and, in fact, many have multiple standards that are often in conflict. While a single metadata standard for all kinds of content is rarely possible or desirable, an enterprise-level effort should be undertaken to integrate the various standards while avoiding redundancies and conflicts. This is something that would fall naturally within the purview of the ETA team—in partnership with the library, if there is one.

In the case of external content, such as social media and professional publications, the enterprise has no control over the metadata applied, which could either be missing or using a proprietary metadata standard. It is still a good idea to develop a complete set of metadata fields and values that can be applied to the external content.

For example, on one project we developed a superset of metadata fields, gathered from about 50 scientific journals. The first step was to normalize the nomenclature—amazing how much difference there was, considering they were ostensibly about the same subjects. We followed up by normalizing the metadata values within the various fields. The last step was to integrate a set of metadata fields that had been developed to describe their internal content, so we could present users with information that covered the entire set of applicable content, regardless of source.

Content Models: Putting Meat on the Bones

Having a well-integrated system of metadata fields is extremely useful, but there is something missing—the actual values that go into those metadata fields. So, in addition to mapping out the metadata fields, it's also important to look at all the existing content resources and structures that are or can be used to fill the values of those metadata fields. These content resources can include:

Level I

- List of keywords (folksonomies)
- Controlled vocabularies, glossaries

Level II

- Thesaurus
- Taxonomies
- Faceted classifications
- Semantic networks/ontologies
- Categorization taxonomies/catonomies
- Topic maps

Level III

- Knowledge maps

The levels are basically defined by the amount and nature of the structure used to organize them.

Level I is *basic language and vocabulary resources*. For text analytics, this level is primarily used as input into the upper levels. This level consists of keywords, glossaries, acronym lists, search logs, and other related resources in which the emphasis is on list of words with very little structure.

Level III is *strategic resources*. An example of this level would be a knowledge map that mapped the key components of knowledge within the organization. One example might be a map that described the expertise within the organization, including both content and people as sources of information. It could also incorporate such concepts as tacit knowledge.

Level II is the level of *semantic resources,* which can be used as a foundation for applications that work with metadata of all kinds. Level II consists of models, such as thesaurus and/or taxonomies, including faceted taxonomies, ontologies, and other models.

There is somewhat of a split within text analytics vendors over whether they use taxonomies or ontologies as their basic model. There are differences, and the main one is that taxonomies are hierarchical, while ontologies have multiple types of relationships. Another difference is that taxonomies are more often designed to model concepts, while ontologies are more often associated with things, events, and other types of entities.

There is as great deal of overlap as you can organize things, events, and people, etc., within a taxonomy, and you can model concepts within an ontology.

For text analytics, the essential point is that both taxonomies and ontologies have categorization rules of some kind associated with them.

Text Analytics and Content Models—From (Almost) Useless to a Power Tool

Text analytics has a role in all three levels of content resources—and those content resources have a role within the development of text analytics—but the most fundamental, both for creating a sophisticated semantic infrastructure and for developing smart applications, is a partnership of taxonomies/ontologies and text analytics.

Level I resources—keywords and simple glossaries as well as search logs—do play an important role in the semantic infrastructure. However, most of them have been underutilized (and will likely continue to be underutilized until they are combined with text analytics). The reality is that resources, like glossaries, are used primarily for reference and have rarely been successfully used to enhance information access or utilization.

Search logs have been around for a long time, but they also have rarely been successfully used to enhance search although that is beginning to change. The one successful use for search logs, aside from a lot of relatively useless reports on the frequencies of certain search terms, is to use those most frequent search terms in the development of an extended "best bets."

Keywords also have a long history of use within search applications, but the level of success has been pretty low. Generating large collections of unrelated keywords, either through some software application and/or authors tagging their documents, have had a very limited impact on improving search results or making that content available for other advanced applications. This is also true, even when these collections of keywords are given a new name (like "folksonomies"). As has been said a number of times—there is no "-onomy" in folksonomies, and until there is, they will continue to sound important but deliver little real value.

Text analytics, however, can add a whole new dimension of value to these unstructured resources of keywords, glossaries, search logs, and other reference resources, such as acronym lists. The way text analytics adds value to these resources is basically by incorporating them into two major text analytics capabilities: auto-categorization and entity extraction. For example, acronym lists, instead of languishing as an underutilized reference resource, can now be incorporated into text analytics entity extraction. This entity extraction can then be integrated into a faceted search to actually improve findability of information.

The other elements such as keywords, glossaries, and search logs can also be used for entity extraction and as input into auto-categorization rules.

Text Analytics and Taxonomies: Let Me Tell You a Story

The relationship of text analytics and taxonomies/ontologies is the most fundamental and the most complex of all the content structures. It is also the foundation for categorization.

The story: When I first got into information architecture (and one of the few full-time jobs I've ever had) working at Charles Schwab on their intranet, I was convinced that taxonomy was the answer to pretty much all findability issues. And not just taxonomy but large enterprise taxonomies.

At the time, enterprise search was still growing (and so was the amount of content), and there was the familiar split between technologists (the search engine does it all!) and taxonomists (search engines are *dumb* without a taxonomy). I was firmly in the second camp and had two wonderful women working for me who were almost as dedicated to establishing the true religion of taxonomy as I was.

Heady days, until a stock market bust and Schwab had to decide—*keep the technologists or the taxonomists?* (Guess which won?) There were other factors as well, such as I was a complete misfit for the corporate culture.

But I didn't lose faith in taxonomy. I began doing taxonomy consulting, and coincidentally, speaking the praises of taxonomy at conferences, such as Taxonomy Boot Camp and Enterprise Search Summit, and writing articles like "Metadata or Not to Metadata,"[1] and the even more prosaic "Taxonomy in an Enterprise Context."[2]

Even then, I saw taxonomies as part of an infrastructure approach to findability and presented what I thought were pretty compelling arguments for developing these enterprise resources. There was just one problem—hardly anyone followed the advice. Actually, there were quite a few problems, but more on that in a bit.

What changed my mind was not so much a loss of faith in taxonomies (although it was severely tested), but rather doing a project that added something to the taxonomy—text analytics, by a company called Inxight.

While doing this project, I learned two things about taxonomies: taxonomies by themselves are not enough—taxonomies are essential to doing good text analytics—and the relationship between taxonomies and text analytics is rich and complex.

Taxonomy's Role in Text Analytics

First of all, taxonomies are typically used as the essential organization for categorization rules. These taxonomies can be large and complex, or a simple list of high level topics. For example:

Each node in the taxonomy will have a categorization rule associated with it. This rule can then be applied to documents of all sorts. Typically, the application of the categorization rule will produce a relevance ranking score that is used to determine if that document is about that particular taxonomy node or concept.

As mentioned earlier, the rules can be as simple as a list of words, or more complex, such as:

```
(OR,
(START_200,(NOTIN,"agriculture@","Department of
  Agriculture"),(NOTIN,"agriculture@",
  "Committee on Agriculture,")),
(START_100,(NOTIN,"food@", "Food and Drug
  Administration")),
(START_100,"crop@"),
(START_100,"livestock@"),
(START_100, "farm@"),
(START_100, "animal@"),
(START_100, "food safety"),
(START_100, "USDA"),
(START_100, "agricultural")
)
```

This rule basically says: Look in the first 100 or 200 words of a document, and if you see words like "agriculture," count it—unless it appears in the phrases, "Department of Agriculture" or "Committee on Agriculture," because those phrases appeared in lots of documents as formal lists of all departments. And then, look for the other words in the rule. Now you have not just a taxonomy sitting there looking beautiful (to some of us) but something that can be applied with little or no effort.

Not All Taxonomies Are Created Equal

Not all taxonomies are equally useful for text analytics. Using taxonomies for text analytics has a number of implications for the best structure of a taxonomy.

Orthogonal Categories

The first, and perhaps most important implication, is the need for orthogonal, or exclusive, categories. It is always a good idea to have well-defined and distinct categories in your taxonomy—but it becomes even more important when you try to develop categorization rules for each taxonomy node.

For example, in the taxonomy in Figure 15.1, there are three categories—information management, information security, and information technology—that overlap to a great extent, particularly as top-level categories. The extent of the overlap becomes very obvious when trying to develop categorization rules that tag documents having to do with information management but not information security or information technology.

Goldilocks Rule

The other major implication of text analytics for taxonomy development is selecting the right size of the taxonomy. The simple answer to "What is the right size for a taxonomy for a text analytics application?" is known as the *Goldilocks rule*—not too big, not too small, but just right. Of course, it gets a little more complex than that when you try to actually design your taxonomy.

For a number of years, organizations developed large enterprise taxonomies, but in recent years there has been a growing realization that this is probably the wrong approach. These taxonomies, with tens of thousands of nodes, can be useful in certain industries—particularly biopharma—and for certain uses, such as a reference resource to index document sets. But when it comes to using taxonomies to enhance findability or build useful applications, in most industries, these huge taxonomies seem to be losing favor due to a number of problems.

Too Big to Succeed

First of all, these large enterprise taxonomies are very difficult to develop—costing upwards of hundreds of thousands of dollars just to create a taxonomy.

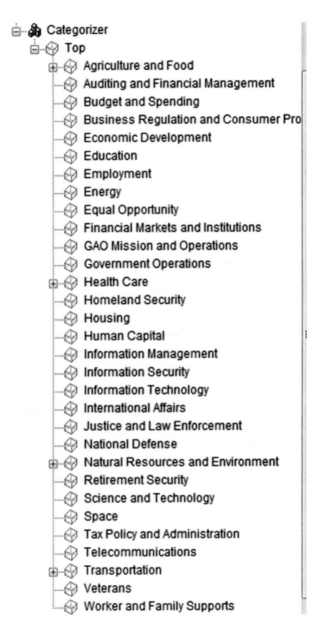

Figure 15.1   Simple Taxonomy

In addition, there are major problems with maintenance for large enterprise taxonomies—as terminology changes, new terms come into existence, old terms are no longer useful—and if the taxonomy is to retain any relevance, someone has to have the job of continually maintaining and refining it.

The problem is that both the original cost to develop and the maintenance costs rise in proportion to the granularity of the taxonomy. Having a simple three-level taxonomy with a few hundred nodes is relatively simple to develop and much simpler and easier to maintain.

These large enterprise taxonomies are even more difficult to actually apply. Basically, the larger and more complex the taxonomy is, the more complex the decision to be made to apply that taxonomy to a document. One issue for the "aboutness" of a document is that very few documents are only about one or two topics. They may be mostly about four or five high-level topics but may also include significant sections containing key information about 10 or more lower-level topics. It can be quite difficult to accurately reflect this complexity, but one thing is certain to not work—counting the times a few keywords appear.

Depth and Complexity: A Trade-Off

The basic trade-off is between taxonomy depth and the complexity of the categorization rules. Typically, a much deeper taxonomy—with much more granular terms—means that you can develop simpler rules for each node, although depending on the nature of the taxonomy, this is not always true. Also, by shifting some of the burden from the taxonomy to the categorization rules, these smaller, more modular taxonomies become much easier to maintain. However, categorization rules also need to be refined, and so the sum of the maintenance task shifts from the taxonomy to the categorization rules.

New Life for Old Overweight Taxonomies

If, on the other hand, your organization already uses large standard taxonomies such as Mesh, it is possible to develop new techniques that reduce the development and maintenance costs of adding text analytics capabilities. One technique is to take a large standard taxonomy, like Mesh, and simply use the top three layers of the taxonomy for your overall text analytics model, then incorporate the lower levels into categorization rules that start with the actual terms of the taxonomy, and build from there. It can be a little more complicated than that, depending on the type of concepts the third level, but it can still be a good starting place.

New Wine and New Bottles

One final implication of text analytics for taxonomies is that for a lot of the applications being developed, there is a need for new kinds of taxonomies. For example, in sentiment analysis you need a taxonomy of products and features, which is fairly straightforward—although it's important to use the kind of features that people are actually talking about. However, these applications also require a taxonomy of sentiments, also known as an emotion taxonomy. For more on these emotion taxonomies, see Chapter 8: Social Media Development.

The Value of Taxonomy and Tagging

By combining taxonomies and text analytics, organizations can realize a number of advantages. Taxonomies provide a consistent and common vocabulary that, when combined with text analytics, becomes an even more valuable enterprise resource, because text analytics enables the integration of a number of smaller, more modular taxonomies, rather than the imposition of one giant enterprise taxonomy.

An even greater benefit of using text analytics with taxonomies is that text analytics also provides the means for applying that taxonomy, along with developing a consistent tagging of documents. The consistency of tagging is something that plagues all solutions that use humans to tag documents, particularly for authors, but even in some cases for librarians. Human tagging, or indexing, is subject to variation both between people—and even within the same person in different situations.

To sum up, taxonomies provide the basic structure for categorization, as well as candidate terms for categorization rules. On the other hand, text analytics provides the power to apply the taxonomy as well as generate metadata of all kinds—hence, the term "catonomy."

Together, text analytics and taxonomy create a platform for tagging that is consistent in every dimension, and creates tags that are higher quality and more economic than traditional ways of trying to apply taxonomy to documents.

Communities—Internal: Peering Inside the Enterprise's Social World

Understanding the people and communities of an organization is essential for developing a fully functioning semantic infrastructure. First of all, it's essential to base any information initiative, whether a new search engine or a new customer intelligence program, on an understanding of what the needs of the people of your organization are. However, when you try to understand the information needs of the people of your organization, the first thing you will discover is that there are major differences and variations within any organization—and even more so for external audiences.

Viva La Difference!

There are a variety of different types of communities within any significantly sized organization. These communities can be formal or informal. Formal communities range from departmental organizations, such as HR or sales, to community-based groups organized around a set of common interests. These common interests can be anything from quasi-organizational support groups to personal interest groups, such as community hikes or community volunteer work (really—lots of companies still support these kind of socially enriching activities).

In some cases, communities can be mapped to specific subject areas, such as vaccines research, or they may be based on functional commonalities, such as sales or technical support.

In addition to a different focus, communities will also have a range of information sources. For example, research communities typically will have well-defined sources of deep information that combine both external sources and internal information, while sales groups may have a variety of more informal sources that rely more on social media content.

Within these communities, there will be a variety of communication channels and different information behaviors. Some groups may have formal communication procedures and methods, while others simply rely on email to keep all the community members in touch.

People often talk about corporate culture, but my experience has been that within the enterprise, there are multiple community cultures—more than a single overarching corporate culture. And these community cultures have different languages, different cultures, and different information behaviors. Capturing these different community cultures is an essential part of developing a semantic infrastructure that can support the variety of types of communication that these cultures need.

The Neocortical Community Communication Model

The neocortical model for community communication came about due to my fascination with how the brain works—in particular its dual nature.

Regardless of the differences amongst communities, they all have certain things in common, and one is that they all have two basic communication needs. The first is *intra-communication*, or communication within the community, and the second is *inter-community* or *inter-silo* communication, meaning communication between communities.

When communicating with other members of the same community, there is a great deal of value to be had using their own native language. That's when newcomers know they have arrived—when what *was* meaningless jargon now seems natural and meaningful. It certainly seems as if the concepts and acronyms, while foreign to anyone not a member, do allow the members of the community to communicate rapidly and deeply. One of the problems with a lot of enterprise solutions, such as developing an enterprise taxonomy or official terminology is that this inter-community communication value is often lost.

At the same time, all organizations have the need for some communication to take place between the various communities. There are a number of ways of dealing with finding the right balance between intra-silo and inter-silo communication, but one good model is what I call the *neocortical model* (at least that's its name when I'm feeling good). This model is based on the organizational structure of the brain's neocortex. I use it mostly because I'm fascinated by the brain, or rather, how much we are learning about the brain. It's hard to beat the brain as a model of organization for achieving a variety of functional activities—just don't take it too literally.

In the neocortex, there are thousands of columns of tightly packed neurons, with multiple connections within the column, but very few outside the column. The neurons that run from column to column, however, tend to be longer. This is very similar to the situation that exists in most large organizations. You have sets of communities that spend most of their time talking and communicating with each other and occasionally talking to people in other communities.

Taking our cue from the brain, rather than trying to impose a single enterprise-wide solution to vocabulary, a much better solution would be to find ways to support this cortical model of communication within the organization. The basic idea is to develop a number of modules that support intermodule communication by capturing the community language in a specialized taxonomy—or catonomy—that can be used to categorize all the community's content. This will enable the community members who know the community language to more effectively communicate. It will enable them to find the precise documents, *without* having to wade through tens of thousands of enterprise documents that might be superficially similar—and could even be used to help write documents by providing quick, in-context look ups or suggested terms.

Finally, for those times when an enterprise perspective and language is needed, an enterprise catonomy can be used to categorize and present enterprise-wide content—or just the content from another community.

Of course, in modern organizations (and in the brain), the situation is even more complex, with an enterprise language that all members share, plus specialized groups within each community and significant collaboration needs with preferred partners. For example, a sales department needs to have access to an enterprise-wide perspective, and they will need to have significant communication with the marketing department—and they may need to have access to the language and concepts of the production group making the things they are selling.

But our modular, neocortical model can easily handle those situations as well. Aside from the whimsy of playing with brain-based models and language, there are a few key ideas we can take from our hypothetical brainy enterprise. The first is just the focus on supporting both inter-community/module and intra-community/module communication.

The second key idea leads to a model that reverses the way a lot of organizations develop the resources to support enterprise and community information needs. The normal model is to develop a rich and deep enterprise taxonomy, with some specialized vocabularies for a select few communities. Of course, it is unfortunately still the case that the so-called real normal is to not do taxonomies at all, but hopefully that is changing.

But both the brain model and my experience suggest that it should be the opposite. It is the small, community taxonomy that should be developed to a much greater degree of granularity to more accurately capture a high level of expertise and the broad enterprise taxonomy that should be relatively shallow and general.

The broad enterprise catonomy should be mostly about connecting the modules—or cortical columns—as well as modeling the higher-level categories shared across all modules/communities.

A third key idea is that the brain seems to have multiple specialized modules, in this case, not organized spatially, but distributed through the brain. These modules perform both specialized functions and the modules can interact in multiple ways to create more advanced functions. In taxonomy design, this idea is most often described as facets.

Every enterprise will be different, but I found that this general type of model works well for most of them. What this might look like in practice is that there will be three high-level taxonomies of organization, communities, and subject. These would be broad—two, or at most three levels deep—and provide a general framework.

In addition, it would normally have information facets like dates, content format, and content type or purpose. The basic idea is that none of these modules—or facets—should be designed to work alone. The real power of this type of model is in the ways in which the module can be combined to better find information and to better utilize information in multiple applications.

What is different about this model is that it can be augmented by numerous specialized taxonomies that capture the depth and granularity needed by specialized communities and/or experts. These specialized modules/taxonomies could be integrated with a broad enterprise taxonomy or maintained separately to reduce the complexity of taxonomy governance. Each specialized module can be organized independently of your organization of the overall enterprise taxonomy.

For example, you may want a functionally based taxonomy organized around tasks, such as how to do a set of standard activities that are important to that particular community.

Which modules are needed will vary from enterprise to enterprise, and even more so for how the different modules can be combined. However, this modular approach works much better than trying to come up with a single hierarchical taxonomy that is broad enough and deep enough to cover all information and communication needs.

Text Analytics to the Rescue—Again / Personalization in Context

There have been various attempts to incorporate personalization into applications, like search targeted news, with varying degrees of success. One of the issues is that many of these efforts focused on individuals, while they offer advantages over a one–size–fits–all enterprise solution, miss the important reality that individuals are part of communities.

Each individual is a member of the enterprise and is a member of one or more communities within the enterprise. So a deeper personalization should take into account the individual, the context of the enterprise as a whole, and the context of the communities to which the individual belongs.

Text analytics can help develop this deeper personalization in a variety of ways. The most basic is by analyzing the documents that a particular person has written and the documents of an entire community to which the person belongs. Using text mining and/or text analytics, a characterization can be built of each set of documents—the individuals, the community, and enterprise. These characterizations can then be combined with additional system metadata coming from an HR database to build much more sophisticated personalization into a variety of applications.

In addition to the largely statistical characterization of these documents an enterprise could get with text mining, text analytics can add additional depth by looking at the context around specific words and phrases in the various documents. Communities can use different words to mean the same thing—and the same words can mean different things—depending on the community.

To use our standard example, the word "pipeline" can be a couple of different things depending on the context. In an oil and gas company, for the production and field people, it could mean the actual pipeline while a research or marketing/sales group, it would mean the products and services that are in the process of being developed.

External Communities—Or, It's a Strange World Out There

Mapping people and communities that are external to the enterprise has some significant differences, but still a fair amount of overlap with internal communities. One difference is what you know about people— and that tends to be much less than within the enterprise. Another is that there is much less system metadata available in the social world than internally.

Also, social communities are significantly different than the communities you find within the enterprise. On the one hand, you have a lot of communities devoted to such profound topics as what George Clooney had for breakfast. But on the other hand, social community's primary focus is communication, and that makes them great candidates for using text analytics to improve their communication.

Social communities also are much more volatile than the ones within an organization, with everything changing at a much faster rate, including changing topics and the expected speed of response. This will have implications for the kinds of solutions that will work in this environment. For example, the balance between automation and human intermediation will be much more on the automated side of the spectrum.

Another difference is that there is much less intercommunity communication than within the enterprise. In other words, there are fewer of those long neurons connecting cortical columns and a much stronger focus on internal communication. Or perhaps they are just "longer" connections. People in HR have to talk with people in most other departments or communities within their organization, but someone who follows Kim Kardashian might also belong to a community devoted to saving the red potbellied albatross.

This distance between communities makes mapping community connections more difficult and also tends to favor a stronger focus on the individual as the focal point for serving up content—no one can predict all the myriad interests an individual might have. There are algorithms to predict similar communities someone might be interested in, but not those far-ranging connections.

Social Communities and Text Analytics: Adding Depth

One solution in this social world, as with the enterprise environment, is a more strategic and infrastructure-based approach using text analytics. It might not be as fully developed a semantic infrastructure as within the enterprise, since there tends to be so much less control over content, metadata, and the pace of change. But the basic focus on depth is the same—depth of the characterization of the content, and depth of the characterization of the community members as well as content. And even more than in the enterprise, the way to achieve that depth is with text analytics.

When you take a semantic infrastructure approach—building full models of the content and the communities of interest, regardless of the specific application (almost), it is possible to build very powerful applications. One good example is *deep personalization.*

Deep personalization, using text analytics, can tailor the huge variety of content in the ever-growing social media world to specific audiences. This deep personalization can be used for everything—from online shopping communities to news aggregation applications.

For example, one company that is focused on news aggregation in a social context, GetWiser, started with the general characterization of some of the main communities of interest in their target market and is now using text analytics to deliver content to different audiences—and to create a more refined map of those social communities.

One way to do this is to track which stories particular people read and use text analytics to characterize the topics of those stories and capture important entities, like people or organizations, and then make recommendations on additional stories of interest. In their application, users also can follow one another and create ad hoc communities around particular stories or themes. In that case, text analytics then also analyzes the stories that all or selected members of that community are interested in.

In addition to story recommendations, the software can also capture the vocabulary expressed in those stories, incorporate them into categorization rules, and capture new entities to enhance their existing people and organization catalogs. This feedback loop drives continual improvement in the personalization feature of their offering.

Text analytics can be used to supplement other social environments. For example, suppose you are writing a blog about your latest, greatest sci-fi idea (say, solving overpopulation by giving people gills and moving them to the 70% of the planet that is water). You write down a few ideas, perhaps an outline, or even a draft. You send that to a text analytics app that analyzes your scribbling, then goes out to find content to help you write the blog and/or find some related ideas that you can use to augment the blog or use for your next blog.

Or, how about the giant of social media, Facebook? One idea might be to have an "add depth" button that goes out and finds the top related stories/posts related to your latest rant—giving you a chance to add material or at least change that embarrassing gaff. It could also suggest the top "creative" links of wild but somehow related stories or posts. The app could also broaden the context beyond your post and analyze threads—or even communities of posts.

A text analytics–powered "add depth" would be orders of magnitude better than a simple "find similar." Imagine in the near future, when you ask for related stories, the app not only brings back a set of stories related to your example story/blog post/social rant, but also characterizes the content as either for or against, positive or negative. In this content would not be the document as a whole, but all the various subtopics that the software found in the document. A kind of sentiment analysis, but much more complex since it deals with conceptual "sentiment," not just positive or negative emotions. It's likely coming sooner than you think.

So, while the world of social media is much different and more volatile than the enterprise, the same infrastructure approach can add depth and breadth in ways that are not all that different.

Inside and Outside: Ever the Twain Shall Meet

However, the most and useful exciting applications are when you integrate internal and external content and communities. Most companies are already doing this to some extent, but to get more deeply integrated applications, text analytics—and particularly a semantic infrastructure platform—is a good solution.

To get an idea of how this integration might work, let's take a look at a basic integration of internal communities and external content and communities. Of course, by the time this book is published, there will be many more and more exciting applications, and some of these ideas might be out of date and/or pretty standard stuff.

Internal communities have long put links to external content—from online journals to relevant blogs, to external community websites. While this is useful, imagine how much more useful it would be to deeply categorize that content beyond the ability of search engines to connect to "relevant" content.

For example, let's say you have a training group that has a general interest in training content. This could be handled with links to training journals and online communities. Using text analytics to categorize that content has a number of advantages.

First, categorized content allows for more precise explicit selections. Online journals and communities contain information on a variety of topics, so to find specific content, even if some of those journals/communities are specialized. So, if you have a group that is interested not only in the latest education research but particularly in the use of new research in cognitive science and how that research impacts education, it's pretty straightforward to provide links to education research—but that will require this group to read/scan a lot of material that will not be of interest. This means a lot of wasted time.

A second advantage of providing categorized content is that it enables the selection of content from multiple journals/communities to be aggregated and presented by topics, not sources. Instead of forcing people to visit multiple sites and exploring within each one, the application can present the information as a unified whole—saving time while also supporting the discovery of interesting connections among the various sources.

In addition to more sophisticated and useful explicit selections of content, a semantic infrastructure approach could be used to automatically or implicitly route internal and external content, based on an analysis of the content of your communities. And, just as in the case of explicit selections, these selections could be based on a rich set of connections between the concepts, not just a general similarity.

For example, text analytics could categorize the writings in community posts or blogs and create a profile of subjects for each person or subgroup of the community—or the entire community. The software can then go out and find content targeted to those individuals or communities. This could be done automatically, but the application could also be designed to present the profile to an individual for their editing—removing inaccurate parts of the profile or adding some explicit choices.

In summary, taking a semantic infrastructure approach supports the development of more much detailed profiles based on a well-developed taxonomy and sophisticated categorization rules. If the application then allows people to select multiple categories and the intersection of categories, you save them time and effort and focus their reading. Of course, serendipitous exposure to articles not in your specified list can be a good thing, just not by forcing people to scan that serendipitous information every time they try to find anything.

A text analytics–based semantic infrastructure approach can support many more ways to integrate internal and external content—insert your favorite here.

ETA: Adding Depth and Intelligence

Throughout this book, I've talked about text analytics adding depth and intelligence to applications like enterprise search and social media analysis. I'd like to conclude this chapter with the deeper dive into what "adding depth and intelligence" is really based on. We are going to dive into the world of language and concept theory, which may seem foreign to many, but it is absolutely essential if you're going to get the full benefit from text analytics and/or ETA.

Information Behavior & Needs/Business Processes & Activities

Mapping out all the varied communities within an enterprise and the even more varied social communities might seem like overkill and/or way too academic an approach to be practical (true if we were engaged in some deep navel gazing social research into general communities and their behaviors), but what this approach focuses on is understanding community communication—and particularly the information behavior and needs of those communities. However, this research looks at how these information behaviors and needs are embedded in the organization's business and/or social processes and activities—and how those information behaviors impact the business.

In general, information behaviors may vary, from the need for deep research-based dives into large complex documents to the need to look up a specific answer to a specific question. Most communities will have a full range of these information behaviors, but the balance between them will vary from community to community.

Theories Are Blooming Out All Over

Just in case you were thinking that we haven't been theoretical enough, I'd like to introduce a very practical use of a broad theoretical construct called Bloom's Taxonomy.[3] It was developed to characterize different learning domains meant to guide the development of education. However, in a very real and practical sense, most of the information behaviors and needs basically involve learning—from simple facts to complex concepts.

This taxonomy starts with three basic domains: cognitive, affective, and psychomotor. For our purposes, we'll focus on the cognitive. No sense in getting carried away with the theoretical (even when it's practical).

The *cognitive* domain consists of six basic activities:

1. Remembering – being able to quote prices or recite the safety policy
2. Understanding – being able to write an explanation for complex tasks
3. Applying – utilizing a concept in a new situation
4. Analyze – see a pattern in a set of social media posts
5. Evaluate – make judgments about the value of concepts
6. Creating – creating new meaning or structure from existing parts

In addition, Bloom's taxonomy discusses three levels of knowledge: factual, conceptual, and procedural. Unfortunately, we don't have a good taxonomy of information behaviors and needs within the business and/or social context, or at least none that I'm aware of (if you have one or know of one, I'd love to take a look). In the meantime, Bloom's taxonomy can provide a great deal of insight. It can be useful for getting a good idea, not only of different kinds of information behaviors but also of the kinds of content structures and applications needed to support these information behaviors.

Remembering or recalling data or information is a basic activity in both learning environments—and in virtually every job within modern information-dependent enterprises. There are significant differences, of course, depending on what information needs to be recalled, including the characteristics of the location(s) of the information, and the business activity within which information needs to be recalled.

One of the key differences is the speed at which the information needs to be recalled/retrieved. For example, even when the activity is looking up a fact, there are wide differences in context or purpose. For example, one case might involve a tech support person having to retrieve a fact to answer a question that an irate customer is demanding an answer to—NOW. Another case might be an employee looking up today's cafeteria menu—still looking up a fact (or small set of facts) but with very different speed requirements.

One implication of the speed at which a fact needs to be recalled is on structure of the user interface. If someone needs an answer in five to seven seconds, giving them a list of relevance-ranked documents that *might* contain the answer somewhere within a list of poorly-titled documents is hardly satisfactory. They need answers not links, and more often than not, the rest of us would appreciate that for many of our searches. I don't want to oversell the capabilities of a semantic infrastructure—by itself it won't lead to answers over links, but it does support the development of an application that provides answers. IBM's Watson is perhaps the best example of what can be done.

The Bloom Deepens and Slows

The second domain of Bloom's taxonomy, *understanding*, more closely describes the sort of deep research information behavior that is perhaps most commonly found in R&D departments but is an activity that is really essential to most jobs or departments. Some examples of this kind of research might include:

- A lawyer looking through a collection of emails (from hundreds to millions) to find any instances of violations of specific company policy
- Detecting recurring problems in customer interactions
- Automatically creating summaries of large documents and then looking for specific issues

In these kinds of cases, having a user interface that consists of links to documents, plus multiple ways of refining results (facets) is exactly what is needed.

The third domain of Bloom's taxonomy, *application*, is used to describe collaborative learning and perhaps is a good description of what goes on in social world as well as within the enterprise.

In the case of information behaviors and needs within business/social processes and activities, there are no established taxonomies or even established methods for organizing these descriptions. So here, even more than in other cases, what is important is that different organizations describe these behaviors and needs in terms that resonate with their organization or audience.

What is important, in addition, is to develop a deep characterization of those information behaviors and needs, mapped to business/social processes and activities and typically to the different target communities. The format doesn't matter, the understanding does.

Cognitive Deep Research: Paying Attention to Theory is Practical

In addition to this basic research, text analytics can be more successful if we also take a much deeper look at the cognitive elements behind the content, the content models, and potential applications the text analytics will be applied to.

For example, modeling how people categorize content within the organization typically reveals a great deal of variation among individuals and specific groups or departments. People in HR, for example, tend to not only use different language from someone in IT, but they also categorize content differently. In some cases, the differences are fairly minor, such as just different levels of granularity favored by each group, but in other cases, the differences are more profound. For example, one significant difference in the types of categories is the use of simple hierarchical subject-matter relationships versus functional relationships.

Panda, Monkey, Banana

A simple example that I like to use at conferences is to ask the audience to group a simple set of three words. The three words are panda, monkey, and banana. The question that I ask the crowd is this: *Which two words of the three go together best?* And I deliberately don't define what I mean by *best*.

I've gotten different results with different crowds. In some cases, most of the crowd raised their hands for panda and monkey. In other crowds, the majority go for monkey and banana. Inevitably, I also get a few laughs by asking how many think that panda and banana go together best (I did get one person raising their hand for this—a lexicographer who pointed out that they both end in "a").

What this little toy example reveals, however, is that some words are related to each other because they belong to the same general subject category, such as panda and monkey are both mammals. On the other hand, in the case of monkey and banana, the two are related by a functional relationship, that is, monkeys eat bananas.

The point of this little demo is simply that there is no single correct way to put words together.

Therefore, it is important to understand how the different people in your organization think, because that will ultimately impact the kind of taxonomies or ontologies that are created as well as the types of categorization rules that are developed.

For example, for the panda-monkey groups, the subject matter hierarchical taxonomy would likely be the preferred solution, while the monkey-banana group might be better served with an ontology structure.

Centrality and Natural Level Categories

Another concept from category theory that I've found to be particularly useful involves what are called *natural level categories* or *prototype theory*. These ideas were first developed by Eleanor Rosch in the 1970s.[4] For something so seemingly theoretical, these ideas actually have a great many implications for text analytics, taxonomy development, and other advanced uses of language.

The two critical ideas are: 1) some members of a category are more central than others, and 2) natural level categories tend to appear in the middle of a hierarchy.

In the case of centrality, a good example would be a chair as a member of the category "furniture," rather than a loveseat or a lamp. One interesting aspect of centrality is that concepts that are not as central can lead to some intriguing results, such as people will take longer to judge whether an ostrich is a bird than to judge if a robin is a bird.

While it is harder to make centrality judgments about more abstract concepts (animals and objects are easy), still the concept can be used to build taxonomies that are easier for users to understand and to use.

Natural level categories are even more powerful tools for organizing concepts. What are natural level categories? A good, simple example of a natural level category as mid-level in a hierarchy is (the three-part hierarchy of) *mammal-dog-golden retriever*. In this case, the concept "dog" is a natural level category.

There are a number of characteristics of natural level categories that have been identified, both in terms of language and also in how language is used in different communities. Some of the basic characteristics of natural level categories include:

- They tend to be short and easy words.
- They are the first level of language named and understood by children.
- They are concepts that have maximum distinctness—dogs are much more different from cats than a golden retriever is different from a golden lab.
- They represent the level at which most of our knowledge is organized.

In addition to their categorical properties, which can be used to develop better taxonomies, natural level categories have a number of implications for modeling communities and for developing applications to support those communities. For example, experts prefer lower, subordinate levels, while novices prefer higher levels—and the general populace prefers a basic level. These preferences show up, not only at the individual level but also for entire communities. In fact, it is often possible to characterize the overall expertise level of a community by analyzing the granularity of the language that they use.

What this means is that experts and nonexperts have very different language needs, even when dealing with the same issues.

One use of natural level categories is to facilitate communication between communities and within different levels of expertise within a community by, for example, developing expertise rules that are similar to categorization rules. So, documents can be categorized, not only by subject but also by expertise level, so users can select the most appropriate documents. Or, expertise level characterization could be added to personalization applications.

Another use might be to add expertise levels to customer intelligence applications, so that, for example, you could distinguish what experts were saying about your company/products versus what novices or the general public was saying.

It is also important to remember that the text analytics team needs to have these advanced linguistic skills and understandings in order to develop more sophisticated applications. It may seem too theoretical for practical business applications, but the reality is this type of deep knowledge of language and concepts can add depth and intelligence to all applications that deal with unstructured text.

Practically Speaking

Semantic infrastructure! Enterprise text analytics! Natural level categories! To a lot of companies, these concepts will seem as about as alien as, say, "Predator IX" versus "Encounters of the Fifteenth Kind," or—at the very least—they are a lot more than they bargained for when they decided to do an enterprise search, or social media monitoring application … or just want to see what this text analytics stuff is all about.

This is particularly true, since a lot of text analytics vendors are too often telling organizations that they don't need any of this. So this brings up the question: What if you can't get support for this approach?

One answer is, of course, have someone in the organization read this book—especially Chapter 3 if the objections are primarily cost. On the other hand, for someone who is skeptical that it can be done, seeing the results of the successful pilot can generate a great deal of support.

And if that doesn't work, one simple—if somewhat sneaky—answer is what I call the *stealth infrastructure approach*.

The stealth infrastructure approach takes advantage of the fact that a lot of the infrastructure elements need to be developed for any single application, so even if your enterprise opts to stick with the "practical" approach, by the time they are done, they will have a number of essential elements of an infrastructure approach in place.

The danger is that these infrastructure elements (taxonomies, categorization rules, extraction catalogs, etc.) will be developed in such a partial way that it will be difficult to develop any enterprise-wide resources on top of them. In addition, the people who have been trained to do the text analytics components may very well be returned to their regular day jobs.

One of the best ways I know to avoid these dangers is something that I look for in all the projects that my company does, which is to find someone on the team who has an infrastructure perspective. My company may have been hired to do a single application, but if we can find an infrastructure perspective champion—someone who understands the advantages of looking beyond a single application—and they can become a champion who'll represent the infrastructure or enterprise perspective.

Being an infrastructure champion involves both spreading the gospel about the advantages of this approach and working to develop specific application components in a way that enables them to function as a foundation for further development. As noted earlier, this sometimes adds a small cost to the initial development, but it will be much cheaper in the long run.

Who are these people—these potential infrastructure champions? Actually, they can come from anywhere, but probably more often, they come from groups that already have an infrastructure mindset—corporate librarians, enterprise database designers, even groups like corporate legal.

I'm always amazed at who has this enterprise/infrastructure perspective. Sometimes, it seems much more psychological than "place in the organization." But no matter where they come from, treasure them, support them, and enable them to add their infrastructure perspective to your project.

Another point to consider is that it is amazing how little extra cost it is to add an infrastructure perspective to a local project. One common number I've seen is that adding an infrastructure perspective to a local project might add 10% to the overall cost of that project, but then every additional project can be built on the infrastructure platform—and they might cost as much as 50% less.

The reality is, of course, we don't really know any of these numbers in any meaningful way. It will all depend on the interplay of your enterprise's environment—what projects have already been done, the extent of your current infrastructure—both IT and semantic, and a host of other factors.

What we *do* know is that this type of infrastructure approach to text analytics is by far the smartest and cheapest approach to take for almost all organizations. Try it—you'll be amazed!

No matter if you start with a simple social monitoring application hosted on the cloud or have multiple enterprise applications that you are determined to build and integrate yourself, the one essential is that you have an overall strategic vision guiding you. Try it—you'll be amazed!

And even if your IT department plugs their ears as the finer points of taxonomy development are being discussed—much less natural level categories—these practical-theoretical ideas can spell the difference between an endless cycle of buying and implementing new software that continues to disappoint. Try it—you'll be amazed!

Endnotes

1. Reamy, Tom. "Metadata or Not to Metadata," *EContent* (October 2004).

2. Reamy, Tom. "Taxonomy in an Enterprise Context." Edocmagazine.com (November/December 2007).

3. Krumme, Gunter. "Major Categories in the Taxonomy of Educational Objectives (Bloom 1956)." www.krummefamily.org/guides/bloom.html. (Note: This contains the original Bloom's Taxonomy as well as multiple resources to explore special topics within the taxonomy and its use.)

4. Rosch, Eleanor. "Cognitive Representation of Semantic Categories." *Journal of Experimental Psychology*.104. (1975): 192-233. (Note: See also Lamberts, Koen, and David Shanks. *Knowledge, Concepts, and Categories*. Cambridge, Mass.: MIT Press, 1997. 100.)

Conclusion

We've covered a lot of ground in this book—from what text analytics is to how to get started with it, to how to develop applications with it, to how to build an enterprise text analytics platform. I hope by now you have a good idea of how powerful text analytics can be in helping us deal with information overload—and get maximum value out of social media and all the other unstructured text that inundates us.

I'm not going to try to summarize all of what we've covered in the book, although I will be experimenting with auto-summarization of individual chapters—for fun and learning, but I won't inflict that on readers.

What I would like to do is conclude by doing a high-level review of the major points of this book. This will be a somewhat impressionistic review of what I think are the most important and/or most interesting.

I will end by exploring some possibilities text analytics for the future—it could be amazing!

Deep Text

Before we cover those themes, I want to more fully describe the overall approach to text analytics that I briefly mentioned in the Introduction, *deep text*. Throughout the book, I've been emphasizing the need to add depth and intelligence to text analytics and adding depth and intelligence to applications through the use of text analytics. I've also lamented the lack of a good name for text analytics itself (as well as auto-categorization being the name for what I consider the most important technique in text analytics).

Deep text describes an approach to doing text analytics, and it also describes the kinds of applications that can be built using this approach.

What Is Deep Text?

There are three essential characteristics of deep text:

- Linguistic and cognitive depth
- Integration of multiple techniques, methods, and resources
- Platform/infrastructure

Linguistic and cognitive depth refers to incorporating the complexities of language and documents into our approach to text analytics—and the applications that we build on this foundation. For text analytics development, that means an emphasis on using the "auto-categorization" functionality as the brains of the outfit. It also means developing new ways and methods of utilizing that linguistic and cognitive depth.

As noted previously, in the last 20 years, we've learned more about the brain than in the last 20,000 years. And there are a number of new initiatives planned to learn even more. A previously mentioned very good book is *Thinking, Fast and Slow*, in which author Daniel Kahneman summarizes a great deal of this amazing period in cognitive science. I highly recommend the book to anyone interested in cognitive science. I also found it interesting that he uses a slightly redefined traditional dichotomy to describe the different features of cognition.

The book is way too big and dense and filled with amazing insights for me to try to summarize, but the basic concept of fast and slow thinking is fairly easy to summarize. First, fast and slow thinking does not refer to a particular part or side of the brain, but rather describes two systems of the brain that are distributed throughout its areas and functions.

"System 1 is fast, intuitive, and emotional; System 2 is slower, more deliberative, and more logical."[1] While this sounds somewhat similar to the old left brain/right brain dichotomy, this model is much more sophisticated and based on much deeper analysis of actual cognition.

Some of the characteristics of System 1 include:

- Generates impressions, feelings, and inclinations; when endorsed by System 2, these become beliefs, attitudes, and intentions
- Executes skilled responses and generates skilled intuitions, after adequate training
- Creates a coherent pattern of activated ideas in associative memory

- Neglects ambiguity and suppresses doubt
- Is biased to believe and confirm
- Sometimes substitutes an easier question for a difficult one (heuristics)
- Is more sensitive to changes than to states
- Frames decision problems narrowly, in isolation from one another[2]

System 2 is described as: "The highly-diverse operations of System 2 have one feature in common: they require attention and are disrupted when attention is drawn away. Here are some examples:

- Focus on the voice of the particular person in a crowded and noisy room
- Search memory to identify a surprising sound
- Compare two washing machines for overall value
- Fill out a tax form
- Check the validity of the complex logical argument"[3]

What is wonderful about Kahneman's book is not just simply division into Systems 1 and 2, but the depth of the exploration into each system, with myriad examples from the cognitive science studies of the last 20 years.

In many ways, a deep-text approach is a lot like System 2, or slow thinking in cognitive science. It is the functionality that enables text analytics to build complex, rules-based methods for analyzing the meaning(s) of phrases and sentences, documents and sections of documents, and corpus of documents. It includes conceptual analysis as well as emotional analysis.

Deep text utilizes semantic models (taxonomies, ontologies, semantic networks) to enable better reasoning about the meanings and emotions expressed in text.

Integration. Just as the brain needs both System 1 and System 2 to function as a human brain, a deep-text approach to text analytics requires the integration of multiple methods and techniques. These methods and techniques include text mining (with all of its advanced mathematical analysis of text), adding in the deep learning of Watson along with cognitive computing.

The key for a deep-text approach is to integrate "fast thinking" (System 1) methods with "slow thinking" (System 2) methods in new ways. It also includes knowing when to use or emphasize which techniques to solve a variety of issues and applications.

Deep text in this context refers to both the methods for utilizing linguistic and cognitive complexity within text analytics and as an approach to integrating those methods with all the other approaches to text analysis to build a "brain" that can understand and analyze text.

Right now we don't know how to add all these different elements together very well, but this is what is needed and what I imagine many of us will be working on in the coming years. In a number of places in the book, I've emphasized the need to focus on certain aspects of deep text, such as rules-versus-automatic categorization—but that is only because that side of the dichotomy seems not to get enough focus. It is important to remember that a deep-text approach to text analytics requires both, and calls out for us to develop new ways to integrate the two.

Platform/infrastructure. Throughout the book, I've argued that an infrastructure platform approach to text analytics is the best way to get maximum value. This infrastructure can include everything from enterprise semantic resources—such as taxonomies—to a full-blown ETA department. It can be as much mindset, however, as organizational structure.

For a deep-text approach to text analytics, it also refers to the fact that text analytics is not only a platform for developing applications but is also a means for incorporating advanced linguistic and cognitive theories, such as natural level categories and prototype categories, into those applications.

For a more complete understanding of deep text, let's take a look at how the concept plays out as we review various themes of the book.

Basic Text Analytics Themes

Text Analytics Is More Than Text Mining

You can do some great things with text mining! You can detect all kinds of patterns in all kinds of text and apply really advanced kinds of mathematical analysis to provide a variety of insights. However, there are two things missing—*language* and *meaning*. Yes, you can use dictionaries to provide a very limited kind of meaning in text mining, but to really dive deeply into what all this unstructured text is about, you need *deep-text approaches to text analytics.*

Deep text gives us the ability to understand complex utterances that are beyond the scope of text mining. Deep text, while not yet at the level of the promises of AI, enables us to deal with the rich semantic contexts that can be found in everything, from formal enterprise documents to the chaotic posts of social media.

The Payoff is Huge!

Probably the hardest thing about calculating the ROI for text analytics is adding up all the different ways it delivers value. From millions of dollars a year in productivity gains within the enterprise, to the early discovery of a potential million-dollar flaw in your new product, to understanding what really drives your customers (and figuring out how to keep them from going to your competitors), to early warnings about what those competitors are getting ready to do—*the only way to lose money on text analytics is not to do it.*

OK, yes—it is possible to do it badly enough to lose money, but you have to work at it and/or listen to the wrong people. A deep-text approach to text analytics will likely cost a little more initially, but the payoff should be even greater, not only because of the higher quality of results, but the greater range of applications that can be built.

Young and Restless

The market for text analytics software is a young and growing market that exhibits a great deal of restless creativity, with new vendors and new approaches showing up almost daily. On the other hand, it is extremely fragmented, with no dominant leader and a huge range of approaches, offerings, and pricing models.

This does pose some dangers when going out to make your text analytics software selection. It means that you have to be careful and do your homework.

Actually, from my perspective, the market is not quite young and restless enough. I'd like to see some major new directions including better integration and better ease of use. This better integration is needed for a deep-text approach to text analytics. Deep text also has implications for selecting a text analytics vendor—you will need a product that supports using an auto-categorization functionality, not only to categorize documents but also flexible enough to add linguistic and cognitive depth to your analysis of text.

Think Big, Start Small, Scale Fast

While text analytics software selection can be complex, if it's done right, you can not only make the best selection for your organization, but you can also create the foundation on which to build your infrastructure and/ or applications.

Doing it right means starting with *self-knowledge*—understanding your information environment and information needs and behaviors—and only then do your standard market research of the text analytics market. However, this is not enough, since text analytics software is different from traditional software in that it deals with all that messy language stuff.

Dealing with the complexity of language means that the *last step in your selection process* should be a *short pilot* or *proof of concept* (POC) to evaluate how the software does in your environment, with your content, with your users, and your applications, both real and imagined. The good news—if you do a pilot and/or POC, you will also create the foundation to build on. This foundation includes developing basic resources (taxonomies, ontologies, catonomies), as well as training people within your organization on how to develop text analytics capabilities and applications.

Or to put it another way, start with a *strategic vision* of what text analytics can do for your organization (Think Big), then develop a quick-win application as a sound foundation (Start Small), and finally, use that sound foundation to develop multiple applications (Scale Fast).

This motto—and approach—fits extremely well with a deep-text approach to text analytics, and it is a motto that I obviously think bears repeating—so I have.

Interpenetration of Opposites

As I mentioned, my degree is in the field of history of ideas, and throughout the history of ideas, there have been many famous and fundamental dichotomies that continue to structure a lot of our thinking today. Some of these dichotomies include:

- Objective – Subjective
- Spiritual – Material
- Ideal – Empirical
- Logical – Artistic
- Communal – Individual
- Left Brain – Right Brain

The field of text analytics is no exception. We have:

- Machine Learning – Rules-Based Learning
- Automatic – Human

- Enterprise – Social
- Infrastructure – Projects

OK, ours are not *quite* so fundamental, but they are based on a similar logic. There is a very famous painting (one of my favorites) that encapsulates the logic of most of these dichotomies: *The School of Athens*.[4]

The painting (shown in Figure C.1) is a depiction of the celebrated Greek philosophers and thinkers and includes some famous models, such as Michelangelo. And while it features one of my favorite philosophers, Heraclitus, the center of the painting depicts the *big two*—Plato and Aristotle. The artist has demonstrated the fundamental difference between their two philosophies, using the positions of their hands—Plato is pointing up to the world of eternal forms, while Aristotle holds his hand straight out, pointing to the empirical world.

While studying these dichotomies, I was drawn to the modern philosopher and historian of ideas, Ernst Cassirer.[5] In both his historical and philosophical works, a central idea was what he called the *interpenetration of opposites*. The basic idea is simple and one that I find still compelling

Figure C.1   Greek Philosophers

in almost all dichotomies—the best answer is usually how to characterize and utilize the interaction of the two opposites. This is, of course, one of the essential characteristics of a deep-text approach to text analytics. It is almost never one or the other side of the dichotomy that is the right answer. With that in mind, let's take a look at a few of the text analytics–related dichotomies.

Machine Learning vs. Rules // Automatic vs. Human

Machine learning (automatic) versus rules (human) is one of the funda-mental dichotomies that permeates the entire field of text analytics. It seems to take on an almost philosophical or religious nature, as adherents of one side or the other claim the mantle of truth and attack the other side as, if not evil, then certainly extremely misguided.

Software companies, as expected, tend to emphasize the software (automatic) solution. Their emphasis is on things like speed, mathemat-ics, and automation. Information professionals with a more linguistic and library science background tend to emphasize rules, the depth of language understanding, and the role of humans. Judging by press cov-erage, machine learning (the automatic side) seems to be dominant. After all, it makes a great story when IBM announces a new break-through in making machines intelligent by beating the two best *Jeopardy* champions—this is much more newsworthy (or maybe just more sen-sational) than the story of the company that achieves better results through the use of a library.

By now I imagine you know which side of this dichotomy I favor or at least emphasize. However, the reality is it's almost never an either/or, rather, the issue is *where* and *when* humans do *what*. No matter what side of the dichotomy you are on, the reality is that AI is not here yet, and so machine learning (or *deep learning* as it is currently being called) needs a lot of human effort.

Even the poster child of machine learning, Watson, takes "an army of people" to implement each of the subject areas to which it is applied. However, a machine learning approach has one big advantage—most of the people it needs are programmers, of which there is an abundance in most organizations. Text analysts and/or librarians, especially linguistically oriented ones, are in much shorter supply.

Another advantage often claimed is that rules are brittle while machine learning can adapt to new content. I have to say that that has not been my experience. Statistically based categorization also needs to be retrained as new content comes in (and getting meaningful feedback about a black-box process can be very difficult). One reason for this claim may be that automatic solutions are most successful, with relatively simple high-level categories—and it is these categories that are flexible because they're so broad—not the underlying categorization mechanism.

Also, if the rules are designed properly, they can be very flexible. This proper design includes creating modular sets of rules, using templates in which the logic stays relatively the same, and where only specific vocabulary needs to be added as new content comes in.

It Depends

As with most dichotomies, the answer is usually how best to combine the two and finding the right balance, or, as in many cases, "it depends."

Specifically, it depends on the application and the content. And in particular, it depends on what the needed level of accuracy is for the application. If all you need is 70% accuracy—and there isn't much payoff for the effort to raise the accuracy from 70% to 90%—then you can be much more successful with machine learning approaches.

For example, if you have a simple high-level list of topics that you are interested in categorizing, it's much easier to develop machine learning–based or categorization by example. Of course, it's also much easier to develop rules for broad high-level topics as well.

Actually, it turns out that high-level topics and low-level topics (such as a level three or four in a taxonomy) are the easiest topics to develop categorization for, whether you use rules or categorization by example. High-level topics are broad enough and usually distinct enough to make categorization easy. On the other hand, low-level topics are usually specific enough so that there's little overlap between the categories, and they often refer to specific things or events.

The difficult ones are the mid-level concepts. And this difficulty is there, for both machine learning and rules-based categorization. This has more to do with the nature of taxonomies and language than your method. And it is here that the issue of accuracy comes into play. My own experience—and that of a number of people I interviewed for this book—is that it's easier to get 75% accuracy with categorization by example, but it becomes increasingly difficult to improve accuracy above that level.

In addition to accuracy, the other big variables are size and speed of the content. If the application is enterprise search/content management, and you might have a few documents published each day by authors that you can communicate with (and therefore control the tagging process), then a hybrid automatic–human tagging solution is probably the best bet.

On the other hand, if the content is external and there are millions of tweets or tweet-sized posts published every day, this calls for more "automatic" solutions. Although, even here, it is usually a good idea to have humans monitoring the process selectively.

Also, it is not just categorization within the automatic-human and the machine–rules dichotomy that is important. More and more text analytics vendors are developing automatic taxonomy-building capabilities. Of course, as we've noted, they are not really automatic. Rather, most companies are developing taxonomy builders designed to enhance human taxonomy building, rather than replace it. For example, Saratendu Sethi of SAS, explained that their goal was to automate 80% of taxonomy development, with the remaining 20% done by human taxonomists.[6]

Even though it seems obvious to me that the best solution is how best to integrate the two approaches, it is not an easy task. It is hard to integrate mathematical and linguistic approaches to categorization and text analytics in general. Not only are the methods different, the people doing the work in these areas speak different languages, so what we need is a good translation program.

Integration of Enterprise and Social

Even though I think there are significant differences between enterprise and social text analytics, as exemplified by my using them as chapter organization schema, the reality is the two areas are merging more and more—and smart organizations are figuring out the best ways to integrate the two.

This integration can be at the application level, with applications that integrate social media and Twitter posts into every aspect of enterprise communication and product development. Or, it might be a voice of the customer application being adapted to become an enterprise listening application.

The best way to support this integration is on a solid deep-text foundation. For example, doing sentiment analysis well requires the same basic techniques as doing enterprise search well.

On way to achieve a deep integration of these areas is by combining multiple methods, including both text mining and text analytics. One of the things that impressed me most about IBM's Watson is how they developed multiple modules, and then, critically, designed new ways to evaluate the output of all those modules to pick the best answer.

Rather than trying to select the best method a priori, the approach was to let them all try and then take the best. Apparently the technique was to do a very fast filtering of thousands of modules to pick the top 100, and then do a second pass on those to pick the best answer. Most of us don't have the luxury of developing thousands of modules, but the idea is still extremely powerful.

As somewhat of an aside, the other thing that really impressed me about Watson is that a great deal of the intelligence was really figuring out what the right context was. I'm convinced that one of the things we need is a much more systematic and dynamic exploration of what constitutes a context—and how it impacts the meaning of the text.

A good example of context and text can be seen in the software I used to write this book—Dragon Naturally Speaking. With training, this software has done a good job of helping me avoid typing. However, one thing I noticed as I used the software is, if I just spoke one word and then paused, the error rate was much higher than when I spoke a full phrase or sentence at a time. The software used the context of the sentence to select the right words.

Move Fast with a Stable Infrastructure

Infrastructure versus projects is another standard dichotomy in text analytics. And as with other dichotomies, the answer for particular applications is usually how best to combine or the "interpenetration" of the two. However, what is too often missing is the infrastructure side of the dichotomy. Also, taking a deep-text approach to text analytics means that an infrastructure approach is all the more important.

Even though it is a harder sell in the United States than in other parts of the world, the reality is that text analytics is an infrastructure technology, and the best way to develop this infrastructure is through an enterprise text analytics approach, or what we've been referring to as an ETA approach. ETA can encompass anything, from a full-blown text analytics department to a couple of people with the right infrastructure mindset, working with partners throughout the organization.

While the historical trend in most enterprises seems to be to reduce the number of information professionals (librarians, taxonomists, etc.), adding text analytics to these information professionals and training them changes the entire value proposition. With the power of text analytics behind them, text analysts can not only fulfill the traditional role of adding quality and depth to an organization's ability to deal with information, they can also be part of the team that creates amazing new applications, both enterprise and social.

Having someone who understands information organization—and a deep language understanding of such things as natural level categories, prototype categorization, and all the complexities of language—should not be seen as a luxury but as a necessity. In an information age, we really need to be able to deal with information with more depth and intelligence, not just more processing speed.

Text Analytics Development and Applications

"Categorization" Is the Brains of the Outfit

It really is too bad that this functionality got called "categorization," because while this is an important use of this functionality, it is only one among many. Just as text analytics adds intelligence and depth to our dealing with the complexity of language, this functionality is the piece that adds intelligence and depth to text analytics.

This is also one of the reasons I favor rules over categorization by statistics—even if you can get good results categorizing what a document is about with statistics, you can't use those statistics for all the other things that rules can provide. These other things include disambiguation for better entity extraction, complex fact extraction, adding intelligence to sentiment analysis by dealing with such things as counterfactuals (and those "but" sentences), and so much more.

We really do need a new name for this functionality. "Contextual analysis" and "content intelligence" are better than "categorization," but there are issues with both, not the least of which is that they are associated with specific vendors. A contest to come up with a new name seems appropriate, as it is at the heart of a deep-text approach—but deep text covers more than just categorization.

Adding Structure to Unstructured Text = Everything

Unstructured text is everywhere and growing like a mutant fungus from a Grade-B horror film—*it's everywhere, it's everywhere!*

This would not be a problem, except that we don't know how to deal with all this unstructured text very well, or even how to utilize it in our applications. The simple answer is: The way to get value from unstructured text is to add, or discover, structure.

Well, I'm glad we solved that one!

OK, it's a little more complicated than that, but we have discovered a number of ways to add structure to unstructured text.

First, text mining has been very successful at discovering all kinds of patterns within unstructured text. Text mining continues to be a major tool in our battle with unstructured text, but it is limited in the kinds of patterns that it can discover.

Text analytics adds three basic tools for dealing with unstructured text: entity and fact extraction, categorization, and the capture and utilization of existing structures of all kinds.

Entity and fact extraction is basically a way of pulling data out of unstructured text. This data can include dates, people, companies, products, and much more. Once this data has been extracted, then we can apply all of our sophisticated data techniques. This is the easiest text analytics technique to develop and apply, but it too is limited since there is so much more in our unstructured text documents than mere mentions of data. And to do it well requires context, not just simple extraction.

Auto-categorization, contextual analysis, sentiment analysis—or whatever we want to call this deeper ability to deal with meaning and context within text—gives us the ability to model, capture, and utilize most or all the information contained within all that unstructured text.

The third tool is to *use contextual analysis to capture various kinds of structures* that are found within so-called unstructured text. As mentioned a number of times earlier, there is no such thing as unstructured text, but it's a handy way to distinguish text from data. These existing structures can include dynamically defined sections of the document, based on everything from text headings to clusters of co-occurring terms.

One promising technique is to combine the two and capture sections, like abstracts or methods, and then cluster within those sections, rather than the document as a whole. These sections can also be used to enhance any text mining applications.

Using the full suite of text analytics capabilities enables us to add and/ or find more kinds of structure—and that enables us to build more kinds of applications that utilize all of this unstructured text.

Customization

The need for customized solutions that depend on content is something that continues to slow down the growth of text analytics. The good news is that more and more text analytics vendors and consulting companies are developing ways to reduce the need for customization. As with most things text analytics, there are multiple methods being tried.

One path is to make more and deeper, generic *catonomies*—or, models of how people in an organization think about content. There are number of companies offering standard taxonomies, and when these are combined with basic categorization, you have a growing set of generic catonomies. Rarely are these catonomies sufficient for advanced applications, but they greatly reduce the amount of time it takes to develop the deep taxonomies needed for these applications.

One technique that makes these generic catonomies more powerful and easier to develop is the separation of the logic of the categorization rules from the specific vocabulary. Finding and adding vocabulary terms is much easier and faster than developing whole new sets of rules. This technique rivals categorization by document training sets for speed and ease of use, while providing much more powerful and accurate categorization.

Another path that a lot of vendors are working on is trying to enhance their auto-taxonomy capabilities. I have to admit I've been skeptical of these efforts, but they really are getting better. This is particularly true if they are approached as tools to speed up and enhance the full development of taxonomies by taxonomists, and not as a substitute.

Another technique that works well is to develop more *productized or systematized* methods of customization. This can include standard research techniques (interviews, work sessions, etc.), as well as integrating advanced text mining techniques. Having well-defined methods can take some of the "custom" out of customization. This is something that my company has been working on for some time.

The Future of Text Analytics

I'd like to close with a look at the future of text analytics. It will be a speculative look at some possible ideas, not an attempted future history of the whole field.

Cognitive Computing and Text Analytics

You can't really talk about the future of text analytics without discussing IBM's Watson and the whole idea of *cognitive computing*.[7] Cognitive computing is an exciting new field that is very closely related to text analytics—and I have to admit that I wish I had thought of the name cognitive computing as a replacement for text analytics.

However, as I learn more about current approaches in cognitive computing, it seems to me that the field needs more of an emphasis on cognitive—and a little less on computing. The situation is a whole lot better than it is for semantic technology, or the semantic web, which really have almost nothing to do with semantics.

However, the "cognitive" in cognitive computing largely consists of machine learning and neural networks (renamed as *deep learning*). And as we have seen throughout this book, machine learning and text mining techniques are limited in the cognitive depth they can achieve.

During SmartData Conference 2015, Sue Feldman gave a great talk on cognitive computing in which she listed the following as the essential characteristics of the field:

- Meaning-based
- Probabilistic
- Iterative and conversational
- Interactive
- Contextual
- Learns and adapts based on interactions, new information, users
- Highly integrated – search, BIA, analytics, visualization, voting algorithms, categorization, statistics, machine learning, NLP, inferencing, content management, voice recognition, etc.

Quite a list, and one that overlaps almost completely the characteristics and applications we've been discussing in this book.

So why not rename *text analytics* as *cognitive computing?* I have to admit I was tempted, especially in light of Sue's focus on the whole concept of context.

However, the big difference I see is in cognitive computing's overwhelming emphasis on machine learning/neural networks as the brains of the outfit. This seems to me to place too much emphasis on *computing*, and once again, not enough on *cognitive*.

As I look at the future, I see the two fields overlapping more and more—perhaps eventually merging. But for now, it seems to me that just as a broadly defined categorization capability is the brains of deep text, so, too, can deep text be the brains of cognitive computing.

For cognitive computing to fully succeed (and to deserve the title "cognitive"), it needs to add many more deep-text capabilities. This is true, for both the analytical techniques applied (more deep-text text analytics and less text mining), and for models of learning. Learning in a cognitive system is much more than simple machine learning and neural networks.

In addition, machine learning has two major flaws. First, machine learning is a *black box*—we can improve performance, but we don't quite know how or why. As one of the leaders of the Watson team admitted, "When it comes to neural networks, we don't really know how they work. And what's amazing is that we're starting to build systems we can't fully understand."[8] The other major issue with machine learning for text is it is very difficult to improve results beyond a certain threshold.

Developing more cognitive models of learning is something that both deep text and cognitive computing need, but is a topic well beyond the scope of this book. (Perhaps the next one?) However, one way to approach developing these models is adding more sophisticated learning into our text analytics capabilities and applications.

For the future, I see (or hope to see) a mutual enrichment between cognitive computing and deep text. The broad definition of text analytics that I've been discussing, including the variety of techniques, the variety of applications, and a lot of the basic concepts—like the importance of context—overlap a great deal with how cognitive computing is defined.

Future Visions

A number of years ago, I was a member of the Futurist Society, an organization for professional futurists, semiprofessional futurists, and amateur futurists. It was a lot of fun, thinking about future directions for a society and the world, and I ended up giving a number of talks at conferences on radical (revolutionary?) changes to education—and what they would mean for society.

It was also fascinating to learn a set of techniques that professional futurists used to elevate what they were doing above pure guesswork. I became disenchanted, however, as I realized that it was mostly about who had the loudest and most creative voice. In other words, it was mostly bullshit.

One thing I did learn, though, is how hard it is to predict the future, and so what follows is not so much a prediction as it is a vision or image of what might be. This image will focus on three areas: 1) a semantic infrastructure, 2) a text analytics developer assistant, and 3) a reading/research assistant. These are more a description of functionality, rather than specific products. At this point it's too early to say how they'll be implemented.

Deep Text Semantic Infrastructure

In the chapters on enterprise text analytics, we explored a number of ideas for adding text analytics to the entire enterprise. One way of looking at the result of an ETA approach is that ETA can be used to create what is in essence an enterprise brain. This brain not only tracks all the content of an enterprise but, in some sense, understands the content throughout the entire enterprise.

This "enterprise brain" knows the primary subject for every document throughout the enterprise, and can also tell you simple things about those documents, like dates and document sizes. It can also tell you which documents mention a particular person or company. It can help you write a report that details all the mentions of a particular company throughout the entire enterprise corpus—and then break that down by types of documents, authors (individual and by department), and date of mentions, including changes in frequency and other statistical variables. It can also relate that analysis to any number of other variables, such as product mentions, broken down by positive or negative aspects, or specific product features.

Our ETA brain can characterize that content, not just at a high level, such as a primary subject of each document, but also break down the documents to describe all the secondary subjects within each document and their relationship to each other. It can also characterize the content in a whole variety of ways, including the level of complexity or generality of each document or set of documents, revealing a great deal about the authors of those documents.

And it is not just documents that it understands, but also the people and communities within the enterprise who use those documents, what they use them for, who wrote what and how that maps to subject areas of all kinds.

No, it is not full-blown artificial intelligence, but a semantic infrastructure adds a level of depth and intelligence that can change the way businesses operate in this information age.

Developer Assistant

Another future possibility would be a deep text–powered assistant that can provide help in two major areas.

The first would be a text analytics development assistant, which could greatly enhance the whole process of developing text analytics capabilities. Currently, it can be time-consuming and require significant effort to develop text analytics resources, including taxonomies and ontologies. It can require even more effort to develop categorization and other contextual analysis capabilities. Rather than trying to develop better "automatic" taxonomies, or categorization rules, it would be much more productive to develop this type of an assistant, which can then enhance the abilities of human text analysts.

For example, for taxonomy development, the assistant could utilize a number of existing generic taxonomies and combine that with clustering—not at the document level or word or phrase level, but at the section level. In this case, "sections" are defined very broadly—and they include everything from actual section headings to clusters, which are defined by different patterns of vocabulary.

These vocabulary patterns could be mapped to the different taxonomies for an additional level of structure. By combining existing conceptual frameworks with pattern discovery by clustering, you get something that works a lot more like the human brain. In other words, it's a lot smarter to find linguistic and mathematical approaches together, than depend on either one alone.

A second function for our deep text–powered developer assistant would be to help people incorporate text analytics into their applications. This could be done by simply making a text analytics development environment that's easy enough for subject matter experts to use.

A deeper approach could also include the ability for the assistant to analyze the new content of the application, then provide everything from a list of major concepts and types of concepts to a mapping of those concepts into existing catonomies and suggested categorization rules.

Reading / Research Assistant

Another possibility would be a kind of "reading and research assistant," powered by deep text.

Imagine, as you start to read an article, that the first step is to ask your assistant to break down the article for you. It would then pull out all the significant entities and concepts of the document. What is significant would be defined, both by sophisticated rules that distinguish between major and insignificant mentions, based on the content of the article and on other contexts as well. It would also include a deep characterization of your past reading and writing.

These other contexts might include enterprise and personal catonomies that are applied to the document, including a judgment about whether this was a purely business document, or it was a personal document that included other concepts.

What you would get at the start and while reading, would be a smart summary that maps out these entities, presents its judgment of what the major concepts of the documents are and how those concepts relate to each other, and/or how they relate to a corporate catonomy.

For certain kinds of reading, a smart summary might be enough, but in other cases, it would just provide an overall cognitive context that can be used to guide your reading.

Another function of our assistant might be to look up words you are not familiar with, or more creative tasks, possibly ranging from "tell me how these concepts relate to my personal catonomy, flagging new concepts for special attention," to fun exercises, like "create a poetic image that will enable me to remember the content of the article."[9]

Making People Smarter

That last example brings up a theme I'd like to end with—while making machines smarter is an important activity, it has many limits. The ultimate goal is to make people smarter, or at the very least, enable them to *work smarter*.

There's been a great deal written about "how the internet is making you dumb," and the sad truth is that there is a great deal of truth behind these articles and books. In a recent article in the *New Scientist*, a number of new studies are cited that make for depressing reading. For example, in looking at the use of computers in education, they concluded that: "But numerous studies have failed to identify a positive impact and have even found negative effects." An earlier study of 250,000 students "show that they performed worse at school if they had a computer in their bedroom."[10]

The same article goes on to ask, "Why? Given what we know from experimental psychology and neuroscience, the negative effects of IT on learning are not surprising: the deeper content is processed mentally, the better the learning. IT seems to result in shallower processing. A study in Science found that online information is less likely to be encoded in memory than that obtained from books or journals."

This is a serious issue, despite skeptics that love to point out that certain learning tasks got worse with the invention of printing, and memory took a hit when writing was invented.

What does this have to do with a deep-text approach to text analytics? Well, it is unlikely that the growth of online reading will suddenly reverse, but it might be possible to make that online reading a much richer experience that is not only encoded in memory more deeply but which actually incorporates multiple cognitive processes. In other words, it might be possible to make online reading as good as, or better than, reading paper books and journals.

It seems to me, however, that the only way to do that is basing those new online reading techniques on a deep understanding of the actual meaning in the documents—and not just by a technical gimmick or by substituting images for words.

And this is what deep text brings to the party—a means of incorporating the whole dimension of semantics and meaning in new, richer, deeper ways that accomplish the ultimate goal—making people smarter.

Endnotes

1. Kahneman, Daniel. *Thinking, Fast and Slow.* New York: Farrar, Straus and Giroux, 2011. (Note: Taken from the jacket blurb.)

2. Ibid, page 105.

3. Ibid, page 22.

4. *The School of Athens.* Raphael. 1509. Painting.

5. Cassirer was a fascinating person, writing in both German and English (he fled Nazi Germany and spent the last twelve years or so at Yale). He wrote dense philosophical works such as the three volume "The Philosophy of Symbolic Forms", multiple historical works such as "The Individual and the Cosmos in Renaissance Philosophy" and a sort of popular version of his philosophy in "An Essay on Man." The reason I know so much about him, is that I planned to write my dissertation on his works before getting seduced by artificial intelligence and going off in a different direction.

6. Stated in an interview done as research for the book. (See Chapter 4.)

7. See: www.cognitivecomputingforum.com/.

8. As quoted in a post on The Platform. (See: www.theplatfomr.net/2015/25 /the-real-trouble-with-cognitive-computing/.)

9. Foer, Joshua. *Walking with Einstein: the Art and Science of Remembering Everything.* New York: Penguin Press, 2011. (Note: This contains a good description of current memory techniques.)

10. This and the following quotes are taken from New Scientist, October 17-23, 2015, pages 28-29.

Appendices

Appendix A

Template for contextual and information interview questions.

Background

1. Describe our part of the project – taxonomy. Brief – our methods, our goals for interview.
2. What is your job? How long have you been in it? With Company A?
3. Who do you work with? In Company A? External?
4. What is your role on this project?
5. Is there anything that you would like to ask or tell us before we begin?

Project / Business Goals

1. What business goals or problems do you see this project (and longer-term projects) addressing? What are your hopes for this project?
2. What elements of the project do you see as critical to success (search, taxonomy, IA, etc.)?
3. How will the success of this project be assessed?
4. Are there any outside factors that might influence the project?
5. How do you see this project fitting in within Company A? What do you think will be its impact? Support for it?

Information Activities / Behaviors

1. Could you describe the kinds of information activities that you and your group engage in (types of content, search, write proposals, research)?

2. Bloom's taxonomy – what kinds of information access are part of your job? How often do you do them?

    a. Looking up facts, specific data

    b. Finding a particular document

    c. Finding a kind of document

    d. Researching a subject area, a topic

3. What is the output of those information activities? Proposals, other?

4. What content (experts) do you work with? Frequently? Importantly?

5. How is that content organized and accessed today?

6. What is right and what's wrong with today's methods?

7. In an ideal world, how would information access work in analytical chemistry?

8. What are the obstacles preventing the ideal?

Content and Content Structure

1. Please describe what content you and your group use in your jobs (databases, unstructured content, and people expertise)?

2. How is this content created and managed today? Who contributes to that content creation?

3. Is there non-text content (pictures, graphs, database numbers)?

4. Are there any existing database or metadata schemas?

5. How frequently in new content generated? What volume?

6. How is the content managed now? What is right/wrong with that process?

7. Do things like joint ventures, acquisitions, divestures, and new ventures affect content?

8. Is there much content exchanged with partners, vendors, or others?

Users and User Behavior

1. Who are the users that will be served by this project? Are there any different groups within that user population? How do they differ?

2. In healthcare, there are four groups – how do they differ? Do they have different information access needs? Different content creation processes?

3. In the rest of Company A, are there other very different groups? How are they different – subject matter or more? What is the difference between market segment people and product line people in terms of information activities?

4. How do users find information today? How do you think they would like to find information?

5. Are there many sophisticated search users today? Do you have a library or research support group to find information?

Taxonomy Construction Helper

1. Have there been any efforts to date to organize or categorize unstructured information?

2. Has your group ever inventoried your content?

3. Do you know of an existing taxonomy that might address your group's interests?

4. Does Company A have or use a thesaurus? How is it used? A glossary?

5. Are there any structured repositories or existing metadata (e.g., in EDRM systems)?

6. What is the quality of the metadata?

7. Any other things that might help (synonym lists, acronym lists, product and service brochures, share drives structure, existing categorization schemes, intranet site map)?

Natural Categories

1. In terms of kinds of topics, how separate is your area from the other healthcare areas?

2. What can you tell me about the healthcare vocabulary list? What has it been used for? How complete do you think it is?

3. Under healthcare, what would be some example high-level topics?

4. Under one of those high-level topics, what would be some next-level topics?

5. When you are writing a proposal (or doing one of the other activities above—also see asset types), would you research/write any of the topics listed in above, or would the main ideas be more specific?

6. Let's take a sample proposal—what would the title topic be? What about chapter headings? What about key ideas?

7. Are there any other large categories or organizational schemas that you can think of that people in Company A use?

Appendix B

Selected List of Text Analytics Companies

The following is a list of text analytics companies. There are quite a few other companies that are not listed, but in my experience, these are the "companies that matter." Some of the newest companies are probably not listed, and some may have gone out of business by the time this book is published. You should update this list if you are interested in adding text analytics to your company.

I have tried to organize them by type, but it quickly became apparent that I could lose a number of friends and potential partners, so here they are in alphabetical order. I have my opinion as to the top 10 or so and will be happy to share with you in private.

Ai-One	LexisNexis
AlchemyAPI	Linguamatics
Attensity	Luminoso
BA Insight	Megaputer
Basis Technology	Multi-Tes
Clarabridge	NetOwl
Concept Searching	OdinText
Content Analyst	Open Text
Data Harmony // Access Innovations	Pool Party
Endeca Technologies	Provalis Research
Expert System (includes Temis)	Rapid Miner
GATE	SAP
HP Autonomy	SAS
IBM	Semantria
Lexalytics	Smartlogic
	Textalytics
	Verint Systems

Free Text Analytics and Text Mining Software

In addition to the commercial offerings, there are a number of free resources, which can be a good way to explore and/or determine if you are interested in building your own. GATE has been the primary source for build it yourself, but it looks like there are some new sources as well.

Apache Mahout	OpenNLP
CAT	Oragne-Textable
GATE	QDA Miner Lite
Gensim	RapidMiner
KH Coder	S-EM
KNIME	TAMS Analyzer
LibShortText	Tm
Lingpipe	Unstructured Information
LPU	Management Architecture
Natural Language Toolkit	

Bibliography

Books
Cognitive Science

Baars, Bernard J., and Nicole M. Gage. *Cognition, Brain, and Consciousness: Introduction to Cognitive Neuroscience*. 2nd edition. Burlington, MA: Academic Press, 2010.

Brockman, John, ed. *The Mind: Leading Scientists Explore the Brain, Memory, Personality, and Happiness*. New York: Harper Perennial, 2011.

Buonomano, Dean. *Brain Bugs: How the Brain's Flaws Shape Our Lives*. New York: W.W. Norton & Company, 2011.

Burton, Robert A. *A Skeptic's Guide to the Mind: What Neuroscience Can and Cannot Tell Us about Ourselves*. New York: St. Martin's Griffin, 2014.

Carey, Susan. *The Origin of Concepts*. Oxford, UK: Oxford University Press, 2009.

Churchland, Patricia Smith. *Brain-Wise: Studies in Neurophilosophy*. Cambridge, MA: The MIT Press, 2002.

Churchland, Patricia, S. Braintrust: *What Neuroscience Tells Us About Morality*. Princeton, NJ: Princeton University Press, 2011.

Churchland, Patricia S. *Touching a Nerve: The Self as Brain*. New York: W.W. Norton & Company, 2013.

Dehaene, Stanislas. *Reading in the Brain: The New Science of How We Read*. New York: Penguin Books, 2009.

Dennett, Daniel C. *Kinds of Mind: Toward an Understanding of Consciousness*. New York: BasicBooks, 1996.

Eagleman, David. *Incognito: The Secret Lives of the Brain*. New York: Pantheon Books, 2011.

Edelman, Gerald M. *Bright Air, Brilliant Fire: On the Matter of the Mind*. New York: BasicBooks, 1992.

Edelman, Gerald M. *Second Nature: Brain Science and Human Knowledge*. New Haven, CT: Yale University Press, 2006.

Edelman, Gerald M., and Vernon B. Mountcastle. *The Mindful Brain: Cortical Organization and the Group-Selective Theory of Higher Brain Function*. Cambridge, MA: The MIT Press, 1978.

Engel, Susan. *Context Is Everything: The Nature of Memory*. New York: W.H. Freeman and Company, 1999.

Fields, R. Douglas. *The Other Brain: The Scientific and Medical Breakthroughs that Will Heal Our Brains and Revolutionize Our Health*. New York: Simon & Shuster, 2009.

Fodor, Jerry. *In Critical Condition: Polemical Essays on Cognitive Science and the Philosophy of Mind*. Cambridge, MA: The MIT Press, 1998.

Fodor, Jerry. *The Mind Doesn't Work That Way: The Scope and Limits of Computational Psychology*. Cambridge, MA: The MIT Press, 2000.

Fodor, Jerry. *The Modularity of Mind: An Essay on Faculty Psychology*. Cambridge, MA: The MIT Press, 2001.

Frith, Chris, *Making Up the Mind: How the Brain Creates Our Mental World*. Malden, MA: Blackwell Publishing, 2007.

Gamble, Clive, John Gowlett, and Robin Dunbar. *Thinking Big: How the Evolution of Social Life Shaped the Human Mind*. London, UK: Thames & Hudson, 2014.

Glannon, Walter, ed. *Defining Right and Wrong in Brain Science: Essential Readings in Neuroethics*. New York: Dana Press, 2007.

Herman, David, ed. *Narrative Theory and the Cognitive Sciences*. Stanford, CA: CSLI Publications, 2003.

Jackendoff, Ray. *A User's Guide to Thought and Meaning*. Oxford, UK: Oxford University Press, 2012.

Kahneman, Daniel. *Thinking, Fast and Slow*. New York: Farrar, Straus and Giroux, 2011.

Lamberts, Koen, and David Shanks. *Knowledge, Concepts, and Categories*. Cambridge, MA: The MIT Press, 1997.

Ledoux, Joseph. *Synaptic Self: How Our Brains Become Who We Are*. New York: Viking, 2002.

Lehrer, Jonah. *The Decisive Moment: How the Brain Makes Up Its Mind*. Edinburgh, Scotland: Conongate, 2009.

Libet, Benjamin. *Mind Time: The Temporal Factor in Consciousness*. Cambridge, MA: Harvard University Press, 2004.

Lynch, Zack, and Byron Laursen. *The Neuro Revolution: How Brain Science Is Changing Our World*. New York: St. Martin's Griffin, 2009.

Minsky, Marvin. *The Society of Mind*. New York: Simon and Schuster, 1986.

Pinker, Steven. *How the Mind Works*. New York: W.W. Norton & Company, 1997.

Ramachandran, V.S. *The Tell-Tale Brain: A Neuroscientist's Quest for What Makes Us Human*. New York: W.W. Norton & Company, 2011.

Shafto, Michael, ed. *How We Know: Nobel Conference XX*. San Francisco, CA: Harper & Row, 1985.

Springer, Sally P., and Georg Deutsch. *Left Brain, Right Brain*. New York: W.H. Freeman and Company, 1981.

Stainton, Robert J., ed. *Contemporary Debates in Cognitive Science*. Malden, MA: Blackwell Publishing, 2006.

Young, J.Z. *Programs of the Brain*. Oxford, UK: Oxford University Press, 1978.

Information

Boiko, Bob. *Laughing at the CIO: A Parable and Prescription for IT Leadership*. Medford, NJ: Information Today, 2007.

Foer, Joshua. *Moonwalking with Einstein*. New York: Penguin Press, 2011.

Shiri, Ali. Powering Search: *The Role of Thesauri in New Information Environments*. Medford, NJ: Information Today, 2012.

Tomaiuolo, Nicholas G. *UContent: The Information Professional's Guide to User-Generated Content*. Medford, NJ: Information Today, 2012.

Internet and Thinking

Carr, Nicholas. *The Glass Cage: How Our Computers Are Changing Us*. New York: W.W. Norton & Company, 2014.

Carr, Nicholas. *The Shallows: What the Internet Is Doing to Our Brains*. New York: W.W. Norton & Company, 2010.

Gershenfeld, Neil. *When Things Start to Think*. New York: Henry Holt and Company, 1999.

Keen, Andrew. *The Cult of the Amateur: How Today's Internet Is Killing Our Culture*. New York: Doubleday, 2007.

Levithin, Daniel J. *The Organized Mind: Thinking Straight in the Age of Information Overload*. New York: Dutton, 2014.

Thompson, Clive. *Smarter Than You Think: How Technology Is Changing Our Minds for the Better*. New York: The Penguin Press, 2013.

Turkle, Sherry. *Alone Together: Why We Expect More from Technology and Less from Each Other*. New York: Basic Books, 2011.

Turkle, Sherry. *Reclaiming Conversation: The Power of Talk in a Digital Age*. New York: Penguin Press, 2015.

Language

Barthes, Roland. *Elements of Semiology*. Translated by Annette Lavers and Colin Smith. New York: Hill and Wang, 1967.

Brown, John Seely, and Paul Duguid. *The Social Life of Information*. Boston, MA: Harvard Business School Press, 2000.

Chomsky, Noam. *Language and Mind*. New York: Harcourt, Brace & World, 1968.

Chomsky, Noam. *Syntactic Structures*. The Hague, Netherlands: Mouton, 1972.

Croft, William, and D. Alan Cruse. *Cognitive Linguistics*. Cambridge, UK: Cambridge University Press, 2004.

Crystal, David. Words in Time and Place: Exploring Language Through *The Historical Thesaurus of the Oxford English Dictionary*. Oxford, UK: Oxford University Press, 2014.

Deacon, Terrence W. *The Symbolic Species: The Co-Evolution of Language and the Brain*. New York: W.W. Norton & Company, 1997.

Donoghue, Denis. *Metaphor*. Cambridge, MA: Harvard University Press, 2014.

Driven, René, and Marjolijn Verspoor. *Cognitive Exploration of Language and Linguistics*. Amsterdam, The Netherlands: John Benjamins Publishing, n.d.

Eco, Umberto. *A Theory of Semiotics*. Bloomington, IN: Indiana University Press, 1979.

Gibbs, Raymond W., Jr., ed. *The Cambridge Handbook of Metaphor and Thought*. Cambridge, UK: Cambridge University Press, 2008.

Hirst, Graeme. *Semantic Interpretation and the Resolution of Ambiguity*. Cambridge, UK: Cambridge University Press, 1987.

Hudson, Richard. *Language Networks: The New Word Grammar*. Oxford, UK: Oxford University Press, 2007.

Jackendoff, Ray. *Foundations of Language: Brain, Meaning, Grammar, Evolution*. Oxford, UK: Oxford University Press, 2002.

Kövecses, Zoltán. *Metaphor: A Practical Introduction*. Oxford, UK: Oxford University Press, 2010.

Lakoff, George. *Women, Fire, and Dangerous Things: What Categories Reveal about the Mind*. Chicago, IL: The University of Chicago Press, 1987.

Lakoff, George, and Mark Johnson. *Metaphors We Live By*. Chicago, IL: The University of Chicago Press, 2003.

Pinker, Steven. *The Sense of Style: The Thinking Person's Guide to Writing in the 21st Century!* New York: Penguin Books, 2014.

Pinker, Steven. *The Stuff of Thought: Language as a Window into Human Nature*. New York: Viking, 2007.

Saeed, John I. *Semantics*. 3rd edition. Malden, MA: Wiley-Blackwell, 2009.

Shlain, Leonard. *The Alphabet versus the Goddess: The Conflict Between Word and Image*. New York: Viking, 1998.

Tannen, Deborah. *The Argument Culture: Moving from Debate to Dialogue*. New York: Random House, 1998.

Tannen, Deborah. *Talking from 9 to 5: How Women's and Men's Conversational Styles Affect Who Gets Heard, Who Gets Credit, and What Gets Done at Work*. New York: William Morrow and Company, 1994.

Tannen, Deborah. *That's Not What I Meant!: How Conversational Style Makes or Breaks Relationships*. New York: Ballantine Books, 1987.

Tannen, Deborah. *You Just Don't Understand: Women and Men in Conversation*. New York: Ballantine Books, 1990.

Wajnryb, Ruth. *You Know What I Mean?* Cambridge, UK: Cambridge University Press, 2008.

Philosophy and History of Ideas

Cassirer, Ernst. *An Essay on Man: An Introduction to a Philosophy of Human Culture*. New Haven, CT: Yale University Press, 1944.

Cassirer, Ernst. *The Individual and the Cosmos in Renaissance Philosophy*. Translated by Mario Domandi. New York: Harper Torchbooks, 1963.

Cassirer, Ernst. *The Philosophy of Symbolic Forms. Vol. 1: Language*. Translated by Ralph Manheim. New Have: Yale University Press, 1953.

Danto, Arthur C. *Narration and Knowledge* (including the Integral Text of Analytical Philosophy of History). New York: Columbia University Press, 1985.

Gottschalk, Louis, ed. *Generalization in the Writing of History*. Chicago, IL: The University of Chicago Press, 1963.

Hoerl, Christophe, and Teresa McCormack, eds. *Time and Memory: Issues in Philosophy and Psychology*. Oxford, UK: Clarendon Press, 2001.

Koselleck, Reinhart. *The Practice of Conceptual History: Timing History, Spacing Concepts*. Translated by Todd Samuel Presner and others. Stanford, CA: Stanford University Press, 2002.

Roberts, Geoffrey, ed. *The History and Narrative Reader*. London, UK: Routledge, 2001.

Searle, John. *Minds, Brains and Science*. Cambridge, MA: Harvard University Press, 1984.

Wittgenstein, Ludwig. *Philosophical Investigations*. Translated by G.E.M. Anscombe. 3rd Edition. New York: The Macmillan Company, 1958.

Systems

Barabási, Albert-László. *Linked: How Everything Is Connected to Everything Else and What It Means for Business, Science, and Everyday Life*. New York: Basic Books, 2014.

Fisher, Len. *The Perfect Swarm: The Science of Complexity in Everyday Life*. New York: Basic Books, 2009.

Gazzaniga, Michael S. *The Social Brain: Discovering the Networks of the Mind*. New York: Basic Books, 1985.

Gleick, James. Chaos: *Making a New Science*. New York: Penguin, 1987.

Gleick, James. *The Information: A History, a Theory, a Flood*. New York: Pantheon Books, 2011.

Goleman, Daniel. *Emotional Intelligence: What It Can Matter More than IQ*. New York: Bantam Books, 1995.

Johnson, Steven. *Emergence: The Connected Lives of Ants, Brains, Cities, and Software*. New York: Scribner, 2001.

Kosko, Bart. *Fuzzy Thinking: The New Science of Fuzzy Logic*. New York: Hyperion, 1993.

Minsky, Marvin. *The Emotion Machine: Commonsense Thinking, Artificial Intelligence, and the Future of the Human Mind*. New York: Simon & Schuster, 2006.

Piaget, Jean. *Structuralism*. Translated and Edited by Chaninah Maschler. New York: Harper Torchbooks, 1968.

Picard, Rosalind. *Affective Computing*. Cambridge, MA: The MIT Press, 1997.

Rheingold, Howard. *Smart Mobs: The Next Social Revolution*. Cambridge, MA: Perseus Books, 2002.

Taleb, Nassim Nicholas. *Antifragile: Things That Gain from Disorder*. New York: Random House, 2014.

Watts, Duncan J. *Six Degrees: The Science of a Connected Age*. New York: W.W. Norton & Company, 2003.

Wolfram, Stephen. *A New Kind of Science*. Champaign, IL: Wolfram Media, 2002.

Text / Data Analytics

Affelt, Amy. *The Accidental Data Scientist*. Medford, NJ: Information Today, 2015.

Allenmang, Dean, and Jim Hendler. *Semantic Web for the Working Ontologist: Effective Modeling in RDFS and OWL*. Burlington, MA: Morgan Kaufmann, 2007.

Feldman, Ronen, and James Sanger. *The Text Mining Handbook: Advanced Approaches in Analyzing Unstructured Data*. Cambridge, UK: Cambridge University Press, 2007.

Fisher, Karen E., Sanda Erdelez, and Lynne (E.F.) McKechnie, eds. *Theories of Information Behavior*. Medford, NJ: Information Today, 2005.

Hedden, Heather. *The Accidental Taxonomist, Second Edition*. Medford, NJ: Information Today, 2016.

Liu, Bing. *Sentiment Analysis and Opinion Mining*. Morgan & Claypool Publishers, 2012.

Pennebaker, James W. *The Secret Life of Pronouns: What Our Words Say About Us*. New York: Blooomsbury Press, 2011.

Pinheiro, Carlos, Andre Reis, and Fiona McNeill. *Heuristics in Analytics: A Practical Perspective of What Influences Our Analytical World*. Wiley and SAS Business Series, 2014.

Pothos, Emmanuel M., and Andy J. Wills. *Formal Approaches in Categorization*. Cambridge, UK: Cambridge University Press, 2011.

Siegel, Eric. *Predictive Analytics: The Power to Predict Who Will Click, Buy, Lie, or Die*. Hoboken, NJ: John Wiley & Sons, 2013.

Silver, Nate. *The Signal and the Noise: Why So Many Predictions Fail—But Some Don't*. New York: Penguin Press, 2012.

Wilcock, Graham. *Introduction to Linguistic Annotation and Text Analytics*. Morgan & Claypool Publishers, 2009.

Thinking

Boulding, Kenneth E. *The Image: Knowledge in Life and Society*. Ann Arbor, MI: The University of Michigan Press, 1966.

Boyd, Brian. *On the Origin of Stories: Evolution, Cognition, and Fiction*. Cambridge, MA: The Belknap Press of Harvard University Press, 2009.

Brown, Peter C., Henry L. Roediger III, and Mark A. McDaniel. *Make It Stick: The Science of Successful Learning*. Cambridge, MA: The Belknap Press of Harvard University Press, 2014.

Burton, Robert A. *On Being Certain: Believing You Are Right Even When You're Not*. New York: St. Martin's Griffin, 2008.

Dobelli, Rolf. *The Art of Thinking Clearly*. Translated by Nicky Griffin. New York: Harper, 2013.

Ford, Kenneth M., Clark Glymour, and Patrick J. Hayes. *Thinking about Android Epistemology*. Menlo Park, CA: AAAI Press, 2006.

Gardner, Howard. *Frames of Mind: The Theory of Multiple Intelligences*. 10th Anniversary Edition. New York, BasicBooks, 1983.

Goleman, Daniel. *Social Intelligence: The Revolutionary New Sciences of Human Relationships*. New York: Bantam Books, 2006.

Hallinan, Joseph T. *Why We Make Mistakes: How We Look Without Seeing, Forget Things in Seconds, and Are All Pretty Sure We Are Way Above Average*. New York: Broadway Books, 2009.

Kowalski, Robert. *Computational Logic and Human Thinking: How to Be Artificially Intelligent*. Cambridge, UK: Cambridge University Press, 2011.

Kurzweil, Ray. *How to Create a Mind: The Secret of Human Thought Revealed*. New York, Viking, 2012.

Lakoff, George. *Don't Think of an Elephant!: Know Your Values and Frame the Debate*. White River Junction: VT: Chelsea Green Publishing, 2004.

Moseley, David, et al. *Frameworks for Thinking: A Handbook for Teaching and Learning*. Cambridge, UK: Cambridge University Press, 2005.

Nisbett, Richard E. *The Geography of Thought: How Asians and Westerners Think Differently ... and Why*. New York: The Free Press, 2003.

Polanyi, Michael. *Personal Knowledge: Towards a Post-Critical Philosophy*. Chicago: The University of Chicago Press, 1962.

Polanyi, Michael. *The Tacit Dimension*. Garden City, NY: Anchor Books, 1967.

Articles and Presentations

"Best Practices Series: Smart Customer Service," *Customer Relationship Management* (June 2014): 21-30.

"Business Intelligence," Wikipedia, accessed January 16, 2015. https://en.wikipedia.org/wiki/Business_intelligence, Last Modified January 15, 2015.

"Business Intelligence and Unstructured Data," BARC, accessed January 16, 2015. www.barc-research.com/business-intelligence-and-unstructured-data.

"Mind the Search Gap: A MindMetre Research Report Analyzing the Gap Between Enterprise Search Expectations and Real-Life Experience," 2011.

"Search-Based Application," Wikipedia, modified July 3, 2014, accessed July 8, 2014. https://en.wikipedia.org/wiki/Search-based_application.

"Twitter Sentiment Analysis & Other Metrics Measuring Social Media ROI," January 12, 2010, accessed October 9, 2014. blog.sourcemetrics.com/twitter-sentiment-analysis-social-media-roi-metrics/.

"What Are the Applications of Sentiment Analysis? Why Is It in So Much Discussion and Demand?" accessed February 16, 2015. www.quora.com/What-are-the-applications-of-sentiment-analysis-Why-is-it-in-so-much-demand.

"What Is a Good Explanation of Latent Dirichlet Allocation?" 2011, accessed February 8, 2015. www.quora.com/What-is-a-good-explanation-of-Latent-Dirichlet-Allocation.

"What's Next for Sentiment Measurement?" accessed February 16, 2015. www.mashable.com/2010/04/19/sentiment-analysis.

Aldhouse, Peter. "'Language of Deceit' Betrays Scientific Fraud," *NewScientist* (September 6, 2014): 14.

Alvarez, Guy. "A Guide to Social Media Compliance," *EContent* (July/August 2014): 30-31.

Askanase, Debra. "Measuring Online Sentiment Is Measuring the Wrong ROI," December 20, 2010, accessed October 9, 2014. www.communityorganizer20.com/2010/12/20/measuring-online-sentiment-is-measuring-the-wrong-roi.

Averill-Snell, Ned. "Search Prowess Is Key to Effective E-Discovery," *KMWorld Supplement* (February 2014): 6.

Barrenchea, Mark. "Information Governance Is Good Business," *KMWorld Supplement* (February 2014): 5.

Bertolucci, Jeff. "E-Discovery Software Helps Organizations Manage the Digital Stockpiles of Unstructured Data They Warehouse in Case of Litigation," Information Week, accessed January 16, 2015. www.informationweek.com/software/information/management/when-big-data-meets-legal-discovery.

Boeri, Robert. "Making the Case for Text and Predictive Analytics," *EContent* (December 2013): 31.

Cambria, Erik, Björn Schuller, YunQing Xia, and Catherine Havasi. "New Avenues in Opinion Mining and Sentiment Analysis," *IEEE Intelligent Systems* (March/April 2013): 15-21.

Cretella, Emily. "Sentiment Analysis: Measuring Social Media and Content Marketing ROI," March 14, 2013.

Del Moro, Karine. "Voice of the Customer: How to Handle Unstructured Data," MyCustomer, March 19, 2014, accessed January 16, 2015. www.mycustomer.com/feature/dara-experience/adding-voc-mix-how-to-get-started-unstructured-data.

Dickerson, Jeff. "New Tools for the Old School: Affordable Early Case Assessment and Information Governance," *KMWorld Supplement* (February 2014): 3-4.

Diggs, Woody, and Jeffrey Stier. "The Tipping Point: The Language of Trust," *Customer Relationship Management* (July 2014): 7.

Farmer, Donald. "A Natural Approach to Analytics," *Wired* (February 7, 2014), accessed May 26, 2014.

Feiler, Bruce. "Statisticians 10, Poets 0," *New York Times* (May 18, 2014).

Fletcher, John, and Jon Patrick. "Evaluating the Utility of Appraisal Hierarchies as a Method for Sentiment Classification," *Proceedings of the Australasian Language Technology Workshop 2005*, Sydney, Australia, December 2005: 134-142.

Fogarty, Kevin. "Test Shows Big Data Text Analysis Inconsistent, Inaccurate," *Computerworld* (January 30, 2015), accessed February 8, 2015. www.computerworld.com/article.2878080/test-shows-bid-data-text-analysis-inconsistent-inaccurate.

Gennarelli, Jane. "Litigation 101 for e-Discovery Tech Professionals: Vehicles for Discovery," e-DiscoveryDaily, November 28, 2012, accessed January 16, 2015. www.cloudnine-Discovery.com/e-Discoverydaily/litigation-101-for-e-Discovery-tech-professionals.

Gingras, Jarrod. "A Guide to WCM: Choosing the Right Tool for You," *EContent* (March 2012): 30-31.

Goldenberg, Barton. "Taking the Plunge into Social CRM," *Customer Relationship Management* (April 2104): 6.

Grimes, Seth. "Social Sentiment's Missing Measures," January 29, 2014, accessed October 9, 2014. www.socialmediaexplorer.com/social-media-measurement/social-sentiments-missing-measures.

Grimes, Seth. "Text Analytics 2014: User Perspectives on Solutions and Providers," Market Study, Alta Plana Corporation, July 9, 2014.

Guiseva, Irina. "What Is Content Analytics and Who Needs It?" *Econtent* (May 2013): 31.

Halper, Fern, Marcia Kaufman, and Daniel Kirsh. "Text Analytics: The Hurwitz Victory Index Report," Hurwitz & Associates report, 2013.

Inmon, Bill, and Anthony Nesavich. "Integrating Unstructured Text into a Structured Environment," accessed January 16, 2015. searchbusinesssanalytics.techtarget.com/feature/Integrating-unstructured-text-into-a-structured-environment.

Jacob, Joel and J.R. Jenkins. "Software Deployment Models Impact Innovation," *KMWorld Supplement* (February 2014): 7.

Kampffmeyer, Ulrich. "EIM Enterprise Information Management," Project Consult, conference presentation, December 2013.

Kellogg, Dave. "ICD's Definition of Search-Based Applications," accessed July 8, 2014. www.kellblog.com/2010/02/11/idcs-definiton-of-search-based-applications/.

Klie, Leonard. "3 Reasons to Boost Your Contact Center's Strategic Value with Analytics," *Customer Relationship Management* (April 2104): 36-39.

Klie, Leonard. "Insight: Social Networking Offers Increased Agility," *Customer Relationship Management* (June 2014): 11.

Lamont, Judith. "Delving Into Customer Thoughts: Text Analytics Provides Insights," *KMWorld* (July/August 2014): 12-13, 20.

Lamont, Judith. "E-Discovery: Sifting Through the Evidence," *KMWorld* (July/August 2014): 16-18.

Lamont, Judith. "Making Sense of Social," *KMWorld* (June 2014): 8-9.

Lamont, Judith. "Search: Power Tools that Leverage Corporate Knowledge," *KMWorld* (April 2013): 12-13.

Lamont, Judith. "Search Technology: A Spectrum of Options," *KMWorld* (April 2014): 8-10, 22.

Lamont, Judith. "Searching for Results," *KMWorld* (May 2013): 12-13.

Lamont, Judith. "Text Analytics Finds Dynamic Growth in E-Discovery and Customer Feedback," *KMWorld* (July/August 2011): 14-15, 24.

Lang, Alexander, Maria Mera Ortiz, and Stefan Abraham. "Enhancing Business Intelligence with Unstructured Data," Report, Advanced Analytics Development, IBM Research and Development Company, n.d.

Leibtag, Ahava. "Social Media: What Are You Waiting For?" *EContent* (March 2012): 19.

LePage, Evan. How to Measure Social Media ROI for Your Business," accessed October 9, 2014. https://hootsuite.com/measure-social-media-roi-business.

Lopresti, Michael J. "Overcoming the Challenges of Calculating Digital Marketing ROI," *EContent* (July/August 2014): 6-10.

Martin, Erik, J. "The State of Social Media," *EContent* (January/February 2014): 20-21.

Martin, John. "Is Your TAR Really Text-Assisted Review? (And Why It Should Matter to You), BeyondRecognition, accessed June 15, 2014. www.beyondrecognition.net/document-u-blog/is-your-tar-really-text-assisted-review.

McMurtrie, John. "Facebook, Zuckerberg Start 'A Year of Books' Project," *San Francisco Chronicle*, January 6, 2015.

Minsker, Maria. "Insight: The 6 Types of Twitter Conversations," *Customer Relationship Management* (May 2014): 13.

Minsker, Maria. "Why Marketers Need a Tag Management System," *Customer Relationship Management* (September 2014): 28-41.

Modha, Dharmendra. "A Computer that Thinks," *NewScientist* (November 8, 2014): 28-29.

Moore, Andy. "E-Discovery and the Cloud," *KMWorld Supplement* (February 2014): 2.

Morrow, Lanny. "Mining Unstructured Data in Forensic Accounting Investigations—Part 2: Components of Text Mining," BKD Forensics.com, accessed January 16, 2105. www.bkdforensics.com/2014/07/15/mining-unstructured-data-in-forensic -accounting-investigations.

Mullainathan, Sendhil. "Why Computers Won't Replace You Just Yet," *New York Times*, July 3, 2014: A3.

Myron, David. "Five Ways to Reveal Your Customer Data," *Customer Relationship Management* (September 2014): 4.

Nelson, Matthew. "E-Discovery Requirements," *KMWorld* (April 2104): 10-11, 22.

Pophal, Lin. "The Technology of Contextualized Content: What's Next on the Horizon?" *EContent* (September 2014): 17-20.

Rasmus, Daniel W. "Analytics for the Rest of Us," *KMWorld* (February 2014): 10-12.

Rosch, Eleanor, et al. "Basic Objects in Natural Categories," *Cognitive Psychology* 8 (1976): 382ff.

Rutkin, Aviva. "Super-Dialects Exposed via Millions of Tweets, *NewScientist* (August 9, 2014): 18.

Saba, Walid "Text Analytics and Semantic Technology—Myth vs. Reality" (March 19, 2014), accessed May 26, 2014. www.agencypost.com/text-analysis-and-semantic -technolgy-myth-vs-reality.

Scheff, Thomas J. "A Taxonomy of Emotions: How Do We Begin?" accessed July 25, 2014. www.soc.ucsb.edu/faculty/scheff/47.html.

Schmid-Subramanian, Maxie. "The State of Voice of the Customer Programs, 2014: It's Time to Act," Report, Forrester Research, Inc., June 20, 2014.

Search Technologies. "The Glass Box Approach to Enterprise Search," Report, 2011.

Seymour, Chris. "All Content Is Personal," *EContent* (July/August 2014): 20-25.

Socher, Richard, et al. "Recursive Deep Models for Semantic Compositionality Over a Sentiment Treebank," *Proceedings of the Australasian Language Technology Workshop 2005*, Sydney, Australia, December 2005.

Springer, Robert. "A Social Media Compliance Update: Ten Years Later," *EContent* (July/August 2014): 15-18.

Springer, Robert. "Personalizing Personalization: It's About More Than Just Knowing Your User's Name," *EContent* (May 2014): 8-10.

Thompson, Mike. "The State of Content Analytics," *EContent* (January/February 2014): 24-25.

Tierney, John. "Why We All Sound Like Pollyannas," *New York Times"* (February 24, 2015): D3.

Whitelaw, Casey, Navendu Garg, and Shlomo Argamon. "Using Appraisal Groups for Sentiment Analysis," *Proceedings of the Australasian Language Technology Workshop 2005*, Sydney, Australia, December 2005.

Whitelaw, Casey, Navendu Garg, and Shlomo Argamon. "Using Appraisal Taxonomies for Sentiment Analysis," *Proceedings of the Australasian Language Technology Workshop 2005*, Sydney, Australia, December 2005.

Whiting, Geoff, and Alesia Siuchykava. "Executive Lessons on Modern Text Analytics." Presentation given at the 13th Annual Text Analytics Summit West 2014, San Francisco, California, November 4-5, 2014.

References Missing

Ananyan, Sergei, and Michael Kiselev. "Automated Analysis of Unstructured Texts: Technology and Implementations."

McNeill, Fiona. "SAS," email to author.

Miller, Ron, "Drowning in Data and Searching for Answers," *EContent*.

Hagelin, Olle. "How to Use Text Mining in Social and CRM to Improve Quality Control and Save Money," Conference Presentation, Sony Mobile Communications, 2014 (?).

About the Author

Photo by Melanie Reamy

Tom Reamy is currently the chief knowledge architect and founder of the KAPS Group, a group of knowledge architecture, text analytics, and taxonomy consultants, and has 20 years of experience in information projects of various kinds. He has published a number of articles in a variety of journals and is a frequent speaker at knowledge management, taxonomy, and text analytics conferences. He has served as the program chair for Text Analytics World since 2013.

For more than a decade, Tom's primary focus has been on text analytics and helping clients select the best text analytics software as well as doing text analytics development projects that include applications such as call support, voice of the customer, social media analysis, sentiment analysis, enterprise search, and multiple enterprise text analytics–powered applications.

Tom's academic background includes a master's in the history of ideas, research in artificial intelligence and cognitive science, and a strong background in philosophy, particularly epistemology.

When not writing or developing text analytics projects, he can usually be found at the bottom of the ocean in Carmel, photographing strange critters.

Index